EXPLORING SPACE–CITY!

EXPLORING

SPACE-CITY!

HOUSTON'S HISTORIC UNDERGROUND NEWSPAPER

Edited by Thorne Dreyer, Alice Embree,
Cam Duncan, and Sherwood Bishop

Designed by Carlos Lowry

New Journalism Project
Austin, Texas

Published by New Journalism Project
P.O. Box 16442, Austin, TX 78761-6442

New Journalism Project, 2021

ISBN 978-1-312-16267-9

Explorers then and now. Clockwise, from upper left: Bill Narum, Dennis Fitzgerald, Judy Gitlin Fitzgrald, Kerry Fitzgerald, Thorne Dreyer, cindy soo, Cam Duncan, Sue Mithun Duncan, Sherwood Bishop, and Victoria Smith.

Art by Kerry Awn, 2021.

Copy Editors: Thorne Dreyer and Ryan Bernard

Production committee: Alice Embree, Thorne Dreyer, cindy soo, Cam Duncan, Sherwood Bishop, and Karen Northcott

Contents

Space City!
Beginnings

20¢
25¢ out of town

vol. 1, no. 1
june 5, 1969
houston, texas

PANCHO VILLA
Born June 5, 1878

First cover: Art by Kerry Fitzgerald, June 5, 1969.

Launching
Space City!

Cover: Art by Vaughn Bode, May 18, 1972.

Exploring Space City!: I Read the News Today, Oh Boy

Thorne Dreyer

It is my honor (to say nothing of great good luck!) to have been a founding editor of *Space City!*. It was a very exciting time and we made some important history back in the day. And it is also an honor, some 50 years later, to be an editor of *Exploring Space City!: Houston's Historic Underground Newspaper*, the book you have in your hands. *Exploring Space City!* has documented much of that rich but often overlooked history that *Space City!* captured. And done so with a lot of passion and humor.

Space City! was an underground newspaper published in Houston, Texas, from June 5, 1969, to August 3, 1972. Though it was relatively short-lived, the paper was widely acknowledged to be one of the very best of the 1960s-70s underground newspapers that had significant impact on mainstream journalism.

The paper was originally called *Space City News* – and that name graced the banner for the first dozen issues – but a UFO newsletter of the same name came out of nowhere and threatened to sue the paper and the name was changed to *Space City!*. (Wikipedia describes the exclamation point on "*Space City!*" as a "graphical design flourish.")

In this book we call the paper "*Space City!*," unless we are specifically referring to one of those early issues before the name was changed.

With this book and in the process of preparing it, we have recovered and recorded significant history that otherwise might have been lost. The project started with an expansive effort to locate and digitize a complete set of *Space City!*, which is now accessible to the public both at the Internet Archive and at JSTOR. (Find links in the Bibliography at the end of this book.)

Exploring Space City! features both articles and artwork from the original *Space City!*, as well as essays written specifically for the book by its editors and others, designed to look back on the historical importance of the paper and to add contemporary perspective.

The underground press was a rowdy bunch of counterculture and New-Left-oriented publications

We have recovered and recorded significant history that otherwise might have been lost.

that started with the *Los Angeles Free Press* in 1964 and the early ones included the *Berkeley Barb*, *The Great Speckled Bird* in Atlanta, the *San Francisco Oracle*, and Chicago's *Seed* — as well as *The Rag* in Austin. Three years later, came Houston's *Space City!*.

The Underground Press Syndicate (UPS), a loose affiliation of alternative tabloids, started out in 1966 with five papers and, over the next few years (mid-60s to late-70s) the number of underground papers mushroomed to as many as 1,000 with multiple readership in the millions. They emerged in cities big and small, university towns, and urban centers — from hip enclaves to high schools to GI bases and gay communities — and ranged in focus from psychedelic to politically revolutionary. Some were beautifully designed with original art while others were roughshod, hap-hazard, and riddled with reprints. But they all had heart and a lot to say. This new kind of journalism was proliferating from coast to coast thanks to the readily accessible and easily affordable photo-offset press.

The 1960s-70s underground press played a major role in bringing to light news that was previously unreported — or underreported (or reported only from a government or "establishment" perspective) — by the mainstream press, especially concerning the War in Vietnam and the growing resistance to it. The papers gave voice to the fast-growing countercultural phenomenon ("hippies" as the media called us; "freaks" as many of us called ourselves) and the New Left and other related movements for social change.

The writing was often subjective, telling stories from the perspective of the writers who were frequently themselves participants in the events they reported on. And the papers had a unique look. Some used multi-color split-fount inking, and most included a new genre of comic art called "comix" – made famous by Gilbert Shelton (who started his Fabulous Furry Freak Brothers at *The Rag*), R. Crumb, Skip Williamson, and many more.

Exploring Space City! is a companion work to *Celebrating The Rag: Austin's Iconic Underground News-*

paper, a 300-page volume released in 2016. Both books were published by the New Journalism Project, a 501(c)(3) Texas nonprofit corporation that also publishes *The Rag Blog* and sponsors Rag Radio which originates on KOOP-FM 91.7 in Austin.

The Rag was one of the first underground papers and among the most influential. It was a pioneer in combining New Left analysis with content appealing to the counterculture, featuring iconic art by Gilbert Shelton, Jim Franklin (surrealist armadillos), and cartoonists Kerry Awn (aka Kerry Fitzgerald), Trudy Minkoff, and Micael Priest.

The Rag was set in a campus environment (Austin was a sleepy college town at that point). Historian John McMillian wrote that *The Rag* "was a spirited, quirky, and humorous paper, whose founders pushed the New Left's political agenda even as they embraced the counterculture's zeal for rock music, psychedelics, and personal liberation." Historian Laurence Leamer called it "one of the few legendary undergrounds."

Space City!, on the other hand, thrived in an urban setting with a bohemian community based in the Montrose neighborhood and in pockets around the lively boomtown. (Houston was already one of the largest and fastest-growing metropolises in the country. Now it's among the most diverse.) *Space City!* gave voice to the previously isolated centers of activism and hip culture and helped unite them into an extended community. It also reported on and served as a voice for a very active "rainbow coalition" of Black, Chicano, and white radical activists.

In a 1972 book titled *Paper Revolutionaries* (see story in the "Reflections" section), Laurence Leamer wrote:

> There is another Houston... a world of black, Chicano and poor-white ghettos; of business and political leaders manipulating Houston's future like a Monopoly game; of drugs and ennui in the suburbs; of hippies and assorted long-hairs building lives within the confines of the city limits. This is the Houston that *Space City!* has covered since June 1969....

Space City! interviewed SNCC activist Lee Otis Johnson, who was given 30 years for passing a joint to a cop, and photographed him in a prison hospital (see photo in this book). We interviewed People's Party II Chairman Carl Hampton, an eloquent spokesman for the Black Liberation movement, approximately 10 days before he was shot to death by Houston Police on Dowling Street. And we worked closely with the militant Mexican American Youth Organization (MAYO) that occupied a church and used it as a temporary center for community activities that included a breakfast program for kids.

The paper ran an "Advice to Dopers" column that offered drug news to Houston's growing countercultural community, warning about dangerous street drugs and giving advice on how to best come down from a bad trip. And the paper provided extensive coverage of rock concerts and music festivals. There were features on Janis Joplin and Muhammad Ali by Jeff Shero and rock and film reviews by John M. Lomax, Gary Chason, Tary Owens, and many more.

Space City! invited Yippie leader and Chicago 8 defendant Abbie Hoffman to speak in Houston and covered demonstrations when Rice University refused to allow him on campus. We supported the large anti-war GI community at Ft. Hood and interviewed Jane Fonda at the Oleo Strut GI coffeehouse about the war and the GI movement that she supported.

SPACE CITY!

VOLUME III, NUMBER 40   HOUSTON, TEXAS   MAR. 16—22, 1972   25¢

35¢ out of town

PSYCHOSURGERY:

The Modern Way
To Peace of Mind
p. 3

Cover: March 16, 1972.

And we did major power structure research uncovering who ruled Rice and the University of Houston, we revealed the financial forces behind construction giant Brown & Root as well as the *Houston Chronicle* and its publisher, Houston Endowment (which was called "the largest single corporate force" in the city of Houston). According to Cam Duncan, one of the editors of this book, "Despite its vast financial and political power, the Endowment had never been investigated or written about before in any Houston newspaper."

We also reported on electoral politics, writing about the campaign of feminist gubernatorial hopeful Sissy Farenthold and racist George Wallace's aborted efforts to remake his image while running for president. And I wrote a long analytical piece about the 1972 Democratic National Convention in Miami Beach at a time when the Democratic Party was energized by progressive politics and the anti-war candidate George McGovern's reformist crusade.

The paper also wrote about resistance to the War in Vietnam, and about the women's movement, labor, Gay Liberation, the movement in Houston high schools, and the Venceremos Brigades to Cuba. And all of this reporting and arts criticism is also featured in *Exploring Space City!*. Major contributors to the art and design of the paper were Kerry Fitzgerald and Bill Narum.

Space City! inspired and helped organize — and offered meeting and work space – to a number of alternative community institutions including a drug crisis center, a community switchboard, a food co-op, and a nonprofit community-run music venue, Of Our Own. *Space City!*'s Dennis Fitzgerald was a prime mover behind Of Our Own. *Space City!* provided support to an underground movement in Houston's high schools and high school underground papers were laid out in our offices. And the *Space City!* headquarters became a center for organizing events, demonstrations, and benefit concerts.

Space City! was democratically run by the editorial Collective. The original Collective had three women and three men, a trend that continued throughout the life of the paper.

We were also the continuing target of right-wing nightriders whose reign of terror included bombing the *Space City!* offices, shooting up the storefronts of our advertisers, and twice bombing the transmitter of

KPFT (Pacifica Radio). The terrorism in Houston drew national coverage in outlets like *The New York Times*, *Newsweek*, and PBS' Great American Dream Machine. Learn more about the Klan's assault on *Space City!* in upcoming pages.

How We Started

Three of the founding editors of *The Rag* — Dennis and Judy Fitzgerald and I — were also founding members of the *Space City!* editorial Collective. The three of us were close friends at Bellaire High School in Houston where we were involved in journalism and the arts, then went to Austin and the University of Texas in 1963. We all, however, dropped out of school into the world of SDS, the civil rights and anti-war movements, and the underground press.

> *Space City!* was democratically run by the editorial Collective.

After leaving *The Rag*, the Fitzgeralds moved to San Francisco where they worked with an SDS Regional Office and I went to New York where I was an editor at Liberation News Service. At LNS I partnered up with Victoria Smith, a radical journalist who was a former reporter for the *St. Paul Dispatch*. Dennis and Judy, who were pondering their next life move (Europe was a possibility), visited Vicky and me in New York and did some volunteer work at LNS. The four of us attended an underground press conference sponsored by Atlanta's *Great Speckled Bird* where we met up with community organizers Cam and Susan Mithun Duncan.

The Duncans had moved to Houston to work for a VISTA (Volunteers in Service to America) project. Cam and Sue were already interested in the underground press, and the six of us unanimously — and with great enthusiasm — decided to make the move to the Bayou City to start *Space City!*

(I had previously proposed to Dennis that we reunite to publish a paper in Houston, but he had written back, "God no, I don't want to go back to Houston," adding that he didn't want to start a paper in San Francisco, either. But, as Cam Duncan recalls, our group of six dug in for an extended session at an Atlanta diner to discuss the project and the growing collective enthusiasm won Dennis over.)

So the six of us converged on Houston where we rented a two-story house at 1217 Wichita Street in an area halfway between the Montrose and Hermann Park — to use as an office — and lived together in a high-ceilinged old Victorian house in the Old Sixth Ward, a primarily Mexican-American neighborhood, for which we paid $40 rent (less than $7 apiece!). The house, with beautiful stained-glass windows, now has a historic designation. (I don't think it acknowledges *Space City!* as part of that history for which it is designated!) In the beginning we lived as a commune, sharing all household chores.

Space City! hit the streets and folks started pouring into the office, wanting to help out. The Collective grew; one new member was Sherwood Bishop who is now one of the editors of this book. (Sherwood brought civil rights activist and future Congressman Mickey Leland — who later died in a mercy mission over Gambela, Ethiopia — to the *Space City!* office and he became a fan and a friend.) Over the paper's lifetime, more than 20 people served on the Collective. A compilation staff box in the back of this book shows almost 200 names of people who wrote for the paper, took pictures, did art, sold advertising, or helped around the office. (And that doesn't even start to count the scores of vendors who sold the paper at Montrose and Westheimer, at local high schools, at Hermann Park, and on the UH and Rice campuses. ("Buy it for a dime, sell it for 20 cents!")

Space City! went through its ups and downs — including financial and political struggles — and even a split where a couple of staffers who thought the paper was becoming too moderate started another paper called *Mockingbird*. One of their objections was our increasing reportage of electoral politics, which many considered anathema in our revolutionary past. Read about those dynamics in reflections by original Collective members Dennis Fitzgerald, Victoria Smith, and me towards the end of the book.

Also read "*Space City!*: From Opposition to Organizational Collapse," by Victoria Smith Holden in Ken Wachsberger's *Insider Histories of the Vietnam Era Underground Press, Part 1*, published by Michigan State University Press (see Bibliography).

Looking back at the *Space City!* experience, it wasn't always a smooth trip and sometimes it was an intense struggle. But we were definitely a force in the city, reporting on very dynamic times, and left our mark.

About the Book

I am an editor of *Exploring Space City!*, along with Alice Embree, Sherwood Bishop, and Cam Duncan.

> **It wasn't always a smooth trip and sometimes it was an intense struggle.**

All of us had worked at *Space City!* except Alice, who had helped start *The Rag* and is now a director of the New Journalism Project. (Along with Richard Croxdale, Alice and I edited *Celebrating The Rag* in 2016.) Sadly, original Collective members Sue Mithun Duncan, Victoria Smith, and Dennis Fitzgerald have passed away in recent years and many others, like Bill Narum, Jim Shannon, Tary Owens, and Gary Chason have also left us.

Carlos Lowry designed this book and many others contributed to its development, including Karen Northcott, cindy soo, and Ryan Bernard who followed me in giving the text a thorough editing. In addition to the editors, Houston-based historian John Moretta (author of *The Hippies: A 1960s History*), musicologist John Lomax III (of the legendary Lomax family), and the late filmmaker and *Space City!* arts critic Gary Chason contributed contemporary essays.

Exploring Space City! is divided into eight thematic sections: Beginnings, Insurgents, Arts and Culture, Power Structure, Special Reporting, Electoral Politics, Reflections, and a closing segment that includes contributors' bios, a bibliography, thumbnails of all 106 *Space City!* covers, and a composite staff box.

Most of *Exploring Space City!* consists of articles and graphics from the original paper, though there are a number of introductions and essays that were written specifically for this book. The reprinted material is edited only for grammar, spelling, and typos. Some headlines may have been changed and the material is organized differently from the original presentation, but we have not edited for content and we have made no changes for "political correctness."

There is language in the book — from the original articles — that many of us would not use today. That might include calling cops "pigs," for instance. Language today has evolved to be more inclusive of gender diversity then it was when we were publishing *Space City!*. Terms like "Gay Liberation" and "Chicano" may sound antiquated in the contemporary environment of LGBTQ and Latinx (or the more fluid Latines). Contemporary essays in this book might have "Black" capitalized, but the original articles from the paper will probably use lower case. The 106 issues of *Space City!* are historical documents and we believe you should see the material essentially as it was originally published.

Art: Gilbert Shelton, March 9, 1972.

There are also articles in the book written by the same person under different names. John Lomax wrote an essay under the byline, "John Lomax III," but his music criticism for the original paper was credited to "John M. Lomax." Jeff Shero would change his name to "Jeff Nighthyrd" and there are bylines in the book with both names. Sue Duncan also wrote and credited photos as "Sue Mithun." Kerry Fitzgerald became "Kerry Awn" in his work at *The Rag*. In the book, we have left the bylines as they originally appeared in the paper.

We've been working on this project for over two years, and it's been a labor of love. We hope you find it to be an educational and rewarding experience – and a whole lot of fun.

Austin
August 2021

The Counterculture and the Underground Press

John Moretta

John Moretta received his Ph.D in history from Rice University in 1985 and has published several books and scholarly articles on both Texas and United States history including his most recent book, The Hippies: A 1960s History, *published by McFarland & Co. In 2020, he wrote an article for the academic journal,* Southwestern Historical Quarterly, *titled "Political Hippies and Hip Politicos: Counterculture Alliance and Cultural Radicalism in 1960s Austin, Texas" and his book on that subject will be published in early 2022. Dr. Moretta is a full-time history professor with Houston Community College and also teaches upper level U.S. history courses at the University of Houston.*

No one can write a thorough history of the 1960s without an in-depth discussion of the importance of the emergence and proliferation of one of the most seminal dynamics that both informed and helped to spread the decade's countercultural rebellion: the underground press. Although not the only source of information on the counterculture, and not necessarily the most reliable, it was, without question, the most creative and distinctive of the hip community's literary and even aesthetic creations.

The underground press engaged two media: words and the visual arts. The counterculture became legendary for its visual presence, with its outlandish, colorful clothing, psychedelic posters, decorated cars and vans, and a variety of other outrageous expressions. Distinctive, striking art and in some instances, equally provocative, risqué, and unfortunately misogynistic "comix" and suggestive portrayals of nude women, defined many publications. Not only were such graphics designed to shock and challenge the staid mainstream media, but also to convey a sense of the sensory and sensual experience which the counterculture strove to proclaim as part of its ethos. The papers' art reflected the multifaceted nature of the decade's political and cultural revolution, and the underground journals were loaded with it.

The various publications became a staple of life for the youth movement, reflecting all the major impulses of both the counterculture and the New Left/SDS: the assertion of subjectivity in all its manifestations, the search for community and authenticity, and an unrelenting critique of the superficial values of "plastic" mainstream culture and society. They featured

The various publications became a staple of life for the youth movement.

political treatises and news of Movement activities; *exposés* on drug use, spiritual enlightenment; profiles of activists or counterculture communities and "happenings"; information and reviews of arts and music events, and even opportunities for personal and sexual contacts with other "liberated" individuals.

As the press proliferated, the need arose for a more coordinated way to disseminate all that was happening across the nation in the hip/radical communities. Thus, emerged Liberation News Service (LNS) and the Underground Press Syndicate (UPS), both of which brought together editors and activists in a series of Movement conferences, with the intent of providing national coverage to smaller papers. Some publications like the *Berkeley Barb*, the *Los Angeles Free Press*, and *Win*, emphasized the more instrumental politics of New Left activism, while others, such as the *San Francisco Oracle* and the *East Village Other*, focused on amplifying and sustaining the hip counterculture. The underground press, in short, reflected the Movement it covered. In its heyday it gave voice to radical activism as well as featuring the hip counterculture and its liberated ethos and lifestyle. It was a medium for the youth counterculture's powerful personal expression. It could also be silly, offensive, and excessive. It filled a social and political vacuum and fed on the energy of its times. It paved the way for journalistic alternatives, broadening the scope of traditional reporting.

Only a handful believed it important to cover both the Movement and the counterculture, believing they were equally essential, if not symbiotic in advancing the cultural revolution. In this capacity, both Aus tin's *Rag* and Houston's *Space City!* became legendary for their respective advocacy of a hip/politico alliance. To Thorne Dreyer, one of the *Rag*'s founding "funnels," the new journalism was "born of necessity" as a medium through which the counterculture could be "visible" and relate to readers "the strange breeze of discovery [that] was sweeping through the land…"

Dreyer believed that the young people who joined the counterculture "weren't just indulgent, hedonistic middle-class mutants seeking inner peace" but rather a much more aware and politically savvy group "that named the institutions of the state the enemy" and "acted on that analysis" by joining the counterculture as a means of mass protest and rejection of the status quo. They needed a forum for their causes and

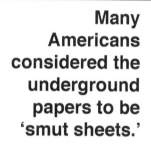

Many Americans considered the underground papers to be 'smut sheets.'

thus the emergence of the underground press, which gave voice to the "kinds of changes kids were going through. The papers were merely extensions of the hip communities [and] mirrored these changes."[1]

By the late 1960s, the underground press had "evolved from the sweetness and light of its early days" to become "culturally outrageous and politically revolutionary. It has produced an anger and fear among those whose interests it opposes. … [They have become] fairly sophisticated and attractive tabloids, beginning to develop a synthesis of the cultural and political aspects of making a revolution in this country." Right-wing attacks pushed them to become even more "consciously subjective" in their reporting and articles, as well as churning out stories that were "rooted in personal experience."

Dreyer proudly admitted that "objectivity [was] a farce," as far as he was concerned, a mainstream media contrivance of meaningless, vapid, pap journalism, and that by contrast the underground papers made no pretense about their biases; they were "upfront" and unequivocal in their positions on the decade's key issues affecting young Americans such as the Vietnam War and the countercultural revolution. Although a few years later Dreyer would "confess" that UPS was organized "to create the illusion of a giant coordinated network of freaky papers poised for the kill,"[2] the underground press was no "illusion;" the papers played a vital and dynamic role in the 1960s political and cultural insurrection.

Many Americans considered the underground papers to be "smut sheets. … Molotov cocktails thrown at the respectability and decency in our nation. … These papers encourage depravity and irresponsibility, and they nurture a breakdown in the continued capacity of the government to conduct an orderly and constitutional society. … They [the publishers] know that the more obscene and dirty their newspapers are, the more they will attract the irresponsible readers whom they want to enlist in their crusade to destroy this country."[3] Such screeds by right-wing individuals such as Texas congressman Joe Pool, only further emboldened the "funnels," editors, writers, and staff of the underground press to continue publishing their "subversive" papers, many of which moved even farther left as the decade wore on.

Beautiful Hair Is Our Thing . . .

STYLES ‡2.25…HAIR TRIMMED $1.00

NORRIS oʄ HOUSTON
BARBER COLLEGE · 10530 EAST EX FREEWAY · · ·
697-2958 HOURS: M-F 10-8 SAT.9-6 CLOSED WED.

Ad: September 14, 1971.

Such a mission informed the founding of *Space City News*, which in 1970 changed to *Space City!* Started by Dreyer, Victoria Smith, Cam and Susan Mithun Duncan, and Dennis and Judy Gitlin Fitzgerald in the summer of 1969, its founders formed a collective, through which they hoped to energize Houston with the same "revolutionary consciousness" and activism that *The Rag* had successfully brought to the fore in Austin and on the University of Texas campus. Most important, the paper's originators believed that not only was the "personal political" but that the "political was personal," and thus, hoped to have *Space City!* become a "focal point" for bringing together the city's radical and hip communities into an alliance as *The Rag* had accomplished in Austin.

As Victoria Smith wrote, "From the start we made it clear that *Space City!*'s central purpose was for movement organizing, and to raise revolutionary consciousness among the city's disaffected — primarily a fragmented youth population that expressed defiance through sex, drugs, and rock-and-roll." Smith, Dreyer, and company believed it was time, via *Space City!*'s articles and editorials, to politicize those among Houston's youth who had embraced the hip counterculture and thus were perceived to be ready to take the next step toward radical, political activism.

As Smith noted, "Sex, drugs, and rock gave us something to go on, but we hoped to infuse that youthful rebelliousness with political awareness as well. As we wrote in an open letter from the Collective in the third issue: 'For us putting out a newspaper can't be an end in itself, and we sure ain't doing it to make money! We want to build a movement in Houston. We want our paper to serve as a catalytic agent, stimulating radical activity. And as a coalescing point, around which an alternative community can grow.'"[4]

Although the paper's initial focus was to help promote and sustain a viable countercultural movement in Houston, such an endeavor proved to be more difficult than anticipated. Several factors contributed to the undermining of this effort. The city's expansiveness and lack of an inner city "core" prevented the development of a hip/radical enclave on the scale of a Haight-Ashbury, the East Village, or Telegraph Ave-

nue. Those neighborhoods provided their respective underground journals a ready-made physical focal point with an established, centralized community that could be easily accessed and energized into political action. Those communities became key distribution points and centers for dissemination of the radical/hip message of the *Berkeley Barb* or *East Village Other*. Although lacking a legendary hip/radical enclave, late 1960s and early 1970s Houston did have, in a much smaller, confined capacity, a bohemian nabe, Montrose, which did serve as a countercultural hub, which gave *Space City!* a key distribution point for its message, with multiple sales outlets and vendor pick-up sites. Nonetheless, most of Houston's counterculturists were intermingled within a city of 1.2 million people in 1970 and spread out over 500 square miles of the greater metropolitan area.

Add to this geographical obstacle, the city's general white intolerance and disdain at that time for the "other," let alone the embracing of diversity, for which today Houston has become noteworthy. A very white, conservative power elite and structure dominated the city, sustained by an often brutal, oppressive white police force, who often looked the other way, if not condoned, the terrorism visited upon the hip/radical community by vigilante groups such as the Klan. As Victoria Smith noted, "As one might expect, Houston in the late sixties and early seventies provided an inhospitable climate for radicalism. Already the nation's sixth largest city, it was growing rapidly and almost uncontrollably, which meant the general population was unstable, and communication and transportation were difficult. Houston was dominated by extreme conservatism," and most important, a small, moribund "white liberal-left movement of a few older anti-war activists, staff members of KPFT-FM, a small Socialist Worker's Party group, and some five or six ex-SDSers who recently had broken with the militant Weatherman group."[5]

Although long a supposedly integrated city, racism and prejudice still defined much of its white demographics in the late sixties and early seventies, as Houston's people of color remained confined to specific wards and barrios. Another important factor handicapping *Space City!*'s countercultural initiatives was that neither of Houston's two major uni-

> **Houston was far from a hotbed of countercultural protest and rebellion.**

versities (the University of Houston and Rice, unlike UT) provided much student assistance when it came to radical politics nor did either have much of a hip community, which could be counted on for action. UH had an SDS chapter and so did Rice, but neither were able to generate the kind of enthusiastic student participation and activism found at UT.

UH politicos had a difficult time rallying their fellow collegians for Movement involvement, primarily because UH was overwhelmingly a commuter school, and thus lacked a stable community of on-campus residents who could be politically mobilized for action. For Rice students, even though the majority lived on campus, a rigorous curriculum and related academic pursuits rather than student politics and activism defined their daily lives. Although Rice called itself the "Harvard of the Southwest," during the 1960s and early 1970s, its students rarely displayed any of the radical politics and activism found on the Harvard campus or at the other Ivy League schools.

In short, 1960s and early 1970s Houston was far from a hotbed of countercultural protest and rebellion as witnessed on the west and east coasts. It was thus difficult to advance the countercultural cause and radical politics without the constant fear of reprisal, which all too frequently visited *Space City!*'s offices in the form of drive-by shootings, car bombings, and one pipe bomb, most of this harassment at the hands of the local KKK, who openly took credit for their actions. Even the paper's advertisers were threatened, and many had their places of business shot up.

The paper wasn't the only target of the "hippie-haters." The gallery owned by Dreyer's mother, Margaret Webb Dreyer, was hit by gunfire with bullets penetrating the front door and yellow paint thrown on an external wall. Equally terrifying, the progressive Pacifica radio station, KPFT, was bombed off the air twice in 1970. Nonetheless, despite the physical threats and general harassment, the paper persevered for three years, successfully, according to Dreyer, bringing together the various countercultural communities that were "in bits and pieces everywhere. Houston is much more of a city now than it was then. What *Space City!* did was to help identify all these pockets of progressive politics and kindred

> **Space City! developed a more sophisticated advocacy journalism.**

spirits, and pull them together in a cohesive spirit... a network of countercultural stuff."[6]

Despite the acts of terrorism that frequented Houston's countercultural community, whether in direct assaults by police or other hate groups on individuals or on the community's establishments or activities, *Space City!* persevered and even flourished for a few years by adapting its purpose to the realities of a very inhospitable urban environment but not wavering in its initial commitment to continue to be a voice for revolutionary change and political activism.

Such dedication was expressed in its August 1-21, 1970 issue when the paper accused the Houston police of the premeditated murder of Carl Hampton, leader of the fledgling People's Party II African-American revolutionary group. The paper declared: "The war on the

people of the world against the Amerikan Leviathan is now, and will continue to be, the most important, the most difficult, and the bloodiest in history. Amerika will not relinquish control without a deadly fight. ... If there was ever a time to get serious, it's now. If ever there was a time to get together, to suspend our ideological differences for a while, it's now. ... We need to re-recognize our common struggle, if any of us are to long continue in that struggle at all. ... If we don't live our lives fighting this American monster that killed Carl, that is killing people all over the world, that is destroying people all over the world, that is destroying the planet, that is twisting peoples' minds — well, then our lives aren't worth shit."[7]

In hostile cities such as Houston, many underground papers, such as *Space City!*, if they hoped to survive such an unwelcoming environment, needed to make constant "adjustments" to their papers' tone, content, reporting, and analysis. Although continuing to fundamentally adhere to the paper's original purpose of conveying the radical message and of trying to bring hip and radical together, *Space City!*'s staff simultaneously developed a more sophisticated advocacy journalism in both content and style, more-in-depth research and investigative reporting, and greater arts coverage. This transition reflected a movement within the second generation of the underground press to remain avant-garde and oppositional to mainstream "objective" journalism, yet concomitantly a desire to be taken seriously as a more legitimate, alternative press.

For *Space City!* the year of "adjustment" was 1971, as Houston's radical movement, which had never been strong, dwindled even further. Although the hip community remained visible and even gained some momentum, its new followers were younger, "plastic" or "life-style" hippies, with little to no interest or commitment in radical

Space City! earned accolades for being 'a well-written, sprightly sheet.'

politics. At the national level SDS dissolved in 1969, the casualty of internecine warfare, and by 1971 the Weatherman faction was operating completely underground. Most important, the mass media was no longer interested in the countercultural phenomenon, either with its hip component, which they had successfully helped to destroy by commodification and disparaging reporting, or the New Left, which the FBI and other law enforcement helped in the self-implosion process by infiltrating its various affinity groups with *agents provocateurs*, who inflamed the existing ideological discord.

This reality forced *Space City!* to become "more of a newspaper, more immediate." As Victoria Smith observed, it was time for the paper to "expand its appeal to include essentially the same audience Pacifica reached: the socially-conscious [Houston] liberal [not exclusively the hip/radical community, which was becoming less cohesive and committed by 1971] and artistic intelligentsia. Editorial changes involved increasing the amount of local news coverage and investigative reporting, plus adopting a more objective tone and consistent writing and editing styles." In short, the paper "moved away" from its focus on cultivating a "radical youth constituency" in order to broaden its "economic and political base of support." Consequently, its staff "altered the paper's entire journalistic strategy, from a combative, oppositional style to a more reasoned, 'alternative' approach.'"[8]

Despite this "changeover," Thorne Dreyer believed the paper maintained its original integrity by "in-depth reporting on city and state politics, significant power-structure research dealing with Rice and the University of Houston and with major institutions like the *Houston Chronicle* and the Jones Endowment that ran it. We reported on police corruption and the right-wing run rampant. To

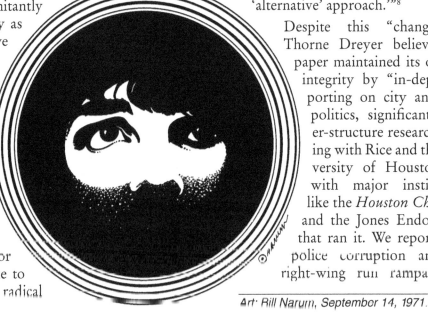

Art: Bill Narum, September 14, 1971.

say nothing of our continuing coverage on Women's Liberation, the Black Liberation and Chicano activist movement, and anti-war GIs. And we covered arts and culture extensively."⁹

Some staff members believed in the end *Space City!* "sold out" or "accommodated" or was forced by circumstances to be "co-opted" by the very political liberalism it originally opposed. However, the paper's ultimate demise in September 1972, was more a result of trying to radicalize a diffuse and diverse youth of a city not only spread across 500 square miles, but also against an overwhelming conservative power structure determined to destroy any and all manifestations of the 1960s countercultural rebellion.

While it existed *Space City!* earned accolades for being "a well-written, sprightly sheet … [that] also had an eye for vivid, telling graphics and poetry of a high level." Reporting that reflected "a solid intelligence to reviews and cultural articles. … It is radical journalism grounded in fact … resolved and balanced in content and full of common purpose." It was also applauded for "major muckraking… and numerous articles challenging the conventional wisdom, either above or underground."¹⁰

It should be noted that the underground papers were written, edited, pasted-up, and published by the counterculture exclusively. They were usually small, usually nonpaying, and usually hand-to-mouth operations. They were unequivocally publications of passion not detachment, and thus no apologies are warranted for their bias, personal, and immersed reporting; they were enthusiastic participants in the culture, society, and politics, that they were covering. As will be readily seen in this anthology of *Space City!*, they represented the clearest declaration counterculturists ever made of their ideals and values.

Houston
May 2021

Endnotes

1. Thorne Dreyer and Victoria Smith, "The Movement and the New Media," at www.nuevoanden.com/rag/newmedia.html (accessed August 17, 2016). Also see Thorne Dreyer and Victoria Smith, "Our Underground Roots," *Space City News*, July 4-17, 1969 (Vol. 1, No. 3), 12.

2. Victoria Smith Holden, "*Space City!*: From Opposition to Organizational Collapse," in Ken Wachsberger, ed., *Insider Histories of the Vietnam Era Underground Press, Part I* (East Lansing: Michigan State University Press, 2011), 306. Also see *Space City News*, ibid. 23.

3. Dreyer and Smith, "Our Underground Roots," 12.

4. Ibid. Also see John Leo, "Politics Now the Focus of the Underground Press," *The New York Times*, September 4, 1968 (Vol. 117, no. 40,401), 49, 95; John Burks, "The Underground Press: A Special Report," *Rolling Stone*, October 4, 1969 (Vol. 43), 12.

5. Smith, "*Space City!*: From Opposition to Organizational Collapse," 307-308.

6. Alice Embree, "Houston's historic *Space City!* to get new life," December 5, 2019. www.theragblog.com/alice-embree-houstons-

historic-space-city-to-get-new-life/ (accessed May 20, 2021); Dreyer quoted in Raj Mankad, "Underground in H-Town," *Offcite*, May 21, 2010. web.archive.org/web/20100524110804/http://offcite.org/2010/05/21/underground-papers-in-h-town (accessed July 21, 2020).

7. On Hampton's murder and *Space City!*'s response, see "The Houston Police Murdered Carl Hampton," *Space City!*, August 1-21, 1970 (Vol. 2, no. 5), 2-4; Also see Victoria Smith and Thorne Dreyer, "Carl Lives!: Power to the People's Party," *Space City!*, August 22, 1970 (Vol. 2, No. 6), 4-5.

8. "A Letter From the Collective," *Space City!*, April 6, 1971 (Vol. 2, no. 19), 2; Smith, "From Opposition to Organizational Collapse," 311-312, 316.

9. Thorne Dreyer to John Moretta, email, May 24, 2021.

10. Hermes Nye, "Texas Tea and Rainy Day Woman," in Francis Edward Abernethy, ed., *What's Going On? In Modern Texas Folklore* (Austin: Encino Press, 1976), 118; Laurence Leamer, *The Paper Revolutionaries: The Rise of the Underground Press* (New York: Simon & Schuster, 1972), 104-105.

Space City! and Houston's Alternative Community

Sherwood Bishop

In June 1969, *Space City News* (later *Space City!*) began publishing in a city that had long considered itself to be exceptional, although Houston was actually a fairly conventional Southern city. A large percentage of Houston's population was Latino or African-American, but like other Southern cities, most of the wealth and political power was controlled by whites.

In 1970, about 25 percent of Houston's population was African-American: one of the largest Black populations of any city in the U.S. Ninety percent of them lived in mostly African-American communities. There was a Black newspaper, the *Forward Times*, a Black-owned radio station, KCOH, and a historically Black university, Texas Southern University. There were many small Black businesses and a vigorous Black economy. However, the Black economy was segregated geographically and socially from the dominant white economy by Houston's laws and traditions.

Houston's Latinx population was about two thirds the size of the African-American population, not including about 70,000 undocumented immigrants. In 1970 there were no Latinx-owned newspapers or radio stations in Houston.

The Houston Independent School District was forced to integrate by the civil rights movement of the 1950s and 1960s, but integration occurred very slowly. To help achieve court-ordered integration numbers, the school district transferred many Latinx students, who were officially designated as "white," to mostly Black schools. HISD only integrated one grade level per year, and it was not finally integrated until 1970.

Of course, there was only one police force, and the Houston police had a long history of brutally supporting Jim Crow laws and robustly acting to keep its non-white citizens subdued. As a result, many of them experienced Houston, and Texas, as a place where whites were the citizens, and Blacks and Lat-

They were called hippies by others, but proudly referred to themselves as 'freaks.'

inx were little more than pretenders. Street frisks and intrusive traffic stops were commonplace.

Despite the similarities of their situations, the Black and Latinx communities were kept isolated from each other by culture, traditions, jealousy, and the machinations of the white power structure. In 1970, Houston's neighborhoods and economy were the most segregated of any major American city.

Fortunately, there were growing numbers of progressive activists: Black, Latinx, and white. Their frustration at their relative powerlessness sharpened their views and their tactics. With the support of civil rights legislation and the courts, their influence grew in the 60s.

In the late 1960s, new refugees began appearing in Houston. Many were semi-homeless although the homes of their families were not far away. They were called hippies by others, but usually proudly referred to themselves as "freaks." In Houston, in the 1960s, freaks were objects of scorn in the media and in public, where they could be yelled at, even threatened, by "straight" folks. Police harassed them just as they did Blacks and Latinx. As their numbers increased, they began forming a community of their own.

By this time everyone, even suburban children, had heard of hippies and San Francisco's 1967 Summer of Love. If a straight couple stopped their car at a traffic light and saw a hippie standing nearby, the adults might lock their car doors, while their children, even those in elementary school, might hold up their hands showing a peace sign.

While young people remained at home or in school, their lives and their looks were strictly controlled. Students in Texas schools could be expelled for growing long hair or not following other dress codes. *Space City!* published stories on October 25, 1969 and November 7, 1969 of a student who was permanently expelled from San Jacinto Junior College in Pasadena for growing a beard. The student, Carlos Calbillo, was eventually reinstated after successfully suing the college.

Space City! introduced itself into this volatile mixture of tradition and turmoil in June 1969. Its stated objective was not only to provide information that was otherwise not available, but also, as written by Dennis Fitzgerald in the first issue, to support the evolution of a community. As Dennis wrote, "A real community is people together — not just people." *Space City!* was a catalyst in that evolution, not just by providing information, but by providing a means of communication, discourse, and consensus. It also provided impoverished freaks with a simple way to earn some cash.

One thing that made Houston a welcoming space for the growing freak community was the availability of very cheap rental space for housing and offices. In the 1950s and early 60s, many middle-class white citizens had moved from comfortable but old homes near downtown into new suburban homes with amenities lacking in their old ones, like central heating and air conditioning, garages, plentiful electric outlets, and large yards. In the old neighborhoods, two-story, four-or-five-bedroom houses could be rented very cheaply. The *Space City!* offices were in one of those old homes at 1217 Wichita Street.

The availability of large but cheap rental houses, and the relative poverty of most freaks led to the development of communes or to less-formal situations where one person with a steady income would rent a house and sublet rooms or even parts of rooms to others. The cheapest houses were in neighborhoods within walking distance of downtown, and freak communities began growing in them.

Newly arriving runaways or castaways would be aware of basic aspects of hippie culture: "peace and love," long hair, colorful dress, and drug use. However, there were wide cultural differences between individual freaks, depending on their backgrounds. Teenagers from towns south of Houston might not have ever met a Black person. In 2000, African-Americans still made up only 1.6 percent of the population of Pasadena.

Newly arriving teenagers had often been outcasts or loners before leaving home. While freaks who had recently left home would invariably have rejected some of their parent's beliefs, they might have retained some of their parent's religious beliefs and even their politics. They may have never discussed these issues with anyone. Nevertheless, they all had one thing in common: they were unhappy with their lives and their prescribed futures, and they were searching for something better.

There were many others living in towns outside of Houston who were seeking new ideas and ways of living. For many of them, a second- or third-hand copy of *Space City!* provided hope.

That is exactly what happened to me. In the summer of 1969, I was working at the Shell Oil refinery in Deer Park. I was an active union steward in the Oil Chemical & Atomic Workers Local 4-367. Unfortunately, I'd become disillusioned with the union, due to the racism and reactionary attitudes of most of the members.

I was a classmate of Carlos Calbillo's at San Jacinto Junior College. The college, or "Spencer High" as we called it, was a miserably reactionary and incompe-

> 'A real
> community
> is people
> together —
> not just
> people.'

Ad: June 19, 1969.

tent institution at the time, and I was not far from dropping out for the second or third time.

My family lived in Houston, but I was estranged from them. I felt that I was an exile. One day a friend brought me a copy of the first issue of *Space City!*. He said, "These people are writing about the same things we're talking about."

Inside was "All You Need is Love" on the problems facing young people who wanted to make the world a better place. On the same page was Dennis Fitzgerald's piece, "On Community."

An article by Victoria Smith, "Radical Rumbling: Workers on the Move," described union scenarios like the ones I faced, but in California, New Jersey, and Michigan. In "From the Other Side of the Bayou," Danny Schacht and Raymond Ellington described Texas labor history that wasn't taught in schools or labor halls.

There were other articles on welfare mothers uniting (Sue Duncan) and on the oppressiveness of kindergarten and public schools (Dennis Fitzgerald). I was enthralled!

A few days later I visited the *Space City!* office. Within weeks my life had been transformed.

Space City! altered the lives of many others in ways that depended on who they were. Inside were articles addressing the interests and lives of women, of young men concerned about being drafted to fight in Vietnam, of students, artists, musicians, gays, prisoners, Blacks, and Latinx. A reader might be drawn to one article or even just the ads and cartoons, but then would move on to read about other people and issues.

The conditions of freak life induced the development of a common culture. Someone arriving in Montrose, the catch-all name for the area where freaks congregated, would need a place to stay, and they'd likely end up in a commune of some sort.

Communes weren't just crash pads. They provided the equivalent of freak families where everyone was a brother, sister, or lover.

People shared information, food, drugs, and philosophies. One or two people in a commune might buy a *Space City!*, but everyone would read it. Communal living entailed group conversations, including discussions of political, moral, or cultural issues. One

of the most basic aphorisms was the idea that people should work together to make the world better, to build a new culture and even a new world.

There were no computers, smart phones, or email. There were three network television stations, all broadcasting mainstream entertainment and news, and freaks saw limited value in them. Instead, people talked, played music, ate, and got stoned together, and talked more. These activities enabled people to learn new information and ways of viewing the world, to exchange ideas and, over time, to develop a new, albeit diverse, culture.

The first two ads by businesses in the first issue of *Space City!* were for Be-In Buttons ("Every Good Cause Deserves a Button") and Captain America's ("Not just a head shop, it's the beginning of a community.")

> **Within weeks my life had been transformed.**

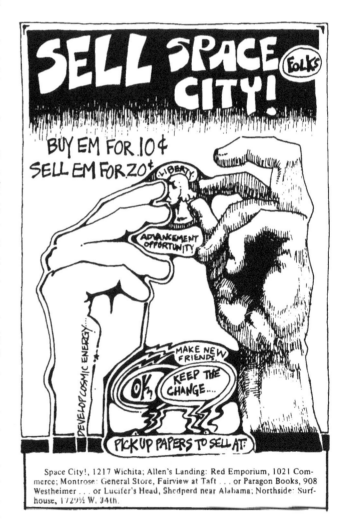

Space City!, 1217 Wichita; Allen's Landing: Red Emporium, 1021 Commerce; Montrose: General Store, Fairview at Taft . . . or Paragon Books, 908 Westheimer . . . or Lucifer's Head, Shepperd near Alabama; Northside: Surfhouse, 1729½ W. 34th.

Ad. Kerry Fitzgerald, November 26, 1970.

The same issue contained an article, "Burger Boycott" by Jane Manning, about the boycott of a Burger King at the corner of Wheeler St. and Almeda Rd. in the heart of a Black community. While a group of Black businessmen had applied to buy the franchise before the Burger King was built, the corporation sold the franchise to a white man who lived in Miami, Florida. The boycott was successful and within a month the franchise was sold to the local Black businessmen.

While the ads in *Space City!* provided money to support the costs of publishing the paper, they also helped support the development of the freak community. Ads in mainstream newspapers like the *Houston Chronicle* were not only very expensive, but they were also hard to see. Ads for movie theaters, musical performances from rock bands to opera, stage plays, and shows for children were all jumbled together in the classified section. On September 4, 1969, a benefit concert for *Space City!* ("Underground Concert... Featuring Bubble Puppy and other top groups") was held on the University of Houston campus. An ad for it appeared in the *Chronicle* on the same page with dozens of other ads. The concert ad was adjacent to ads for the film *Valley of the Dolls*, a live stage production of *Cabaret* at Jones Hall, a screening of *Oliver Twist* at the Alley Theatre, and ads for several XXX theaters.

In contrast, ads in *Space City!* were much cheaper and were targeted at *Space City!*'s readers. There were ads for rock concerts, night clubs, head shops, hip clothing shops, new folk or rock albums, bookstores, restaurants like the Family Hand that catered to freaks, record stores, bicycle shops, astrologers and healers, and various small freak owned businesses.

Because *Space City!* ads could be much larger, it was possible to include graphics and stylistic effects

The ads also helped support the development of the freak community.

Ad: Kerry Fitzgerald, June 5, 1969.

that communicated what they were. Such ads and graphics generally weren't allowed in conservative papers like the *Chronicle*.

If freaks, gays, or young hip Houstonians wanted to know what was happening in town, *Space City!* was the place to find out. *Space City!* not only became a forum for sharing information about businesses, activities, and ideas for freaks or liberal whites, it came to serve the same function for many Blacks, Latinx, gays, high school and university students, and others.

Each *Space City!* issue contained articles about activities in those communities: interviews with Black or Latinx activists, articles about organizations like the Mexican American Youth Organization (MAYO), People's Party II, the Welfare Rights Organization, Pacifica Radio, the Red Coyotes, high school groups, and many more. And *Space City!* didn't aim for journalistic neutrality, it was dedicated to advocacy of ideas and causes, and it supported the causes of organizations like the ones listed above. Because of this, those organizations could use *Space City!* articles to help them in their efforts. This exposed people in those communities to *Space City!*, and over time they came to read it and trust it.

Organizations that served minority communities, including *Space City!*, were different in nature than those in the dominant economy. The purposes of *Space City!* were advocacy and to provide information, rather than to be a financial investment. There was no one owner, publisher, or editor. It was managed by a collective of men and women who shared in all activities from writing and editing to sweeping floors. It was officially published by the Lyman Padde Educational Project, owned by the Collective. Lyman Padde was a dog.

Each member of the Collective had equal power in running the paper. Because straight media reporters often assumed that there must be a male publisher or editor, the Collective eventually decided that female members would be the representatives to the media.

Over the years, new members were added to the Collective, and some left. Management and editorial decisions made by the Collective often involved long discussions. Because of the social volatility of the times, small decisions, such as whether to use a specific graphic, were sometimes complicated by concerns about sexism, racism, and politics. This could result in a slow, clumsy, decision-making process, but because the Collective took these concerns very seriously, it was an educational process as well.

Decisions made in this way affected *Space City!*'s readers and its community as well. As *Space City!* came to be seen as the voice of the "alternate" community, readers often expressed great indignation or outrage at specific graphics, articles, or even sentences they found objectionable. The opinions of different readers were often dialectically opposed. When the concerns had been discussed by the Collective before publication, it was much easier to respond to these letters. During the last months that *Space City!* was published, some questions, such as whether there should be more cultural coverage or more political analysis, became persistent and divisive issues that contributed to *Space City!*'s eventual dissolution.

Many other freak businesses and organizations shared, to varying degrees, *Space City!*'s nonhierarchical management structure, and its aspiration to serve rather than to profit. Switchboard was a free phone-in forerunner of Wikipedia that provided information as well as eclectic aid to those in need. The University of Thought, Inlet Drug Crisis Center, the North Side People's Center, the Settegast Medical Center (see August 1, 1970 "Settegast Clinic: Community Control"), the Draft Counseling Service, Pacifica radio station KPFT, and the Job Co-op all provided free services (donations welcome!) and were managed with various experimental organizational structures. (See "Building Community.")

The People's Community Center & Clinic, created by People's Party II under the direction of Carl Hampton, opened and provided free services after Carl's murder. Community Bread was a member-operated food co-op that grew to include a farm run by volunteers, a kitchen/bakery that produced bread, tortillas, yogurt, and other simple foods. The co-op offered classes on nutrition and cooking and operated a day care center. It eventually grew to over 20 locations in the Houston area.

Some small freak businesses also experimented with group ownership or management, like Family Hand Restaurant (see "Family Hand: Some Changes"), Turtle News Book Store, and Of Our Own, a large live music venue. (See "Of Our Own, an Exciting Experiment.")

All these organizations operated successfully for a time. None of them exist today, except for the Pacifica radio station, KPFT.

They all eventually succumbed to the same set of problems: lack of financial capital, conflicts among the owners/staff, and especially, the eventual dissolution of the freak community itself. Most of the old Montrose houses are now gone, replaced by office buildings, multi-story apartment buildings or converted into condominiums.

However, Houston itself, now a twenty-first century city, is in some ways more like the old Montrose than the old Houston. The Houston metropolitan area has become the most racially/ethnically diverse large metropolitan area in the nation, although there are still large, relatively segregated areas. It is politically progressive and culturally audacious, and many of its residents look and act surprisingly like freaks.

San Marcos, Texas
June 2021

Promo: Kerry Fitzgerald, October 17, 1970.

The
Klan

Cover: April 13, 1971.

Under Siege: *Space City!* and the Nightriders

Thorne Dreyer

A frequent feature of *Space City!* was the "Letter from the Collective," the Collective being the editorial board and decision-making entity of the paper. These informal thought pieces were communiques to our readers, to keep them advised about what was going on with the paper and what we were thinking about events around us. I was a member of the *Space City!* Collective for its three-year run, from June 5, 1969, to August 3, 1972.

The Collective's dispatches often reported on the latest attacks by the local Ku Klux Klan on our offices and our community.

A "Letter from the Collective" in the June 19, 1969 issue of the paper, published after a Klan raid on the office, ended like this:

> One final note. If you gave us poetry anytime in the last few weeks, we no longer have it. The Klan stole the Poetry Box! How fiendish can you get?

Bombing the office is one thing, but stealing the Poetry Box? Couldn't they write their own freaking poetry? Well, come to think of it… probably not. Maybe they wanted to use it for *The Rat Sheet*, their occasional mimeographed throwaway. (Incidentally, the Klan also stole the *Space City!* subscription files and other items from Judy Fitzgerald's desk.)

The following is an example of *Rat Sheet* prose:

> The vulgar *Space City!* (formerly *Space City News*) hippie-type newspaper filth sheet of Houston recently ceased publication; with its death came cheers of delight from the community's decent citizens, who have become irate with that paper's degeneracy, and with the adverse effects it has had on the youth of our city…
>
> Let us examine the activities of some of the undesirables who complement-

Bombing the office is one thing, but stealing the Poetry Box?

ed [sic] *Space City!*'s staff, symps, and associates. KBI (Klan Bureau of Investigation) leads give the *RAT SHEET* reason to believe that these misfits, biocruds, and outpourings of a cesspool, are now using their money to stockpile arms and ammunition with which to instigate a revolution.

In addition to the purple nature of their prose, the Klan's journalism wasn't very reliable either. *Space City!* had not "ceased publication," but was on a short hiatus. That issue of *The Rat Sheet* was published in April 1971, more than a year before *Space City!* closed shop.

The Rat Sheet singled out my family: Martin Dreyer, the *Chronicle* reporter; Margaret Webb Dreyer, the artist, gallery owner, and peace activist; and their son, your humble correspondent.

They called us the "Infamous Dreyer Rats." After *The Rat Sheet* attacked us, my parents and I charged down to the next city council meeting where we expressed our outrage about the Klan and its actions.

To understand Martin Dreyer, *The Rat Sheet* suggested, "look for the most ultra-lib or leftist-slanted article the *Houston Chronicle* has to offer in its *Texas Magazine*… Yep, father of our little Thorne." In a statement, my father responded, "I feel that the Klan's shrill attack on me, its attempt to intimidate me in my writings for the *Chronicle*, is an attack on the freedom of the press. This is certainly true as the Klan also shoots its venom at *Space City!*, Pacifica, and other media."

My mother, after noting her "patriotic" bona fides (she was eligible for membership in the Daughters of the American Revolution should she care to join), said: "I think that it is ironic that they call themselves patriots… To me patriotism is being concerned about my fellow man. In fact, I consider my opposition to the War in Vietnam to be an expression of my patriotism."

About "little Thorne," this *Rat Sheet* was concise: "Now here's a rat if there ever was one!"

At City Council, Houston Mayor Louie Welch called *The Rat Sheet* one of the "filthiest pieces" he had ever read. The same mayor, it should be noted, who sat on his hands while the nightriders rode roughshod through his town.

Space City! was under attack from the Klan during its entire run, from first issue to the final number, as was most everybody else on the Left in the Bayou City. And the Klan's idea of the Left was pretty broad.

The *Space City!* office was hit with a military-style concussion grenade, cars outside were firebombed, nightriders shot bullets into the office multiple times. Several staffers were sitting on the front steps when a car pulled up and fired a half-dozen shots above their heads. Another time, a car stopped in front of the office and a man shot a hunting arrow from a crossbow into the front door. It had a sticker that said, "The Knights of the Ku Klux Klan *is* Watching You." (Sherwood Bishop, who was in the office at the time and saw the whole thing, said that two police cars were cruising the block, appearing to run interference for the nightriders.)

"In the wee morning hours of Friday, April 9 [1971], nightriders made the rounds of the Montrose area, firing numerous steel pellets through the windows and glass doors" of *Space City!* advertisers, reported the paper's Dennis Fitzgerald. "Several hours later the vandalized merchants received similar phone calls 'If you don't stop advertising in *Space City!*, you'll lose more than a window.'" None of the advertisers were intimidated; some even increased their level of support in response to the threats.

> 'If you don't stop advertising in *Space City!*, you'll lose more than a window.'

The Klan also shot up Dreyer Galleries, threw paint on the façade, and slashed a hammer and sickle on an outside wall. They shot a bullet through the front door and it lodged into a mosaic wall inside. Instead of repairing the damage, my mother painted a circle around the bullet hole, marking it as a badge of honor.

Space City! and SDS invited Yippie leader Abbie Hoffman to come to Houston to speak about the Chicago 8 at an April 1970 series of events at Hermann Park, Rice University, and the Continental Club. The right-wingers' hair caught fire over the thought of Abbie Hoffman in their fair city and threats were flying. They included a series of phone calls from an unidentified woman who promised to blow us up within 12 hours, if we didn't call off Hoffman's appearance. She kept calling, counting down the hours before our imminent demise. Either she was bluffing or they got cold feet — and we, of course, didn't cancel Abbie's visit.

Blackbelts John and Rick — who led our community karate class — volunteered to be Abbie's bodyguards, sticking to him like glue everywhere he went. When Abbie was leaving town, we presented him with a souvenir: the arrow that had been shot from the crossbow into the *Space City!* front door.

And it was more than just *Space City!* that was being attacked. In the August 28, 1969 number (only our fifth issue), we posted a "Letter from the Collective" that reported on attacks against local members

Infamous Dreyer Rats. Photo by Victoria Smith, April 13, 1971.

of the Students for a Democratic (SDS). Homes were being "broken into, ransacked and robbed" and an SDS apartment was shot up; an arrow was shot into an SDS house; car tires were slashed, a car firebombed, and other movement cars were riddled with bullets.

The article also reported that,

> The night before our [Space City!] office was bombed, a local SDS house received a phone call from a man who identified himself as the Grand Titan of the United Klans of America. He talked for two hours, attempting to scare local movement people with the extent of his knowledge about their activities. And he was, indeed, very well versed. One local activist was told information about himself that he thought only his mother knew.

Fred Brode, then chairman of the Houston Committee to End the War in Viet Nam, was a frequent Klan target, with, according to *The New York Times*, "20 bullets being fired into his home within five months and a fire started underneath it." He literally sandbagged the outside of his house for protection.

Another ongoing recipient of Klan wrath was Debbie Leonard, Socialist Workers Party candidate for mayor. About Debbie, *The Rat Sheet* wrote: "[Leonard] is linked with the Women's Liberation movement and is a staunch advocate of legislation for the Texas Abortion Coalition's 'legalized child murder' proposition." It called her a "hard core leftist and a proponent of the Gay Liberation Front." "Sounds sort of queer to us," they added.

An employee's car was bombed at *The Forward Times*, a Black community newspaper and publishing company that printed *Space City!* and several other college and neighborhood papers. The Klan's *Rat Sheet* called *The Forward Times* the "Jungle News," and referred to another paper published at its print shop as a "jungle bunny Rag." The Black Panthers had automatic weapons fired into their office as did the Carl Hampton Free Clinic.

Numerous countercultural institutions also found themselves on the Klan's enemies list. Nightriders set off a firebomb on the front porch of The Pagan Church, and the Family Hand Restaurant, a popular community gathering spot, was attacked with Molotov cocktails and bombed with a homemade explosive device that knocked out two doors. The Sport Cycle Shop "was attacked because it sold Czech bicycles." The Family Food Co-Op and the Drug Crisis Center were also harassed.

According to a report by Gary Thiher in October 1970, "At least a hundred such incidents have occurred in the last year or so. Yet the Houston police have not made one arrest in any of these cases."

KPFT-FM was bombed twice in its first six months of operation.

KPFT-FM, Houston's Pacifica radio station, which worked closely with *Space City!*, was bombed twice in its first six months of operation; both times the attacks took out the station's transmitter. That's two bombings more than any other radio station in the history of this country. The bombings occurred on May 12, 1970, and October 6, 1970.

After the transmitter was dynamited the first time, KPFT, noted for its commitment to free speech, offered Klan Grand Dragon Frank Converse a weekly program, which he eagerly accepted. As then KPFT news director Mitch Green remembered, "They did [the show] for a couple of weeks but [Converse] realized that nobody was listening to them, so they got pissed and went out and bombed us again."

With most of the acts of violence and intimidation against the Left in Houston at the hands of the Klan and other right-wing organizations, justice was slow in coming — when it came at all. *Space City!*'s Tom Hylden, in a June 6, 1971 article about a Grand Jury investigation of the Klan, wrote, "I don't feel too confident that the District Attorney and the Police Department are particularly serious about getting to the bottom of recent terrorism in Houston."

Space City!'s Richard Atwater asked Harris County Assistant District Attorney Warren White if his Grand Jury investigation "had uncovered any evidence of collusion between the police and the Klan." White denied that such collusion existed. "Maybe they didn't look too hard," wrote Atwater. It would, in fact, become widely documented that the KKK was heavily involved with the Houston Police Department.

Hugh Aynesworth, in a feature article in *Newsweek* magazine, wrote, "Not surprisingly, the beleaguered leftists are coming to regard the police as much a part of the enemy as the Klan."

On November 3, 1970, *The New York Times* reported:

> Representatives of a coalition of 12 liberal and radical groups, most of them anti-war, accused the Houston Police Department today of protecting two "nightrider" members of the Ku Klux Klan who allegedly committed vandalism.

> The coalition spokesman said that the two men had been seen committing acts of vandalism but that the police had refused to bring charges against them. Policemen apprehended the two men just before dawn last Thursday driving around Houston without lights.

> The automobile contained three semi-automatic rifles, a quantity of ammunition, a walkie-talkie radio, a container of gasoline, and some KKK literature, the police said. However, no charges were made against the two men.

> "This incident, among others, raises serious questions about the relationship between the Ku Klux Klan and the Houston Police Department," the coalition said in a formal statement.

Space City! later reported:

> [Klansman Louis] Beam said that the two were in the neighborhood that night for the purpose of watching the *Space City!* office, which is located a few blocks from the site of their arrest. Beam described *Space City!* as "a local underground communist newspaper published here." He said he had been keeping an eye on *Space City!* and other leftist organizations for some time, and had frequently turned over information on these groups to the Houston Police Department.

When young progressive Fred Hofheinz was elected Mayor of Houston in 1974, he was the first political figure to at least begin addressing the issue of Klan infiltration of the police.

It is nothing short of a miracle that no one was killed or seriously injured in the terrorist actions against Left groups at the hands of the Houston KKK. The Klansmen with whom we at *Space City!* had the most interaction were Mike Lowe, who attempted to infiltrate the *Space City!* staff, Jimmy Dale Hutto, who successfully infiltrated SDS and for a time lived in an SDS house with *Space City!* staffer Gavan Duffy and others; Louis Beam, who, according to the Southern Poverty Law Center, became a national leader in the white supremacist movement; and Klan Grand Dragon Frank Converse, who ran a North Houston gun shop.

It is nothing short of a miracle that no one was killed or seriously injured.

As I later wrote in a retrospective piece for *The Rag Blog*:

> Frank Converse admitted that the Klan had members working undercover in the police and city government. And, "for over two years we kept Klansmen working in the SDS," he said, but added that they had pulled them out for fear their cover would be blown...

> The Klan attempted to infiltrate the *Space City!* staff but scrawny and clueless Mike Lowe didn't fool anyone for long. In what — through the coolness of retrospection — seems genuinely knuckleheaded, a couple of staffers actually went to a cross-burning and photographed Lowe in full Klan regalia. *Space City!* ran the photos in the next issue. The next time he came to the office to volunteer, Dennis Fitzgerald and Cam Duncan chased him down, tackled him cleanly, and held him in a headlock. A picture of this textbook takedown would also grace the pages of *Space City!*"

In 1993, a "Michael Lowe," identified as Grand Dragon of the Texas Knights of the Ku Klux Klan, showed up in the national news and is clearly the same Mike Lowe we came to know in Houston as a lowly Klan soldier (or so we assumed). It looks like he, at least in the 1990s, was still going strong, though I must admit,

Lowe would have seemed an unlikely leadership candidate. [See Victoria Smith's *Space City!* feature on Mike Lowe elsewhere in these pages.]

The *Houston Chronicle* later reported that,

> Three Klansman were arrested in the [Pacifica] bombing. Jimmy Dale Hutto of Pasadena, the only person to stand trial in the bombings, was arrested on his way to California, where he allegedly planned to blow up KPFT's sister stations KPFA in Berkeley and KPFK in Los Angeles. Hutto was convicted in 1971 and sent to prison. The other two suspects testified for the government and never stood trial.

In addition to Hutto, Louis R. Beam Jr. was arrested for the Pacifica bombing and a machine-gun attack on the local Communist Party headquarters, but those charges were dropped. Also arrested in the Pacifica bombings were Peter Lout Jr. and Paul William Moratto.

In 1973, Mike Lowe received a 10-year probated sentence for possessing components for a home-made bomb. He admitted before a Grand Jury to bombing the *Space City!* office, the Family Hand Restaurant, and an architectural firm, but was granted immunity on those charges for testifying against others.

Other than that: Zilch.

Considering all their acts of violence over such an extended period of time, the Klan gang just weren't very effective terrorists. Or we weren't very good at being terrorized. We remained (perhaps foolishly) fearless and ever-more-committed to our cause — and the community around us just supported us all the more as the actions took place. If anything, the bombings and shootings brought more attention, sympathy — and readers. Frankly, these events simply pulled more people into the movement and made the community tighter.

The SWP's Debbie Leonard said that the terrorist attacks only served to draw socialist

and liberal organizations and individuals closer together. "We know each other now," she said, "and we aren't going to continue to take this sort of harassment quietly."

All the media attention created embarrassment for the city officials and highlighted the issue of how intertwined the Houston police was with the Ku Klux Klan.

One of the many attacks on the *Space City!* offices occurred at 2:30 a.m. on June 8, 1971. The paper reported that "the attackers shot several BB-type pellets into an upstairs office from a passing car. The pellets barely missed artist Kerry Fitzgerald [also known as Kerry Awn], as he was laboring away on a cartoon."

"Kerry hit the floor until the shooting was over, and then calmly resumed his work," the story said.

During all these heated times, *Space City!* just kept on truckin'.

Austin
May 2021

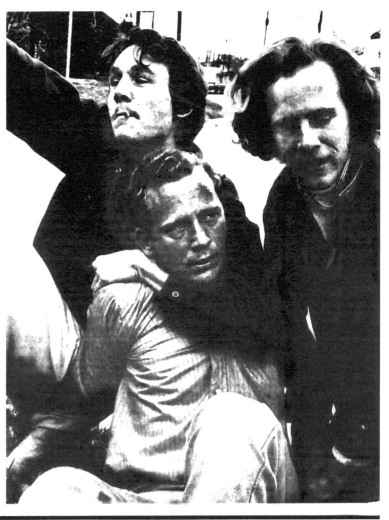

Cam Duncan, left, and Dennis Fitzgerald chase down Klansman Mike Lowe. Photo by Sue Mithun, June 1, 1971.

GIs Blasted Enroute

Space City News Staff • October 1, 1969

A car bringing GIs from Ft. Hood to participate in the anti-imperialist rally at Hermann Park, October 4, was riddled with bullets from an M-16 rifle.

The car, a yellow '68 Mustang owned by Austin civilian Dave Pratt, was one of four cars bringing 20 GIs to the rally. The cars had left the Oleo Strut GI coffee house in Killeen early Saturday. The GIs planned to attend the Houston rally to express their opposition to the Vietnam War and their support for the Movement.

However, most of the GIs did not arrive until long after the rally had ended.

This time the man in the back seat shot twice.

When the car driven by Pratt was about 13 miles past Temple, heading for Houston, a red and black '66 Fairlane cut in front. A man who looked like he weighed 250 pounds leaned out the back window with an M-16 automatic rifle, the kind used in Vietnam. He shot at their car and missed.

(Pvt. E-2 Roderick Hawkins was a passenger in the GI car. He told *Space City News* that the man driving the Fairlane had been in the Oleo Strut earlier in the day. He had identified himself as a Houstonian, and had been sitting in the coffee house listening to the GIs discuss the rally and their plans for attending it.)

Pratt's car sped ahead, attempting to shake its assailants. But the Fairlane passed them again; this time the man in the back seat shot twice, hitting the car's radiator and oil filter.

Pfc. Jim Carter, a passenger in a red Volkswagen who was following close behind Pratt's car, reported that the VW was also shot at, but was not hit.

Shortly past 3 p.m. that same afternoon, *Space City News* received a long-distance phone call. According to Richard Atwater who answered the phone, the caller had a smooth, gravelly voice.

"Hello friend," he said. "Understand you have a peace rally today. Well, some people came down from Killeen and ran into machine gun fire."

"I want to tell you right now that this is the Klan talking to you. The next time we're going to bury those people."

Although Pratt's car was put out of commission, most of the guys from Hood made it to Houston. They arrived at the *Space City News* office about 8 p.m. and were greeted by cheers and applause from the more than 30 people who had come there after the rally.

One private, a red fist stenciled to the back of his t-shirt, told us; "We knew we were going to be too late for the rally, but we decided to come anyway. We didn't want to let the Klan have the pleasure of keeping us away!" -30-

Art: Stogsdill, June 5, 1969.

Space City! Goes to a Cross Burning

Bill Casper • October 17, 1970

Last Saturday night (October 10) another *Space City!* staffer and I got dressed up in some of our straightest-looking clothes, combed the curls back off our ears, and headed for Northeast Harris County to the Ku Klux Klan rally. The rally was in a field about 10 miles this side of Crosby on Highway 90. When we got there we were pretty nervous, but we loosened up considerably when we got up in front of the crowd and saw other people filming and taking photographs.

About 400 people were gathered to one side of a long flatbed truck. The truck was all decked out with Klannish flags and paraphernalia, complete with uniformed Klansmen. As we walked up, Reverend Kitt, a right-wing fundamentalist who is head of the Louisiana Klan, was rapping out some racist Sunday School lesson. In fact, the whole atmosphere was revival-like. There were frequent interjections of "Amen," or "Tell it like it is," or "That's right" from the audience up front. The women's auxiliary sold coffee and cupcakes nearby, and several dozen kids were running around.

A real family thing, you know.

The main attraction at the rally was Robert Shelton, the Imperial Wizard of the United Klans of America, by far the largest Klan organization today. Shelton's speech was pretty standard Klan rhetoric, interspersed with a variety of racist jokes. Most of his comments were directed at "educational problems," since that's what's most on the minds of Southern (and Northern) racists right now. He laid out: how integration and bussing are part of the anti-Christ conspiracy designed by the Communists and financed from "Jew York City;" how drugs from Red China are being smuggled into Amerika thru Cuba in order to demoralize the minds of today's youth and create a generation gap; how the "nigras" are putty in the hands of the International Communist Zionist Jew Conspiracy, which aims at breaking down the faith of the Bible Belt; and blah, blah, blah.

Frank Converse, the Grand Dragon of the United Klans in Texas, was a little more interesting than Shelton, but he didn't come through with what he had been promising in the media. For the past week Converse had been on radio and television news saying that he would "expose" Houston City Hall at his rally Saturday night. But Saturday night Converse didn't expose anything but his own bullshit; he had worked the media for some pretty good advertising though. His most pertinent remarks were on the Klan's growth in Harris County: "We have them (members) in the police department, in the sheriff's department and up in City Hall, and these people are working to build up the United Klan." Converse had high praises for Houston police chief Herman Short and Harris County Sheriff Buster Kern.

But why is there now enough interest in the Klan for them to hold a political rally (the first in Harris County in three years) when they're still saying the same old shit? Why did 400 people drive up to Crosby to hear Shelton's same tired, old rap? Most of those people were either working people or petty bourgeoisie (shopkeepers, farmers, very small-time businessmen, etc.). It is easy to say that these people are dupes of Klan-type rhetoric or to say that they are incurable racists with their dander up about civil rights and school integration. Certainly, an Amerikan education and a fundamentalist upbringing don't give you a highly developed critical facility, and certainly the rally-goers were racists. But if we say only that, we risk indulging our own middle-class biases and we also risk missing some other reasons why these people might turn fondly toward the right wing.

I would guess that those people (and lots of other lower-middle and working-class whites) have a lot of unanswered questions in their heads: Why are our taxes so high? Why are we spending so much money and so many lives in Southeast Asia without winning? Why is there so much welfare and low-cost housing for minorities when we work our asses off and just get by? Why are college kids and hippies using these weird drugs and raising so much hell?

At the same time, these people are the ones who are feeling the pinch of the high taxes for a drawn-out war. They are getting screwed by rising unemployment and rising prices. They think that black and brown workers are getting the jobs that they are missing out on (this being a myth of rather gigantic proportions, as are the myths of welfare and low cost

> **Silk-sheeted Klansmen with torches slowly circled the gasoline-soaked cross.**

housing). They have had to work hard and they have no love for people that they believe won't work (hippies, welfare recipients, etc.).

The Klan comes to these people with a line that answers all their questions and at the same time appeals to all their racial and religious prejudices: white supremacy, anti-Semitism, anti-Catholicism, etc. Not only that, but the Klan has all the stylistic appeal of the other fraternal orders: flashy costumes, exciting titles (Wizards, Dragons, Kleagles, Exalted Cyclopses, etc.), far-out rituals, and a feeling of sticking together, "klannishness." A pretty attractive bag to fall into.

After all the speeches it was announced that there would be a cross-burning and most of the crowd hurried over to get a good look. About two dozen silk-sheeted Klansmen with torches slowly circled the gasoline-soaked cross and then a couple of them walked in and lit it. All the while, "The Old Rugged Cross" was blaring out of the p.a. system back at the truck (really funky organ music, you know, the kind you get on TV soap operas). Everybody watched the fire in silence until the music stopped and then they left. It was very bizarre.

We hung around for a few minutes to get a picture of an old "friend" we had recognized under one of the sheets, and then we split, too. eager to get back to the city. -30-

The Klan freaked out when
Abbie was coming.
Ad: Art by Kerry Fitzgerald,
March 28, 1970.

Newsweek Says Civil War in Houston

Thorne Dreyer • May 4, 1971

Check out the May 3 *Newsweek*. It has a spread on Our Town.

The article, which covers more than a page, is headed "Houston's Civil War." It is the latest in a series of features on right-wing terrorism in Houston that have appeared in major national publications.

Previously, magazines such as *Esquire*, *The New Yorker*, and *The Nation* have run items on the subject. And National Educational Television's "The American Dream Machine" did a live telecast of Pacifica radio's return to the air after the second bombing that included a Houston repression wrap-up.

But the *Newsweek* number appears to be the one that finally got the mayor's goat. Mayor Louie told the local television audience that the article was inaccurate, poorly researched. *Newsweek* Houston bureau man Hugh Aynesworth, who penned the piece, says fiddlesticks. And from where we stand, this is probably the most accurate article on the subject yet distributed nationally.

The top of the page (p. 54, incidentally) is adorned with three photos: Fred Brode standing in front of his sandbagged house; the good mayor in the middle; and, on the far right, Klan Grand Dragon Frank Converse, standing behind the counter at his Airline Gun Shop.

The article sketchily details the events of right-wing terrorism over the last few years. It also points something of an editorial finger at the police and city officials for their consistent inaction.

"For reasons best known to itself, the Houston Police Department has managed to make not a single arrest and efforts even to dampen the violence have been notably ineffectual."

After giving the cops the benefit of the doubt (like the city's so big and the police force is so small, and things are tough all over), Aynesworth concludes:

"Not surprisingly, the beleaguered leftists are coming to regard the police as much a part of the enemy as the Klan. 'If these things were happening to right-wingers,' says a white activist, 'you'd see a dozen long-haired cats and blacks in the pokey in 24 hours.'

'...the leftists are coming to regard the police as much a part of the enemy as the Klan.'

On the record, the statement does not seem unreasonable."

He quotes anti-war activist/harassment victim Fred Brode: "The police spend most of their time investigating the peace movement instead of the Ku Klux Klan. You see everything the police do fits a pattern. They agree with the bombers; it's that simple."

About Mayor Welch, the article adds: "The mayor, a four-term politician named Louie Welch who peddles real estate as a sideline (as do the police chief and several city officials) has refused to investigate the local Klan and contents himself with periodically counseling both right and left against acts of violence."

There's also a quote from Converse that should perk up a few ears. (Dragon Frank's been coming on with a line of cool moderation in most recent interviews.) Says Frank: "To me, if you kill a man overseas for being a Communist, you should kill him over here. I don't see any difference."

Pretty heavy. -30-

Lowe-down: Portrait of a Klansman

Victoria Smith • June 1, 1971

We last saw Mike Lowe, young Waco carpenter and known Klansman, just a few weeks before he was arrested with materials to make a bomb.

He and some friends dropped by to purchase some papers Saturday, May 8. Lowe was smiling and cocky, as usual. We were downright hostile, angrily snapping photographs of him and his colleagues. After it became clear to them that we were in no mood for playing games, they left in a hurry without even paying for the papers.

This encounter was certainly not the first. We've known Mike Lowe for nearly two years. He has been around *Space City!* from time to time just about as long as *Space City!* has been in Houston.

The story of our acquaintance with Lowe is at times comical, more often hair-raising, but generally revealing. He has visited us more often than have [notorious Klansmen] Jimmy Hutto, Louis Beam or any of the others, sometimes under the cover of night, sometimes in broad daylight when he would drop in for a little chat. And while he never openly admitted what he was up to, he was apparently so taken with himself that he could scarcely conceal it; we got the message through innuendo and thinly-veiled threats.

We were barely into our second month of publication when Mike first came by the *Space City!* office. He told us he was a carpenter and wanted to help. But he seemed more interested in just "hanging around" and eyeing people as they worked than in performing the little tasks we set out for him.

He especially liked to hang around Judy Fitzgerald's office, where most of the business and subscription records were kept. Lowe gave Judy the creeps from the very beginning.

One day, late in July of 1969, after Mike had spent the day watching Judy work, the subscription files mysteriously disappeared. The next morning, the tires on one of the staff cars were slashed. But no one was particularly suspicious of Mike, and he just kept hanging around.

The following evening staff members Sherwood Bishop and Gavan Duffy were working downstairs

'You're going to be dead motherfuckers if you don't quit messing around.'

in the office when there was a strange noise at the front door. Sherwood went to investigate. He found a funny-looking cylindrical package just inside the door. Fortunately, he didn't pick it up, but stepped outside to catch sight of a figure beating a hasty retreat to a car parked in front of the office. The license plates were covered with white cloth. Then the little package exploded. Glass in the front door and in most of the downstairs windows shattered. Smoke filled the office.

Gavan called the police and summoned the rest of the staff which was meeting at a nearby home. When we arrived the place was crawling with police, who were busily probing through the debris with flashlights. Just then the phone rang. Gavan answered it and nervously conveyed the caller's message: "You're going to be dead motherfuckers if you don't quit messing around."

"I know who it was, too," Gavan whispered. "That was Mike's voice." (Lowe has a distinctive voice: deep, deep Southern accent complicated by what sounds like a speech impediment, making it difficult to understand what he's saying. He also maintains a saccharine-sweet intonation that bugs the hell out of you.)

But we didn't tell the police; we didn't want to get any possibly innocent people in trouble. (Little did we know that it would prove next to impossible to get any possibly *guilty* people in trouble with the Houston police.)

We should have listened to Gavan. He was an SDS member that summer and was living in an apartment with Bartee Haile and Jimmy Dale Hutto, a rather odd couple as it turns out. Hutto was also "an SDS member" that summer. That was the summer that SDS was trying to organize a work-in and Hutto was a worker at Shell and how was anyone to know that he was a Klan infiltrator? Gavan says he was suspicious of Jimmy Dale from the beginning.

Some of us stubbornly refused to jump to nefarious conclusions about Lowe until a few months later when Cam Duncan, then a member of the *Space City!* Collective, met up with him at a high school rally at Jubilee Hall. Cam and Mike took a little walk into the night, during which Mike, in his own inimitable manner, made some pretty provocative statements. Cam, while a little nervous about his physical safety during the jaunt, courageously persisted in his "investigation," and returned convinced that Lowe was involved in right-wing terrorist activities.

On October 4, 1969, SDS and *Space City!* held an "anti-imperialist" rally in Hermann Park. Several carloads of anti-war GIs from Ft. Hood, traveling in caravan to Houston for the rally, were attacked and fired upon in broad daylight on the highway near Temple. (The attack was extremely nervy.) One car was seriously damaged, but no one was hurt.

Interestingly enough, the GIs' description of one of the occupants of the car resembled that of our friend Mike. The victims said this man had been hanging around the Oleo Strut GI coffeehouse near Ft. Hood, asking about the rally. (Lowe's physical description, like his voice, is rather unique: moderate height, wavy reddish-blond hair, and startlingly piercing blue eyes. When he smiles, you just know he's not your friend.) Later, when we showed the Strut folks our photographs of Mike, they said they couldn't be absolutely positive, but they thought it was the same man. They also described the attacker's car as deep red with a black vinyl top, a vehicle that was to become all too familiar to us in the next several months.

Mike put in another appearance at the *Space City!* office November 8, 1969, at a meeting to discuss a large anti-war march and rally scheduled for the next day. There was quite a little flurry as Mike sauntered in. It was a large meeting and those of us who knew Mike went around whispering to those who had not yet had the pleasure. Lowe seemed amused. He kept asking me which one was Dennis (presumably Dennis Fitzgerald, another *Space City!* Collective member). I told him coldly that I didn't know any Dennis.

Klansman Mike Lowe with Rev. Kitt at Klan rally near Crosby, Texas. Photo by Bill Casper. June 1, 1971

The meeting broke up and we all moved outside. I overheard Lowe asking someone why the *Space City!* people were so uptight. He also told this same person that he knew the guys that shot up those GIs on the highway. It was a clear case of he knew what we were thinking, and we knew he knew, and he knew we knew he knew...

So, there we were, sitting around on the front porch, exchanging abstruse but leading comments about guns and paranoia, when all of a sudden Mike stood up, bid us an abrupt farewell, and split. We watched him walk down Wichita St. and turn the corner at San Jacinto. The instant he passed out of sight, Kerry Fitzgerald took off like a shot after him. But he had disappeared, seemingly into thin air. There was no chance of trailing him.

Early the next morning, a car was burned and gutted outside the front of the *Space City!* office. Lest this sound too incriminating, we still don't know who did it. But we have our suspicions.

We didn't see much of Mike until the beginning of 1970. It was Christmas vacation time and Thorne Dreyer and I were just about the only *Space City!* people in town. We were sitting around the office one afternoon when Mike came by, ostensibly to purchase some papers. He and Thorne (or "Thornton," as the Klan is wont to call him) fell into a heavy discussion.

The message was increased terrorism and the medium was snide innuendo. Mike spoke extensively of right-wing groups, particularly the Minutemen, but he never used the first person plural. It was always "them," with the "we" heavily implied. In addition to the usual right-wing analyses (like it's the Communists who are stirring up all the trouble among the blacks), Lowe submitted that the right wing was using Houston as a sort of testing ground, to demonstrate how a city could be purged, one way or another, of leftist elements. He also told Thorne that he thought the terrorism would quickly rise to more serious levels; they're going to start killing people, he said. He painted a vivid picture of one of these "nice young girls" around *Space City!* being whisked away one night and later turning up with a slit throat.

Well, we just didn't know what to think. We felt that Mike was bluffing, but then, one couldn't be too cautious. After all, the man was clearly mad as a hatter. No telling what he might do. After that, we forsook those lonely evening walks, travelled everywhere in pairs, religiously locked doors and windows. And you can be sure that we always knew where to find a shotgun quickly.

The next time Lowe made the scene, however, we were ready for him. He appeared one afternoon in February, 1970. Dennis Fitzgerald kept him occupied with idle chatter downstairs while Judy Fitzgerald contacted Cam and Sue Duncan on the phone. "Mike Lowe's here," she said. "Get over here with your camera." Cam and Sue took the long route, via the Sears parking lot, where their suspicions were confirmed. There was that notorious red late model car with a black vinyl top: the license plate spelled out, most appropriately, NEVER.

Sue snapped a few pictures of the car as well as some of a couple in the car parked next to it. Sue said she had seen the people, a man and a women, observ-

True to his word, Lowe was apparently no longer our 'friend.'

ing anti-war demonstrators at a peace march some months before. When the couple realized what was going on, they became angry and chased Cam and Sue's Volkswagen up Fannin to Wichita where the VW turned off and the other car drove on.

Cam and Sue burst into the *Space City!* office with the camera. Mike started getting a little jittery. Cam suggested that Mike let him take his picture, but Lowe didn't go for that idea at all. He dropped his papers and darted out the front door, with Cam, Dennis, Sue, and the camera right behind him. The *Space City!* folks caught up with the suspect a few blocks from the office. Cam and Dennis wrestled him gently to the ground while Sue snapped his picture. They said that Lowe kept telling them that he "couldn't be our friend" after this. Was he mad! (We later traced the NEVER license plate to a Waco registration under the name of Michael Lowe and the plate on the other car to a Houston firm, the Brown Fintube company.)

Later that night, Mike and his friends drove by a few times in the never, never car. At one point, the intrepid Lowe marched up the front walk to reclaim the papers he had lost earlier. Every time the car drove by, we stuck a warning shotgun out the upstairs window. We didn't notice the Klan hanging around for several months after that. Forewarned is forearmed, and all that.

Never: Mike Lowe's nightrider car. June 1, 1971.

DO YOU WANT TO STAND OUT FROM THE CROWD?

THEN SUBSCRIBE TO...

SPACE CITY NEWS

1 year ★ 5 BUCKS   Servicemen ★ 3 BUCKS

Ad: Art by Kerry Fitzgerald, May 23, 1970.

peace-love stoned freaks, that we strongly believed in armed self-defense, particularly where right-wing terrorism is concerned.

I have since learned that they call him "The Kid" in the Klan and that he is generally considered to be pretty wacko. In fact, when Klan Grand Dragon Frank Converse was interviewed recently by Pacifica radio's Gary Thiher, he said, "I hope that little sonofabitch gets what's coming to him." Converse claimed that Lowe was an upstate Klansman and had never been a member of a local Klan "unit," and that even the Klan considers him pretty crazy.

Whether that's on the level or just Converse covering his tracks, we don't know. It's kind of hard to read those folks. But we have to agree with Converse on one point: Mike Lowe certainly is a crazy son-of-a-bitch! -30-

True to his word, Lowe was apparently no longer our "friend." We would only see him at large public gatherings, like anti-war rallies. The notorious red and black car was replaced by a goldish-brown car, which always seemed to be cruising around whenever bullets or arrows were fired at our office.

One of our cagey short-haired photographers did manage to snap a shot of Lowe in United Klans of America regalia posing with a right-wing minister at the Klan rally near Crosby last year. "Here, Reverend, let me take your picture with the nice young Klansman here." They both beamed (no pun intended.)

At any rate, we were happy when we found that Lowe had been picked up by the police and put behind bars.

We don't have much of an analysis of this man, except that he's dangerous, disturbing, and probably very sick. We never could quite figure out what drove him to play those games with us, to blow his cover almost from the first time he came around. Surely he must have known that we weren't your traditional

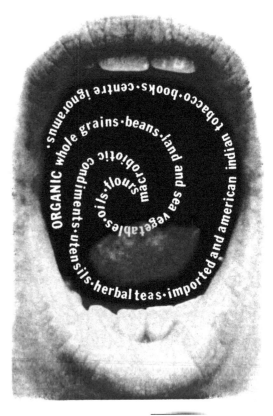

Ad: October 20, 1971.

Guilty on 3 Counts:
Jimmy Dale Hutto Convicted

Karen Northcott • September 14, 1971

The courtroom grew quiet as the judge walked solemnly to the bench. As the six men and six women entered in single file, the spectators inhaled as one, moved to the edge of their seats, turned to look at the jury in whose hands the fate of Jimmy Dale Hutto rested, and then settled back down to hear the reading of the verdict.

Jimmy Dale sat there, smiling the same vacant smile, registering little or no emotion as the foreman announced that he had been found guilty of conspiracy to destroy the transmitters of the Pacifica [radio] stations in Los Angeles and Berkeley and two counts of violation of the Federal Firearms Act — offenses which could cost him up to 12 years in prison and/or $25,000.

The jury had deliberated a little over three and a half hours following several hours of often passionate and inflammatory summations.

Charges and countercharges marked the closing statements of both the prosecution and defense. Asst. U.S. Attorney Edward McDonough opened the argument for the government and listed some of the offenses involving Hutto besides the conspiracy and gun charges.

He cited the October 6 bombing of the Pacifica station's transmitter here which knocked the station off the air for the second time. (Hutto and Louis Beam, a self-proclaimed Klan intelligence agent, are indicted in state court for that bombing.)

"There was no burning in California because the conspiracy was frustrated by the arrest of the parties," McCullough said. He said that the government had the choice of following them (two young Pasadena men, Russell A. Rector and Ronford L. Styron were arrested along with Hutto but were not prosecuted because they "had blown the whistle") across the country at 105 miles per hour, maybe having a flat tire, or get in the way, or maybe not catch him until he set fire to something.

"Hopefully, when you get wind of a crime, you nip it in the bud," he said.

> ## Hutto and Beam 'remind me of a couple of witch doctors trying to drive the devils out of the land with loud noises and blinding flashes of light.'

Phillip Cyphers, Pasadena attorney for Hutto, asked the jury not to convict his client for his beliefs. He said that if a conspiracy existed it was between informants Rector, 18, and Styron, 20, and FBI agent Edward Stork, all of whom had served as government witnesses in the trial.

J.B. Stoner, lead counsel for the defense, charged that the government was attempting to destroy the Klan. He said that the government was trying to appeal to the jury's biases and prejudices by dragging the Klan into the case and the indictment. "When you find this man not guilty, you aren't condoning his acts, because he hasn't done anything," Stoner told the jury.

"Because Jimmy Dale Hutto doesn't like any of these Communist Revolutionary organizations that are carrying on a revolution against us today," he railed, arms flailing, "that doesn't mean that he would go out and use bloody violence against them."

"It seems to me that when you have a revolution going on like we are today the Justice Department should have the revolutionaries on trial rather than Jimmy Dale," he thundered. "The government is placed in the position of having to protect the revolutionaries," Stoner added.

Stoner refuted the government's charges that Beam and Hutto were up to no good the night they were arrested in the vicinity of *Space City!* and KNUZ. "The government is trying to make a case because Beam had guns, flares, and newspapers [*Space City!*, *The Texas Observer*, and Klan publications]. The government is trying to put prejudice in your minds," he told the six men and six women, "not just prejudice, but concrete prejudice."

Asst. U.S. Atty. Ellis McCullough, lead counsel for the government, alternately roared and mimicked as he ripped apart Hutto's testimony in his closing argument.

He said that Hutto and Beam "remind me of a couple of witch doctors trying to drive the devils out of the land with loud noises and blinding flashes of light."

Jimmy Dale's defense to the gun charges (illegally purchasing a weapon because he had been previously declared a "mental defective" and making a false statement in the purchase of that gun) was two-pronged: first, that no gun dealer had read him the government form that requires that a buyer be neither a felon nor a person with a history of a mental defect and second, that his parents had told him that his records concerning his stay at two mental institutions had been expunged by the court.

"He can read, can't he?" thundered McCullough. "Then he says, 'Momma told me it didn't count.' He wasn't going to get a gun legally after that anyway — he was going to be convicted but he chose the insanity route." (Hutto said he had previously feigned insanity in 1965 to keep from going to jail for a minor offense.)

McCullough said that the bomb plot was not "a Halloween prank."

"The most dangerous animal in the urban guerilla war is not the junkie, but is the terrorist. Fortunately, there aren't too many of them yet," he added. "How many innocent people are going to be burned and bombed?" he asked, pounding his fist on the desk, his voice raising to a high emotional pitch. "But it's you and me that are going to be in the middle, if the victims start fighting back," he warned. "It's our duty to put a halt to this by convicting Hutto," he finished fervently.

And convict him they did. -30-

Art: Kerry Fitzgerald, September 7, 1971.

Space City!
Insurgents

CARL LIVES!

CARL HAMPTON, murdered by Houston police, July 26, 1970

PEOPLES PARTY II PLATFORM

1. We want freedom. We want power to determine the destiny of our Black Community.

We believe that black people will not be free until we are able to determine our destiny.

2. We want full employment for our people.

We believe that the federal government is responsible and obligated to give every man employment or a guaranteed income. We believe that if the white American businessmen will not give full employment, then the means of production should be taken from the businessmen and placed in the community so that the people of the community can organize and employ all of its people and give a high standard of living.

3. We want an end to the robbery by the capitalist of our Black Community.

We believe that this racist government has robbed us and now we are demanding the overdue debt of forty acres and two mules. Forty acres and two mules was promised 100 years ago as restitution for slave labor and mass murder of black people. We will accept the payment in currency which will be distributed to our many communities. The Germans are now aiding the Jews in Israel for the genocide of the Jewish people. The Germans murdered six million Jews. The American racist has taken part in the slaughter of over fifty million black people; therefore, we feel that this is a modest demand that we make.

4. We want decent housing, fit for shelter of human beings.

We believe that if the white landlords will not give decent housing to our black community, then the housing and the land should be made into cooperatives so that our community, with government aid, can build and make decent housing for its people.

5. We want education for our people that exposes the true nature of this decadent American society. We want education that teaches us our true history and our role in the present-day society.

We believe in an educational system that will give to our people a knowledge of self. If a man does not have knowledge of himself and his position in society and the world, then he has little chance to relate to anything else.

6. We want all black men to be exempt from military service.

We believe that Black people should not be forced to fight in the military service to defend a racist government that does not protect us. We will not fight and kill other people of color in the world who, like black people, are being victimized by the white racist government of America. We will protect ourselves from the force and violence of the racist police and the racist military, by whatever means necessary.

7. We want an immediate end to POLICE BRUTALITY and MURDER of black people.

We believe we can end police brutality in our black community by organizing black self-defense groups that are dedicated to defending our black community from racist police oppression and brutality. The Second Amendment to the Constitution of the United States gives a right to bear arms. We therefore believe that all black people should arm themselves for self-defense.

8. We want freedom for all black men held in federal, state, county and city prisons and jails.

We believe that all black people should be released from the many jails and prisons because they have not received a fair and impartial trial.

9. We want all black people when brought to trial to be tried in court by a jury of their peer group or people from their black communities, as defined by the Constitution of the United States.

10. We want land, bread, housing, education, clothing, justice and peace. And as our major political objective, a United Nations-supervised plebiscite to be held throughout the black colony in which only black colonial subjects will be allowed to participate, for the purpose of determining the will of black people as to their national destiny.

YOU CAN KILL A REVOLUTIONARY,
BUT YOU CAN'T KILL THE REVOLUTION

Poster: August 1, 1970.

Women's
Liberation

Cover: March 28, 1970.

Space City! and Women's Liberation

Alice Embree

In early June 1969, when *Space City!* began as *Space City News*, Women's Liberation was beginning to reverberate across the country. Women were demanding an end to sexism in the underground press. Houston's newly minted underground newspaper was ahead of the curve.

The original Collective had a gender parity that was uncommon at the time. Women's participation in collective leadership never faltered, and Victoria Smith was a prodigious writer, contributing over 70 articles over the course of *Space City!*'s three-year run.

The coverage of Women's Liberation began with two consecutive articles co-authored by Victoria Smith and Judy Fitzgerald. These articles explore the dawning consciousness of Women's Liberation, focusing first on gender roles and barriers, then on women as objects of marketing in a society shaped by consumption.

The first article appeared in the June 19, 1969 issue with artwork by *Rag* artist Trudy Minkoff. The title was "American Woman: You've Come a Long Way, Baby." In the July 4, 1969 issue, Victoria Smith and Judy Fitzgerald focused on "The Woman Market." In December 1969, a comic drawn by Trudy Minkoff provides a remarkable crash course in Women's Liberation consciousness at the time, all captured in a centerspread graphic.

Coverage of women's issues was continuous and diverse. It reflected an intersectional approach long before "intersectionality" was coined by Kimberlé Crenshaw in 1989 to describe the way forms of oppression, such as race, class, and gender, intersect. *Space City!* certainly covered contraception and abortion, but also the issue of forced sterilization. There was recognition that reproductive issues included the right to have and raise a child as well as the right to terminate a pregnancy. Welfare rights, health care access, and child care all received coverage. As women pounded on the doors of employment restrictions, *Space City!* reported on demonstrations, conferences, and lawsuits filed.

Coverage of women's issues was continuous and diverse.

Contributor Karen Northcott began writing for the paper in April 1971. Both Northcott and Smith covered many topics, including police repression and prison rights. Beginning in July 1971, Northcott began coverage of a major complaint and subsequent lawsuit filed against the University of Texas for sex discrimination, detailing salary disparities, representation of women in faculty positions, and barriers to promotion.

Coverage of women's issues included treatment of women prisoners, GIs and their relationship with Asian women, labor organizing by women employees at Ma Bell, Chicana organizing, lesbians, and the role of women in Cuba. *Space City!* also delved deeply into women's history as it was being unearthed. Before gender studies became a thing, the paper was publishing a history of International Women's Day, the fight for suffrage, and telling the stories of Harriet Tubman, Elizabeth Gurley Flynn, and Helen Keller.

Space City! also had a cultural component, including the poetry of Diane di Prima, Margaret Randall, and others; book reviews; film criticism, including a cover story on Greta Garbo; the ideas of actress turned activist Jane Fonda on Women's Liberation; and Joe Hill's tribute song, *The Rebel Girl*.

Marie Blazek wrote a number of book reviews in 1971 that included Firestone's *The Dialectic of Sex*; J's *The Way to Become a Sensuous Woman*; and Greer's *The Female Eunuch*. In October 1971, Blazek responded to a *Space City!* article by columnist Saundra Wrye who usually covered cooking and food in the paper. Wrye had written instead about the characteristics of Yin and Yang. Blazek provides a feminist perspective, prescient in its recognition of fluid gender roles and clever with its critique of archaic stereotypes.

In the last issue of *Space City!*, Blazek remembers her own trajectory from Houston's Harriet Tubman Brigade. She provides a panoramic picture of Houston's vibrant and diverse women's movement in 1972. Only five months after *Space City!* ended, the

National Women's Political Caucus brought 1,500 women to a Houston convention.

Space City! ads reveal an aspect of life before Roe v. Wade for women seeking an abortion. "Low Cost, Safe, Legal Abortion in New York, Scheduled Immediately" was a recurring ad. Women were, of course, getting abortions before Roe. The question, as it has become today, is how safe were the abortions and how much access did poor women have. Money and time made it possible to schedule a legal abortion in New York.

Austin
May 2021

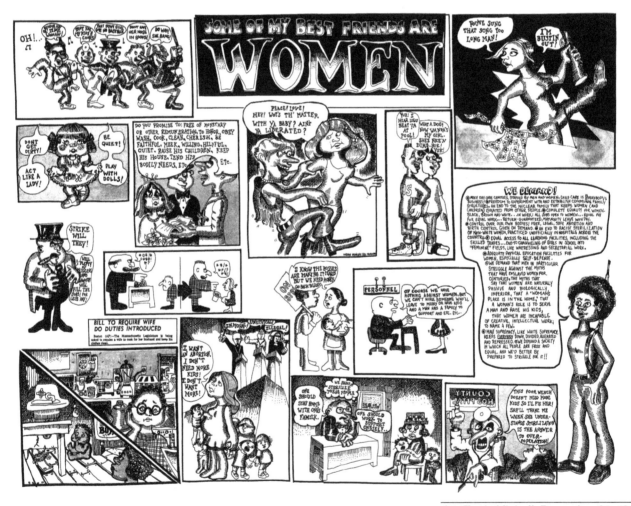

Art: Trudy Minkoff, December 20, 1969.

American Woman: You've Come A Long Way

Victoria Smith and Judy Fitzgerald • June 19, 1969

I have a Bachelor's degree in French literature. The smartest thing I ever did, however, was to take a typing course my junior year in high school; without it I would never be able to find a job. *(Secretary, age 24.)*

Ever since I had Kevin I lie in bed at night and plan what I'm going to do the next day. When I go to the drugstore to buy some more Pampers, that's a big thing. I plan my whole day around it. I can't believe that's become an excursion out for me now. *(New mother, age 21, college graduate.)*

Ye Gods, what do I do all day. Well, I get up and out of bed at 6 a.m. I get my son dressed and then get breakfast. After breakfast I wash dishes, then bathe and feed my baby. She's three months old. Then start the procedure of house cleaning. I make beds, dust, mop, sweep, vacuum. Then I do my baby's wash. Then I get lunch for the three of us. Then I put my baby to bed, and the little boy to bed for his nap. Then I usually sew or mend or wash windows and iron and do the things I can't possibly get done before noon. Then I cook supper for my family. After supper my husband usually watches TV while I wash dishes. I get the kids to bed. Then — if l m lucky — I'm able to sit down, watch TV, or read a magazine. Then I set my hair and go to bed. *(A 22-year-old housewife, quoted in* Workingman's Wife.*)*

Do these unhappy testimonies, originally cited by Marilyn Salzman Webb in *Motive* magazine, give an accurate picture of American womanhood? Not quite. The total picture is even worse.

American society is structured in such a way that women are given a certain limited range of roles to play.

In most cases, no matter which role she choses or is forced to choose — that of housekeeper-babysitter, expensive mistress-whore, working girl — she will eventually experience deep feelings of dehumanization and frustration. And the role that all women, rich or poor, black or white, are required to fill is that of the heavy consumer.

The stereotype of the neurotic housewife, the frustrated sex-kitten, and the bitter old maid is something of a great joke to the American society. But it's no joke to the millions of women who have to play these parts.

Many women think that their problems are individual ones. Women have it good in this society, you may say. Something must be wrong with me, if I'm so dissatisfied. So, women continue to accept their roles as domestic drudge, they continue to work for inferior wages, they let themselves be used as sexual objects.

But the problem doesn't lie in any one woman's head. In fact, there is now in this country a growing political movement of women who are meeting together to discuss their common problems.

We are probing the causes and seeking to develop solutions. Most important, we are organizing, coming together.

Although we are still a small minority, we are realizing that our problems are political and must be understood collectively. The roots of our discontent lie in an oppressive social structure and the solution is not to try putting our own minds at rest, but to do something about that structure.

Now, this may sound strange, even ridiculous, to people who think women "rule the world," or that American women are the most privileged in history.

Some people claim that women's rights were won long ago by the Suffragettes.

But we think a careful examination of American society and the function women must fulfill in it may change some minds.

> **Many women think that their problems are individual ones.**

all women are oppressed

This is the first installment in *Space City News* of a series on American women in which we will try to uncover the sources of women's oppression. We want to show not only how, but why, women are screwed around (so to speak) in American society. And we think we can develop some ideas for constructive action women can take against the ways in which they are used.

This series is written for all women.

We know that many housewives express very real frustrations, especially the younger ones whose great expectations have been shattered by the reality of mops, pans, and diapers.

And many working women — the assemblers, operators, waitresses, typists, and nurses' aides — are fed up with having to work at stupefying jobs for wages few men would accept.

But professional women, the journalists, lawyers, and social workers, tend to feel that they have "made it" in spite of their sex. If they were to examine their

Our problems are political and must be understood collectively.

real status and opportunities in relation to their fellow male workers, they might see that they have more in common with their sisters who keep house or type letters than they do with the men who run their businesses. This series is for them, too.

We also went to the large Houston hip community to listen. Hippie girls usually think they have transcended the false material and sexual values of American society. Yet many still spend their meager funds on Yardley eye makeup and hip clothing made by Levi Strauss. Often they find that their most acceptable position in the world of freaks and fun is prone. And they are too often the pretty, silent partner who accompanies the studly freak on his beautiful adventures.

This series is not directed exclusively toward women. Men might listen too, lest they be caught with their pants down. American men are living under a grand illusion that is ensnaring them almost as painfully as it is us women.

Art: Trudy Minkoff, June 19, 1969.

Insurgents 41

identity in hair dye?

Important to emphasize is that the movement for Women's Liberation is not grounded in a hatred of men. That analysis would be too simple, because it would mean that men are naturally evil and women naturally good.

We have to keep in mind that women's oppression is rooted in an irrational social system which must use and manipulate people to maintain itself. It uses men, it uses women.

But the many ways in which it uses women as women suggest that we are highly important to the American economy and crucial to certain key institutions, like the cellular family structure.

"Be SomeBody," commands an advertisement for panty hose. It depicts the lower half of a slinky, long-legged body. Long legs, a crotch, and no head. The message of the ad? Buy our stockings, be somebody. Your brain's between your legs, baby,

A large part of the consumer industry is directed toward the female buyer. Think of how many ads in popular magazines promote women's clothing, cosmetics, jewelry, and household goods. Those people know that women can actually be deluded into thinking that they're finding an identity through buying. As an ad executive interviewed by Betty Frieden put it:

> Properly manipulated (if you're not afraid of that word), American housewives can be given a sense of purpose, creativity, identity, the self-realization, even the sexual joy they lack — by buying things.

Not only does business exploit us as a domestic market, but through advertising, it promotes our image as sexual objects and then binds us to that image.

That image is useful — to business. A woman's body sells cars and liquor to men and it sells "beauty products" to women. We're supposed to buy these beauty products to make us more appealing to men, and hence, more successful.

The measure of our success is how easily we can catch and hold a man — although we probably need a little help from our friends at Revlon, Maidenform, Clairol, and Bobbie Brookes. Being naturally dependent crea-

Men might listen too, lest they be caught with their pants down.

tures (so goes the myth), we can't be whole women unless we have a man to wrap ourselves around.

And what about the woman who, through necessity or aggressive desire, steps into the working world?

the working girl

If she's not white, she might have to settle for an assembly line job. Statistics show that she's the last to be hired and the first to be fired. Despite "equal opportunity" laws, her working conditions are worse and wages are generally lower than those of men doing the same kind of work.

If she's a clerical worker — the largest percentage of working women — she is stuck with some of the most demeaning and boring work the job market has to offer. Even if she's an executive secretary, she's little more than a big man's petty servant.

Or she performs service work — waitressing, bartending, cooking and housekeeping — for which she generally gets low pay and tired feet.

Ad: May 11, 1971.

If she's lucky and educated, she might be a professional. For most women this means school teaching, nursing, or medical and dental technician work.

Only a very small percentage of working women hold positions as engineers, doctors, lawyers, scientists, and journalists — not because there aren't openings in these professions, but because a woman encounters so many obstacles on the way.

For instance, a *Newsweek* executive once confided to us that a woman can never be promoted to a top editorial position on his magazine, no matter how competent she may be, because she is a woman.

So where does a woman "find" herself? In the home, of course, serving her man, raising his kids, making his house a pleasant place for him to come home to.

marry or die

Marriage is a must for every girl, regardless of her social stratum. Even the most independent young woman is haunted by the pressure to marry. It's acceptable for a man to stay a bachelor, but who can tolerate an old maid?

From the time they can comprehend language, girls are taught that what they really want is a man, a home, and a family. Little wonder a woman gets uptight if she isn't married by her early 20s.

Many people, particularly men, argue that home-making and child-rearing comes "naturally" to women. But there is nothing innate in women to suggest that they are best suited for these often-unsatisfying tasks.

Women as a group are not naturally inferior to men in intellect or emotional stamina. Whatever intellectual or emotional deficiencies women may seem to possess are acquired through socialization, not through birth.

(How many women feel compelled to "hide" their intelligence so as not to threaten the masculinity of the man they're trying to attract? And woe betide her if she beats her boyfriend at some sport!)

But there are real reasons why this society insists that a woman's place is primarily in the home — and it's not just for propagation of the species.

> **Even the most independent young woman is haunted by the pressure to marry.**

First, men have a premium on performing the "work of the world." Women are allowed in selectively, as the economy permits, but the gates are never opened wide, lest a flood hit the labor market. The work force must be controlled and manipulated.

Second, women, throughout recent Western history, have been stuck with the responsibility of feeding the workforce, raising the children, keeping the household. (Historically, this has not been true in some societies.) But in male-dominated American society, it's not hard to persuade a woman to accept her stay-at-home role. Someone has to keep the home fires burning.

Third, in contemporary American society, the housewife provides a booming market for corporate profits, especially if she is convinced that she has to be her husband's glamour girl as well as his housekeeper.

our buried history

In terms of world history, women, like the non-white races, have been screwed royally.

Several men have told us that, of course women are inferior to men. Why, all the great writers, scientists, artists, poets, and musicians in history have been men.

What these men forget is that all those great men have also been white men. Given the scientific facts, these men are hard put to claim that black people, for instance, are genetically inferior to whites.

In American schools, history is presented as a series of wars and other adventures performed by "great (white) men." And this textbook tradition sticks, despite wide criticism leveled by educational reformers at this one-sided view of history.

Women, however, despite the fact that they have largely been kept by men in the world's shadows, do have a history. This history, like that of black Americans, has been suppressed so far.

In this series on women, we will look more closely at each of the roles women play and what forces, which institutions, make them play these roles.

The next article will talk in depth about woman as consumer and sex object. -30-

Art: Trudy Minkoff, July 20, 1971.

The Woman Market

Victoria Smith and Judy Fitzgerald • July 4, 1969

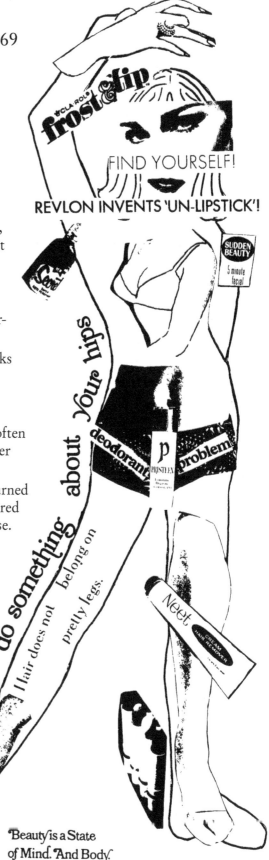

Women may serve a variety of functions in American society, but a function all women serve is that of a domestic market.

And they serve it faithfully, almost eagerly, it would seem.

American women, perhaps more than any other women in the world, must fulfill their role as heavy consumer. If they don't, their whole identity — an identity created primarily by business and advertising — will be shattered.

When a woman reads in her favorite woman's magazine that, "Unfortunately, the trickiest deodorant problem a girl has isn't under her pretty little arms," she starts to worry. Is my vaginal area ("the most girl part of you," the ad gurgles) giving off offensive odors? she wonders.

"Could you be the last woman to be using just ONE deodorant?" an ad for another vaginal deodorant queries.

She may not smell all that bad, but just to make sure, she picks up a container of FDS (feminine deodorant spray) and Alberto-Culver Co. scores another point.

Alberto-Culver and other companies in the woman market understand the American woman. They know she's insecure, often unhappy with the narrow perimeters of her life, desperate in her efforts to catch and/or keep a man.

So, the company anticipates a female insecurity that can be turned into a need, and creates a product to fulfill that newly-discovered need. If the product is successful, the company's profits increase. If not, there's always another "need."

Basically, there are two problems with corporate America's approach to women — which can apply to its approach to all people.

First, business can hold no real concern for women as human beings. It must objectify all women as a "market" in order to increase growth and profits. Business is concerned only with the ways in which it can get women to buy. Whether the products sold are of any real use, or meet real needs, is unimportant.

Second, American business creates excessive waste of resources, particularly through products made for women. People do not need 50 different kinds of soap to choose among, or 100 different types of lipstick. But American companies continue to produce dozens of variations on the same useless themes, and thus divert energy, resources, and money from more productive human goals.

"Beauty is a State of Mind. And Body."

Art: July 4, 1969.

In 1968, for instance, $3.1 billion was spent on television advertising, twice the amount spent on the poverty program in the same year.

The advanced technological era that America has recently entered should make for greater freedom for Americans.

But American technology has generally granted the opposite effect, and American women are the most alienated from and enslaved by it. As a group, women have little control over production and planning. They relate to the technological society primarily as a consumer market.

Of course, there is nothing inherently wrong with consumption. But in American society, women are forced to consume large quantities of goods and services they really don't need or want.

Advertising is the mouthpiece for the companies that create products for the woman market.

On a very basic level, the advertising and editorial content of women's magazines like *McCall's*, *Seventeen*, *Cosmopolitan*, and *Mademoiselle* are insults to women as human beings. So are the women's sections in newspapers and daytime television.

Let's look at some of these insults and the ways in which they are used to keep women in their place as a domestic market.

get 'em young

Teenage girls are a market in training.

The people who run *Seventeen* magazine, the slick, top-selling teenage publication, understand the importance of the youth market.

An ad in *The New York Times*, June 18, 1969, reads:

"The *Seventeen* award to American industry for its investment in the country's young women under 20.

"Once again advertisers have demonstrated their realization that youth sets the pace.

"And once again *Seventeen*, their magazine, has broken all publishing records for a single issue.

"This August is a new high, carrying 357 advertising pages, 245 in four/color.

"*Seventeen* is the biggest circulation magazine in the young women's field — for 16 consecutive years it has carried more advertising than any other woman's monthly magazine.

"That's the strength of *Seventeen*."

Teenage girls are a market in training.

The "strength of *Seventeen*" is not that it informs or educates young women, but that it sells advertisers' products.

The ad congratulates American industry for "investing" in these young women, much as if industry were investing in some kind of new automobile or hairspray.

The focus of the advertising and editorial in Seventeen is fashion — clothes and cosmetics.

The projected image is young, super slim, tall, carefully made up to look "natural," tastefully (and not inexpensively) dressed and (despite an occasional anglo-looking black model) white. The impossible teenager.

And the youth market booms.

Young American girls move into young womanhood with a number of insecurities, mostly about sex and boys.

Seventeen and the youth marketers have a beautiful answer. It lies in the right kind of clothes, and makeup. You "pamper" your skin, "cultivate the flowery look that becomes you," and "highlight your hair, especially if it's brown on the shady side." (*Seventeen*, June 1969).

In America, a young woman's buying habits and personality develop side-by-side. Corporate America ensures that the two will not be separated. What she wears and what she puts on her face become as important to her as what she studies in school and how she relates to other people.

If the advertisers play it right, a girl will no more abandon her Revlon blusher or her Clairol "Born Blonde" than she would abandon her fondest dreams.

And industry can even help formulate her dreams for her: Wallace Sterling, De Beers Diamonds, Lenox china, Springmaid linen. The makeup, the clothes, the diets, the hair pieces and hair colorings for an individual girl all point to one goal — to catch and keep a man. This typecasting of women is so obvious in the women's magazines that it never has to be made explicit.

the breakaway girl

As the young female consumer grows so does her spending power. Industry summons its resources to meet her new "needs."

Whether she's going to college or working in an office, she is told that she must maintain, even amplify, the image created for her as a teenager.

Her magazines are *Glamour*, *Mademoiselle*, *Cosmopolitan*, especially if she's white and middle-class.

Glamour calls her the "breakaway girl," independent, energetic, strong-willed and, of course, chic. The breakaway girl is an important market, *Glamour* tells advertisers.

In fact, she has broken away from nothing. She may not rush out of high school directly into marriage, but she still fits herself into whatever image industry creates for her in a given year.

A fashion article in the June issue of *Mademoiselle* begins: "During the big jump from high school grad to freewheeling college frosh, the look changes. Adapts, chameleonlike, to the college spirit. Not only clothes — hair and faces, too."

Mademoiselle tells her she's "freewheeling," so she can flatter herself that she's independent while being told what she must wear to college.

With *Glamour* and *Mademoiselle* hitting the college market, *Cosmopolitan*, perhaps the closest thing to the girl's version of *Playboy*, confronts the working girl.

The magazine's editorial policies and advertisers use the image of the sexually-liberated young woman to sell products.

American women are far from sexually liberated, a fact that publications like *Cosmopolitan* effectively betray. For instance, the lead article in the July *Cosmopolitan* is "39 Men Tell a Nice Girl Like You What Turns Them On." Another article discusses the best tactics to use in seducing married men. The magazine never talks about genuine love among human beings.

Sex is just another sales gimmick. The "breakaway girl" is liberated just enough to buy micro-skirts and transparent clothing. She's experimental enough to try fake curls and false eyelashes, but nothing more significant. And she has the leisure time (or thinks she does) to spend two or three hours a day ornamenting herself to fit the image.

Not only does the "breakaway girl" provide an excellent market, but she herself is a product, packaged and sold with the help of industry and advertising, to the man of her choice.

As the young female consumer grows so does her spending power.

marriage is good business

Marriages mean good business. Every new household is a new consumption unit, *TV Guide* indicates in a *New York Times* ad, November 6, 1968.

"Nothing makes markets like marriage. There's setting up the house, and future business in raising a family. All together it's big business, appliances and house furnishings to bigger cars."

As a middle-class housewife, a woman is a ready market not only for the beauty products she has grown accustomed to wanting, but for myriad household soaps, cleansers, and appliances.

Her new image is that pretty, efficient homemaker, lovingly choosing her family's bathroom tissue and toilet bowl cleaner.

And if she becomes hassled by the routine of meals-dishes-laundry, business offers her headache remedies and time-saving cleaners to ease the situation.

The more hassled she becomes, the more she demands a life beyond the home, the more receptive a market she is.

"Why is it never said that the really crucial function, the really important role that women serve as housewives is to buy more things for the house?" writes Betty Friedan in *The Feminine Mystique*.

"In all the talk of femininity and woman's role one forgets that the real business of America is business. Somehow, somewhere, someone must have figured out that women will buy more things if they are kept in the underused, nameless-yearning, energy-to-get-rid-of-state of being housewives."

Since as a homemaker the American housewife can have no control over the world outside her home, she is effectively cut off from the rest of society, particularly by the media.

Her world is the home. Her magazines — like *McCall's*, *Ladies Home Journal*, *Woman's Day*, *Redbook*, and *Good Housekeeping* — talk almost exclusively about children, beauty, food, and housekeeping

The July issue of *McCall's*, for instance, includes articles on California and New Or-

Art: Trudy Minkoff, August 28, 1969.

leans patios; Beauty; The Sun Catchers, Menus for the Family Reunion, The Church Social and Supper at the Sea; A New Life, a New Love: Audrey Hepburn at 40; The Case Against Little League Mothers, and the Faith of Mamie Eisenhower.

Only one article — *The Revolt of the Young Priests* — breaks through the perimeters of the woman's world.

Television is much the same, with day-time TV — prime viewing time for house-wives — taken up with inane quiz shows and soap operas.

In 1967, for instance, during the Ful-bright hearings on the Vietnam war, CBS made a rather major decision about housewives.

"Fred Friendly, who was working with the News Division at CBS at the time, quit over the decision," writes Alice Embree, in an article for a yet unpublished book on women. "CBS broadcast an *I Love Lucy* rerun instead of the Senate hearings — not because the rerun was part of television folklore, but because the commercials surrounding it involved money.

"Friendly reports in his book, *Due to Circumstances Beyond Our Control*, that one of the unpublished reasons for the CBS decision was the fact that housewives, not 'opinion leaders' were tuned in at the hour, and housewives weren't interested in Vietnam."

The daily work of the American housewife is generally boring and repetitive — and certainly doesn't require much thought. Business is aware of this. But rather than trying to alleviate her work so she is free to do other things, corporations in the woman market bind her even more by creating new household problems and then new products to "solve" those problems.

All people desire creative forms of self-expression, and business knows housewives can be convinced that their homemaking tasks are creative.

As a motivational research expert put it:

> In a free enterprise economy, we have to develop a need for new products. And to do that we have to liberate women to desire new products. We help them rediscover that homemaking is more creative than to compete with men. This can be manipulated. We sell them what they ought to want, speed up the unconscious, move it along.

Men like this motivational manipulating. They understand that there is a gap to be filled in the house-wife's life — not by helping to create conditions and institutions that would give her life more meaning, but by selling her things to replace that meaning.

So, housewives are told, of course, your work is meaningful and important. Why, mother is important to the family. She is the protector — she protects her family from germs by using Lysol spray disinfectant and by cleaning the toilet bowl regularly with Sani-Flush. Of course, her life has meaning. She keeps her family healthy by feeding them "Wonder Bread to make the most of their wonder years."

The daily work of the American housewife is generally boring and repetitive.

do blondes have more fun?

Although most advertising is aimed at the white, middle-to-upper-middle income American, industry will sell to anyone, rich or poor, black or white, as long as she pays the price.

So we have scenes like the one we observed on a New York subway: a poor Puerto Rican woman, with children squirming around her, reading the latest issue of *Vogue* magazine.

We have worked with young girls from poor families, often of racial or ethnic minorities, who read *Cosmopolitan* and *Glamour*. They learn that the way a woman makes it is by looking like the models in the ads. And they spend large parts of their salaries on clothes, cosmetics (which they apply too generously) and synthetic hair pieces that fool no one.

Or if a woman simply can't afford all the regalia of success — the beauty products, the clothes, the household appliances — she may see herself as a failure as a woman, as inferior to the glamorous magazine creatures who swish around in long scarves, go on high protein diets, or decorate their living rooms in Italian provincial.

American industry doesn't even pretend to meet the needs of these American women. Beauty and feminine success is a white thing, a thing that requires money.

But this doesn't mean that poor or non-white women should struggle to fit the image created by business and advertising. If a woman can afford the image financially, she cannot afford it in terms of her humanity. We just want to point out the class and racial nature of the woman market.

captive consumers

An excerpt from *Forbes Magazine*, April 15, 1968, puts the whole crass process on the line: "One Harvard grad recalls his on-campus interview with a P&G (Proctor and Gamble) recruiter several years back. 'We sell products that aren't much different from anyone else's,' the recruiter told him. 'We sell them because someone will buy them, not because they are socially good. If we could put s--t in a box and the customer would buy it, we'd sell it.'" (The censored word is shit.)

And an ad for the Magazine Publishers Association, run in *Advertising Age*, April 21, 1969, helps clarify the intent of advertising:

"'But mother,'" (says a Beautiful Blonde modeling a 'nude look' fashion) "'Underwear would hide my fashion accessories.'"

"It wasn't long ago that all exposure was indecent. Today it's vogue. Admittedly spunky. But not spurned even in the safe suburbs.

"How did it happen?

"Magazines.

"Magazines turned legs into a rainbow. Magazines convinced a gal she needed a flutter of fur where plain little eyelashes used to wink.

"Magazines have the power to make a girl forget her waist exists. And the very next year, make her buy a belt for every dress she owns...

"Magazines help distressed damsels remake their wardrobes, faces, hair, body. And sometimes their whole way of being.

"And the ladies love it. And beg for more.

"When she gets involved with herself and fashion, in any magazine, she's a captive cover to cover...."

When you're a "captive cover to cover," all the talk about "breakaway girls" and happy homemakers with more free time, more money, and the powers of femininity sounds pretty irrelevant.

And the "ladies" really don't "love" being captives; they are afraid not to play the game. The roles a woman can hold in American society are so limited that to relinquish her function as consumer (and all that involves) would be very threatening.

So as captives, American women continue to carry a heavy social and economic burden that allows American corporations to expand markets and increase profits.

It is ironic that as little as an American woman may think of herself, business brains think she's great, in somewhat the same way that Standard Oil of New Jersey, which holds heavy interests in Latin America, thinks the Venezuelan workers are great.

It is useless and absurd to ask corporations to think of women as human beings. Corporations cannot possibly do this.

In fact, as long as there are markets, prices, buying and selling and profits, technology cannot be used in human ways. As long as technology is controlled by men pursuing profit and corporate expansion, human beings, especially women, cannot participate except as investments and markets.

Alice Embree clarifies the transformation of woman as human being to woman as object:

> "A woman is supposed to be a body, not a person — a decorated body. If she can successfully manage that transformation, then she can market herself for a man. The commercial creates commercialized people in its own image; and the marketed commodities create people who think of themselves as marketable commodities."

Think about these things the next time you pick up one of your favorite women's magazines. Perhaps your human (and naturally beautiful) face will tingle from a corporate slap. -30-

THE   LATEST...

(from Newsweek)

For the girl who may or may not have everything, there is something new on the market—bosom make-up put out by New York hairdresser **Kenneth**, 41, who sells a line of cosmetics besides sculpting hair-dos for Jackie and other famous customers. His bosom kit includes everything from a "cleavage delineator" to "tip blush," a red liquid "which is drawn across the tips in a circular motion to achieve a glistening, rosy hue." Why bosom make-up? "I think of it really as a bedroom product," said Kenneth. "Or I suppose you could say it's for women who want to look their best when they get uncovered, for whatever reason."

Sidebar: July 4, 1969.

Women Moving More Than Ever

Marie Blazek • August 3, 1972

Since I am a feminist and great admirer of my sex, thinking about Houston women startles and bedazzles me. Where else but here can one see a shagged head above a suntop, pedalling hurriedly by a bouffant blond in a convertible, who just dropped off her black maid at the bus stop where she'll wait to ride home with her peers — heading east. At home her sleek black Afro'd daughter will welcome her with the day's confidences.

Meanwhile, in some other part of the city, feminists plot the proceedings of the "women's movement" — taking us all in, from barefoot to bouffant. Is it presumptuous to assume that women share enough to be included in one movement? A movement to include 52 percent of the population?

When I came to Houston two years ago, I joined the Harriet Tubman Brigade, an organization of radical women, united mainly behind our participation in other radical heterosexual organizations. The HTB was never a priority for its members; we never accomplished anything for ourselves or for other sisters. We just mainly got together and felt guilty because we were doing nothing for women, since we were busy "making the revolution" with men. The HTB died in its sleep in the spring of 1971.

Meanwhile the National Organization for Women was beginning to pound loudly on the door of the male establishment, demanding entry and equality. NOW is the longest-lived feminist organization in town. It is and has been involved in seeking equal employment opportunity, educational opportunity, and legal protection.

Currently, NOW is involved in filing complaints of sex discrimination against more than a hundred employers advertising in the sex-segregated want-ads of the *Houston Chronicle*. Also three large banks in Houston — Texas Commerce, Bank of the Southwest, and First City National Bank — have been charged with sex discrimination in hiring, promotion, pay, benefits, leaves of absence, advertising, and training. These complaints have been filed with the Department of Treasury as a violation of Revised Executive Order Four. NOW is also investigating the

> **The main result of this effort was several consciousness-raising groups.**

lack of credit for women. (For information contact Susan Butler, 666-9534.)

With the demise of the Harriet Tubman Brigade, another broader women's organization developed, Houston Women's Liberation. The main result of this effort was several consciousness-raising groups, which a number of women used to their advantage for many months. HWL, too, died an early death after numerous efforts to start a women's center and study groups.

Between the summer of 1970 and today, there has been one consistent development in the women's movement, the Trotskyites. Women who are members of the Socialist Workers Party or Young Socialist Alliance have used their organizational skills and contacts to influence Houston women, through campaign support for women, participation in women's groups, and especially the local abortion action groups.

The Houston Women's Abortion Action Coalition is a local chapter of the Women's National Abortion Action Coalition. Its members are presently involved in Rep. Bella Abzug's effort to get an abortion bill through the legislature. A "tribunal" is planned for late October, at which time several persons will be tried for their support of harsh abortion legislation, performance of bad abortions, or participation in tactics which are "anti-women."

The Women's Equality Action League is a recent group in town. Its members are currently conducting a three-part study of private employment agencies in Houston and their policies regarding sex discrimination. Interviews with the managers of these agencies is the first part of the study, to be followed by statements from clients and employees. For more information, contact Barbara Farley, 461-6075.

Another new group providing leadership is the Housewives for Collective Action. This group is actively pursuing a meat boycott to counteract Nixon's failure to control prices, especially of meat. Be advised: the boycott begins on August 6, next Wednesday. No fresh meat should be purchased (this excludes birds). For more information, contact Carol Durram, 733-7198.

Finally, there's another local group, the Women's Workshop, which has recently organized to build a women's center. It is bringing women together to do a women's news program each Wednesday night at 7 p.m. on KPFT-FM 90.1. It will also be sponsoring a women's poetry reading in September and, we hope, a series of speeches and raps with local women in politics. For more information contact either Pat Dowell or Marie Blazek at 224-4000.

In retrospect it seems that the women's movement can and does include an incredible variety of Houston women. It also seems to be stronger than ever before, unlike most political groups today. Houston women seem to be organizing for their own survival. The changes that have happened nationally in the past two years in the terms of employment opportunities, birth control possibilities, day care facilities, less sex role indoctrination in schools and media are also happening here at an active pace. Houston may be farther behind in this regard, but, even so, changes are coming.

The breadth and heterogeneity of the women's movement here and elsewhere is especially encouraging. The National Women's Political Caucus is a good example. It is playing an important role in both major political conventions this summer. Legalization of abortion is an issue which affects all impregnable persons very directly.

In answer to my own question: Yes, women do share enough to be included in one movement. -30-

Art: Trudy Minkoff, July 20, 1971.

Harriet Tubman Brigade skit at NOW rally. Photo by Cam Duncan, September 5, 1970.

Anti-war
Resistance

Cover: April 13, 1972.

Art: May 11, 1972.

Vietnam: Nixon's Latest Escalation

Jeff Shero • May 11, 1972

President Nixon's smarter than his people give him credit for. Like Mayor Daley, Louie Welch, David Cassidy, and Lawrence Welk, he touches sentiments in America that his hipper critics fail to appreciate.

Nixon's no longer the man from Anaheim with a used car salesman's mind; he's a crafty political veteran who understands the use of brinksmanship. Faced with the collapse of his Vietnam policy, and with it the chances of reelection, his newest escalation has aroused the support of frustrated mid-America which wants decisive action. Thus, he has gained more time to maneuver, and a chance to obscure the principal issues of the war. All in all, not bad for one speech.

It's good to examine the situation in which Nixon found himself to appreciate his short term tactical brilliance and his long term failures.

The war has entered its final phase. The Vietnamese offensive is rapidly proving to be the administration's Dien Bien Phu. Despite massive air support, not to mention billions in aid and arms, the Thieu government in Saigon was headed for collapse, and with it, Nixon's prestige.

The military situation finds Hue surrounded and about to fall. The Central Highlands to Binh Dinh province on the coast have been won, cutting Vietnam in half. An Loc and Highway 13 have been a meat grinder chewing up reinforcements and imperiling Saigon. In the Mekong Delta the pacification program rapidly crumbles.

Even more ominous, the South Vietnamese army has abandoned over 25 bases — in Hoi An neatly stacking arms before fleeing — and except for a few elite Ranger and Paratrooper units, they have broken and fled in many major battles. An army consisting of approximately 120,000 North Vietnamese and perhaps another 100,000 guerrilla and regional forces is humiliating an army four times its size. American air power, navel shelling, unlimited supplies and advisors have not forestalled the collapse.

The fatal contradiction between concentration and dispersal faced by the French is now being faced by Nixon and Thieu. Prestige dictates that provincial capitals must be held, so troops are dispersed throughout Vietnam and clumped around cities. Military needs demand concentration of forces to defeat the smaller but better grouped and more dedicated revolutionary force. As with the French, General Giap has been able to take advantage of this situation by coordinating a three-front offensive and guerrilla attacks, so that Saigon's strategic reserves are rushed about the country, attempting to save first An Loc, then Kontum/Pleiku, then Hue. At no time massed in decisive battle, instead they have been slowly whittled away and demoralized.

Before Nixon's escalation speech, it appeared the worsening military situation would force President Thieu to resign in four to six weeks. This would set the stage for an interim Government of National Accord — consisting of one third Saigon administration, one-third neutralist, and one-third revolutionary makeup — which the National Liberation Front has been seeking in Paris. This interim government would draw up plans for new elections. The brewing crises forced the Administration to act. The next domino after Thieu in Saigon could well be Nixon in November.

The Dreariness of Past Lies

More than three years ago, Nixon was elected with a "secret plan" to get the United States out of the war. Instead, as troops were being pulled out, the air war was being escalated and Vietnamization was being sold like GL-70, a wonder ingredient to maintain American influence for years to come. George McGovern said at the time, "Vietnamization is not a formula for ending the war. It is a formula for ending the criticism at home."

Two years ago Nixon, facing a deteriorating situation in Vietnam, expanded the war to Cambodia to "destroy the Communist Command Headquarters." The result was a wider war, Kent State, and more time for Thieu. One year ago, using the same phrase ("decisive military action"), he expanded the war into Laos "to destroy the North Vietnamese capability for a military offensive." The resulting rout of the Saigon forces was passed off as a victory. In the last year, Nixon has escalated — in violation of the 1968 agreements with bombing raids (labeled "protective reaction strikes") against North Vietnam.

> **Nixon was elected with a 'secret plan' to get the United States out of the war.**

Three months ago, when a much-heralded Central Highlands offensive to coincide with Nixon's trip to China didn't materialize, pinpoint bombing was credited with breaking the enemy's capability. One intelligence report assured that only 14 percent of the supplies entering the Ho Chi Minh trail were arriving in the South. At the beginning of the offensive the enemy's capability (and goal) was judged as possible seizure of one provincial capital. Either we have the world's worst intelligence, or the public has been lied to, to suit the administration's political ends.

Nixon's Speech and Escalation

The threat of Thieu's collapse and the Vietnamese gaining on the battlefield what the United States refused to concede at the negotiating table, set the stage for Nixon's escalation. The dramatic measures of mining North Vietnamese harbors and bombing the railroads and other military targets will have little effect on the battles in the South. Supplies take approximately five weeks to reach the South, and Australian communist correspondent Wilfred Burchett reports North Vietnam has a five month stockpile of supplies.

A study released by Sen. Mike Gravel of Alaska shows that, despite bombing and mining, enough supplies can be brought in by railroad and over highways to meet North Vietnam's military needs. The military operation seems to be, then, an attempt to win the public and buy time, while forcing the big powers into solving the war. By offering significant new peace proposals — such as a cease fire, withdrawal of troops in four months in exchange for the Prisoners of War, and letting the Vietnamese settle their own affairs — Nixon might be trying to extract himself, while silencing his right-wing critics through increased military action. (This is the most optimistic interpretation.)

A scenario which includes behind-the-scenes negotiating with Russia, five to six weeks of fighting in the South (at which time the Vietnamese agree to a cease-fire while holding large amounts of territory), and the withdrawal of American forces in four months, is not impossible. In fact, the four-month troop withdrawal would have Nixon out about next October. Not bad timing for a man who claims his duty to protect American honor comes before his desire to be reelected to the presidency!

The pessimistic scenario views Nixon as the cold warrior to the last. Many suspect U.S. armed forces will be kept next door in Thailand and aid will continue to be given to Saigon. The NLF remembers what happened in 1954. After defeating the French and negotiating terms for elections in Geneva, the United States intervened and set up a permanent government in Saigon.

The rhetoric of this speech was aggressive and had the ring of personal affront. Nixon called the North Vietnamese "International Outlaws," as well as "insolent," "arrogant," and "insulting." He declared, "abandoning our commitment in Vietnam would mean turning over 17 million South Vietnamese to Communist terror and tyranny."

Perhaps Nixon's attempting to trick the Vietnamese into stopping the offensive, while preparing new plans to shore up Saigon, possibly by landing Marines in the North. Then again, Nixon may indeed have developed a quality of balanced statesmanship. Or, deep down, he may still be the knee-jerk anti-communist he once was, when he made statements like this in the 1952 presidential campaign: "I call on Adlai Stevenson to renounce his previously expressed ideas and declare unequivocally that he opposes the recognition of Red China and supports free China... Unless he does this, he forfeits the right even to be considered for the Presidency."

The Vietnam war has created a whole 1984 Newspeak. The words used to describe what's going on have little resemblance to the truth. In his speech, Nixon justified the escalation of the war on two principals, both untrue. He claimed the offensive had "gravely threatened the lives of 60,000 troops still in Vietnam." Yet last Sunday's paper carried an article sighting the disaffection many South Vietnamese military personnel feel because American bases aren't being attacked. It pointed out that American installations in Da Nang, Phu Bi, Bien Hoa, and Saigon had been spared mortar and rocket attacks. The NLF seems to feel U.S. troops have no will to fight and just want to return home. They think attacks would motivate the spirit of combat in the troops, and high American casualties would turn sentiment against the NLF in the United States.

> **The pessimistic scenario views Nixon as the cold warrior to the last.**

Second, Nixon claimed, the "North Vietnamese arrogantly refuse to negotiate anything but an imposition by the United States of a communist regime." The NLF and North Vietnamese peace proposals have never called for a communist regime. They have called for a Government of National Accord, elections, establishment of a non-aligned foreign policy, and respect for all religious and ethnic minorities.

Because North Vietnam has been built up over 18 years on a socialist basis, reunification has been proposed as a long range effort to be worked out between the two halves of the country, with mutual development and planning. What the NLF has insisted, is that President Thieu is

Ad: April 20, 1972.

a puppet of the Americans and a traitor, because all his life he has fought for foreign powers against the Vietnamese. They refuse to take part in a government with Thieu controlling the machinery of police state power.

Nixon and Russia

Newspeak became double think when Nixon spoke of the Soviet Union. He stated solemnly, "There is only one way to stop the killing, and that is to keep the weapons of war out of the hands of the international outlaws of North Vietnam." He refused to recognize (or acknowledge) that another way to stop the killing would be for the United States to withdraw its troops and stop the bombing. Studies show U.S. bombing has killed more people and created more refugees than all the ground fighting put together.

Instead of blaming the defeats in South Vietnam on the lack of will to fight in the Saigon army, Nixon has blamed Russian aid. CBS television news showed that, by liberal estimate, Soviet aid to North Vietnam is only one-tenth of U.S. aid to South Vietnam.

The blockade of Vietnamese ports and the resulting danger to Russian and Chinese shipping is a bad gamble. If there is no showdown with Russia, at least the spirit of cooperation has been undermined. One can imagine a Russian President Nixon saying, "We have three alternatives — withdrawal, negotiations or decisive military action. Let us not destroy Soviet honor by withdrawing support from North Vietnam. Negotiations are getting us nowhere because the United States has proved to be arrogant and intransigent. The only course left is decisive military action."

Using Nixon's doctrine of self-interest, the Russians might justify going half way around the world to blockade Guantanamo, the hated American base on the coast of their ally Cuba. It would be interesting to see how President Nixon and the American people would respond to this defensive threat to their shipping. As mines were being dropped, Breshnev might say to Nixon on Soviet television, "Our two nations have made significant progress in our negotiations in recent months. We are near major agreements on nuclear arms limitations, on trade, and on a host of other issues. Let us not slide back toward the dark shadows of a previous age."

If this escalation isn't a cover for new negotiating terms, Nixon has sacrificed long term possibilities for peace, and risked serious confrontations with Russia

and China to protect a corrupt dictatorship in Saigon a little longer. The American honor that will be preserved is the honor of the gunslinger, not the honor of the just. The all-out bombing campaign, which has included the use of anti-personnel pellet bombs, will account for tens of thousands of deaths.

If this campaign of mass terror bombing has no end but to protect this administration, then American policy comes down to the same genocide that was waged against the American Indian. It flows from the same inhuman sensibility shown by government agents who made "peace" with the Indians and gave them blankets which had been infected with smallpox. It results from the racist sense that every man, woman and child who is a gook, a dink, a slopehead, or an Indian is less human than the chosen white man, and any who resist the white man's will, deserve death.

The world is smaller now, and what worked against the Indians may prove hazardous in Vietnam. If we bomb the Chinese engineering battalions who build roads and rail lines in the north of North Vietnam, we might find ourselves at war with another major power. If we shoot down Russian aircraft, or blow up her ships bringing in anti-aircraft missiles (as Nixon said, "Let us, and let all great powers, help allies only for the purpose of their defense"), then the militarists of Russia might push for a showdown, too horrible to contemplate.

Nixon appears to have won wide support in this country for his decisive actions. But the euphoria will pass quickly as people begin to realize the implications of his escalation of the war. If negotiations and a ceasefire don't develop soon, then we know that Nixon has moved from the darkest impulses of the human spirit. In that case, his military madness should be resisted with every bit of sanity and strength people can muster. -30-

> Newspeak became double think when Nixon spoke of the Soviet Union.

Ad: April 8, 1972.

Danny Schacht Jailed:
Wore Army Uniform in Skit

Tracey Oates • September 27, 1969

Danny Schacht, a Houston radical activist, has been sent to Seagoville, Texas, federal penitentiary, where he is serving a six-month sentence.

Schacht was charged with wearing parts of a U.S. Army uniform during a skit outside the Houston Induction Center. He was tried and convicted February 15, 1968. His appeal to the New Orleans district court was turned down on May 14 of this year.

The skit, sponsored by SDS, was part of national Stop the Draft Week activities in early December, 1967. It was produced by the Bong-the-Cong Repertory Theater. The military uniforms, worn by Schacht and another activist, Jarrett Smith, were a mixture of current and surplus military and civilian garments.

(Smith was given a suspended sentence and fine on the condition he would not participate in activities of SDS or the UH Humanist Club.)

The defense during the trial pointed out that military uniforms are often and legally worn in theatrical productions.

The prosecution refused to accept the Bong-the-Cong theater as real theater. Said Assistant U.S. Attorney Fred L. Hartman, 'They (Schacht and Smith) did it to discredit the Army, this country, and the people in it. That's why I say, 'If you don't like it, get out'."

The defense claimed, however, that Schacht and Smith were being prosecuted "because they dared to speak out against the war in Vietnam."

After Schacht's appeal to the district court was turned down, there were plans made to bring the case before the U.S. Supreme Court. Schacht's lawyer, however, neglected to file for an appeal within the 30-day limit, reportedly because his fees hadn't been paid. Schacht had known nothing about the expiration date until it was too late.

On August 29, he received notice to report to the Harris County Rehabilitation Center to start serving his sentence. His father, Ezra Schacht, stated that the issue of the right to dissent is crucial, and therefore, despite the tremendous cost of some $6,000, Schacht and his new attorney, David Berg, have decided to continue the case.

Earlier this week the case was presented to the U.S. Supreme Court for consideration. Money for the defense is scarce. Any contributions should be sent to the Danny Schacht Defense Fund, American Civil Liberties Union, 1819 Dunstan. Personal letters can be sent to Danny in care of Seagoville Federal Penitentiary, Seagoville, Texas. -30-

Demonstration against Defense Secretary Melvin Laird. Photo by Cam Duncan.

Chains Chains Chains:
Civil Disobedience in Houston

Thorne Dreyer • April 20, 1972

Last Friday, April 14, eight people chained themselves to the front door of Houston's federal building and subsequently became political prisoners.

Their action was another frustrated response to The War That Won't Go Away. It was an act of defiance, a symbolic protest, a publicity stunt. The week before, on April 6, 200 people had marched on City Hall; they followed in the beleaguered footsteps of thousands — in Houston and throughout this embattled nation — who have said their piece against the war.

The vast majority of the people in this country want the United States out of Indochina and fast. Yet, last week Richard Nixon bombed Hanoi and Haiphong harbor, a significant escalation of the war ("reckless" to quote two democratic presidential hopefuls). Vietnamization is a total flop; Thieu's soldiers of fortune are clearly incapable and/or unwilling to defend anything. Emperor Nixon is naked as a jaybird. His response now is no different from the one that made LBJ a one-term president. His goal is still a Vietnam-in-our-image (and the mirror does not flatter) or no Vietnam at all.

So eight people chain themselves to the door of the federal building. Maybe a futile gesture. One that will just bog down people's energies in fundraising and legal defense. Or perhaps the spark to ignite a dormant peace movement at a time when a loud noise must be heard.

Whatever else Friday's action may have done, it has spawned a legal battle that bears watching. All eight demonstrators face misdemeanor charges — trespassing and obstructing a public entrance. And four — the four men — have been saddled with heavier charges, forcibly opposing, impeding, and resisting a U.S. Marshal. This is a felony count and carries a possible three years.

This trial is already teaching interesting lessons about U.S. criminal justice. Like the fact that the women — whose actions, by everyone's admission, were the same as those of the men — were treated from the beginning with a sticky deference. The wom-

en were released on personal recognizance, while the men spent the weekend in the clink, unable to make their $2,000 bond each.

During the April 18 hearing, at which felony charges were given an exclusively masculine gender, the women were continually referred to as "girls." This was es-

> **The women were continually referred to as 'girls.'**

pecially annoying to Elizabeth Frei, who is 47, and Yvonne Hauge, 31. Nina Wouk is 22 and Jan Warness is 24.

Another interesting sidelight has been the treatment of Mickey McGuire, chairman of the local Angela Davis Defense Committee. McGuire, the only black defendant, appears to have been singled out for special attention. Much has been made of his past scrapes with the law, yet there has been little notice of the fact that several other defendants have arrest records from politically-related activities. U.S. attorney Novack made an attempt to get McGuire's bond raised to $15,000 cash; his request was denied.

Ad: April 6, 1972.

The other men charged are Cliff Bain, 21, Mark Wilson, 19, and Wayne Vogel, 25. The eight chained themselves to the Federal Building door at 11:40 a.m. Friday, April 14. Father James Barnett, a Catholic priest and chaplain at the University of Houston, then read a statement to the assembled crowd, many of whom were press.

Defendants said they were treated roughly by federal marshals, but not by Houston police, who eventually arrested them. As the chains were cut, the demonstrators put their hands on their heads and were marched off, POW style.

Three of the defendants used their one phone call to dial Pacifica radio, and they were heard live during the Briarpatch show. Wayne Vogel told the KPFT listening audience that some of the Houston police "say they're against the war. We're trying to get them to do something."

He went on to explain why he felt their act of civil disobedience was justified:

> It's hard to find anyone who thinks we're doing anything there (Vietnam) of value — yet it continues. The President refuses to stop. The Congress apparently is incapable. I think that the people are just going to have to do it themselves.... We just couldn't keep silent anymore. I guess the spokesmen for the Pentagon can call a press conference and get hundreds of newsmen and give them all the official propaganda and it gets printed up in all the newspapers. We have to go out

and get arrested — chain ourselves to the federal building — in order to get people to listen to us.

One weird bit of irony we shouldn't fail to mention. As the demonstrators were awaiting the arrival of the Houston police, they did a few rounds of "Give Peace a Chance" and "We Shall Overcome." As they sang the words, "We shall overcome some day; Oh deep in my heart, I do believe..." a weird moan filled the air, producing an instant counterpoint to their melody. It was Houston's air raid siren, doing its regular Friday noon practice run. Pretty eerie, that.

*****

People wishing to show their support for the eight and their opposition to Nixon's war should come to a demonstration Friday, April 19, at noon outside the Federal Building, 515 Rusk. The action is sponsored by the People's Coalition for Peace and Justice and the Houston Peace Action Coalition. (There will be major anti-war demonstrations in Los Angeles and New York Saturday.)

There will also be a demonstration in Houston Wednesday, April 26, at the annual General Electric stockholders meeting, at the Sheraton-Lincoln Hotel. There will be guerrilla theater, a picket line and a press conference; it's all to express opposition to GE's involvement in the war, and activities start at 9 a.m. (See article this issue.)

For more information about these actions and about defense activities for the eight defendants in the Federal Building chain-in, contact the Peace Center, 227-1646. -30-

Ad: Art by Dennis Kling, April 13, 1972.

Vigil at Mecom Fountain

Karen Northcott • May 11, 1972

As reports poured into town Tuesday night about the anti-war protests erupting violently across the country in the wake of President Nixon's announcement of his intent to mine the North Vietnamese harbors, a crowd of approximately 400 gathered in the First Unitarian Church to decide what they would do to protest the most dramatic and extensive escalation of the war to date.

Various actions were suggested, ranging from the passing of resolutions at the senatorial district conventions condemning the President's move, to telegramming congressmen asking them to nullify the President's orders, to a massive legal peaceful march on Saturday, to taking to the streets. Then followed what may prove to be one of the most effective anti-war actions in Houston. Two hundred demonstrators marched to the Mecom Fountain across from the Warwick Hotel, and vowed to maintain a vigil until early Thursday morning when the mines are scheduled to be activated.

The marchers, many participating in their first anti-war march, encircled the fountain, placed their candles on the curb, and sat down with quiet determination. They would be seen. And heard. It was a moving sight, a ring of candlelight reflected in the water of the fountain, now red in symbolic representation of the war's bloodshed.

As cars drove by, the demonstrators talked to the occupants, decrying the unconcealed aggression of the President's act and voicing their opposition to a long future of continued horror and killing. Their choruses of "join us" were often met with the peace sign or a clenched fist. Occasionally, someone would park their car and come sit on the grass. A few guests from the Warwick came over: some to ask questions, one to stay.

As word spread through the crowd of the shooting of two students at the University of New Mexico, the demonstrators grew somber, remembering the deaths at Kent State, Jackson State, and Augusta. Reporters and photographers came and went, their questions answered seriously and without leftist rhetoric.

Representatives of the Clergy and Laymen Concerned, Peoples' Coalition for Peace and Justice, Vietnam Veterans Against the War, Houston 8 Defense Committee, Angela Davis Defense Committee, United Farmworkers, La Raza Contra La Guerra, and more than a smattering of McGovern people gathered at the base of the fountain to discuss further means of demonstrating opposition to the war. A debate centered on the viability of nonviolent civil disobedience as a tactic. -30-

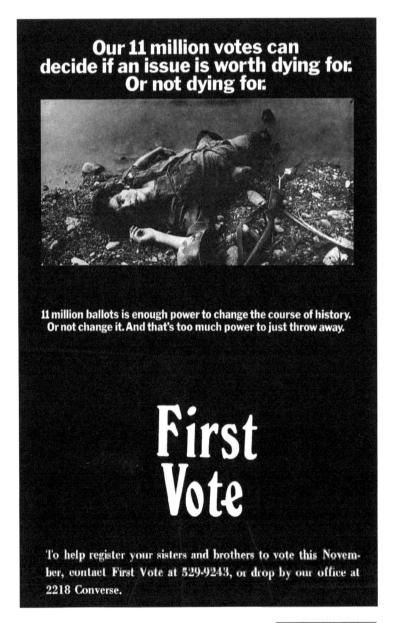
Ad: August 3, 1972.

GI
Resistance

Cover: October 25, 1969.

GI Resistance

Alice Embree

Space City News featured the Oleo Strut in Killeen in its ninth issue with a cover story by Karolyn Kendrick about the GI coffeehouse at Fort Hood. Named for the stabilizing device in a Huey helicopter, the Oleo Strut was the third GI coffeehouse to be organized in 1968. It was adjacent to one of the largest deployment bases in the country and became one of the most important sites of GI resistance to the war in Vietnam.

The scale of resistance taking place in every branch of the U.S. Armed Forces has been erased from most historical accounts. But the memory of that resistance was well known to David Zeiger. He had worked at the Oleo Strut and helped put out the newspaper, the *Fatigue Press*. His documentary *Sir! No Sir!* was released to critical acclaim in 2006.

Space City! reporters covered the Oleo Strut throughout the paper's existence, but covered national GI resistance as well, from uprisings to courts martial and arrests — in Fort Dix, Camp Pendleton, Presidio, and other locations. A previous section on the Klan includes the harrowing account of a GI car caravan fired upon as soldiers made their way from Killeen to Houston. An article by the New York Asian Women's Coalition appeared in the October 28, 1971, issue. It delves into the racist stereotypes of Asian women that GIs heard from their chain of command while in Vietnam.

The in-depth coverage of the anti-war GIs at the Oleo Strut and in Vietnam Veterans Against the War (VVAW) reflects the leadership role that GIs played in the anti-war movement. Returning GIs could speak with compelling first-hand authority about the war and their criticism influenced public opinion and ultimately military policy.

Articles on demonstrations, boycotts, and reprisals against Oleo Strut staff and anti-war GIs at Fort Hood appeared throughout the newspaper's run. Several were chosen for inclusion in this section. An account by *Space City!* reporter Karen Northcott on the VVAW's 1971 actions in DC provides an inside look at events that included soldiers returning medals they had earned for service in Vietnam.

Austin
May 2021

Ad: Art by Kerry Fitzgerald, July 17, 1969.

Oleo Strut: Ft. Hood GI Haven

Karolyn Kendrick • October 25, 1969

KILLEEN, TX — Amid the pinball machines, the used car dealers, and the pawnshops — in the rot of Killeen, Texas — the Oleo Strut sits unobtrusively, serving Ft. Hood, a huge, sprawling armored post of 50,000 men. The third GI coffee house to open, the Strut has been in operation since June 1968 — the "Summer of Support" when the movement began to recognize GI's as victims of the system rather than as willing perpetrators of it.

Once a TV repair shop, the cavernous room that houses the Oleo Strut is now a bright yellow movement center, filled with political posters and movement literature. To the left as one enters is the snack bar where coffee, tea, soft drinks, and sandwiches are served. To the right is a literature table that contains an excellent selection of GI and underground papers from around the country.

When *Space City News* folks arrived, people in the Strut had just learned that Pfc. Bruce Bowers, who had spoken at the Moratorium Day rally in Austin while wearing his fatigue uniform, had been charged with being AWOL when he returned to the post. Wearing fatigues off-post is illegal, but the military brass, perhaps to forestall charges of political repression, had busted him for being AWOL instead of for engaging in political activity while in uniform.

The Strut's first major action was a love-in held on July 4, 1968.

Small groups of men gathered around the oil-cloth-covered tables to discuss the fine points of the code of military justice or to compose the latest issue of the *Fatigue Press*, the Ft. Hood GI's underground paper. Other men sat alone, divorced from the bustle, reading papers and sipping their drinks. A Military Policeman and a Killeen cop sauntered in, walked midway into the room, turned, and walked out. They had been doing this every night for the last week, a GI said. They didn't hassle anyone, just let their presence be known.

In the past, though, the Oleo Strut has suffered harassment from both military and civilian cops, as well as hostile townspeople. The Strut's first major action, a love-in held in the town park on July 4, 1968, was busted up by cowboys, who were spurred on by the Killeen cops.

The next month, on August 23, when organizers from the Strut and a GI — Bruce "Gypsy" Peterson, the editor of the *Fatigue Press* — were preparing to leave for the Democratic convention in Chicago, both Josh Gould, an organizer, and Peterson were busted on rigged dope charges.

The case against Gould was dropped, but the charges against Peterson were transferred from a civilian to a military court. A trace of marijuana had been found in a car in which Peterson was a passenger. Only Peterson was arrested; neither the owner of the car nor any of the other passengers was charged with possession.

Several weeks later Peterson was searched by Killeen cops because he was a "known dope user" — that is, he had been charged previously although not tried. The cops found some lint in one of Peterson's pockets, which they claimed was marijuana. The lint was destroyed in its analysis.

Under the Texas Minimus clause, which states that a person must be carrying enough dope for use before he can be charged with possession, Peterson would have been released. The charges, however, had been transferred to a military court. A chemist testified that the lint was grass. Under cross examination, the chemist revealed that he did not even know of two of the chemical tests that must be performed to determine if a substance is marijuana.

Art: July 17, 1969.

Peterson, who is now in the Leavenworth penitentiary, was sentenced to eight years. His case has been appealed to the Court of Military Review where it is expected to be overturned.

However, once he is freed, Peterson will have a new charge to face. Military authorities claim they discovered a bag of marijuana in Peterson's foot locker during an inspection.

Twice before, Peterson had discovered grass planted in his footlocker, had removed it and had signed sworn affidavits that it had been planted. People at the Strut stress that this charge is political in nature, and not a simple marijuana case.

The same night of August 23, 43 black soldiers — the Ft. Hood 43 — were arrested on the post. The Oleo Strut organizers claim that they were busted because they were black and were discussing griev-

Pfc. Richard Chase was arrested for refusing riot control training.

ances. At the time, rumors were rampant on the post that Ft. Hood troops would be used to quell riots. The GIs had gathered to discuss this issue and the question of racial discrimination at Ft. Hood. They were never given a direct order to disperse; MP's surrounded them and arrested them.

Half of the men were tried by special court martials, in which the maximum sentence is six months, and half by general court martials, in which the maximum sentence is five years. The type of trial is left to the discretion of the commanding officer. Some of the most active organizers of the demonstration were tried by special court martials and acquitted.

Only three weeks ago, Pfc. Richard Chase was arrested for refusing riot control training. From the time of his arrival at Hood, Chase had been afford-

Oleo Strut collective: Mike Keegan, David Clinc, Terry Davis, Jay Lockard, and Josh Gould. Photo by Cam Duncan, October 25, 1969.

ed an unofficial conscientious objector status in his company because his sergeant and commanding officer knew that he would refuse to participate in the training. Recently, a new first sergeant and captain have refused to recognize this tacit arrangement because of Chase's increased political activity.

The captain called Chase in and gave him a direct order to report for riot control training. Chase refused and now faces a general court martial, which is rumored to be set for October 23. The defense will argue that it is illegal for an officer to order a man to perform a duty he knows that man is incapable of performing.

Four months ago, organizers at the Oleo Strut formed a commune. Josh Gould, 24, and Jay Lockard, 23, have been at the Strut since it opened. Dave Cline, 22, and Mike Keegan, 23, were stationed at Ft. Hood and stayed to work at the coffeehouse after they were discharged. Terry Davis, 21, came to the Strut after she was suspended from the University of Wisconsin at Madison for her political activities.

During the last few months, the Strut has undergone a complete change in appearance, symbolizing the collective's new attitude toward its role. After the arrests, people were afraid to come to the coffeehouse. Rumors were spread on the post that the Strut was off-limits. Because of its psychedelic appearance, the coffeehouse had become the headquarters for Ft. Hood's heavy druggers, who among other things enjoyed tripping out on the Strut's two spinning lights.

The collective decided that they needed to create an atmosphere in the Strut that would reflect its political purpose. Their decision to remove the lights prompted the formation of a spinning light caucus protesting the alteration. The physical change has led to a change in the type of men attracted to the coffeehouse. Now many of them are from working-class backgrounds and are of a lower rank in the army. More Chicano soldiers come in, although the number of blacks has remained about the same.

Jay Lockard expressed part of the Strut's transformation in a more concrete way when she spoke of Strut organizers' increasing disapproval of dope and desertion. "Desertion," she said, "draws men away from the United States where the work's got to be done." The

Radicals in the army face continual harassment from the military.

collective feels that the excessive use of drugs in the army is the main reason why most GIs don't rebel against irrational authority.

The collective sees its purpose as building organizers in the army and providing support for them. They say that they see no basis now for a mass movement in the army, but believe that the movement is slowly growing. A substantive movement in the army can't exist without a large civilian movement, they feel.

Radicals in the army face continual harassment from the military. Essentially, there is nothing they can do once they have become radical. The collective worries that most of the men have undergone no more than an intellectual radicalization. Repression and day-to-day harassment in the army lead to fear and intimidation. This situation limits the collective and the soldiers to a frustratingly slow, rap-type organizing.

Mike Keegan feels that GI coffeehouses are most valuable in introducing people to the movement who later continue working in it as civilians. The collective tries to maintain contact with the soldiers after their discharges and to encourage them in political work. A major limitation that Terry Davis sees is the mobility of the soldiers and the constant cycle of political education as new troops come in, are made aware of conditions, and then are transferred or discharged. -30-

Ad: Art by Dennis Kling, April 27, 1972.

Ft. Hood GIs Lead Space City March

Victoria Smith • November 22, 1969

About 1,500 people, led by a contingent of nearly 100 GIs, marched through the streets of Space City, Sunday, November 9, to demonstrate opposition to the war in Vietnam.

We marched about three miles under the hot Houston sun from Emancipation Park in the Third Ward to a rally in Hermann Park, where we were met by another thousand people. The turnout was pretty impressive for this town; it was probably the largest display of discontent with the war ever seen here.

The events were organized by the Houston Mobilization Committee against the War, the leadership of which is fairly moderate. But the tone of the rally was for the most part militant.

The militancy stemmed largely from the active presence of the anti-war GIs from Ft. Hood near Killeen. Because of the GIs, people couldn't forget that one of the major issues of the day was "support for GI rights and GI rebellions."

The GIs led the march, along with the Mobilization people. They bolstered the spirit, as well as the political level of the rally with fist-waving and revolutionary song-singing led by folksinger Barbara Dane.

As she and the GIs gathered around the speaker's mike to sing, Dane said that "for every GI here today, there's 10 back at Hood" who wanted to come but couldn't make it.

The reason the others couldn't come to Houston that day makes an interesting addition to the continuing tale of military suppression of dissident GIs.

The staff of the Oleo Strut, the Ft. Hood GI coffeehouse in Killeen, lined up four buses several weeks ago to transport GIs to Houston for the march. Suddenly, three weeks before the trip, the bus company told the Strut that buses were no longer available.

The Strut attempted to charter buses with other coach companies, but the story was the same. First, the company would agree to rent the buses, and then, a few days later, would cancel the contract.

The militancy stemmed largely from the active presence of the anti-war GIs from Ft. Hood.

The Strut collective finally made what it thought was a binding agreement with Transportation Enterprises, Inc., in Austin. But when they went down to pay the $50 deposit, the deal was off. According to Jay Lockard of the Strut, the company manager said that the FBI had paid him a visit, and advised him not to rent them the buses.

He told them the FBI called Strut people "disreputable," and warned him that there would probably be narcotics on the bus, Lockard said. The FBI reportedly said that the buses would probably be impounded and that the company could be implicated in felony charges. So naturally the company was unwilling to rent the buses.

But in case intimidation of bus companies failed to detain the anti-war GIs, the Army had a few more tricks up its sleeve.

Many of the men planning to go to the march were put on extra duty that weekend. A whole company was placed on standby two days before the march, although the men weren't told why they were standing by. (After the Strut broke the story to the Texas press, this order was revised to say that the men were restricted to the base that weekend.)

So after these last-minute obstacles were thrown in their path, only about half of the 170 GIs who had planned to come to the march actually made it.

Lockard said that some of the brass had openly indicated their knowledge of the GIs' plans, so the restrictions placed on them were not mere coincidence. She also said that she thinks the brass was attempting to discredit the Strut by making it almost impossible for them to fulfill their promises to get the GIs safely to Houston and back. But the attempt failed. The Strut commissioned two buses from a church in Austin, and the GIs enjoyed good accommodations in Houston at Autry House and the First Unitarian Church.

But this is not the first time attempts have been made to prevent Ft. Hood GIs from attending movement events in Houston. Several carloads of GIs, en route to an SDS rally here October 4, were shot at outside Temple, Texas, by right-wingers who later called *Space City News* and identified themselves as members of the Ku Klux Klan.

Ammunition from an M-1 rifle was fired into the engine of one of the cars, putting it out of commission.

The Klan also made a presence around the November 9 action.

Several days before the march, the home of Fred Brode, a key organizer for the Houston Mobilization Committee, was riddled with automatic rifle fire.

And at 6 a.m., November 9, a car parked in front of the *Space City News* office was firebombed and completely demolished. The car belonged to a local SDS member. People in the office rushed outside, but the bomber had vanished. They did see two police cars, however, hovering a block away, watching.

While the rally was going on, the Klan was slashing tires on dozens of cars parked near the scene. One observer counted a total of 27 sabotaged cars within a three-block stretch, although the toll was even higher since tires of cars parked around Emancipation Park were also slashed. On the windshields of many of the cars was a handwritten note: "This is the work of the Silent Majority."

Strangely enough, several Houston policemen were patrolling the area around Hermann Park during the rally, but they "didn't notice a thing."

> ## While the rally was going on, the Klan was slashing tires on dozens of cars.

Many of those who returned to find their tires slashed had not even been to the rally. These Sunday afternoon park and zoo goers, some of whom probably consider themselves part of Nixon's Silent Majority, must have been pretty surprised to find that things aren't so peaceful within the ranks of the S.M.

A burned fuse was found attached to the gas tank of a mobile truck belonging to radio station KYOK, a local soul station. The truck was not damaged.

The march and rally, despite moderate leadership, were enough to rile the blood of any self-respecting Houston Klansman.

Behind the GI contingent marched anti-war veterans, the Mexican American Youth Organization (MAYO), the Young Socialists Alliance, supporters of SDS/RYM-II (Revolutionary Youth Movement) and groups of high school and college students. Banners were raised high, many of which demanded the immediate withdrawal of U. S. troops from Vietnam.

There wasn't a significant black presence at the march or the rally. It seems the Mobilization hadn't tried to bring members of the black community into the planning of the events, even though the march started in that community's own Emancipation Park.

"Peace Now!" was the most persistent chant of the march, but other chants rose out of different contingents like "Tax the Rich, Not the Poor!" "Viva Che!" and "Free Bobby Seale!"

As we marched past a restaurant on Fannin, we noticed a group of black female workers clustered at a window, watching the march. The SDS contingent broke into a chant of "Power to the Workers!" One of the women raised a timid fist, timid perhaps because the white management was gathered in front of the restaurant, reprovingly watching the parade, and clucking, "Here come the hippies!"

A man stationed along the route of the march was greeted with fists, V-signs and cheers as he held up his sign reading "I'm One of the Silent Majority and I Say Bring the Boys Home."

Speakers at the rally included a black high school senior from Phyllis Wheatley; a Dallas businessman; Josh Gould and David Cline of the Oleo Strut; Bartee Haile of SDS/RYM-II; Andy Vasquez of MAYO, and Dr. Howard Levy, an Army doctor

Ad: October 28, 1971.

who was court martialed and jailed for refusing to train Green Beret medics for Vietnam.

None of the speakers were women, except for Barbara Dane, who gave a short rap about the Strut, even though moderator Ed Crane announced that she was going to sing while "everyone stretches their legs for a minute." Dane immediately told us to sit right back down, and she and the GIs delivered some entertainment as revolutionary as any of the speeches.

It seems that the Mobilization had some female speakers lined up but the engagements fell through. But the next time events like this one come up, we think people are going to have to try a little harder to avoid an all-male program, as the Women's Liberation movement develops strength and leadership here.

Most of the speakers raised the political level of the rally from simple anti-war consciousness and relat-

> **Levy came down hard on U. S. aggression in other parts of the world, and talked about the need for a revolution.**

ed such issues as U. S. imperialism, racism, and GI rebellions to the War. Gould from the Strut talked about Richard Chase, the Ft. Hood GI who is facing a court martial for refusing to take riot training (see story in this issue).Vasquez noted that the percentage of brown soldiers killed in Vietnam is considerably higher than the percentage of brown people in the country.

Levy came down hard on U. S. aggression in other parts of the world, and talked about the need for a revolution in America. He brought cheers from the crowd when he said that "Nixon shouldn't worry about being the first president to lose an army."

Levy told the crowd that the skills the GIs are learning now will not go unused, and concluded, amid applause and fist-waving, by predicting the formation of a people's army.
-30-

Fort Hood United Front. Photo by Cam Duncan, May 25, 1972.

Vets Move on D.C.

Karen Northcott • April 27, 1971

On April 24, between 200,000 and 500,000 persons (police estimate) marched in Washington — once again — for peace in Vietnam. The march climaxed a week of anti-war activities in many parts of the country and served as a prelude to perhaps even more massive demonstrations in the next two weeks. Below, Space City! reporter Karen Northcott describes the activities of Vietnam veterans in Washington during the week leading up to April 24.

WASHINGTON, D.C. — As the Spring offensive winds up its first week, I find myself coming back again and again to reflect upon the role of the Vietnam veterans in the anti-war movement. The vets have by far been the most personally involved in this, the first week of demonstrations: describing the atrocities they had heard about or seen or personally committed while in Vietnam. The rage, the frustration, the chaos and the divisiveness that the war has inflicted upon this country has been graphically illustrated by the vets this past week.

It hasn't been a pleasant week; it's been sort of a purgatory. The days have been filled with lobbying with the congressmen, or whomever else would listen, marches to the Pentagon to turn themselves in as war criminals, testifying before the Senate Foreign Relations Committee, the House subcommittee on prisoners of war, and Ron Dellums' ad hoc committee on war crimes. Then there has been the continual hassle concerning the campsite, which made sleeping the radical position of the time. The following is a day-by-day account of the Dewey Canyon III activities. [The name Dewey Canyon comes from the tag given the first American intervention into Laos.]

Fifteen hundred veterans and their supporters, many wearing battle fatigues, marched to Arlington Cemetery Monday morning for memorial services. Following the service, the five-member delegation of two gold-star mothers, a veteran's wife, and two veterans were refused entrance to the cemetery when they attempted to place two wreaths commemorating the American and the Vietnamese dead. The angry vets, many of them in tears, vowed to return to the cemetery every day until they were admitted.

Veterans and their supporters, many wearing battle fatigues, marched to Arlington Cemetery

Not until later in the day were they given a reason for the gates being closed. The deputy superintendent of the cemetery said later that government regulations prohibit unauthorized demonstrations. After the cemetery, the vets marched back through the mall to the Capitol. Dressed in battle fatigues and chanting anti-war slogans, the vets converged on the Capitol steps where they were met by a sympathetic group of Congressmen.

In the afternoon the protestors broke up into state delegations and began lobbying with individual senators and congressmen. The vets demanded congressional action on a 16-point list of demands, including immediate withdrawal of all troops and CIA personnel from Southeast Asia, the establishment of a drug rehabilitation center for veterans, and the establishment of some kind of job training and placement program for veterans. Late in the afternoon the vets learned that the United States Court of Appeals rescinded a lower court ruling which had barred them from camping on the mall. The new order allowed sleeping on the mall as long as there were no open fires and no tents for sleeping purposes.

Late Tuesday morning the first guerrilla theater search-and-destroy missions were staged on the steps of the old Senate Office Building and on the east steps of the Capitol, while scores of tourists looked on. At the Capitol three girls wearing straw coolie caps attempted to run away from a squad of infantrymen armed with toy M-16's. With a burst of simulated automatic fire, the girls clutched their stomachs and plastic bags of red paint splattered on the Capitol steps. "Waste 'em, waste 'em," and "Get the body count," cried some of the raiders as the rifles cracked and the girls screamed.

At the old Senate Office Building a group of 40 vets approached the building in combat formation and wrestled two men in civilian clothes to the ground shouting, "Keep on the gooks" and "Everyone is considered a suspect — then we check I.D.'s" Squad leader Bill Crandall of the 199th Infantry Brigade, and now a student at Ohio State University, said that the demonstration was a portrayal of tactics used in Vietnam to get civilian suspects. Crandall said that the huts are often burned on such missions, but not when the press is around.

Later in the afternoon the vets returned to Arlington Cemetery, bitter about being refused entrance on Monday. Around 300 vets clad in battle fatigues marched silently in single file up the cemetery roadway; a woman whose son had been killed in Vietnam carried wreathes. As they marched up the hill, a leader explained that they were not there to make speeches but were there to honor the dead.

As the last of the men moved up the hill, a volley of rifle salutes from a burial in a lower field was heard followed by bugle taps. The marchers knelt under a tree as a woman placed the wreathes, one of them marked "Allies" and another, "Indochina." The vets then silently filed out, many of them raising their arms in a clenched fist and military salute.

Tuesday evening rumors filtered throughout the campsite that President Nixon had estimated that 35 percent of the demonstrators were not veterans, but merely hippies with long hair. A White House spokesman has denied the rumor. Nevertheless, the vet leaders began collecting discharge papers, military identification cards, draft classification cards, or anything else that would prove that they were indeed vets. One leader estimated that over 1,000 documents had been collected and placed in a box at the mall campsite for public investigation.

That same night Chief Justice Warren Burger, acting on an emergency petition from the Justice Dept., reversed the U.S. Court of Appeals and banned the GI's from camping on the mall. Burger, acting in his capacity as Circuit Justice for the District of Columbia, reinstituted a preliminary injunction against the campout granted Friday, April 16, by United States District Court Judge George L. Hart, Jr. The Justice Department gave the veterans until 4:30 Wednesday to leave the camp.

On Wednesday morning all sleeping gear was packed, but the vets vowed to remain on the campsite during the night. Sen. Edward Kennedy showed up at the camp in the morning and thanked the veterans for their service in Indochina, adding that their presence in Washington had done more than all previous marches. He said they were having a tremendous impact on Congress, because of their first-hand reports of the war.

The first arrests of Dewey Canyon III, in the early morning, came as protestors tried to enter the Supreme Court during hearings on the Justice Dept. injunction. They were stopped by guards in the hallway outside the court and sat down and vowed to stay until the court ruled on the constitutionality of the war in Vietnam. Author Mark Lane was among the 11 people arrested. Another protestor was ejected from the Supreme Court chamber when he refused to remove a Vietnam Vets Against the War button. When told to leave, he raised his fist in defiance.

When told to leave, he raised his fist in defiance.

A 4 p.m. general meeting was later called. California Congressman Ronald Dellums, Joe Howard of New Jersey, Bella Abzug of New York, and Shirley Chisholm spoke in support of the vets and promised their offices for the campers should they be evicted from the mall. Journalist I.F. Stone compared the eviction injunction to Herbert Hoover's eviction of the bonus marchers in 1932. Ramsey Clark announced that the eviction notice had been affirmed by the entire Supreme Court. Al Hubbard, executive secretary of the VVAW, suggested to the vets that those who were physically able should abide by the "no sleeping" law and simply stay awake for the remainder of Dewey Canyon III. The California delegation proposed that instead, the vets should act in civil disobedience.

The meeting was adjourned into state caucuses to vote on the two plans.

The vets reconvened at 6 p.m. and the voting of the caucuses was read to the crowd by John Kerry. The vets voted to sleep by 480 to 400, supporting the civil disobedience of the California group. After the meeting all people not officially connected with the protest were asked to leave.

Wednesday night marshals patrolled the camp, expecting a bust which never materialized. Despite a

cold rain, most of the veterans slept, defiant of the court order.

Thursday morning 107 Vietnam veterans and their supporters were arrested as they chanted and sang on the steps of the Supreme Court building. The arrests climaxed a morning of protest at the court building where the vets had gone to demand that the court rule on the constitutionality of the war. Later, U.S. District Court Judge George L. Hart, Jr., at the last minute request of the Justice Dept., reversed himself and lifted a ban on the encampment of the vets on the mall. Judge Hart also criticized the Nixon administration for degrading the federal judiciary by refusing to enforce the bans that the high court upheld Wednesday.

The veterans returned their medals to the government which had sent them to Vietnam.

Later in the evening 2,000 veterans and supporters marched four miles to the White House for a candle-light vigil. The veterans, some of them wearing POW shirts, marched down Pennsylvania Ave., circled the White House, and returned to the campsite.

Originally, the names of the war dead were to be read, but the veterans decided that it would be too painful and difficult to hear the names of their slain brothers again. After the march the vets returned to their campsite for much-needed sleep.

Friday, the last day of Dewey Canyon III, the veterans returned their medals to the government which had sent them to Vietnam. A line of vets stretched from the west steps of the Capitol back to the mall campsite as they moved single-file up to the make-shift wire fence which had been erected Thursday to protect the Capitol from the April 24 marchers.

Jack Smith, a Marine veteran from Connecticut, read a declaration from the Vietnam Veterans Against the War, saying, "We now strip ourselves of these medals of courage and heroism, these citations for gallantry and exemplary service. We cast these away as symbols of shame, dishonor and inhumanity." As the medals were being tossed onto the Capitol steps, other vets were preparing to leave the campsite.

Friday afternoon the 107 veterans and their supporters arrested Thursday for disorderly conduct were acquitted and were going through the processes of reclaiming their bond money. -30-

Ft. Hood: GIs Hit the Streets

Thorne Dreyer • May 23, 1970

Ford Hood, Texas, for several years the scene of growing GI dissidence, experienced its first large demonstration May 16.

According to staff members of the Oleo Strut, Killeen's GI coffee house, between 600 and 800 people marched through the streets of that small, central Texas town. Less than a hundred were students and civilian supporters: the rest were active duty soldiers.

The Killeen march was the high point of nine days of concerted anti-war activities at the Oleo Strut dubbed the Nine Days In May and was part of a nationally-coordinated series of Armed Forces Day activities.

Nationally, the actions were coordinated by the GI Task Force of the New Mobilization Committee to End the War in Vietnam. Demonstrations, organized primarily by active-duty GIs, took place May 16 at military bases throughout the nation.

The Nine Days in May, sponsored by Ft. Hood's underground paper, the *Fatigue Press*, built dramatically to the May 16 march. In addition to a series of nightly educational forums at the Oleo Strut, there was a court battle over a parade permit, and the much-publicized appearance of actress Jane Fonda.

Fonda, who has become actively involved in the GI anti-war movement over the last few months, appeared at the Strut May 10. She spoke on Women's Liberation, along with Vicky Smith of *Space City!*, Evelyn Sell of Austin, and Terry Davis of the Strut staff.

The next morning, she entered Ft. Hood to distribute leaflets publicizing the May 16 demonstration. She was immediately stopped by an MP and informed that she was violating a military regulation. To distribute leaflets at Ft. Hood, you must apply for permission seven days in advance and submit the leaflet for approval.

Fonda told the MP, "I've never been aware of the fact that the Constitution says one has to apply for permission to have freedom of press and speech and assembly." She passed out leaflets and was immediately arrested and taken to the Provost Marshal's

The Killeen march was the high point of nine days of concerted anti-war activities.

office. She was then given a letter of expulsion and informed that, should she attempt to reenter the base, she would be subject to a $500 fine and/or six months in prison.

She left the base and gave a press conference at the Oleo Strut. There, she stressed the upcoming demonstration. She also talked about the recent mass gathering at Washington protesting the U.S. invasion of Cambodia, where she was one of the speakers. She said that every speaker at the rally, attended by more than 100,000 persons, discussed the GI movement and the planned Armed Forces Day actions. In addition, one half of all money raised there went to the GI movement, the other half being donated to the Black Panther Legal Defense Fund.

But, she pointed out to the newsmen gathered around her, none of this information made the newspapers or radio and television newscasts. "There was a complete blackout of news of the GI movement." she said. "This shows' how uptight the establishment is and how very important the GI struggle is."

Concerning GI rights, Fonda said. "I think it is appalling that men who are sent overseas to fight and die for their country are denied the constitutional rights, which they are supposed to be defending."

She also commented on the recent Kent State killings. "It is easier to slaughter Vietnamese people when they're thought of not as human beings, but as gooks. It is easier to shoot students when our heads of state brand them as bums and buffoons. As far as I'm concerned, Nixon is as guilty of pulling that trigger as the National Guardsmen."

At the time Jane Fonda was in Killeen. it appeared there would be no parade permit granted for the May 16 march. The city council nixed the street march request and plans were to march on the sidewalks. But the day before the demonstration, thanks to the effort of Odessa attorney Warren Burnett, a parade permit was won. A judge in Belton declared the Killeen parade ordinance unconstitutional.

So Killeen experienced its first anti-war demonstration, and right down the middle of the street. And, according to the Strut folk, it was quite an impressive affair.

Many of the local citizenry felt slightly different, however. The police were mobilized in force: all of Killeen's 30 cops, plus another 120 from nearby towns, including a contingent of Texas Rangers.

In addition, there was a counterdemonstration of 100 local super-patriots, many duded up in cowboy garb and brandishing Amerikan flags. One right-winger attempted to rip off a Black Panther banner from a black GI and another black GI was attacked by a counterdemonstrator. The patriotic types attempted to start fights several times and caused the rally after the march to be shortened significantly.

According to the Strut, there were more than 1,000 sympathetic mostly GIs who looked on from the sidewalks. but were too intimidated by the cordon of cops and by the right-wing hecklers to join the demonstrators in the streets. Many GI's were also restricted to the base for the day.

One of the most popular chants was "FTA All the Way!" (FTA means "Fuck The Army!") Also: "Vietnam Love It or Leave It!"

The official demands of the march were: "U.S. Out of Southeast Asia Now." "Free Bobby Seale and All Political Prisoners," and "Avenge the Kent State 5."

-30-

Boycott on Avenue D

Sue Mithun • July 6, 1971

It's a street that goes by many names. You'll find it in every military town. It's usually a couple of blocks long. Garish, hastily constructed shops selling flashy clothes, jewelry, and skin flicks. There's a pool hall, some finance companies and auto rent places, a drug store or two featuring Archie comics and Playboy, several pawnshops, an arcade of pin-ball machines, and rifle ranges.

GIs call it Rip-Off Alley. In Killeen, Texas, the town closest to the Army's huge military installation of Fort Hood, it's Avenue D. And right in the middle of Avenue D is Tyrell's Jewelers Inc., a worldwide jewelry chain with stores in towns near almost every U.S. army base around the world.

— An ex-GI once stationed at Fort Hood

'GIs call it Rip-Off Alley.'

KILLEEN — Tyrell's specialty is getting young GIs, many of them away from home for the first time, to buy an expensive piece of jewelry for the girl back home: whether it's mom or a girlfriend.

Throughout the years they have developed a sales technique designed to exploit the loneliness and alienation of GIs in Army towns. Each new salesman gets a 20-page manual that includes detailed scenarios of sales pitches with word-for-word dialogues to be memorized.

As part of their spring offensive this year, anti-war GIs at Fort Hood decided to blow the whistle on Tyrell's. At the Armed Forces Day demonstration May 15, the Spring Offensive Committee (SOC) called for a GI-civilian boycott of Tyrell's. They made four demands of the jewelry chain.

- Stop sidewalk soliciting and high-pressure sales;
- Stop exploiting GI homesickness;
- End Army intervention and cooperation on payments — the Army deducts the money GIs owe Tyrell's from their paychecks;
- Remove the hypocritical "Honor Roll" ("We salute and honor these brave men, our customers, who have given their lives in the Vietnam conflict.")

The boycott began with leafleting and picketing in front of the store a few days before the monthly payday weekend at the end of May. By May 31, Tyrell's having done no business on a payday weekend, Killeen's business community was in an uproar. When the picket line was resumed the next day, June 1, police moved in and without warning arrested everyone on the line — eight GIs and two civilians — and charged them with parading without a permit and participating in a secondary boycott (a 1947 Texas anti-labor law that says only people actually employed by the company can call a boycott and picket). The 10 are now out on bail.

SOC called for a demonstration and picket line against Tyrell's to protest the busts and challenge the secondary boycott law for 7:30 p.m., June 30. Usually open until 9 p.m., Tyrell's closed at 7 p.m. that night. The 100 or so demonstrators, mostly GIs, held a spirited victory march up the sidewalk of Avenue D to Tyrell's and back down the other side of the street to the Oleo Strut Coffee House, promising to come back the next night. Tyrell's closed again the next night as 50 or so picketers approached the store.

On July 2 and 3, the committee returned to just leafleting, and Tyrell's stayed open, still

Police moved in and without warning arrested everyone on the picket line.

soliciting. The Honor Roll has been removed from the window, however.

Similar picket lines took place at Tyrell's stores in San Francisco, Newport, R.I., and Fort Bragg, N.C. last week. Fort Bragg GIs report that the store was closed more than it was open all week. A representative of Tyrell's national office came to Fort Bragg and talked to the boycott organizers there. He said they were taking down the Honor Roll in all their stores and talked about the bad publicity the Killeen bust had given them. Evidently they closed down in Killeen this time to avoid a possible confrontation and/or bust which would again make them look bad.

Tyrell's is obviously hurting. They seem to be playing it cool hoping perhaps to outlast the interest and energy behind the boycott. The boycott will continue and perhaps be expanded to other rip-off stores.

The 10 picketers busted June 1 go on trial for the parading-without-a-permit charge July 7, at the Killeen City Hall. On July 9, a pretrial hearing for the secondary boycott charges will be held in the Bell County Courthouse in Belton, Texas.

A committee to defend the Right to Boycott has been organized and needs funds.

Write P.O. Box 1265, Killeen, Texas 76541. -30-

Ad: Art by Kerry Fitzgerald, October 25, 1969.

Jane Fonda at Fort Hood. Photo: Thorne Dreyer, May 23, 1970.

Space City! Interviews Jane Fonda
They Shoot Soldiers Don't They?

Victoria Smith and Thorne Dreyer • May 23, 1970

The following interview with actress Jane Fonda was conducted by Space City! *staffers Victoria Smith and Thorne Dreyer at the Oleo Strut GI Coffeehouse in Killeen, Texas.*

Fonda, who was recently nominated for an Academy Award for her role in They Shoot Horses, Don't They?, *has in the last several months become involved in the radical movement, especially in the struggle for GI rights and the American Indian Movement. She was in Killeen to speak on a Women's Liberation panel at the Oleo Strut. The next day, she was arrested and briefly detained for distributing leaflets to GIs on the Ft. Hood army base.*

Fonda was accompanied by Elisabeth Vailland, widow of author Roger Vailland, who vocally opposed French involvement in Indochina.

SPACE CITY!: You're been involved in the GI movement and the Indian movement for several months now. How'd that all happen?

JANE FONDA: My family has always been liberal, so I was brought up as a white middle-class liberal involved in the various groups on a sort of fundraising thing... therapy money, guilt money. It always disturbed me to sort of live one kind of life then go in and lay some money on some people and then go away again. But that's where my head was then. I never realized the connection between any of the problems in this country and my own life — which is the problem that I am facing now every day when I talk to white middle-class liberals. I got married when I was 25. Fortunately I held off as long as that. And lived in Europe. Living there at the outbreak of the Vietnam War, I had access to information that doesn't come through here.

The most obvious kind of thing that can get someone involved is the news of the atrocities. I was seeing film on French television showing that American bombers were bombing North Vietnam, and instead of dropping the leftover bombs into the ocean as they are supposed to, would unload them on villages in which there is nothing but churches and hospitals and schools. Seeing what bombs — which are called

"lazy dogs" which send off hundreds of thousands of steel splinters — do to babies and women and old men and sick people.

I frankly couldn't believe it. Somewhere, despite the kind of political background that I had, I felt that Americans were exempt from this kind of criminal... what we said we stood for was at least what we tried to stand for. I came more and more to the awareness that in fact we're not exempt from it. And what makes it worse is we pretend to be so much else.

All countries have been guilty of war crimes — what France did in Algeria and Indochina, what the Germans did. All countries are guilty of this. But we promise liberty and justice and democracy and so forth and practice exactly the opposite and this is what makes us so hated abroad. And I can tell you, as someone who has been living there, that we are hated. And it became very difficult to stay there and defend the country and the policies. So I came back because I decided it was more important to come back and live here and try to work here.

> **'Lazy dog bombs send off hundreds of thousands' of steel splinters.'**

Before I came back, I was what I guess you would call a dropout. I just said, "Oh fuck it all" and went to India and was into that whole thing. But while I was in India, I started to become concerned about the political situation there and the poverty and the starving. And literally, one day, I said, "What am I doing here? This kind of thing is happening in my country. There are Indians in my country who are starving and suffering the same oppression."

So I came back and it coincided with all the publicity about Alcatraz. And so I decided that the best thing to do was to go there. I've learned after a long time that you can't learn anything from reading anything but underground papers. So I went to Alcatraz and I started reading a lot about Indian things. There's a particularly good book called *Our Brother's Keeper* by Edgar Cahn which really lays it on the line in terms of what's happening today and what the BIA [Bureau of Indian Affairs] are. I went to the state of Washington to find out about the fishing problem which has been going on there for about 15 years and other places.

The more I saw, the more I learned, the more I realized that the kind of help that I had been thinking of, fundraising, trying to exert pressure on Congress and so on, was very superficial and piecemeal. That it was the system itself which is at fault and is the problem and until something is done about the capitalist system, that everything else is really superficial and meaningless.

At the same time, I was in Europe when everything came down on the Panther Party, all in one fell swoop, and because I had been away for so long, I didn't understand what the Panther Party was all about and I didn't understand why they were getting it more than any other black group — Ron Karenga's group which is much more blatantly racist, for example. Why the Panthers?'

So I began to contact Panthers and I began to meet Panthers and talk to them and discovered that they are not in fact racist and that is one of the reasons they are getting so much harassment. The idea that a militant group will unite all oppressed peoples scares the establishment to death. They are organized, they're disciplined. Their rhetoric is violent, their actions are not violent. They are armed in self-defense.

I think that it is important for people not to listen to their rhetoric, but watch their actions. In fact, they are feeding hot breakfasts to kids of all races in the ghettos, they are setting up free medical clinics, and so forth.

SPACE CITY!: How did you get interested in the GI movement?

FONDA: One of my dreams has always been to drive across the country. At various stages of my life it took on different forms so where at one point it was to dig nature and at another time it was to dig other things. I decided two months ago that it would be a political trip. When I first decided to do it, it was just to find out what was happening between the two coasts that I knew very well. I hadn't been anywhere between those for a long time and I had really lost contact with the country and I wanted to find out what was going on.

At a party in Hollywood, I was talking about this trip and how I was planning to go to Indian reservations and so forth. Fred Gardner was there, who was one of the original organizers of the GI move-

ment and has recently written a book which is about the Presidio mutiny called *The Unlawful Concert*, I think.

And he said, why don't you go to some GI coffee houses — and at that time I didn't even know what a GI coffee house was. So he briefly explained the movement to me and I said I wanted to find out more, what would I be doing and what kind of role could I fulfill and all of that. And so I sort of took a crash course on the GI movement.

> ### 'If 10 percent of the army refuses to fight there is no more war.'

Every night I had meetings with different people, young lawyers involved in military law, some of the organizers of the movement. And I started going to coffee houses ... in Monterrey, in Washington and other places. And the more I work with GIs, the more I find out what kind of oppression they suffer within the military, the more I learned about what military indoctrination does to the heads of lower class boys who have no education — not just while they are in the military but, since there's no debriefing, when they come back from the war as trained killers with a tolerance for violence and a tolerance for having their constitutional rights taken away from them, the more I realize how important it is to get these guys political so that when they come out of the military they come out fighting, they come out not puppets, they come out not able to be manipulated by the government, by their bosses, by their friends and their parents.

I am convinced — I have been convinced during the three months that I have been working with the movement — that it is, of all of the different organizations of the peace movement, at least one of the most important if not the most important. I am told that if 10 percent of the army refuses to fight there is no more war. That's all it takes is 10 percent. This bumper sticker that says "What if they gave a war and no one came" — I'm beginning to think it's not just a pipe dream.

Obviously, I'm not wrong. The Army, the Pentagon, the government is really uptight. This is shown by the fact that despite the fact that every single important speaker that spoke at the rally yesterday [May 9 in Washington D.C.] in front of over 100,000 people, mentioned the fact that the money that was being raised there, half was going to the GI movement, the other half to the Panther Legal Defense Fund. In press coverage, not one word was mentioned of the GI movement. It's obviously a boycott, a national boycott, against the movement. Which only points up the fact that they're scared to death and they're scared to death because it's so important.

It's a very new movement; it's a whole new concept — the idea that guys within the military can buck the military system. For a long time, anyone involved in the peace movement thought that when you were inducted, once you went over and put on a uniform, you were enemy and that the whole thing was to go. More and more, people are beginning to realize that it is important if you have to go, to go and organize. For example, if I were 18 and male right now, I'm not so sure that I wouldn't enlist on purpose to go in and organize from within. That's how important I think it is. We don't advocate desertion, we don't advocate AWOL because they'll just get hung and for every guy who deserts, there is someone else who comes and takes his place. We say, stay in and organize.

So what I've been doing over the last two months is visiting Indian reservations, army bases, GI coffee houses and Panther headquarters all across the country. And the more I see, the more I learn, the more I realize that I don't have any solution, I don't know what the end result is. And that's another reason why for a long time I didn't really lay myself on the line in any way because I thought in order to do so you had to know what you were working for — specifically an "ism" of some kind.

All I know is that despite the fact that I am one of the people who benefit from a capitalist society, I find that any system which exploits other people cannot and should not exist. It's very difficult to make people realize that. I have a lot of friends who are liberal who are working for peace senators, who feel that if you take the bad guys out and put the good guys in office, it's going to change something. I think if you had a whole lot of saints in office in Washington it still wouldn't make any difference because the system is corrupt from the bottom up and this is something that we have to make people aware of. That it's not just poor white people and black people and brown people and red people that are oppressed, we are all being exploited and we are all being oppressed. It's easier to see it in terms of minorities than it is for those of us who are white middle class people. We must realize that we are getting it just as bad as everybody else.

> **'When the entire society is changed there will be true equality.'**

I am only beginning to realize now the importance of the Women's Liberation Movement in terms of this kind of struggle. Just in terms of numbers for one thing. Any time you get people to move, you always do it around their oppression. Getting women political has to be done around showing them the ways in which they are being oppressed. As Evelyn [Sell] said tonight, it's not just a matter of some crazy movement off on one side that is trying to get out of the kitchen. In order to be valid, in order for it to really succeed, it is locked in with every single other area of the struggle which will eventually change the entire society. And it is only when the entire society is changed that there will be true equality between men and women, between sexes, between classes, and between races.

SPACE CITY!: Will you tell us about some of the specific things you have been doing in terms of the GI movement, especially. The places you went. I think you were kicked off a couple of bases, weren't you?

FONDA: I went onto Fort Lewis in Washington to invite guys to come to the Shelter Half Coffee House. I was arrested; I was given expulsion papers which said that I had broken a law and, as a result, I was banned from several military installations. When I asked what I had done that was against the law, they said, "We don't know." As a result, I am suing the Secretary of Defense, Melvin Laird, the Secretary of the Army, and the Commanding General of the fort for depriving me of my constitutional rights of assembly and speech and due process of law.

Because before you can be accused and convicted for breaking a law (I was given an expulsion paper, it is the equivalent of a conviction) I should have been able to have a trial and I was denied that. As I pointed out, well I really didn't need to point it out, it was quite evident to the GIs who came to the coffee house that night, that Bob Hope and Martha Raye, and anyone who is mouthing military rhetoric and urging guys to go to Vietnam, are welcomed on the base with open arms and the red-carpet treatment. If someone's coming on who is speaking to the GIs and showing them an alternative, they are banned, they are discriminated against and harassed.

Besides Fort Lewis, I was also in Colorado Springs at Fort Carson. We went there with a group of civilians and some CBS television and other people to support the guys who had gone out on sick call strike during the moratorium. The commanding general of the fort tried to coopt us by inviting us onto the base and then showed us the stockade, which was a heavy scene. As CBS was filming through the grill — only four of us were allowed on base, the others had to stay outside, we kind of went in as a delegation — we walked through the stockade, the commanding general at our side. We were giving peace signs and saying "Power to the People," and they were all giving them back, and he was really shaken up.

Of course, the place was completely cleaned up because they knew I was coming. And all of the guys in the stockade pointed out to me that this isn't the way it usually is. I was taken in maximum security which is really hair-raising. It's all black, you can't see anything and since all the prisoners were black, all you could see was their teeth and their eyes. And they were all in there for political rea-

> **'The First Amendment doesn't become invalid because somebody puts on a uniform.'**

sons, some for AWOL, some of them because they were political organizers. Some of them had done nothing more than refuse to do KP and were in for like two months.

They thought that they had gotten all the heavy people out, but they had forgotten one black guy who had been beaten so badly and kicked in the ribs so badly the night before that he could hardly move or speak. He should have been in a hospital and he was just left there lying on his bed.

SPACE CITY!: How do you think you've best been able to help political prisoners in the Army?

FONDA: What I say to GIs and what I try to do in terms of working outside of the coffee houses, is to raise money for their legal defense, which is really the way civilians can help the most. They are really risking their lives by bucking the system and by becoming political in any way. There is an incredible shortage of young lawyers who know anything about military law to defend them. In most of the places I've been, there are maybe one or two lawyers who have to come a great distance to defend these guys and they're totally swamped with work. We need training of military lawyers, we need volunteers, we need military law libraries. All of these kind of things.

Along with Dr. Spock and many other people, I have been trying to raise money in various cities for this. Trying to get the GIs to learn about their rights, their legal rights. We always tell them that whatever they do they should do it in as legal a way as possible so that they're not going to get sent to prison. I try to do as much as I can to talk to civilian people about the movement and how important it is and how they need civilian support.

Tomorrow I'm going to try to go onto Fort Hood, I'm going to drive up with leaflets and when they ask what I'm doing (it's an open base, by the way), I'm going to tell them that I want to leaflet about the demonstration that is happening on May 16. They will say to me, "Have you requested permission to do this?" And apparently you need to give them a week or so before they can give you permission to distribute something on the base and they have to see it and everything like that. To which I will say that I didn't realize that the constitution made any provisions, that you don't have to request the right of freedom of speech and press.

END THE WAR!
March on Nov. 6

Freaks: Join the Montrose Contingent

The First Amendment is something guaranteed everybody and this doesn't become invalid just because somebody puts on a uniform. By having the press there, we are trying to make it a dramatic point and emphasize the kind of isolation and discrimination that's been forced on the GIs and also call attention and publicity to the fact that there is this nationwide demonstration happening May 16.

SPACE CITY!: Up until the last week or two, your involvement has primarily been with GIs and Indians. I remember seeing a picture of you in the paper at New Mexico State and someone was tying an arm band on you or something. What do you think about what happened at Kent State? What are your feelings about what's been going on the last week or so in the country?

FONDA: I had just arrived in Santa Fe, New Mexico, when Nixon gave his Cambodia speech and I had heard some things about the University of New Mexico, that there was nothing happening and nothing had been planned, so I asked them if I could speak. I'd never spoken at a university before. It was done

Jane Fonda at Oleo Strut. Photo by Victoria Smith, June 6, 1970.

on very short notice and I didn't expect there to be very many people.

But because of the speech and because it happened the evening of the day the four were killed at Kent State, there was an enormous turnout. And it ended up being a meeting in which they hammered out five demands that they were going to make and we went to the dean and so on and so forth and the university is now closed down and there have been some bad incidents.

I think, as someone said at the rally yesterday in Washington, that Nixon might as well have pulled the triggers himself as far as Kent State is concerned. Just as it makes it easier to slaughter Vietnamese civilians by thinking of them not as human beings but as gooks and slopes, so it is that much easier to kill students when the chiefs of state and heads of state brand them as buffoons and bums.

I think that Spiro Agnew and Richard Nixon, because of their racist attitude and demeaning rhetoric towards students and all of those who are protesting, make it easy for the National Guard to think of protestors as that: as bums, as subhumans, as animals to be shot. And I think that Nixon and Spiro Agnew are as responsible as the National Guard in killing those four students.

One thing that upsets me is that it takes four white students to be killed for the nation to rise up. The black school in Texas where there were a lot of black students killed and wounded by the National Guard and nothing happened. And the three black students who were killed about two years ago in South Carolina in a peaceful demonstration, killed by State troopers and nothing happened.

I think that Nixon is bringing the war onto the campuses. He's calling all his conferences about why are students reacting this way and what has to be done. As usual there is outside agitation and it's communist infiltrated, blah, blah, blah, blah. He's just an idiot if he doesn't realize why these things are happening. It's just so obvious. The fault is his. His and the system's.

But it's happening all the time. This kind of thing gets the nation going, but people mustn't forget that there are black people slain all the time, every day, framed-up, slaughtered, gunned down with military weapons that the police don't have any right to carry anyway. I don't think we have to wait to get worked up about things like that, they are happening all around us. We just have to be more aware of them. -30-

Space City! Interviews Jane Fonda: Part Two

Victoria Smith and Thorne Dreyer • June 6, 1970

SPACE CITY!: Some of our friends seem to feel that your latest film, *They Shoot Horses, Don't They?*, is a very strong indictment of capitalist society and it seemed to be the primary message there. Some people didn't get that at all. You're an actress and you're involved in that whole world in Hollywood. And I assume that you're going to continue to relate to that world. How do you see bringing the understanding you are gaining about what's happening in the world into your work in movies?

FONDA: I wish that every movie I make could be a political movie, a very heavy political movie. I can tell you that it's hard enough just to get a good part in any kind of movie. And we do have to eat, contrary to what most people think. All movie actors aren't particularly rich, especially if they're as dumb as I am as far as money is concerned and I frankly don't really care that much.

There are not enough writers that are involved in writing political movies that really mean anything, although that's changing more and more. I know that right now Don Duncan, an ex-Green Beret and a very big organizer of the GI movement, is writing an anti-war movie involving the GI movement.

This kind of thing should be done more, but since there is a dearth of these kind of scripts the important thing I think for myself and any other actress who is political, is to find ways of making the good scripts as political as possible. Someone who has done this very well is an actress whom I admire enormously, Vanessa Redgrave. She's a very political actress. She always manages, no matter what kind of movie she's in, to get in her politics.

What I'm saying is that it is important — especially now that I've become aware of how movies I've made promote male chauvinism — to be sure when I agree to do a picture and when I choose my scripts that, maybe they're not going to be the heaviest political pictures, but I want to make sure that they're not going to go the other way and do the contrary of what I'm trying to do in my life. And then the second step is to try, in whatever way possible, to make in some way a political statement. It ain't easy and I'll probably be working less, but that's what I have to do. And then also constantly try to find people who do know how to write movie scripts, who are political and who can say things political through movies because that is one of the most important media.

SPACE CITY!: Will you make some specific comments on *They Shoot Horses?* What that was really about?

FONDA: I don't think that any of the people involved in making that movie really thought of it directly as an indictment of the capitalist society, but in fact because it was about the depression and because it showed the misery and oppression of people in a capitalist society, that's what it ended up being. Another thing that it did, as far as I'm concerned — although not too many people thought about it that way — it showed how society creates problems and when people try to find their own personal solutions for them, society condemns them, whatever the solution may be.

In the movie, the character that I was playing was a really down-and-out girl who had been oppressed on every level all of her life and was totally, desperately, hopeless and could not continue. And killing her was the only way. There was no other answer for her. And yet, the man who killed her out of an act of generosity was condemned for it. And this kind of thing happens all the time. Society creates problems and then condemns people for trying to solve them.

SPACE CITY!: I'm trying to get a sense of what you mean by a political film. Could you mention some films that you think have contributed more to progressive politics?

FONDA: I personally think that *Easy Rider* is a political movie. I know that my brother and Dennis Hopper were aware of this, but I don't think they were aware of the degree to which it was a political movie. I think there certainly have been much more political movies, but the important thing is that it was such a huge success seen by a mass of particularly young people who related to it and who realized through it that racism, for example, is not just limited to black people and minorities. It's not just a racial thing.

The best political movie that I've ever seen is the *Battle of Algiers*. There is also *Z* which is not as heavy a picture but has been seen by many more people and this always has to be taken into consideration. A lot of people consider it a kind of Hollywood-type movie. For Americans it's pretty radical, but for very political people and European people, it really wasn't that radical.

As far as I'm concerned, the important thing is that it was seen by people who normally would never have seen a movie like that. That's something else that has to be taken into consideration. It is not that difficult to make an underground political picture, but nobody sees it.

The important thing is to make a movie — *MASH* in its own way is a very political picture — which has been seen by many people. One would hope to make a movie which would be extremely successful which right away means that it's not going to be very radical, it is not going to be heavy, heavy, but in a subtle way is going to reach middle America and touch them in some way.

SPACE CITY!: A lot of people who are in the Movement think that though there are certainly positive things that come out of political movies that are distributed through Hollywood, there is the whole thing about the medium being the message and that as long as you're making big commercial films — that are making lots of money for Hollywood, that are the whole kind of spectacle thing — that you're never going to really accomplish anything very basic and that maybe we have to build different kinds of institutions. Certainly the movement filmmaking groups like Newsreel are very limited in what they can do and they're not technically that adept. Do you see any possibilities for establishing cooperatives of radical movie makers to somehow make and distribute films themselves so they don't have to face the limitations that people face in Hollywood?

FONDA: There are cooperatives. Unfortunately, they're not very political. It's something that I would like very much to see. There's always such a shortage of money for anybody involved in these things. No matter what kind of movie you're making it does take a lot of money. Newsreel can make movies for hardly any money, but on the next step up you start getting into a couple of hundred thousand dollars and that's always hard for the radicals to raise.

It's true, if you're going through a large Hollywood studio you're promoting the capitalist system in a way, but don't you think it may be necessary to use the system against itself for a while? People have to be reached and if Hollywood movies are one way to reach them and Hollywood movies still do exist, then those of us who have access to Hollywood movies have to try to make them more and more pertinent. I think that's very important.

I would like to say just one thing that has nothing to do with movies. I get this a lot. I wasn't aware, since I've been out of the country for so long, the degree to which young people have become discouraged at the idea of protesting and the idea of petitions and all of those kinds of things since 1968. People who were political have just dropped out, they say "What's the point?"

When we were fasting in Denver during the Moratorium, young people were just coming by all the time saying "what's the use?" All I can say to these people is first of all, if you're waiting for big immediate results, forget it. That's not where revolution is at. It's slow, patient, day-to-day work. It takes discipline. It's something that a lot of people are not willing to do, but they must realize that that is the only way to do it.

One example of how effective petitions can be, I read three days ago that the president of Bolivia is going to reexamine the Regis Debray case and perhaps free him simply because of all the pressure that has been put on him over three years by the French intellectuals and all the people who have been protesting in France and sending petitions there. A man's life may very well be saved. And I refuse to become discouraged and lose hope. This is the way things have always been done. History proves us right, that that is the way things are done and to think that because it's not happening immediately it's never going to happen is just defeatist and wrong.

SPACE CITY!: Many people are looking for new forms of protest. On certain levels you can't work within the system. You can't have the ultimate faith that if you petition the system it's going to change itself, there has to be more basic change than that. Many people have thought that various kinds of terroristic actions stimulate people, like the bombings in New York. What do you think about this kind of action? Where demonstrations on campuses end in burning ROTC buildings.

FONDA: I think it's a very misguided idea of what revolution is all about. First, I'm opposed to violence, it's ineffective right now anyway. It gets people hurt for no reason. David Dellinger said it very well yesterday at the rally in Washington. He said breaking windows or smashing people here in Washington means nothing, just as this rally here is not to let off steam, it is not a safety valve, it is not the expression of anything. It is the beginning.

And what it's all about is all of you going back to the communities from which you came and working and organizing and talking and getting it together and keeping up the momentum. This is not a safety valve. I think of the people who are spouting rhetoric and blowing their noses in the American flag and talking about, in one breath, revolution and pot. I think it's just silly. I think it confuses the issues. I think a lot of people who think there is an incredible group, certainly not a majority, that if suddenly everybody goes out in the streets armed and ready for violence that there is going to be a huge uprising.

There's not. They're just going to get exterminated, wiped out. That's not what revolution is about. It's organization. Any revolutionary knows that. Lenin constantly said to the workers, no, not now, wait.

Revolution in this country is such a freaky idea, everybody's so comfortable. I've been talking to workers and lower income people. They've got an ice box and they've got a mobile home and so they'll have to spend the rest of their lives paying for it. But they don't realize the fact that they're exploited. They bicker a bit. As far as they're concerned, our country right or wrong. These people are the people who have to be educated and until they are, until they become political, there's no point in going out in the streets and bombing and stuff like that.

And hopefully, that won't be necessary and hopefully it will never be necessary. It would be marvelous to never have to kill anybody. Besides the bombing faction, there's the other faction, the dropouts, the let's-go-to-Maoui-and-live-on-the-beach-and-let's-go-to-New-Mexico-and-live-in-communes. I visited those communes and I think it's a false utopia, it's extremely egotistical. I very well understand and am frequently tempted by that whole thing. You think this is where it's at. We will go and we will live off the land and that's beautiful except that it solves nothing and I think it's wrong to put your head in the sand and to forget about what is happening to the people in the ghettos and to forget about the people who can't dress and can't eat and who can't feed their children.

I was there two days after Nixon made his speech on Cambodia. Those people didn't even know about it. That's not what life is all about. If everybody doesn't find out the truth and what their role is in terms of showing other people the truth and working and joining the struggle, then how can you get up in the morning and look at yourself in the mirror? And disappearing into nature isn't the answer. It's very tempting, but as I said before, it's a very egotistical thing to do.

I also think that dope is not the answer. It's an ego trip. I think the government will probably legalize marijuana simply because it keeps people oppressed; it keeps people passive and happy. It's very hard to go out and organize when you're stoned. Given a choice, between the two, between protest or dope, they'll legalize dope. I think young people have to become aware of the fact that this is something that is being and will be used to keep them passive and in a manipulative position. -30-

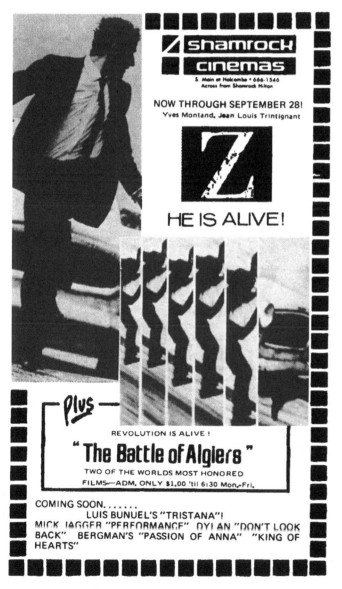

Ad: September 21, 1971.

Gay
Liberation

GAY LIBERATION

Gay people are an oppressed minority in America today. We have been forced into ghettos, the only place we can find one another, and into the few jobs and professions where we can get by. We often have to meet in dehumanizing gay bars; or on the streets where some of us have been beaten and murdered and arrested by plainclothes cops who entrap us. Often we never meet, but if we do come out to each other, most of us are compelled to lead double lives.

We hide and feel guilty because this society says we are "sick," and to varying degrees we believe it. America allows us to live only one way, in shame of our so called "unnatural natures."

The Gay Liberation movement has been formed all across the country to fight the lies and myths perpetuated by this society. We are following the examples of third world and women's liberation movements by rejecting what

we are told we must be. We are not sick. We are making love with people of the same sex. We feel good and whole about our love and we want to remain gay.

Gays will no longer tolerate the bad trip that America puts on us. We are uniting to fight for a free society, where love between people can be a reality. We join with all oppressed peoples in the struggle against this materialist, racist, sexist, imperialist country because we know that we can be free only when all people are free.

This special Gay Liberation supplement has been put together by members of Houston Gay Liberation. All of the material has been written by gay people, some by local people and some by gays in other parts of the country. We hope that it will help to better explain the Gay Liberation movement and that it will generate interest in the movement among both straight and gays.

Queer . . . fairy . . . homo . . . pansy . . . dyke . . . fruit . . . faggot . . . pussy sucker . . . queen . . . gay . . . lesbo . . . cocksucker . . . limp-wrist
The homosexual is a case of retarded emotional development.
It's unnatural to love someone of your own sex.
But what can two women do together?
All you need is a good fuck.
Only massive childhood trauma could cause such distortion of natural development.
Homosexuals are child molesters.
You can't be a lesbian; you're too pretty!
Why don't you be a hairdresser or interior decorator?
Only women love men; only men love women — make your choice: are you going to be a woman or a man;
Homosexuals are sick and can be cured.
Homosexuality is a crime against nature.
She just couldn't get a man.
I thought people like that shot themselves.
Isn't he sweet?
She must be a truck driver!
He'd rather swish than fight.
Faggots are afraid of their mothers.

Check this box if you've had any homosexual tendencies.
Some of my best friends are homosexuals, but I wouldn't want my son to be one.
The Chicago 7 defendants are turning our children into freaking fag revolutionaries!
Any man with long hair must be queer.
It's all too disgusting to talk about.

BUT NOT ANY MORE

It's too disgusting to even talk about.

BUT NOT ANY MORE!

As homosexuals we must deal with our collective alienation and destroy the barriers built up in our own minds — and other people's minds — about who we are and whether or not we matter to the world. Every time we accept the word "queer" as a factual label or a clever joke, we confirm our own image of ourselves as different, other than human.

We are different — and it's good.

Special Pullout Section

June 15, 1971.

Space City! and Gay Liberation

Alice Embree

Gay Liberation was coming into its own in 1969, the year of the Stonewall rebellion in New York City. *Space City!* covered Gay rights marches, the legal challenge to the sodomy law in April 1970, Gay Liberation dances, and lesbian music. A four-page spread in the June 15, 1971, issue featured articles, poetry, and an announcement of a Gay Pride Conference at the University of Houston. The October 7, 1971, issue of *Space City!* included a Houston Gay Liberation political action plan for "Confrontation Politics," with strategies for inclusion in anti-war events and electoral politics. The terminology of Gay Liberation quickly morphed to Lesbian and Gay before it continued its path of gender identity inclusion, LGBTQIA, with "Queer" becoming a term of community pride.

Austin
July 2021

Sodomy Law Challenged

Bill Casper • April 11, 1970

Recently Houston attorney Ben Levy received a court assignment to defend James Dawson, a 38-year-old white man accused of sodomy. Dawson and a 13-year-old black youth were reportedly discovered by a University of Houston security guard in the back seat of a parked car on the UH campus. The two were allegedly engaged in sodomy.

Dawson is being prosecuted under Article 534 of the Texas Penal Code, which makes sodomy a crime. According to the code, sodomy consists of carnal copulation with a beast, or use of the mouth on the sex parts of another for carnal purposes, or carnal copulation with an opening in the human body other than the sex parts, or etc. (Note: For the purposes of the State of Texas, your "sex parts" are exclusively between your legs.)

Although the law makes no distinction between homosexual and heterosexual, the law has been used almost exclusively to prosecute and persecute homosexuals. In his research, Levy has found occasional instances where the statute has been invoked against farm boys for making it with one of their animals, but he was unable to find any instance where it was invoked against heterosexuals. The statute clearly could be used against heterosexuals, though even married couples having oral-genital relations in the privacy of their own home could be prosecuted (and sex-re-

searcher Kinsey estimates that 80 percent of all married couples do engage in such).

Recently a three-judge federal court in Dallas declared the law unconstitutional and restricted its enforcement by the Dallas district attorney. The court was acting on a motion to intervene filed by a Dallas married couple. (A motion to intervene is a motion to have some law declared unconstitutional prior to prosecution under that law.) The grounds upon which the law was stricken were that it interfered with husband-wife private communications. This is protected under the free expression provisions of the First Amendment.

Accordingly, Levy has filed a motion to intervene on behalf of a Harris County married couple. This motion will go before a three-judge federal panel sometime next week. This panel consists of Judges Singleton, Ingraham, and Hannay. (Ingraham and Hannay are conservatives, so it is difficult to predict the result of the hearing.)

Levy has also filed a petition for injunctive relief on behalf of Dawson. This seeks to enjoin the Harris County district attorney from prosecuting under the law because it is unconstitutional with respect to single couples, and is viewed as a class action for homosexuals. Both motions are in point of fact class actions for homosexuals, since homosexuals are practically the only persons prosecuted under the present enforcement patterns of the law. -30-

Gays Spend Nite at Riesner St.

Jim Shannon • November 26, 1970

Five gay brothers from New York who are traveling around the country talking to people about Gay Liberation and especially about the Revolutionary Peoples Constitutional Convention, received an ample dosage of southern hospitality here recently. They were the weekend guests of the Houston Police Department down at city jail Nov. 14-16.

Apparently, the sight of three white freaks and two blacks in a Volkswagen bus with out-of-state license plates was too much for the oinkers — the five were stopped twice before one porker had the brilliant idea (flash!) to run them down to 61 Riesner Street, where they spent the weekend.

Although they weren't charged with any specific crimes, they were held on suspicion of forgery (they had some credit cards borrowed from a friend) and suspicion of narcotics (there were some funny little pills; nobody could figure out what they were). Anyway, this gave the pigs the opportunity to thoroughly harass the quintet, something they had apparently wanted to do since they had laid eyes on them.

Besides eating shit food and being packed into a tank

The other prisoners seemed impressed by their solidarity.

with 80 other men, all five encountered severe oppression, both sexist and racist. Richard Koob, Giles Kotcher and Jimmy Fouratt were the subject of verbal pig attacks and "faggot-baiting" — especially Jimmy, who has super long, beautiful blonde hair. Douglas Batts and Ron Vernon were doubly hassled, since they are both gay and black.

They said the other prisoners seemed impressed by their solidarity in the repressive atmosphere of the jail, and they dug on the way the brothers drew on each other for energy and strength that was sorely needed.

After much hassling by some good movement lawyers (Ed Mallett and John Sayer), the five were released late Monday afternoon, Nov. 16. They soon split town to continue their trip, helping to spread revolutionary gay consciousness in Amerika. Before they left, we were able to interview them, and they had some very interesting things to say about revolution, Gay Liberation, Third World Gay Revolution, and Houston pigs. -30-

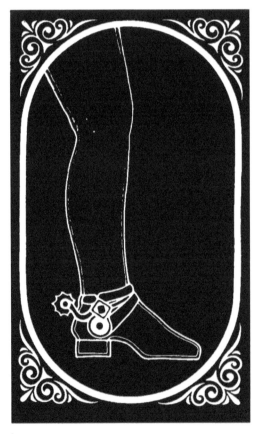

Come Out! An Interview on Gay Liberation

Jeff Shero and Jim Shannon • December 12, 1970

[Five brothers from the New York Gay Liberation Front and Third World Gay Revolution were in Houston recently to talk with local GLF people and members of the Red Coyote Tribe. On their way out of town, the quintet was busted, held for two days, then released without charges. Following their release, they talked with Pacifica reporter Jeff Shero and Space City! ace Jim Shannon. Following are excerpts from that talk.]

I think one of the things that's striking is here: you're a mixed group, both black and white, coming to Texas, which is probably the most uptight, or one of the most uptight places, in the country in terms of masculine roles and role playing. Were you particularly worried when you came to Texas and thought that problems might be a lot different than in New York?*

Yeah, well I had sort of a big paranoia about coming down south. I didn't relate too positively to it at all, because most of my experience of knowing anything or finding out anything about the South was very negative, and once I got here, I found the feelings were justified.

You found they were justified?

Pretty much so, by being arrested, you know.

How were you treated when you were arrested? Differently than you would be in New York or Chicago?

Well, a pig is a pig, but I think I was... I don't know how much differently I was treated. I was more worried about how they were going to react to me. I know that in other experiences with pigs I was more forward and direct with them, you know, than I was here, probably because I was afraid of being killed down here. What was different in the way the pigs dealt with us was that the racism was right out front. It wasn't the subtleness which I've experienced in New York. And the sexism. Before they knew we were gay, they treated us all — the whole police, the whole pig mentality, which was so sexist anyway   they were just so incredibly sexist.

What did they say specifically?

I feel like when we were first brought into the station to be booked for the charges it was like this whole mas-

> **I think they are part of the death culture.**

querade of the repression of gay sexuality in the death culture. It was like the pigs themselves were homosexual in the old sense of the word, in a deathly repressed way. I mean, they made us drop our pants, and they kept talking about "you can have a date with the one with the long blonde hair later," and everything that was gay about us, everything that didn't personify male supremacy, was completely fucked over and completely denigrated.

Do you think that what makes the cops so uptight like that is that they're afraid to deal with their homosexuality?

I think that many pigs are homosexuals — I don't know how many — but I'm sure that some of them are. And this facade that they have to present — this big male supremacist type thing that they have to present forces them into this type thing anyway. Because they have to deal with the system, you know.

I don't think there's any hope in changing them because I really think they are part of the death culture, and it's constantly making me aware as I'm dealing with them how that is dying — how that has to die — how that cannot win. But the change will come for them when the fundamental changes start happening in this society. They are almost the most heightened example of the repression — the sexual repression — in this society.

I don't think it's so much repressed homosexuality. These people are reacting to any kind of intimacy. I'm sure their heterosexual relationships are very messed up too. Because they can't be intimate at all. Everything becomes purely — the whole rap seems to be a very sexual kind of thing, related to getting their sex. Real sexual abuse, without realizing or admitting any kind of intimacy.

I think that when we're talking about their homosexuality — or any kind of homosexual impulses — we are absolutely not indicating that they're gay. Because there is a great deal of difference in someone being homosexual in the old sense of the word and someone being gay.

What is the difference?

Well, we feel that gay means being sexually free.... Right now we feel that our struggles represent a sexual liberation. And that we in our consciousness are proceeding toward liberation, and we are in the vanguard of that process of sexual liberation.

There are a lot of negative things that we can go into that happened to us while we were in jail. Not only in relation to being gay but just the racism and oppression that goes down there. But there were also some positive things for us as five people. And that came out of our solidarity as five gay people — knowing that each other was gay and knowing that we could relate to each other in a way that did not have to go through the games that all the other prisoners and the jailers and the sadists were going through.

I was told that most of the prisoners in the tanks that you were in were black. Did you get into any raps about what GLF meant and what their lives were like inside the jail?

You have to talk to the level of the people that were there, and the level was not to talk about Gay Liberation. It has to be understood that when you get in that enemy zone — that "Man" zone; that's what prisons are about — the role-playing that goes on is so extreme and so heightened that all the prisoners were playing out their versions of being very masculine. Because their masculinity — every time a guard came in — was threatened. So, what would happen was their reaction would be to act super masculine among each other….

And I felt that in many ways there seemed — in the way people seemed to appreciate us after a while, and just how free we were with one another, and being really exemplary, and how we were just laying our heads on one another's laps, touching one another. Things they were so uptight about. You could see that they really wanted to do it and eventually it happened and this brother laid his head on another brother's lap and it was really beautiful. Because there was no sexual thing to it — it was just all out of him.

Third World Gay Revolution

Another thing that I would like to rap about is Third World Gay Revolution, which is a part of Gay Liberation in New York and Chicago and other cities. This is composed of Third World people — that being four-fifths of the world's population which is not Northern European white. We're really having a struggle in relating to each other, and it's a very positive and very beautiful right-on thing.

Also, in turn, dealing with the consciousness and raising the consciousness of our white brothers because we share a common oppression, that is, being gay. Third World Gay Revolution in Chicago was formed because

the black people that had joined Gay Liberation at the beginning found it necessary to split because of the domination of male whites at the meetings and things like this, and also because Third World people, can best relate to the Third World community. More so than my white brothers coming into my community trying to relate to Third World people which is really what's been happening all the time in the system, and we don't want that to fuck it up. So we've taken a different approach.

What do you think of the statement on Gay Liberation made by Huey Newton?

The importance of that statement for all of us as gay people was that it was a vanguard statement. It had never been said before by any revolutionary — that includes Cuba, Mao, Russia — no one has ever taken gay people into the revolution and really seen how sexism is a right on oppression. So, it opened up dialogue. Not only with Black Panthers, but it opened up dialogue with all revolutionary groups.

In New York we had much better contact with the Young Lords Party than we had with the Black Panther Party prior to the statement. After the statement of course all revolutionary groups had to begin to relate or begin to deal with Gay Liberation, because Huey P. Newton is respected as a right-on revolutionary leader. And so one of the things we have recently done is visit the national headquarters of the White Panther Party — brothers from New York and Chicago, and

Art: Charles Arthur Turner, January 31, 1970.

Ann Arbor — and confront them on the sexism we felt was rampant in the party, and that was very productive. We've been dealing with other political parties. We now have the strange problem of a lot of people saying right-on Gay Liberation but having no idea what that means, having no idea how that affects them, and we say there is no such thing as "Right on Gay Liberation."

What sort of responses do you think people should have to Gay Liberation?

I think that Gay Liberation — and Third World Gay Revolution — is looking for people to start dealing with feelings and not stereotypes. Because in the movement a big thing — one of the biggest biases of revolutionary people against Gay Liberation — is that they think in terms of a white, middle-class group of people, of homosexuals. And that is by no means right on. Because Gay Liberation is made up of many, many classes — well, all classes — and we're struggling towards the elimination of classes. I think we'd just like to see them start relating to each other — not necessarily meaning that all men go around jumping into bed with each other, but that all men start dealing with each other's feelings.

We suggest that men engage in consciousness-raising groups — as gay people have done in Gay Liberation — and get to the roots of their feelings and how they've been made to play certain roles and just the part of them that they've given up and just how they feel restricted. To build intimacy and love for members of the same sex. And I think that would also in many ways improve the relationship between the sexes. Just men coming into contact with who they are.

The only product of that can be a more human person. And just as our gay sisters are relating to Women's Liberation, and the way that all women whose consciousness is being raised are relating to each other, to define what is women-identified as women — not male-identified women — that women are going to tell us what they want to be and how they're going to define their own identity. Men also have got to start to challenge what this society has laid upon them as men.

It doesn't mean that men are not going to relate to women. But right now the only way that men are going to be able to relate to women in any human sort of sense is when they begin to struggle with relating to each other. That can only mean for better relationships between people. All kinds of people — men and men, women and women, men and women.

I think I can relate personal experiences as to how I was like for a long time very straight-identified and con-

sidered myself as bisexual and had a certain arrogance about that and what that simply means is...

What do you define as bisexual?

It's giving in to the pressures of the society to be ... All the pressures of the society upon us as gay men is to be straight, to be heterosexual. "Okay," you say "so I'm a little queer. I'm a little homosexual, but no one's going to know. I'm going to relate to women. I'm going to show how much a man I can be." And damn it, you've got to off that. That's not how men should relate to women. That not the point of relating to women: to be a man. To prove that. The point of it would be to love women.

Bisexuality assumes these two camps that you cross over. You know that there's always this balancing act, this tightrope walk. You slip on this side sometimes. You slip on that side sometimes. There's always those two sides. What we want to work for is the time when there's no sides.

When there's no roles at all?

Right on.

The question that Women's Liberation is bringing up to all women … We feel that Gay Liberation — particularly the men in Gay Liberation — has got the same kinds of question to ask of all men. And the kind of questioning that will go on will bring about what we feel will be the new person — both man and woman — who in the new society will not be caught into these camps called "heterosexual" and "homosexual." We won't have these camps. People will just be sexual.

See, so many, many people you talk to in Gay Liberation really date themselves from when they got into Gay Liberation. They'll say, "I'm one year older" or "six months old," and it may sound a little riffy, but it's really not, because to have had to hide all your life and to have had to be some double image and suddenly to feel liberated … how it feels to be liberated and feel in touch with yourself and feel your energies being productive.

I know for myself having been active in the whole hippie movement in New York and Yippie and that kind of thing. It wasn't until I got into Gay Liberation that I really felt that I was, as Richard said, relating to my own oppression. That I could relate openly to my brothers and sisters — both my straight brothers and sisters and my gay brothers and sisters. And it's just fantastic 'cause I feel so alive now. And I feel so totally committed to this vision that I have of what I think we're all struggling for in the revolution — the vision afterwards.

Kate Millett in *Sexual Politics* I think really says some fine right-on things about the power of politics, the sexuality … And well, we can sit here and feel good, because there's the five of us together, and we have this solidarity in the Collective that we're in. And we have solidarity with our beautiful brothers and sisters in Houston. But still the world outside is very real and the sexual politics of it is that heterosexuals hold that and that gay people are the minority and gay people are the odd people out in that power struggle.

It is one of the reasons why gay people and all people have to identify with being gay. To get over that heterosexual chauvinism that goes down. Because as long as you can identify yourself as straight — as long as a man or woman can say … you know, that's what I was talking about, that liberal sort of "Right on, Gay Liberation." As long as a person says that and sits there with the security of being straight: "I know that I'm normal. I know that I'm in that power position."

It may not even be conscious. We want to bring up those unconscious feelings. Because no one, we feel no one, can come from that point of view. Because anyone that comes from that point of view — no matter how right on they are, no matter how liberal they are with us — is our oppressor. Until they start dealing with their own gayness. -30-

Gay Liberation and Political Confrontation

Houston Gay Liberation Political Action Committee • October 7, 1971

"Confrontation politics" is the thrust of the Political Actions Committee [of Houston Gay Liberation]. Discussion and planning of "ZAPS" are underway. Plans call for confronting candidates for the upcoming November elections and questioning them about their stand on such issues as the sodomy laws, harassment of gays. In just a few weeks, when all candidates have declared, the "Zapping" will begin. Their responses to these questions, whether favorable or unfavorable, will be given the widest possible publicity.

In addition, a letter is being prepared to the candidates questioning their stand on the gay civil rights issue. Copies will be circulated so that gays and persons supporting gay civil rights may use it as a guideline to write the candidates.

Anti-War Regional Conference

On Sunday, Sept. 26, there was a regional anti-war conference at the University of Houston. About 200 delegates representing Texas, Oklahoma, and Louisiana were there. The purpose was to coordinate plans in the region for the upcoming anti-war demonstration in Houston on Saturday, Nov. 6. Activists emphasized that this would be a legal, peaceful demonstration.

Representatives of several Gay Liberation groups were there, including Houston Gay Liberation. The following resolution was submitted by the gays and overwhelmingly approved by the delegates:

> The Texas-Oklahoma-Louisiana Peace Action Coalition (TOL PAC) commits itself to offering full support to the Gay Liberation movement. At the last Na-

tional Student Mobilization Committee Conference, approximately a year and a half ago, SMC voted to "support the long-overdue struggle for freedom for its homosexual sisters and brothers." Since that time, the Gay Liberation movement has grown at a phenomenal rate. Gay Liberation groups are now active in all sections of America and in a number of other countries.

This dynamic new movement represents a valid political response to real oppression and a healthy breakthrough against repressive and irrational sexual attitudes and behavior.

We are demanding self-determination and our full human rights.

We gay women and men will no longer submit to our oppression. We are angry. We are proud. And we are demanding self-determination and our full human rights. As Gay Liberation develops, links are developing with other movements for freedom — Black Liberation, Chicano Liberation, the GI movement, the high school movement, and the anti-war movement. Gay Liberation cuts across all forms of oppressive role playing, cuts through all layers of society, and gives a new impetus to the other liberation struggles.

The TOL PAC condemns the news media for refusing to recognize the participation of gay persons and the gay movement in the anti-war movement or at best distorting our participation. An example of this is the refusal of the TV cameraman this morning to film the "Gay People Against the War" banner even though he filmed all the other banners.

Participation of gay contingents has already substantially increased anti-war demonstrations. However, the full potential of this movement, involving tens of thousands of people and potentially millions in motion, has yet to be tapped by the anti-war movement.

We believe that the following concrete proposals will constitute real support for the Gay Liberation movement and by maximizing gay participation, help to end the war in Southeast Asia NOW.

1. All speakers for all rallies and meetings must be made fully aware that Gay Liberation is supported by the anti-war movement, and that antigay remarks will not be permitted.

2. Gay Liberation speakers must be included on an equal basis with other segments of the anti-war movement.

3. TOL PAC should make an effort to include gay groups in active participation in the anti-war movement, and encourage gay contingents in anti-war demonstrations.

4. The Gay Task Force and other gay groups and individuals must be defended against political attack. The struggle of gay people against repressive laws and other forms of social oppression is part of the broader struggle for democratic rights which the anti-war movement must wage to protect its own right to exist.

5. Gay Liberation should be mentioned in all literature on an equal basis with other movements.

6. TOL PAC should distribute pamphlets, leaflets, buttons and posters relating gay people and the gay movement to the war and anti-war movement, all material to be written by gay anti-war activists.

7. A permanent gay task force is to be established within TOL PAC.

8. On all regional organizing trips, gay literature will be taken and displayed at literature tables and an effort will be made to include gay anti-war activists on all trips.

9. Gay anti-war activists will establish the Gay Task Force office within the TOL PAC office, organize gay people throughout the region to attend the Nov. 6 march and support the fall calendar and organize gay participation in the Nov. 6 march.

10. Discussions will continue with the Gay Liberation organizations on the possibility of organizing a "Gays Against the War Day" during the Peace Action Week. If such an activity is called by the Gay Task Force, it will be fully supported and endorsed by TOL PAC.

Women's Cranky and the Bellaire High School Yearbook

Sasha and George • October 7, 1971

How we got into the yearbook without even registering:

So there we were, surrounded by muttering hoards of angry male high school students armed with camera and male ego — we being five innocent females come to bring the word about women to Bellaire. Our weapons were hammer, nails, scissors, tape, tambourine, drum, kazoos, washboard, and the faithful Women's Cranky.

The cranky is a big wooden frame containing two rollers on which is wound a scroll depicting the history of womankind. After playing and marching along with the school band for a while, we unfurled the cranky, accompanied by a historical narrative and musical sound effects, in front of five classes.

Two common reactions to the demonstration were, "Did it ever occur to you some women like to be oppressed?" and "I agree with you but …" After a few minutes of discussion these women would nod solemnly, agreeing with us a little more. With two or three exceptions, the males produced howlers like:

"I'd rather date a feminine queer (sic) than a woman who'd been digging ditches all day getting brown and hard." (What's this racist got against brown women?)

"Y'all remind me of animals with your overalls and frizzy hair." "You're oppressing me by making me

Art: June 15, 1971.

listen to things I don't want to hear." "When a child is brought up with more adults in the house than just its parents there is bound to be some resentment." "I don't oppress women."

The less articulate just said, "Wanna ball?" and "Wanna suck my dick?" Both sexes lapsed into shocked silence when one of us mentioned that she is gay. It was a big upper that after most of these emotional discussions were ended by the bell, some woman from the class would come up to us and say "Thanks for coming. I really agree with you."

Well, we did it, and we're going to do it again. At the risk of being tarred and feathered, no doubt. So if one day you see a band of women marching (in time?) down the street, playing washboards and such, open your ears; you have nothing to lose but your minds.

By the way, the guy with the camera was from the yearbook, so all you Bellaire students check it when it comes out for a picture of two women kissing. Horrors!

We'd love to do the cranky for you, sisters. Reach us at 524-2217 for more information. Any of the high school sisters who agree with us and want to get together with other high school women can call too. We love you. -30-

Art: September 7, 1971.

High
School

Cover: August 28, 1969.

The High School Connection

Alice Embree

Five issues into the paper's three-year run, *Space City News* (later *Space City!*) featured high school uprisings in the August 28, 1969 "Back to Skool" issue. The extensive coverage signaled the importance of outreach to Houston area high school students. A recurring feature, "High School Rap-Up," carried updates from multiple schools.

Space City! offered technical assistance to high school students who wanted to produce newspapers and legal assistance when high school students suffered consequences for selling *Space City!* and distributing campus newspapers. The *Space City!* staff nurtured strong relationships with high school student reporters. A few of those reporters became major contributors to *Space City!* Waltrip High School student Jim Shannon later joined the *Space City!* Collective.

"High School Actions" in the October 1, 1969 issue reflects the sprawling diversity of schools and school districts: Bellaire, Davis, Lincoln, Sharpstown, Westbury, and Madison (Houston ISD), and other districts, MacArthur (Aldine ISD), Rayburn and Pasadena (Pasadena ISD), Spring Branch (Spring Branch ISD), Clear Creek (Clear Creek ISD), and Spring Woods (Spring Woods ISD). *Space City!* covered the working-class schools MacArthur and Hambrick Junior High, the Davis vocational high school, and schools with the advantages of white privilege, including Olympic-size swimming pools.

A deep-dive interview with members of the North Side Student Association at Douglas High School appeared in August 1969, and in September, another interview appeared with Black students at San Jacinto High School. These provided insight into Houston as Jim Crow segregation was giving way. Students described the disparities in opportunity, punishment, expulsions, the racist enforcement of dress codes prohibiting Afros, and the unspoken color barriers for Homecoming Queens. Students revealed their understanding of repercussions as they began to break barriers.

Space City News covered MacArthur High School's North Side Student Association (NSSA) in the August 28, 1969 issue. An end to corporal punishment topped their list of demands:

> We demand an end to beatings of students by school administrators and teachers. We believe the beatings are brutal and sadistic, a possible outlet for latent sadistic tendencies in school administrators.

The NSSA also demanded the creation of a student court, an end to dress codes, support for free speech rights, and the opening of

Art: September 12, 1969.

the library to the community. A photo showed students raising fists in front of a racist North Side hangout, the Swamp, that sported a "whites only" sign.

A sidebar in the same August issue reported unrest at Clear Creek and Westbury where students were protesting "puppet" student senates and dress codes. The August issue also carried the announcement of a "free school" to be operated by and for high school students. The alternative learning format later became The University of Thought. cindy soo, now a New Journalism Project board member, was a recent Westbury high school graduate when she penned an announcement for the University of Thought in the August 31, 1971 *Space City!*.

> **Space City! maintained a steady stream of reporting on high schools.**

The "Back to Skool" issue also carried demands of the Mexican American Youth Organization (MAYO) and a call for a Chicano walkout on September 16, the 159th anniversary of Mexico's independence from Spain. The walkout was part of a national action by high school students that saw historic turnouts in southwestern states.

The full list of MAYO demands, which included initiating Chicano history and culture courses and stopping the practice of "pushing out" students who had disciplinary problems, is included in Dennis Fitzgerald's article in this section.

In the September 12, 1969 issue of *Space City News*, Gregory Salazar, a recent graduate of Reagan High School, wrote about the boycott tactics. In the fall of 1970, as part of MAYO, Salazar was part of a demonstration at the Houston ISD meeting. Nine MAYO members were indicted by a grand jury.

Space City! maintained a steady stream of reporting on high schools, usually heightened at the beginning of the school year. Eager high school reporters gathered stories from many schools and several campus-based papers emerged: *Armas* at Marshall Junior High and Jeff Davis High School; Bellaire High School's *Plain Brown Watermelon*, and *Pflashlyte* at Sharpstown HS. A citywide newspaper, *Little Red Schoolhouse*, began publication in the fall of 1970, and several articles in *Space City!* carried the "Little Red Schoolhouse" byline. Harrell Graham reported on a national high school conference in Chicago in July 1970, and on the newly created Cooperative High School Independent Press Service (CHIPS).

The countercultural revolution in Houston high schools was obvious. Special rules for female students were described by Carolyn Evans in her December 12, 1970 "Day at Dobie," citing the absurd double standard allowing very short skirts on cheerleaders while non-cheerleaders attending the rallies had to submit to skirtlength checks.

High school students were suspended or arrested for selling their own newspapers or *Space City!*, and in September 1970, *Little Red Schoolhouse* issued special advice in an article entitled, "If you are busted." The free speech fights that made it into the court system were covered by *Space City!* Harrell Graham, Paul Kitchen, and Jim Shannon all were disciplined by their schools for selling newspapers. Jim Shannon's article on Waltrip student Paul Kitchen is included in this section and in a July 6, 1971 article, "Decision favors HS vendors," E.F. Shawver, Jr. reports on the outcome of one of these cases.

Another court case made it onto the February 3, 1971 cover of *Space City!*. Divorced high school student, Soni Romans, sued Channelview ISD in federal court when she was barred from extracurricular activities. E.F. Shawver, Jr. reported on the court victory.

Austin
May 2021

Art: Bill Corbin, February 14, 1970.

High School Students Unite

Dennis Fitzgerald • September 12, 1969

Hundreds of kids were suspended from the Houston public schools last week, and countless others were threatened with the same if they don't come around.

It wasn't a situation which made the daily papers. In fact, if all you know is what you read in the *Post* or the *Chronicle*, you're probably going to be terribly shocked at some point during the next few weeks or months. Because all of a sudden, high school students aren't taking it lying down anymore.

For some curious reason — maybe it's the fluoride in their drinking water — they're saying that they "ain't gonna work on Maggie's farm no more."

Out in the middle-class suburbs, when up-tight principals surveyed the new hairstyles cultivated during a summer-long boycott of barbershops, and ordered, "Cut if off!," a half dozen organizations of resistance sprang up. And when the administrators of black and Chicano (Mexican-American) high schools attempted to reassume control of their academic estates, still more groups bloomed in the urban wilderness.

Because of the difficulty of gathering information from several dozen different sources, any list of high schools here is bound to be incomplete. But we do know of specific activities at Bellaire, Westbury, Waltrip, Austin, Milby, Davis, Reagan, MacArthur, and several junior highs.

Is that moon dust out of NASA infecting the minds of high school students? Could be — though nervous administrators are currently blaming it on international communism.

But maybe the best way to talk about the situation is to examine the movements at two very different high schools, Bellaire and Jeff Davis.

Bellaire is the largest school in the Houston system, with an enrollment of approximately 3,600. Its students are drawn from middle- and upper-middle-class families — professionals, managers, business owners, skilled technicians. A sizeable percentage of the students are from Jewish families; the majority are solidly Protestant. Only a handful of Chicano

All of a sudden, high school students aren't taking it lying down anymore.

students attend Bellaire, and until a year or two ago there were no blacks at all. (It is no exaggeration to say that the only blacks with whom most Bellaire students are likely to have had any real contact are their families' maids.)

The school and the community exist in isolation from the rest of the city. Most of the kids there would be lost the minute they were set down on the north or east sides of town (as is no doubt true in reverse) — few probably are even aware of Houston's ghettos as more than an abstraction.

The social and academic pressures at Bellaire are extremely intense — and with significant results: Bellaire consistently turns out a disproportionately high number of National Merit finalists and semi-finalists; graduating seniors move in large numbers to the nation's elite universities.

But "excellence" is sometimes defined differently by students and administrators. To many students, efficiency and scholastic competence don't carry as much appeal as the less orderly values of personal freedom and equality.

For many of those students the point of rebellion — but by no means the sole or even primary complaint — is the school hair and dress codes.

A group of Bellaire students distributed a leaflet at sophomore orientation prior to the opening of school. The leaflet, entitled "Finally," cautioned incoming classmates that attendance at an excellent school carried the additional obligation for excellent obedience — like sporting the correct hair style and accepting the powerless student council.

"Yes, Bellaire is out in front of the other schools," said the leaflet, "but it's time somebody asks where that puts it. We believe a school's excellence depends on its students, all its students. Not their grades, but their involvement; not their trophies, but their concern for the community. What can we as students do about our problems?"

"Finally" was followed by a second leaflet on the first day of school, Tuesday September 2, which urged students to get together in their demands for school reform. As a first step, it was suggested that as many people as

Photo: Larry, August 28, 1969.

possible attend the next open Student Council meeting and present their positions.

Privately the leafletters expressed doubt that the Council could influence administration decisions on any topic more controversial than the flavor of punch to be served at the St. Valentine's Dance, but they stressed that "you have to show people what a farce that is, and, who knows, maybe something will happen."

On Wednesday an after-school watermelon rally was held on the football field to rap out the importance of attending the council meeting. About 200 kids showed up to eat the free watermelon and to make a physical show of support for the leafletters. Other students, for whom even eating watermelon seemed too great an act of defiance, passed by smiling and speaking cautious approval.

Next day the rally was the topic of everyone's conversation, and on that day also the administration chose to acknowledge that something was happening.

Principal Harlan Andrews warned over the PA system that further distribution of unauthorized literature would not be permitted and that disciplinary action would be taken if the leafletting continued.

It was also rumored (though not yet confirmed) that the Student Council meeting had been closed.

The "Watermelon Committee" countered the administration's offensive by forming a squad of 15 or 20 boys and girls who grabbed mops and buckets that afternoon and proceeded to clean the notoriously filthy school bathrooms.

An undertone to the week's activity was the insinuation that communist agitators were backing the students. Teachers questioned people about where the money was coming from (as if a few thousand mimeographed leaflets and 20 watermelons were beyond the financial capacities of kids who drive Thunderbirds to school.)

Andrews confided during interviews with the students that he "knew" SDS (or occasionally *Space City News*) was the real force behind these disruptions. As additional proof he cited a fire which broke out in one of the school's temporary buildings on the first day of school. Speculation even persisted that the FBI had been called in, and soon everyone was certain that his or her phone was tapped (and who's to say...?).

The Bellaire group isn't speculating on what their future moves may be. They only smile and say, "We'll see," and one doesn't dare try to second-guess the potential of kids who after 10 or 12 dreary years are finding school fun ... finally.

Students at Jeff Davis High School, on the north side of town, see their problems a little differently from their south side brothers and sisters.

About 70 percent of the students at Davis are Chicano. Most of the remainder are Anglo, with a smaller proportion of blacks and a few Orientals.

The community is predominantly blue collar working class. Thirty percent of the families earn less than $3,000 a year and one source estimates that 27 percent of the male labor force is unemployed. Nearly 30 percent of the housing in the area is substandard and an additional 42 percent just barely meets acceptable low-standard classifications.

Davis is about half the size of Bellaire, with an enrollment of 1,600 students. There is not a strong vocational training program (like the one that exists at Smiley High School, for example), but the students live with the expectation that they are the manual laborers and assembly line workers of their generation — just as every Bellaire student is aware that a college education is part of his birthright.

Though Davis is overwhelmingly a Chicano school, only two teachers and one administrator, the assistant principal, are Mexican-Americans. Students say that the two teachers are unsympathetic to their conditions; the assistant principal reportedly refers to himself as a Spanish-American, a term which Chicano students regard as abusive of their history.

Davis students, seeing the poverty which surrounds them and watching the school prepare them for their race's usual lot in America, tend to think of appeals for

The walkout was called for by the Chicano Student Confederation of the Southwest.

longer hair and shorter skirts as pretty frivolous. In fact, there is often a resentment towards and a lack of understanding about those other students whom they tend to think of as "hippies" — just as among Bellaire students there often exists strains of racism and feelings of superiority in relation to their lower-class counterparts.

The students at Davis, organized under the name of Advocating Rights for Mexican-American Students (ARMAS), are pushing for a massive walkout of all Chicano students on September 16, the anniversary of Mexico's independence from Spain.

The walkout was called for by the Chicano Student Confederation of the Southwest and is expected to involve thousands of students in several states.

The students who publish *Armas* told *Space City News* that the purpose of the walk-out will be to develop student support for the following demands:

1. Initiation of courses on Chicano history and culture, taught by Chicanos, into the regular school curriculum.

2. Stopping the practice of "pushouts" — that is when counselors whose main concern is to keep order in the school advise students who are disciplinary problems to drop out of school.

3. Hiring of more Chicano counselors, who understand the special problems of Chicanos in high schools, who understand why only 2 percent of the students at the University of Houston are Chicanos while they comprise over 14 percent of the city's population.

4. Elimination of the "pregnancy list" at Davis High School, a publicly posted list of all girls who have left school because of pregnancy — a vicious form of personal degradation.

5. Lengthening the 20-minute lunch break allowed at Marshall. All other schools get at least 30 minutes.

A spokesman for the group says that he hopes Chicano students in other Houston schools will walk out in solidarity with the Marshall and Jeff Davis students. "The walk-out will be a test of student support — with the support of all Chicano students we will go on to implement the demands."

As a voice for their organization, the students at Davis and at Marshall Junior High published *Armas*, a monthly newspaper. On the first day of school, the August issue of *Armas* was somehow slipped into copies of the approved Davis High School newspaper. As at Bellaire, the principal wasted no time in charging that it was definitely communists who had perpetrated this fiendish crime.

Students from other schools, who are faced with the same charge, might take a pointer from the response AR-MAS made to that: "Your remarks are welcomed. Could you define communism for us? Or are you so brain-washed by the system that you dig their poor excuses and labels?"

And for any students who might question the low-er-class schools' claim to a heavier oppression, *Armas* is an excellent eye-opener. An excerpt: The assistant prin-cipal "is so chickenshit in getting revenge with some of the boys he kicks out, espe-cially when he turns in their names to the draft board for likely draft material. Some of these boys have problems and need to stay home; some support families and have to work. You call this democracy?"

The students at Davis, like the students at Bellaire, and like the students at many other Houston high schools are fighting their oppression where it hits them hard-est.

The students at all schools perceive some of the injustices of their particular situations, but their isolation from stu-dents of other economic classes at other schools prevents their understanding of the larger system of injustice.

There is a growing awareness among the rebellious high school students that they need a cross-fertilization of ideas and observations. The students at Davis need to recognize the suffocating irrele-vance that accompanies Anglo affluence. And the students at Bellaire should know that a struggle for the freedom of person-al self-expression is primary only when there's a refrigerator full of food at home.

Students are not a class unto them-selves, but they are fellow prisoners in an institution which gives them more com-mon ground with one another than they will ever have again in their lives. And it is such shared experiences which must be used if people are to reach across class lines to discover a common humanness, if they are to recognize the one system which oppresses them all — though not all equally and not all in the same manner.

This hard and bitter coming of age strikes at rich kid and poor kid alike. Each is realizing that he can neither stay what he was nor become what he started out to be. That's something worth talking about. And acting upon!

Oh, and a word to you moms and dads out there in tee-vee land: if you don't know what's happening, don't worry about it. It's bound to be just that same, small mi-nority of troublemakers (less than one percent) who are messing things up for the rest of us all over the world.

Isn't it? -30-

Cover: Photo by Thorne Dreyer. August 31, 1971.

Principal Doesn't Cotton to Kitchen

Jim Shannon • January 16, 1971

The long legal hassle continues for Paul Kitchen, Waltrip High Skool student suspended last October 20 for selling copies of *Space City!* to his friends before skool. Although he was off skool grounds at the time (before skool), he was suspended for "distributing underground papers." Gordon Cotton, unpopular principal at Waltrip, was confronted by Kitchen, who knew he was getting fucked over by this brutal denial of free speech. "There's bigger issues involved here," Cotton agreed," so I'm suspending Paul for the rest of the semester."

When Kitchen came up by the skool one morning the next week (October 26) to sell the rest of his newspapers, Cotton came running out screaming threats of police intervention if Paul didn't split immediately. By this time, Paul wasn't about to let this principal interpret the constitution for him, so he stayed put. Eventually, the pigs arrived, and at Cotton's insistence, hauled young Kitchen off to the North Shepherd Police Substation. He was soon released, since all the charges were just the ravings of Cotton, with little or no relation to fact.

Even though he was out of jail, he still wasn't back in skool. On November 24, Kitchen's attorney, Robert Hall, obtained a temporary restraining order against the skool, ordering the immediate re-admittance of Paul Kitchen. Hassles continued after he returned to classes, and within a few weeks, they were back in court again, this time getting a further TRO against Cotton, ordering him to permit Paul to make up the work that he missed. He also had to appear before a special closed hearing of the so-called liberal skool board, the members of which seemed more concerned with enforcing their liberal-fascist rules, than with abiding by court rulings having direct hearings on these affairs.

The temporary restraining order was issued pending settlement of a lawsuit filed with U.S. District Judge Woodrow Seals, charging Cotton and friends with violation of the ruling made in 1969 in the famous *Pflashlyte* case at Sharpstown high skool (also known as the Sullivan decision). It is interesting to note that the judge and attorney in the first case are the same ones involved here, namely Judge Seals and attorney Hall. That doesn't seem to deter Cotton and the skool board lawyers, who just keep on harassing Paul and his friends, even going so far as to drag students who were going to be his witnesses down to the office and intimidating them by repeated questioning and harassment.

It looks like the case will be coming up on Seal's docket soon, so a decision should be coming before too long. Paul has grown impatient with all this bullshit, and told one *Space City!* reporter he will be glad when this thing is over so he can sell some more *Space City!*s. As for Gordon Cotton (remember him, he's the principal). Well, it looks like his troubles are just beginning. We heard of a group of Waltrip students working to put out their own underground newspaper, called *Sunshine*. It looks like some more stories will be coming in from Waltrip soon, so stay tuned.

Right On! -30-

Cover: Little Red Schoolhouse, August 31, 1970.

MAYO y
El Movimiento

Cover: Art by Kerry Fitzgerald, June 20, 1970.

MAYO y El Movimiento

Cam Duncan

In May 1972, a Chicano boycott against the Houston School District collapsed after nearly two years of successful protest. Later that year, the Houston branch of the Mexican American Youth Organization (MAYO), the Chicano corollary to the Black civil rights movement's Student Non-Violent Coordinating Committee (SNCC), broke into factions. It's no wonder that many observers considered the early 1970s the end of the Chicano freedom movement. But rather than ending in 1972, the movement in many cities evolved into a more mature civil rights struggle.

MAYO was formed in San Antonio in 1967 to fight for Chicana/o rights and played a key role in the Houston movement in the late 1960s and early 1970s. Houston MAYO — or, as its members called themselves, "*barrio MAYO*" — developed in one of the most diverse U.S. cities, with an entrenched history of anti-Black and anti-Latina/o racism.

MAYO leaders were open to coalition building and practical politics, supported the Welfare Rights Organization, and received the support of white liberals and Rice University students. *Space City!* reported on the Chicano freedom struggle and MAYO, its militant arm, with in-depth coverage of the 1970 Northside church occupation, a two-year-long school boycott, the Houston Chicano Moratorium against the Vietnam War, and the farmworkers boycott of Safeway.

By 1970, Houston's population was 1.2 million, of which 12 percent was Latina/o. A vibrant Chicano movement emerged in 1968-69 to fight poverty, school segregation, and especially police murder. *Space City!* documented the MAYO protests following police killings in 1970 of Dr. Fred Logan Jr. (an Anglo physician beloved by the Chicano community in Mathis) and Mario Benavides in Corpus Christi.

The first national Conferencia de Mujeres por la Raza in Houston. Photo by Dua Milhun, June 1, 1971.

Houston cops were notorious for their brutal treatment of youth of color. In April 1970, Bobby Joe Conner, a Black teenager, was stomped to death in the Houston Police Galena Park substation. Connor's death caused an angry response and began to stir activism in the Black and Latina/o communities. *Space City!* condemned the Houston police beating of Cesar Aguilar in an editorial Viewpoint, calling for "a workable program of community control of police."

The Feb 28, 1970 issue of *Space City!* covered the start of a long 20-day MAYO occupation of the Juan Marcos Presbyterian Church in Northside Houston. The article showed how white Presbyterians and MAYO negotiated the politics of a neighborhood transitioning from white to Black and brown families moving into the barrio, and how they debated the role the church should play in social change. The dramatic takeover, as a way to claim space and offer social services after failed negotiations to open a community center in the church, received almost daily media coverage and helped transform MAYO from a relatively unknown organization to an important player in Houston's civil rights politics.

As historian Felipe Hinojosa observed, in this first big action and with a supportive community, although they were finally forced by a court order to evacuate the church, MAYO was able to bring one of the city's wealthiest institutions — the Presbyterian Church — to its knees. MAYO relocated its Northside Community Center to a different site three months later and continued to provide free breakfasts, Chicano history classes, and office space for social service agencies.

The paper published MAYO's analysis of the new Center's campaign for clean streets and efficient garbage pickup. The group also had their eye on bigger struggles in the city. But MAYO's legacy will always be grounded in the Northside *barrio* and the small church where community care and activism were launched

Strikes, boycotts, and litigation sparked the efforts of the Chicano community to end discrimination and racism in the schools. These actions, covered in a series of *Space City!* articles in 1970-71, responded to the school district decision to circumvent a federal desegregation order by classifying Mexican American students as "white" and integrating them with Black students — leaving Anglos in segregated schools. MAYO took center stage in the fight to gain legal recognition for Chicana/os as a minority group.

The political mobilization over the next two years for access to quality public education highlighted the emergence of a new type of grassroots ethnic leadership committed to community control of schools and to inclusiveness of diverse ideological interests within communities of color. MAYO, for example, played a leading role along with more moderate groups in the three-week-long strike in September 1970, of Houston schools by 3,500 students.

During the struggle over the desegregation order, *Space City!* reported on September 19, 1970, on a contentious school board meeting when a so-called "mini-riot" broke out in the HISD boardroom. Several MAYO members were beaten by police and were arrested. The "MAYO 9" were charged with felonies, including conspiracy to riot. The charges were eventually dropped.

The strike to achieve an equitable desegregation plan evolved into a year-long boycott in January 1971, when the Mexican American Education Council (MAEC), a loose confederation of Latina/o groups, created *huelga* schools in three Northside churches where volunteer certified teachers — and MAYO leaders and VISTA lawyers — helped teach mainly Chicano students. The boycott would continue until the end of the 1972 school year, with mixed results.

Both politically pragmatic and confrontational, MAYO's legacy is also notable for forging an alliance with People's Party II (described in the section on Black Insurgency). The alliance they called the Rainbow Coalition included a group of Anglo activists, the John Brown Revolutionary League, and was formed out of a realization that members were already struggling for common goals but were doing it separately and within their ethnic groups. Each organization rallied its base to call for the release of imprisoned allies such as Lee Otis Johnson, Angela Davis, and Los Siete de la Raza.

The coalition fought for community control of schools, political representation, pushback against urban renewal, and especially an end to police violence. The life of the Rainbow Coalition was short because of the assassination of PPII Chairman Carl Hampton by Houston cops. It was Hampton's ability — along with leaders of MAYO and JBRL — to build coalitions across racial lines, connected to a sophisticated critique of capitalism, that was most inspiring to youths of color and most threatening to the city's power elite.

Space City! gave these communities and their coalition a voice and made their freedom struggle known to a broader audience of allies.

Santa Fe, New Mexico
August 2021

MAYO Liberates Church

Sherwood Bishop • February 28, 1970

Midnight at revolutionary headquarters. The third day of the people's occupation of the Christ Presbyterian Church is beginning. The building has been renamed The Northside People's Center.

The small band of MAYO (Mexican-American Youth Organization) activists inside is in a festive mood. The police and paddy wagons have not come back since the first morning of the takeover. The nervous talk about prisons and police dogs and strange noises outside in the dark has stopped. The people inside are now talking about what they will do with the building.

The Northside People's Center is in a Houston neighborhood that was completely Anglo 20 years ago. But, as in many other American cities, when the houses grew old and began to crumble, the white homeowners moved out, and brown and black tenants moved in. The houses and land in this part of town are still mostly owned by Anglos — the ones who work in the skyscrapers on the other side of Buffalo Bayou. They are waiting to sell the land in a few years when the prices will be a lot higher. Meanwhile, they are renting the houses for as much as they can get and paying fewer taxes every year as the property "depreciates."

As the whites moved out of the North Side, the Christ Presbyterian Church lost its congregation. The new members of the community were not welcome. The Rev. Jim McLeod, pastor of the church when it dissolved, said it dissolved because "the congregation had no real desire to work with the Mexican-American community surrounding the church."

Early last year, MAYO members attended church services and told the worshipers that the church must begin meeting the needs of the community or face the consequences. When the building was finally abandoned, MAYO immediately began negotiating to make the building available for community use. Many groups such as the Welfare Rights Organization (WRO), Political Association of Spanish Speaking Organizations (PASSO), League of United Latin American Citizens (LULAC), the United Organization Information Center (UOIC), and ELLA, a Chicano women's organization, needed places to meet and work. MAYO and the other organizations worked together to try to rent, lease, or otherwise obtain the building.

The Brazos Presbytery, owners of the building, were full of promises and kind words from the beginning. But the people got nothing but red tape from them. They also began hearing rumors that the building was for sale. The Presbytery denied the rumors, and two month's ago put up a sign in front of the church saying, "This property is not for sale. It will remain here to be used by the people who live in this community."

MAYO regarded the sign as a contract between the church and the community. They continued meeting with the Presbytery to try to make some concrete arrangements.

Finally, the Presbytery representative, Robert Frere, told MAYO representatives that the building would probably be given to the congregation of the Juan Marcos Presbyterian Church which is near White Oak Park on Johnson Street. Frere said that the Juan Marcos congregation would have to make the decisions about who would use the building. So, MAYO set up another meeting on February 1. This meeting was attended by Frere, the elders of the Juan Marcos church, MAYO, and several other Chicano organizations which needed workspace. At this meeting

Art: Gregorio Salazar, February 28, 1970.

MAYO presented a plan for the use of Christ Church for the implementation of social programs to improve the northside community. These programs would be initiated by MAYO and then their control would be turned over to the participants.

Things should have been fine there. The small Juan Marcos congregation is Chicano and should've understood the problems and needs of the neighborhood. They would only need to use the chapel of the church building — and they would only need that once a week. Unfortunately, if religion is the opiate of the masses, the Juan Marcos people are really drugged. The congregation is composed almost entirely of very old people who are strict believers that all private and social problems should be solved by prayer and pure living.

At one point during the meeting Frere remarked that the sign outside the church had been put up to stop bad publicity in the papers, and was not intended as a message to the people of the community. Frere had apparently talked to the Juan Marcos congregation about MAYO before the meeting. They suggested that MAYO come back in a month or so and talk some more.

A few days after the meeting MAYO delivered a letter to the Rev. Reuben Armandarez, pastor of Juan Marcos. The letter, signed by MAYO spokeswoman Yolanda Garza de Birdwell, demanded an answer to MAYO's proposal by Feb. 14. It read in part, "Nothing in this statement should be construed as leading to conditions that would interfere with the use of Christ Church for worship and spiritual growth. Should your answer to our proposal be negative; MAYO may not use Christ Church for the implementation of social programs to be controlled by the participants, MAYO will take appropriate action to insure the interests of the community are not neglected. Every day a decision is delayed, a Northside resident goes hungry or is pushed out of school. We can wait no longer. The time to act is now."

On February 14 MAYO met with Juan Marcos for one last futile attempt at "going through channels." The occasion began with people from MAYO and UOIC sitting with the church elders and some other male members of the congregation at one large table, with some women members of the church scurrying around pouring coffee and moving ash trays. When Yolanda, the head of the MAYO group, asked

Every day a decision is delayed, a Northside resident goes hungry.

the women to join the meeting, one of them answered, "Oh, we couldn't sit at the same table with the elders!"

The Rev. Armandarez then read a 30-minute speech answering the proposals which said in effect, "No!"

It became evident that Frere was playing Chicano against Chicano to get the pressure off his own back. The MAYOs' frustration after months of fruitless work came to a head. They left the church in anger. Later that night the members of Houston MAYO voted unanimously to take over the building and begin the people's programs immediately.

Twelve noon Tuesday at the Northside People's Center. The third day of the people's occupation is halfway completed. The building is buzzing with activity. Food is arriving for tomorrow's free breakfast. People are reading telegrams of support from organizations in other parts of the country. Welfare recipients are donating time, food, even money. Newspaper and TV reporters have gotten the latest news and have returned to their offices. Some of the more "respectable" members of the community are beginning to sneak in the door saying, "Nice place we've got here."

There is still a long, long way to go. All power to the people.

Pass the Bacon and Serve the People

The events occurring since the MAYO takeover of the Christ Presbyterian Church have been amazing and beautiful. In six short days an oppressed, poverty-stricken community has awakened to the first joys of controlling its own destiny. The church building has become the Northside People's Center.

In the first few hours after the takeover, MAYO members drove a loudspeaker-equipped car through the neighborhood inviting the people to come see the building. A few people cautiously accepted. They talked with the MAYOs as they toured the rooms. When people spoke of their troubled lives, the MAYO members answered, "Let's do something about it!"

Soon, the building was filled with the people of the community. Some brought food for the hungry MAYOs. The children played in the halls and classrooms. The adults talked about problems. The MAYOs repeated over and over, "This is your building. Use it any way you want."

At first, people voiced wishes. Later they began making plans. Plans quickly became reality. On the night of the takeover a Welfare Rights Organization (WRO) class was held.

The next day an art class was held. Some of the children had never held a paint brush. Soon the MAYO posters were joined by dozens of children's masterpieces.

On Tuesday, February 17, the third day, some of the Chicano children mentioned having problems with the black children at the center. One eight-year-old said, "I thought this was supposed to be a Chicano place." Some MAYO members had a quick meeting with the younger Chicanos. They explained that the center belongs to the entire community, not just the Chicanos. They also suggested that the children talk over the problems with their black friends.

The next day, several MAYOs and a group of black and brown children, aged 7-13, held a meeting. It was an amazing affair. The children talked about particular incidents. Both "sides" told similar stories, such as, "He pushed me off my bike and I hit him. Then they all jumped me." The atmosphere was friendly and some of the stories were funny. The kids talked about how everything "works both ways."

The MAYOs mentioned that the children's problem was racism and that some people, especially the rich whites that run the country, wanted them to be racist so that they couldn't work together for the things they wanted.

The kids agreed that racism is bad. After talking some more they agreed to stop ganging up on each other, to start playing together instead of apart, and to spend the next week being especially "nice to each other" so they could get to be better friends.

On Wednesday morning, another group of children met. They came in at 7:30 and ate the first free breakfast to be served at the center. The free breakfasts, served daily, are organized and prepared by the people of the community. Before this, many of the children did not eat until lunch; some of them did not have lunch either. Now they start each day with eggs, bacon, tortillas, toast, beans, and fruit juices.

The free breakfast program brings out an interesting point. The MAYOs consider themselves to be catalysts for action, not administrators. They are developing community leadership as rapidly as possible

so the community can run the programs. MAYO will then leave to develop community leadership in other neighborhoods.

By Thursday, the fifth day of the takeover, the people were making almost continuous use of their center. About 40 children ate breakfast, twice as many as Wednesday. After breakfast, the WRO met to plan a demonstration against welfare cuts. Some of the MAYOs baby-sat for the welfare mothers' children. Later there were the daily art classes and sports for the children. The same afternoon, the first of a series of Chicano history and culture classes took place.

They explained that the center belongs to the entire community.

The main event, however, was Thursday night. The Juan Marcos Church elders, seeing that the community was solidly allied with MAYO, had announced their desire to meet and discuss the use of the building with community representatives. The elders called for a meeting at 7:30 pm, Thursday, at Juan Marcos Church.

MAYO had always expressed willingness to meet with the Juan Marcos congregation, but MAYO insisted that the meeting be held at the people's center so the community could attend. At 7:30, the meeting room was filled with people. Some of the MAYO men were caring for the children in another room. No one from Juan Marcos showed up. At 8:00, two community representatives drove to Juan Marcos to see why they had not come. They returned later with nothing but bad news. The elders had refused to come. They wanted everyone out of the building. Otherwise, it appeared, the MAYO's would be thrown in jail.

The people were angry. One neighborhood woman stood and shouted, "They're not throwing us out of our building. If they arrest anybody, they'll have to take us all!" Everyone cheered. One by one, people spoke. Brown, black, and white people said over and over, "We'll all go together. Poverty has no color!" "They'll have to take us all!" "They'll have to take my kids, too!" "I'm so happy I'm crying!" "I'm tired of eating dirt. Just let 'em try and take us!" "Right on! Right on!"

The people waited together. The police never came.

Sunday evening, representatives from Juan Marcos came to the Northside People's Center and began talks with the people. A MAYO member stated, "We will never compromise on the issue of community control." The meeting progressed from there, and other talks are scheduled.

Meanwhile, the people continue to develop their center and themselves. Food, paint, books, and utilities all cost money. If you are willing to make a contribution, please bring it by the center at 3600 Fulton or mail it to:

Northside People's Fund
c /o Space City!
1217 Wichita
Houston, Texas 77004 -30-

Church occupation led by MAYO. Photo by Cam Duncan, February 28, 1970.

MAYO Leaves Church

On March 14, 1970, an article in *Space City!* reported:

> On March 5, Juan Marcos officials agreed to negotiate with the community over the proposed programs. The next day, at the Presbytery's request, a Harris County Court issued a temporary restraining order telling the occupants to leave the building. Although MAYO members and other community people had always been ready to go to jail, that now seemed unnecessary. MAYO's lawyers signed the restraining order, agreeing to leave the building until a public hearing could be held. Meanwhile, the community programs could still be held, and Juan Marcos could move into the new building. The community people and MAYO cleaned up the building and left.

....

Exactly what MAYO, or for that matter Juan Marcos church, will do now is uncertain. The free breakfasts will still be served in Moody Park across from the church. There will, of course, be more demonstrations like the one that 200 people held Sunday, March 8, in front of First Presbyterian Church on S. Main.

But the people will not be satisfied until they have won their struggle.

As the leader of Houston MAYO, Yolanda Birdwell, said to the cheering crowd Sunday, "We will be back again and again! Today we demonstrate, tomorrow we revolt! Tierra o muerte! Land or death!"

[On May 18, 1970, MAYO would open a new Northside People's Center at 1501 Brooks. See stories on these pages.] -30-

MAYO Opens Community Center

Gloria Rubac and Alex Rodriguez • June 6, 1970

The Northside Peoples' Center, 1501 Brooks, was started May 18 by the Mexican American Youth Organization. The building will serve as a community center for the people living on the northside of Houston.

MAYO leased the building after receiving confirmation of funds to operate the center for a year.

A community board is being established and this board will decide to what use the center will be put. MAYO is only making the center available and the community will have the power to decide what their needs are and what they will do to help themselves.

Some ideas were discussed at the first community board meeting on May 25. A breakfast program, Chicano and black cultural classes, Boy Scouts, cooking for learning and for fundraising, family counseling, and children's programs were brought up.

The center will also be used to organize the people to do something about garbage service, the lack of a public swimming pool, and other municipal services that are not up to par in the neighborhood.

MAYO stresses that the Northside People's Center must also be an information center. People will be able to come to the center and get information on welfare, jobs, education, scholarships, and anything that can help them.

Present at the first community meeting were representatives from the funding organization, a family counseling representative, a Boy Scout master, 15 people from the community, and the MAYOs.

Many things need to be done before the center can begin total operation. People who want to help can contribute the following: paint, sheetrock, nails, hammers, dishes, cooking utensils, chairs, desks, tables, light bulbs, lamps, extension cords, inside and outside trash cans, soap and cleaning detergents, mops, brooms, paint brushes, turpentine, and dish rags and towels. -30-

MAYO activists at Northside Community Center. Photo by Cam Duncan, June 20, 1970.

Northside People's Center: Off Garbage!

Walter Birdwell and Yolanda Garza Birdwell • June 20, 1970

The Northside People's Center, 1501 Brooks, was organized to serve the people. Those who are associated with the center, mostly members of the Mexican-American Youth Organization and participating residents of the Northside, serve the people by meeting community needs that existing institutions do no work with. Since the center is controlled by residents of the community, those who associate with it are free to work on any problem the community wants solved. The center is further prepared to use any means the community thinks necessary to solve the problems.

One of the earliest functions of the center was to serve as a meeting place for various community organizations. The Welfare Rights Organization has regularly scheduled meetings there. WRO is composed of welfare recipients who don't want to be treated like animals because they are casualties of a society that does not benefit all who compose it.

Members of the Equal Employment Opportunity Commission, about 30 including the officers, met with MAYO and neighborhood residents at the center on June 5. The people got to meet members of a government agency who are supposed to be concerned with the rights of the people. The EEOC's desire to visit the center shows more concern than that shown by other government commissions who have recently visited Houston.

On Sunday, June 7, the center was the scene of a *menudo* and tamale sale, organized by Mrs. Bertha Hernandez, to raise money for the center. This project was very successful; all the food was sold.

Many existing agencies are interested in obtaining space in the center where a branch office would be operated. Some of these agencies will be granted space in the near future as soon as the community determines which will be of service. Political education, leadership training, Chicano history and culture classes, and academic tutoring will be started shortly. The center also will function as an information agency.

During a community meeting on June 6, three ladies complained about the lousy trash pickup service given the residents of the Northside. Heavy trash is supposed to be picked up every other Thursday. The trash was piled up in front of people's houses four and five feet deep because it had not been picked up for over two months. Telephone calls to the City of Houston brought responses, the following of which is typical: "We're running a little behind, just leave it there and we'll get around to it." It was also determined that the city wanted the trash in plastic bags. Have you ever tried to put a ten-foot 2x4, an old sofa, washing machine, or refrigerator into a plastic bag? This attitude shows us how interested our "public servants" are in serving the people (you and me).

> **The trash was piled up in front of people's houses.**

On June 8, a four-year-old girl, Diana Gutierrez, was permanently crippled when she injured her foot on this trash that was supposed to have been picked up. Her parents had to pay a $415 doctor bill. Petitions were collected on June 8 and 9, demanding that the trash be removed, and warning of appropriate community action if it were not. Two hundred and seventy-six signatures were collected. At a scheduled City Council meeting on June 10, MAYO and other community residents presented these petitions and photographs of the trash piles. Four-year-old Diana was introduced to those attending.

Gregory Salazar told the Council that the people were sick and tired of the trash in their neighborhood, and that such trash was not found in River Oaks, Memorial, Westbury, or Sharpstown. The Council was told that if nothing was done, appropriate action would be taken. [Mayor] Louie Welch, displaying his usual brilliance, stated that the residents of River Oaks took care of the trash themselves. What this means is that most of the residents of River Oaks get rich off the labor of working people and it's no skin off their ass if services the people pay taxes for are provided or not. Welch's response had no relation to the problem of the trash pickup on the Northside.

Louie warned that our appropriate action had better be legal. Actions by the people from now on will often be legal and will always be effective. The city was given until noon on June 12 to begin pickup.

Louie did not wait to find out if the "appropriate action" would be legal or not. The trash pickup started on June 11 and is continuing. One of the first piles collected was in front of Diana Gutierrez's home. No other child will be crippled, but it is too late for Diana.

The solution to a problem of the people has been shown here. There are many problems to be solved, and all will be. Each new victory makes the next solution a little easier. Serve the people.

Any person or group interested in starting a community center to be controlled by the people in the neighborhood should contact MAYO, People's Party II, or the John Brown Revolutionary League for help in getting one started. Remember, centers controlled by the community can use any methods to solve any problems or meet any need.

*****

Quizá haya alguien que domine el idioma español y se interese en dar clases en español — Será bienvenido — Una de nuestras miras es el de conservar nuestro idioma — Ya que esto es de suma importancia para el movimiento Chicano — ; Ya que generalmente el enemigo no lo entiende y le molesta de sobremanera verse ignorante.

VIVA LA RAZA UNIDA

-30-

La Raza vs. School Board

Cam Duncan • September 19, 1970

We're boycotting because we can't just let ourselves be thrown around and called white, when we're not - we're BROWN! Many people say we're just fighting because we Chicanos don't want to get mixed with the Blacks, but it's not true. We've been living with them all our lives. Besides, these *huelga* schools are much better than public schools - you learn more here.

— 9th grader, Huelga Enrichment Center

I think we Chicanos are boycotting because we don't like the idea of the school board using us as whites. This school is really cool. I like the teachers and you do learn. I think we all should just build one of our own.

— 9th grader, Huelga Enrichment Center

From 22 I see my first 8 weren't.
Around the 9th, I was called "meskin."
By the 10th, I knew and believed I was.
I found out what it meant to know,
to believe...before my 13th.

Through brown eyes, seeing only
brown colors and feeling only brown
feelings ... I saw ... I felt ... I hated ...
I cried ... I tried ...
I didn't understand during these four.
    I rested by just giving up.

At 22, my problems are still the same but now I know I am your problem.

—from 22 MILES by Jose Angel Gutierrez

The biggest problem facing the Houston Independent School District in implementing its court-ordered desegregation plan is a city-wide boycott of public schools by an estimated 3,500 Mexican-American students.

The strike was called by the Mexican-American Education Council (MAEC) following a meeting with the school board on August 27 concerning HISD's proposed pairing plan. The plan has zoned neighborhoods so that Chicano students, considered "white" by the federal court, are integrated with black students, leaving anglo schools largely unaffected and still lily white.

Northside Community Center free breakfast program.
Photo by Sue Mithun, February 28, 1970.

The boycott has involved most parents in their first organized protest against political authority. In the first two weeks of the strike, both parents and students have been subjected to police harassment and intimidation by school officials.

Arrests

A Chicano was arrested in Denver Harbor for trying too hard to convince a mother not to register her child with HISD. A picketer, Joe Navarro, was arrested for "failure to move on" in front of Reagan Sr. High School on September 8. Another striker, Valentine Flores, was arrested after a scuffle with a policeman at Washington Jr. High on September 9. Mrs. Gutierrez was arrested while picketing Jackson High on September 10. And three MAYO members, including Andy Guerrero and Hector Almendarez, were arrested for unlawful use of a bullhorn while publicizing the boycott from their car.

The involvement of a large part of the Chicano community in the boycott is obvious — picket lines at most schools on the North Side are manned faithfully by strikers and parents. The school administration has used threats and physical intimidation to undermine support for the strike.

The school board "warned" boycotters that students under 17 must attend a state-accredited school to avoid fines. This warning was made shortly after HISD had agreed to a demand made by MAEC for amnesty for all student strikers. It is reported that some Mexican nationals have been admonished by school officials that they would be deported if they participated in the strike. Many schools have locked their doors during class hours so that students may not speak to picketers — an action reminiscent of the September 16 Chicano high school walkout last year in Houston, when school doors and gates were chained after school began each morning.

The Demands

The MAEC, a surprisingly unified coalition of Chicanos ranging from conservative groups such as LULAC to the more radical MAYO, had made 20 demands on the school board. The demands are listed on this page followed by the school board's response, as of this writing.

At the end of the second week of the boycott, MAEC had not won its main demand: that the school board enter the MAEC suit, the "Narciso Rodriguez intervention in the Dolores Ross case," filed in Judge Conally's court. The suit asks the court to recognize Chicanos as an identifiable minority and to issue a new desegregation plan for the district. (The Dolores Ross case is the original desegregation suit against HISD filed by the NAACP.)

Leonel Castillo, MAEC spokesman, feels that, although the main demand has not been met, HISD has made important concessions to La Raza. Demand 10 means that HISD has committed itself to hiring 1,000 Chicano teachers during this year. (There are now about 150 Chicano teachers in HISD.) Although they can't formally accept Demand 9 because a delay in pairing the schools would violate the court order, HISD has informally agreed to halt further pairing action, according to Castillo.

Boycott

"The present pairing plan has served to increase segregation in Houston schools — by isolating white children from black and brown schools under the guise of equidistant zoning," Castillo told me. He claimed that HISD is misleading the public when it says that it has no latitude in implementing the court order, since the court couldn't penalize the district for doing a better job of integrating than they were ordered to do.

Castillo feels that a strong bargaining point for the MAEC has been that the district loses $1.60 a day per child for each of the boycotters. He estimates the total cost of the strike to the district at between eight and 10 thousand dollars a day.

HISD's most recent ploy to get strikers back in school was Superintendent Garver's announcement last week that the administration does consider Mexican-Americans a separate minority. Many parents called the MAEC to ask whether this meant the boycott was over. However, the district made no mention of appealing or changing the present pairing plan. MAYO spokeswoman Yolanda Birdwell says that the announcement was made to deliberately confuse parents about the issues in the boycott.

Huelga Schools

The most important immediate consequence of the strike, of course, has been the *huelga* ("strike") schools set up by the MAEC for striking students. Nearly 20 elementary freedom schools are held in Chicano churches and community centers, staffed by volunteer teachers and funded by donations. At this time *huelga* schools offer few textbooks and school supplies, although this will certainly change if the schools become permanent.

Art: December 16, 1971.

I visited a *huelga* school at San Felipe Church off Wallisville Road in northeast Houston. The school had an enrollment of 200 first-through-eighth graders and was coordinated by a 19-year-old student. Classes seemed to deviate little from the standard "three R's," although some classes used copies of *Papel Chicano*, a Houston newspaper of Chicano culture, in their reading and writing lessons.

The students I talked to expressed little understanding of the demands the MAEC is fighting for and of the consequences of the present pairing plan. I asked one class of fifth graders to write a paragraph on why they are boycotting and how the *huelga* school is different from public school. Typical responses were: "We go to *huelga* school because we are protesting." — "We don't have any books and there's not as much homework." — "There are no colored people in the *huelga* school." — "We have better teachers and have lunch and air-conditioning."

That night I visited the senior high strike school, the Huelga Enrichment Center, at Holy Name School, 1913 Cochran. The school has about 500 students and 25 teachers. Classes are held from 6 to 10 p.m. daily, and most courses offered by HISD are taught here, as well as classes in social problems and Chicano history.

The school's principal, Eliseo Cisneros, who teaches at Washington Jr. High during the day, insists that the school is apolitical and exists merely to keep working students from falling behind in their public school classes. He declined to discuss the MAEC

HISD negotiations and demands at a recent assembly of the school.

Some of the teachers, all of whom are volunteers, and many of the older students feel that the *huelga* school cannot be apolitical and are trying to make their classes more relevant to the Chicano. In a course in business law taught by a Vista lawyer, students rapped about who the legal system serves and about Huey Newton and Reies Tijerina. A social problems class taught by a MAYO member discussed the farmworkers' strike in California. And there was talk of holding a students' meeting this week to discuss what students should be learning in the *huelga* schools.

The underlying racism in many students' decision to boycott, however, was obvious again at the Enrichment school. One ninth grader told me he was boycotting because "the niggers always get what they want — Chicanos never do!" A common feeling was that the students were afraid of going to schools that were predominantly black because "black kids are always bossing us around, picking fights."

What Does The Strike Mean?

Despite the fact that the MAEC has taken every opportunity to announce publicly that the reason for the boycott is not to prevent the transfer of Chicanos to black schools and vice versa, it appears that the *huelga* schools are not dealing effectively with the racism of many students and parents, nor educating the people on all of the issues in the strike. Like talking about why blacks are not boycotting, about what a really progressive education could be offered at *huelga* schools, about what community control of schools means and how it could be achieved.

MAEC spokesman Castillo admits that the *huelga* schools are not doing all they should be doing and that many are striking out of a racist feeling against blacks. He attributes many of the difficulties to the incredible administrative problems involved in setting up a volunteer school district for 3,500 students in one week. Castillo expects the boycott to continue for at least another week, probably longer. Court action is a long process, and the school board liberals seem afraid to take action on their own to change the pairing plan.

Although most progressive blacks have concentrated on raising the consciousness of black teachers instead of fighting for integration through the courts as an end in itself, Castillo says that "the MAEC is for integration on an honest basis." He sees the strike as the first step in involving parents directly in actions which will ultimately lead to community control of schools.

"We need at least three conditions for community control," explained Castillo. "We need a clearly defined and constant geographical student body area; a cohesive bond between teachers, principals, and community; and a community that will demand authority to hire and fire. We've got a long way to go, but maybe this is a beginning for *La Raza*." -30-

Cesar Aguilar Beaten by Police

Space City! Viewpoint:

Who Polices the Police?

Space City! Collective • April 13, 1971

On March 21, Cesar Aguilar was drinking a beer in El Social Ballroom, a Chicano nightspot, when two off-duty policemen employed by the club approached him and attempted to take him outside.

"He wasn't passed out. He wasn't drunk. He wasn't bothering anyone," said Dolores Martinez, a witness. "They just picked him up, twisted his arm, and marched him outside."

Aguilar protested that he wasn't doing anything. In return he received a fractured skull and a charge of assault on a police officer. In their official report, the police stated they were attempting to remove Aguilar, "who had passed out on the table." One of the officers, Charles G. Malone, said that Aguilar kicked and punched him several times, tore his shirt, and ripped his tie off.

Martinez said that about 1:30 a.m., a man named "Phil" came to the table which she and several other people were sharing with Aguilar. Phil was drunk and passed out at the table. The two policemen passed by the table, noticed Phil, but took no action.

Shortly afterwards, two other men also seated at the table helped Phil outside and into his car. The cops then returned to the table and attempted to oust Aguilar.

When asked if the police had perhaps mistaken him for Phil, Aguilar replied, "Yeah, maybe, maybe" — sounding unconvinced that there was any rationality in the cops' actions.

Aguilar's mother, Julia Aguilar, filed a formal complaint with the mayor's office the following Tuesday, charging that her son was pistol-whipped without provocation. As is the procedure with such complaints, it was forwarded to Police Chief Herman Short's office for investigation.

On Wednesday, March 31, William G. Aguirre, representing the American GI Forum (Aguilar is a Vietnam veteran), appeared before Houston City Council to press the complaint further.

By this time, however, Mayor Louie Welch had received the report from the Police Department in response to Julia Aguilar's complaint. Replying to Aguirre's testimony, the mayor cited witnesses who had given the police statements to the effect that Aguilar was resisting the officers and that "he got what was coming to him."

Acting on a separate complaint, the FBI reportedly made an investigation into the incident. But as of April 9, the U.S. Attorney's office had not received the FBI report. (The FBI is required to submit reports to the U.S. Attorney's office on all investigations it conducts.) When contacted by phone on April 8, the Bureau would not release information on the status of the investigation or even acknowledge that such an investigation was being conducted.

At this date it appears that the case of Cesar Aguilar will come to a not uncommon end: the victimization of the victim.

There is an ancient Roman saying, the sort of thing they used to inscribe on the portals of public baths and the like: *Quis custodiet ipsos custodes?* Who Guards the Guardians? Increasingly, Houstonians are asking that very question. Who polices the police?

The March 28 raid on Milby Park and the March 21 police beating of Cesar Aguilar (see story elsewhere in this issue) are two recent incidents which indicate that the Houston police do frequently act with excessive force and with discrimination against racial and cultural minorities.

But that's no news to the people most affected by such police actions. What is significant in the aftermath of the two incidents is that there was no readily available, unbiased agency for investigating charges made against the police. And there certainly is no way to assure that such acts will not continue to occur.

Complaints against the Houston Police Department are investigated by the police department, except 1) when circumstances exist to force the entry of the FBI or 2) when a case appears sufficiently interesting to attract the attention of a grand jury.

The FBI is normally reluctant to enter cases which might result in the embarrassment or indictment of police, or cases which they choose to define as strictly local in nature. This is true even when precedents exist for FBI intervention. The Pacifica bombings, and the difficulty the station had in obtaining FBI cooperation, illustrate the impracticality of this route for the normal citizen.

Of the three available means for handling complaints, the grand jury offers the most hope for a just resolution. But grand juries are notoriously law and order enforcers, not usually given to indicting police officers and public officials. (The Bobby Joe Conner case is remarkable for its singularity.) Grand juries are also untrained in investigative techniques, often naive about political and social conditions, and often

subject to manipulation by district attorneys. This latter is so often the case, in fact, that there is a special name for independent juries — "runaway grand juries."

The community control amendment can be the first step towards real democratic change.

Two alternatives which other cities have investigated are police review boards and community control of the police. Police review boards have been instituted in several major cities. Most suffer from the same handicaps as grand juries, in particular a too-exclusive selection process. But insofar as the boards offer an opportunity to publicly sound complaints and present evidence, they are an improvement over the secret proceedings of a grand jury.

In the recent Berkeley city elections, a proposition for community control of the police was defeated by a 2-1 margin. However, during the course of the campaign, radicals presented a comprehensive and workable program for establishing community control, in itself a significant step from rhetoric to reality.

Art: Adolfo Mexiac, May 18, 1971.

An introduction to the proposition stated that the community control amendment "can be the first step towards real democratic change in city structure. The Amendment is special because it proposes to give power to the people instead of simply making reforms in administrative structure. The essential difference between Community Control of Police and other proposals for reform is the element of grass-roots democracy. Rather than trusting the officials who caused the problems in the first place to now turn around and solve them, community control would place power in the hands of grassroots councils of ordinary people, involving them in the settling of their most fundamental problems."

In Houston, the guardians guard themselves. It doesn't work. It is foolish to expect it to work. -30-

Chicano Moratorium in Houston

By Pedro Vasquez • August 1, 1970

Sunday, July 26, Chicanos from the Houston barrios and from across the state took to the streets of Magnolia for the first time over the Vietnam issue. Approximately 1,200 Raza participated in the march and *junta* (rally) at Hidalgo Park.

Art: September 19, 1970.

The *junta* consisted of a cross section of the Chicano community. As the march proceeded down the avenues of the barrio, both young and old were attracted to the spectacle of La Raza Unida marching in respect for the Chicano brothers who have fallen in Vietnam and marching to demand that our brothers be brought home — immediately and not in pine boxes.

Marchers carried banners, 29 crosses representing the Houston Chicano dead, and a black casket that symbolized the total 8,000 Chicanos dead in Vietnam. The spirits of Quetzalcoatl (Aztec Sun God) and *chile picoso* (fiery hot pepper) stirred in our bronze people as they chanted, "Viva La Raza," "Raza Si — Guerra No!" and "Chicano Power."

Speakers included Bertha Hernandez (WRO), Yolanda Birdwell (MAYO), Alberto Pena (County Commissioner of Bexar County), Raul Gutierrez (Barrios Unidos), Olga Rodriguez (UH MAYO), and an Austin Chicano striker.

Near the end of the rally the *Teatro Chicano* of Austin performed and drew much approval from the crowd. The *Teatro* does skits which speak of the lives and conditions of our people. Often these are performed for people right in their homes or workplaces.

Thus, the first Chicano Moratorium ended, but *La Causa* continues.

Pedro Vasquez, *por mi raza*

-30-

Black
Liberation

Cover: Photo by Cam Duncan, August 1, 1970.

Police on Wheeler Street after TSU police riot in 1967. Photo by Richard Pipes, April 27, 1971.

Houston's Black Insurgents

Alice Embree

The Black insurgency in Houston was multi-faceted, and *Space City!* covered the local leaders, the student and community organizers, and the unrelenting fights against brutality by the Houston police. The June 19, 1969 issue of *Space City News* (later *Space City!*), demonstrates this range of reporting.

In that issue, the second one, the paper reported on the trial of Lee Otis Johnson, the Student Non-violent Coordinating Committee (SNCC) organizer charged with passing a joint to a police detective. In 20 minutes, the jury found him guilty; in another 10 he was sentenced to 30 years in prison. Subsequent issues carried interviews with Lee Otis and updates on the campaign to free him.

The same issue also carried a story on community organizing at the Shepherd Gardens housing project and the acquittal of Johnny Coward who lost an eye in an incident with Houston police and was then charged with aggravated assault on a police detective.

And the paper documented the physical violence and threats faced by Eugene Locke, a University of Houston student organizer of the Afro-Americans for Black Liberation (AABL).

Space City! also covered Black Theater and Welfare Rights Organization actions in Houston and strikes at Black radio stations and by restaurant workers at private venues that didn't allow Black members, and carried features on Black activists like Larry Jackson, a leader at Austin's Community United Front. Throughout the paper's run, there was continuing coverage of the repression of the Black Panther Party (BPP). Panther leaders were targeted by grand juries and some charged with conspiracy. The trials and court appeals of Angela Yvonne Davis, Huey P. Newton, Bobby Seale, and the Panther 21 were covered and featured on covers.

Space City! carried an interview with Carl Hampton, who had emerged as a major leader, on July 18,

1970. Only days after the interview ran, he was murdered by Houston police snipers. Fifty years later, Houston's *Forward Times*, a Black-owned weekly founded in 1960 that also printed *Space City!* — and survives to this day — described Carl Hampton's impact this way in an article by Jeffrey L. Boney dated July 29, 2020:

> On July 26, 1970, Carl Bernard Hampton, was assassinated at the ripe age of 21, after stepping up to the plate to improve the lives and conditions of Black people in Houston and across the entire United States.
>
> The targeted assassination of Hampton is still a difficult pill for so many Black Houstonians to swallow, as his life and legacy continue to be remembered and commemorated 50 years later.
>
> Hampton was a Black man who spoke with conviction and power and regularly rallied people around the issue of police brutality and murders that were prevalent amongst Black people at that time. He was a strong Houston revolutionary and committed organizer, who helped establish the People's Party II in 1969 — a group that was modeled after the Black Panther Party (BPP).
>
> Born December 17, 1948, Hampton grew up in the Greater Houston area and got engaged in the struggle and plight of Black people at an early age. Prior to returning to Houston to establish the People's Party II, Hampton did substantial work with the BPP out of Oakland, California.
>
> Because the BPP leadership decided not to open new chapters because they believed they were unable to manage growth, a disappointed Hampton decided to establish the People's Party II, out of respect for the BPP — an organization he recognized as the original People's Party.
>
> Because of his influence, Hampton was quickly able to galvanize Black people and was able to gain their sincere respect and commitment

On August 1, 1970, *Space City!*'s cover headline was: "The Houston Police Murdered Carl Hampton." The impact of his death on *Space City!*'s Collective was profound. A year later, the Collective reflected on his loss and his continuing impact. Carl Hampton's death demonstrates the disproportionate, and often deadly, violence faced by Black activists, particularly those who stood up and called out Houston police violence.

Space City! continued to report on repression at the Carl Hampton Clinic, ongoing police violence, and criminal charges against two people injured the night Carl Hampton was shot. Bartee Haile, a white member of the John Brown Revolutionary League, had been wounded and then charged with assault with intent to murder a police officer. Haile's case went to trial in 1971 and resulted in a hung jury. Black activist Johnny Coward, also wounded that night, faced similar charges. He was convicted and served time.

Chairman Carl Hampton was shot by Houston police on July 26, 1970, and died early in the morning on the 27th. The murder occurred only seven months after Black Panther Party Chairman Fred Hampton (no relation to Carl) was murdered in his Chicago bed by Chicago police and the FBI.

Cam Duncan draws attention to a striking parallel between Carl and Fred:

> One of Carl's most notable contributions was to lead in the formation of Houston's Rainbow Coalition, which although it had a short lifespan was a significant expression of multiethnic political unity in a city dominated by a brutal, racist police and political establishment. Carl mentions the Rainbow Coalition in the interview included in this section. Fred Hampton had also founded a Rainbow Coalition in Chicago a few months before Peoples Party II was launched.

The story of Fred Hampton was made into a movie, *Judas and the Black Messiah*, premiering in 2021. The story of Peoples Party II and the murder of Chairman Carl Hampton is not as well known. That is one of the reasons this book is so important.

Austin
July 2021

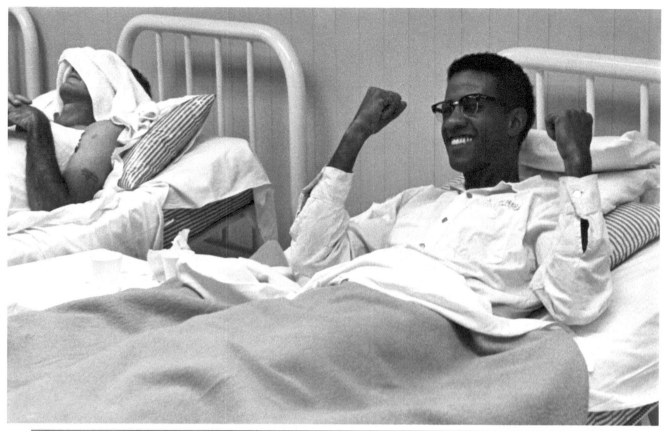

Lee Otis Johnson celebrates his 31st birthday in Ramsey Prison Unit Hospital. Photo by Cam Duncan, July 18, 1970.

Lee Otis Johnson:
Support Your Brothers and Sisters

Thorne Dreyer • June 19, 1969

Lee Otis Johnson, leader of Houston SNCC (Student Nonviolent Coordinating Committee) before he was put away, and University of Texas prof Larry Caroline, were perhaps the movement's most eloquent spokesmen in Texas.

Caroline called for a revolution and got his job pulled out from under him. Johnson led his people in the struggle at Texas Southern, but being neither white nor a respected member of an academic community, he lost more than a gig. He got 30 years for supposedly passing a marijuana joint to a black undercover cop.

Caroline is still calling for a revolution up at UT, but Lee Otis can hardly get a doctor into his cell.

The case of Lee Otis Johnson, and those of a number of other Houston activists, black and white, demand more notice than they have received — especially on the part of Houston's growing movement community. One of the state's most obvious tools

of counterinsurgency is to snatch off leaders, taking away articulate spokesmen and, more important, intimidating everyone else.

And as long as our reaction is to stay in the house and lower the shades, they'll succeed chuckling at our stupidity. They'll pick us off one by one as we quietly do our thing.

It's very important that we support our brothers and sisters who have been earmarked by the law. At the very least, we should remain continually informed about the status of trials and appeals: appearing in court to show our solidarity, coughing up bread if we have it, making it a little harder for the state to do its thing.

Lee Otis Johnson would never have received 30 years, a sentence which even the Houston grand jury says is outrageous, if he were not also a prominent black militant... Dispossession is a credible charge against most any young person these days. And what better way is there for the police to get troublesome radicals out of circulation? — Kaye Northcott, in the *Texas Observer*.

And they'd tried lots of other ways. The word had been out to "Get Lee Otis."

In the spring of 1967, as a result of SNCC activities on the TSU campus, Lee Otis was placed under a $25,000 peace bond. After pressure was applied, the bond was lowered to $1,000. He was forbidden to make public speeches, or even to gather with more than three people.

Police ransacked, at gun point, a car in which Lee Otis and his attorney were riding. The attorney complained to the City Council and was told by Councilman Bill Elliot that if he associated with Johnson, he should expect that kind of treatment.

In May of 1967, Houston police fired hundreds of rounds of ammunition into dormitories at TSU. One cop was killed, probably by a ricocheting bullet. But this was one rap they couldn't pin on Lee Otis. They had thrown him in jail earlier in the week for his role in demonstrations at a local high school.

Lee Otis was relentlessly harassed and shot at by cops and the Klan (often one and the same).

In following months he was indicted five times on trumped-up charges. All indictments were dismissed for lack of evidence.

On April 17, 1968, a secret indictment was filed, charging Johnson with passing a joint to a cop (sale, by Texas law) six weeks previous. They got the "goods" on him, then waited around for a month and a half until they decided it was time to put him out of action for good. His trial was held August 26, 1968. The jury deliberated 20 minutes: guilty; ten more minutes: 30 years.

The trial was a classic railroad. Despite a deluge of negative publicity about Lee Otis in the local media, a change of venue was denied. The state's only witness was the cop to whom the joint was supposedly passed. The defense attempted to subpoena Mayor Welch and Police Chief Short to prove there was a conspiracy to get Johnson, but they were "out of town" and the judge refused to grant a postponement.

The case is now being appealed, but it will be at least two years before Lee Otis has much chance of being freed. -30-

OCTOBER 8 MUSIC HALL

8:00
TICKETS - ALL DISC RECORDS - MARC'S RECORDS - THE PAISLEY CO.
$3 ADVANCE
$3.50 AT DOOR

Ad: October 7, 1971.

required reading for radicals

Ad: October 25, 1969.

Carl Hampton Raps About Peoples Party II

Judy Fitzgerald and Sue Mithun • July 18, 1970

[People's Party II is a revolutionary black organization, active in Houston for the last six months, with a platform similar to that of the Black Panthers. They have recently opened a community information center at 2828 Dowling in Third Ward. The following interview with Chairman Carl Hampton was done by Space City! staffers Judy Fitzgerald and Sue Mithun.]

How long has the center been open, and what kind of response have you gotten from the immediate community?

Well, the center has been open actually for about two weeks. The main things that have been going on in here really is cleaning the place up, and trying to get equipment that we need in order to start information going out to the community. Like there will be day-to-day leafletting in the community coming out of the center. We'll have political education classes. We'll have a liberation school for the younger blacks.

As far as response from people in the community, at this point it's been beautiful. We've had several people come in and express concern. People feel that, you know, this type of thing should have been started long ago. People seem very responsive to the programs, especially the youths, like the youths that were in here just now. This is an everyday thing and they're in and out of here all day and ask a lot of questions and find out a lot of things. A lot of the younger blacks are very familiar with the Panther Party, familiar with Huey, Bobby, Eldridge, you know, and they express grave concern about these brothers. I couldn't ask for any more response than we've had. I feel that the longer we're here, the more support we'll build from the people in the community.

What kinds of things are you planning on doing with the center?

Well, first of all, in the past week, we've had like a free clothing drive. We got some clothes donated from concerned people in this area, from a church. We've had parents come in and get things that they need. We

Brothers will patrol the police while they are in our community.

had things like waffle irons, coffee pots, things like this.

And we plan in the near future, before school starts, to have like new clothes, for a back-to-school sort of thing, so the kids will have some clothes to wear to school. And this is a thing we will have initiated before the last part of August.

The first program that we plan to work on out of the center will be community police control. We already have petitions with something like 2,500 signatures. After we acquire enough signatures, say about 10,000 signatures, we will then come to some kind of agreement, work out some kind of thing with the mayor or city council to see if police harassment that goes on in our community can be stopped. If it can't be stopped, then we will initiate the police patrol program with brothers from the organization and other concerned brothers from the community will patrol the police while they are in our community, both day and night.

We're also still working with this thing concerning Bobby Joe Conner. We're watching this very closely. Brothers from the community where this brother lived came by, and, matter of fact, since this brother was stomped to death we've had several brothers from Fidelity and Clinton Park communities to come by and even join the organization. So now we are planning to organize some sort of action to make sure that the officers that were involved in this incident are properly punished, not only the two Houston policemen but also the Galena Park policemen that were reinstated.

Can you tell me more about the police patrol? Like, if nothing results from the mayor or the police department, what specifically the patrol will do?

Well, actually we don't expect for the city council or mayor to all of a sudden change their nature. Because people have been expressing their concern with police brutality and this kind of thing but it's continued to go on.

The petitions that we have, we call it exhausting all legal means, by showing the people that the only recourse that we have to end this type of thing is self-defense and community control. So, the police patrol itself will consist of brothers riding in cars, brothers patrolling police in certain base areas in different communities. This will be a thing like where people will simply ride around if someone is arrested, if someone is stopped by the police, the brothers will stop and check it out, and stay our legal distance away from the police, which is 10 feet, and we will not interfere with the legal duties of any police officer. But if the police act in a criminal-like manner, then we will treat them like criminals. But I wouldn't want to go into any exact tactics about the program, because I think this will be dealing too much with our security.

But we are sure this police patrol program will be put into practice, because we feel — we know — that this is the only way that those police actions can be stopped.

Do you have any plans for like a free breakfast program?

Yes, we're trying to decide right now whether we're going to start a breakfast program in here, or in another community where there is greater need. It is needed here, but we feel that one of the other communities, such as Fourth Ward or Fifth Ward, where, you know, people are really suffering from hunger. But it is definite that we will have not just one breakfast program but several of them started by the beginning of the next school term.

What about any programs or actions around local schools, the quality of education and stuff?

First of all, as far as the educational system that exists now that's controlled by the establishment, we feel that it has to be completely revolutionized — changed from the bottom to the top — before it can be effective at all. Books will have to be rewritten, the teachers will have to be changed and everything. Because the teachers have been miseducated and they miseducate others.

As far as the crossover, forced integration and this type of thing, we're completely opposed to it. We're not opposed to blacks and whites attending the same school, but we are opposed to forcing people to go to schools they don't want to go to.

But we feel that the first thing as far as black people are concerned — in the educational system black

people are not taught their identities, are not taught the knowledge of themselves, their position in society. And without this knowledge, without a person understanding who they are and where they are, well, they can't move successfully. And this thing the educational system of the United States hasn't dealt with — teaching people knowledge of themselves. We feel that as far as some of the things that could be changed in the educational system right now would be black history, black studies programs.

Forced integration, we're completely opposed to.

We feel that the main question in the world today, the main question that concerns our people is of a political nature and the schools don't deal with this type of thing. And if they do, well it's so whitewashed that people still don't get a correct knowledge of what's going on. But really, I can't deal too much with the educational system that exists because it was founded to serve one purpose, which is to serve this system. And schools are set up in communities where a certain amount of factory workers come out, a certain amount of people with technical skills come out. And this is a systematic thing — schools serve the system and not the people. And so that's why we say that the schools have to be completely revolutionized so they serve the people and not the system.

This deals with point number five of our platform and program. For instance, the liberation schools plan to bring out and expose the phony education that our children are exposed to.

What are your general ideas about the center?

Due to the way things are happening now in the United States we feel that, well, we're actually way behind here in Houston as far as the movement is concerned. We feel that this center can very well serve the community. This is the whole purpose in an information center — to serve the community. Whatever the people's needs are in the community, well this is what we're going to work towards. And we know that this will stay right in the contents of our platform and program. Because the platform and program deals with the basic needs of our people. This is why we're so concerned about the breakfast program. Even some of the younger kids who have been coming around the center express great desire for the breakfast program to be started. A lot of kids spoke of only eating corn flakes every morning and this type of thing. And they don't have the protein and things in the morning.

Also, the information center will be used as a riot control type of thing. We feel that this will be a great service to the community. Because at this point in Houston it wouldn't take but a couple of hours to go out in the community and talk to black folks and see the attitudes they have as far as the conditions they live in and as far as the things that are happening to black people on a day–to–day basis. Our field marshall James Aaron said that he didn't see how Houston could get around a riot this summer unless something has changed. We don't want to see any type of riot or anything like this happen.

So, this is a function that the information center will serve. In keeping our people toned down and, you know, moving spontaneously and getting a lot of people hurt and getting small stores and things in our community destroyed where we have to go to other communities to get food and this type of thing.

It will be like a good term that someone used in the *Space City!* paper — like a clearinghouse — an information clearinghouse. All of the distortions that the people hear over the media. The power structure has the ability to like program people, with the papers and television and so on. And if they want to start a riot or have a riot started — well they have the equipment to do this. By simply flashing certain things over the TV and showing certain things and simply putting police out in the community. Do things like they're doing now and these are the things that start a riot.

And the riot is exactly what we're going to try to stop. Because we feel that the riot is more to the advantage of the power structure than it is to the people. Because they are prepared and organized to deal with this type of thing.

Have you been harassed at all since you've started?

No. We've been under very close surveillance by the Houston Police Department and the Red Squad, who seem to have a regular route by here every day. But as far as them stopping to check it out, they haven't. I believe they've sent a couple of people over to, you know, take a look inside and see what was going on, but they haven't started any harassment yet.

We feel that — in checking out the history of brothers moving to change conditions in our community — that we know that eventually they feel that we are becoming more and more of a threat to the status quo,

well, then they will start their campaign of eliminating our program. But we're not concerned about this and we don't even give it a second thought about what they can do. We take the position that Bobby takes — if we worry about what's going to happen to us and what they're going to do then we won't be able to accomplish anything. So, we only worry about what *we're* going to do and fuck what *they're* going to do.

You were asking about the Switchboard earlier. What do you think about that idea in terms of getting information out, and to draw people together, and to get people to start working together?

I think it's a beautiful thing. It can be very effective. We'd like to have real close communication between the Switchboard and the information center. And any information that we get concerning events in the black community affects the white community and really anybody in all communities.

Are there specific things you need to get the center going?

We need as much help as we can get to get the center started. We need tables for children to sit at, we need chairs, folding chairs, we need a couple of large desks, we need filing cabinets, we need a mimeograph machine, we need all types of office equipment for the center. This is the main problem we have at this point, getting the equipment that we need to make the center functional. And we need all types of donations.

Donations can be sent to 1310 Isabella, No. 1, in the name of Peoples Party II. Or if you have equipment you want to give us, call Switchboard (522-9769). -30-

> # We've been under very close surveillance by the Police Department and the Red Squad.

Carl Hampton Shot on Dowling Street

Victoria Smith • August 1, 1970

It's not because I'm in People's Party II that I'm oppressed, it's because I'm black and in the United States.

Carl Hampton made that statement in a speech shortly before his death early Monday morning, July 27.

The 21-year-old chairman of People's Party II, a revolutionary black organization, was killed, not because he was in People's Party II, but because he was black and in the United States, because he was a revolutionary whose interests resided in his people, the oppressed people of the world.

Carl was shot down by police snipers in an ambush Sunday night, July 26, near the People's Party II headquarters at Dowling and Tuam streets. He died in Ben Taub General Hospital about four hours later.

Several others were wounded in the battle, including other members of People's Party and a man from the John Brown Revolutionary League (JBRL), a white organization. (People's Party II, JBRL, and the Mexican-American Youth Organization formed a Rainbow Coalition several months ago.)

Carl was murdered; shot down in cold blood.

The leadership he exerted, the ideas he represented, and the practice he engaged in so threatened the power structure of the city that Carl could not be permitted to live. The police wasted no time. The People's Party Center had been functioning for less than a month when Carl was killed.

We want to make this clear from the start, because there is no doubt in our minds Carl's death resulted from premeditated murder. Our facts, our knowledge of Carl and People's Party II, our understanding of the nature of repression in Amerika lead us to believe that the "first shot" that police claim started the gun battle that occurred Sunday night did not come from a People's Party or JBRL gun.

The events surrounding Carl remain somewhat unclear at this point. But we think that the Houston police department, as represented in the local commercial media, has lied to Houstonians about the incident. Maybe we can clear things up a little.

Carl was shot down by police snipers in an ambush Sunday night.

Around 6 p.m., Sunday, two brothers were arrested on weapons charges inside a church just around the corner from the Center.

Police had harassed people at the Center continually for more than a week before Carl's death, beginning with an incident Friday, July 17, in which pigs and People's Party members and supporters held guns on each other for about 30 minutes.

We talked with Carl Sunday afternoon, only several hours before his death, and he told us that two Party members had been busted that week, that police had warrants out for the arrest of him and two others, that police surveillance helicopters had hovered continually over the headquarters, that police were spreading false rumors in the Third Ward community about People's Party.

Later that evening People's Party held an impromptu rally outside the Center to gather support for the Party and for the brothers in jail.

A man who has related to People's Party but is not a member gave Space City! the best account we have of the events surrounding Carl's death.

As Carl was addressing the group of some 150 people, Ovide Duncantell, of the Central Committee for the Protection of Poor People, another militant black group, approached Carl and told him that an unmarked police car was parked in a lot at St. John the Baptist Church, a building some 300 yards north of the Center.

Carl relayed the message to the crowd. Two black men, armed with shotguns, ran toward the vicinity of the church.

Some minutes later, Duncantell reported that there were two pigs on the roof of St. John's Church. Duncantell's next message was that someone had shot at the pigs.

Our witness said he heard a shot, but he recognized it as the unmistakable sound of a .22-caliber weapon, not a shotgun. The obvious conclusion is that the brothers who had left for the church could not have fired the shot, since they were armed only with shotguns. (People's Party policy, like that of the

Black Panther Party, forbids firing on police unless in self-defense.)

Carl and another man ran down the street to check out the scene. Apparently, they moved into the street or into some position in which they were exposed. So they evidently crossed the street to hide in an alley near a business building.

Gunshots rang out. Most of the crowd in front of the People's Party Center dispersed and the rest, including members of JBRL and People's Party, moved inside the Center to get their weapons.

The first shots were apparently the ones that felled Carl.

Art: December 2, 1971.

Our witness moved across the street where he stationed himself with Carl's wife, Maggie. He said he saw JBRL member Bartee Haile dash out of the center.

Bartee later told KPFT-FM, Pacifica radio, that three or four men were running toward the church. Bartee, who was trying to get to Carl, hid behind a parked car. Others with guns moved up behind him. There was an exchange of gunfire and Bartee was shot in the arm.

"The same sniper that got Carl hit me," he said.

It is also possible, however, that Carl, because of his apparent location, was hit from a window in the church.

Bartee, bleeding profusely, ran back to the Center, all the way dodging bullets that were bouncing on the sidewalks.

As to who started the shooting, Bartee said, "I don't for any moment believe that People's Party II members and supporters went down there and opened up on snipers who had such a superior firing angle on them."

The logic of this situation is virtually inescapable, although the Houston Police Department and the commercial media managed to ignore it.

People's Party II and JBRL members are not trigger-happy romantics looking to die glorious deaths in the streets by provoking armed confrontation with the pigs. They have guns, they know how to use them and they have used them only for self-defense.

The police claim that some "black militant" opened fire on them. J.O. Norris, of the Criminal Intelligence Division (Red Squad), who says he was on top of the church, was quoted in the *Houston Chronicle* as saying that one man shot at him and his buddy. "We didn't return the fire then. Two Negro males ran across the street and started shooting at us again." At this point Norris claims he and the other policeman shot the men. This report makes no sense.

St. John's Church is the tallest building in the vicinity. There is no way that a person on the street 30 feet below could "snipe" at police virtually hidden on a rooftop, with a strategically useful parapet.

The shooting started sometime after 10 p.m. and lasted less than an hour.

Artice "C-Boy" Vaughn, writing in the *Forward Times*, claims a call went out over the police radio saying, "We got eight under fire. Put some more light on that building because we are going to do some killing.

"Hey, we got two of them. Wait a minute, I think that we got the leader. Yes we got the leader."

An unidentified person in a Volkswagen drove through a hail of bullets to rescue Carl. According to one report, the car was fired on in earnest and it wheeled away, leaving one man, who had been trying to get the wounded Hampton into the car, holding Carl over his shoulder.

The man escaped with Carl. Carl somehow arrived at Ben Taub Hospital by car, shortly after 11 p.m., in very critical condition.

One thing should be abundantly clear. The pigs were out to get Carl and they apparently didn't care whether or not they killed any of the others, except possibly Bartee, who is also a marked man in Houston. (Bartee says he was fortunate not to have been shot in the heart. Gunshot hit his left arm, and he thinks the pigs were aiming for his heart.)

Carl didn't have a chance. *Space City!* learned that he was shot several times in the chest and once in the liver, which at a distance of some 200 feet required excellent marksmanship and intent to kill. The pigs who claim to have shot Carl have even admitted in the media that they shot to kill.

Several others were wounded, but none critically. One of the wounded, however, Johnny Coward, was shot in the ankle and has lost his foot. Coward had lost an eye in a battle with police two years ago. At least eight men were shot, possibly more.

Most of the people remaining in the Center escaped out the back. The injured were on their way to hospitals.

******

Police began to cordon off the area, and initiated a systematic occupation of the community which eventually extended over a 20-square-block area. Two whirlypigs with spotlights hovered over the area.

The men that killed Carl were part of a special sniper unit. The sniper squad technique had not been used for three years, since the police riot May 6 and 7, 1967, at Texas Southern University. (At that time, police swept through the campus, shooting up a men's dormitory. The riot resulted in one death, that of a pig, who died out of the direct line of fire from student-held territory. He

was probably killed by a ricochet pig bullet. More than 300 rounds of ammunition were fired in that incident.)

After the shooting was over and the pigs had secured the area for themselves, they entered the People's Party headquarters and gleefully trashed the place. They entertained themselves by drawing moustaches on posters of Chairman Mao and writing graffiti on the wall, like "Fuck Huey" and "Wallace in '72."

They confiscated a few arms and some literature.

> **The men that killed Carl were part of a special sniper unit.**

After the police had secured the area north of Elgin on Dowling, a squad of at least 120, possibly more, formed at the corner of Dowling and Elgin.

A crowd of some 300 people began to gather in the area, one of whom was Don Gardner, former news editor and associate manager of KPFT-FM. Gardner was doing volunteer work for the station at the time.

"People weren't harassing the cops," Gardner told us. He likened it to a crowd of people watching a wreck or a fire. The crowd was all black, except for two other KPFT reporters.

Suddenly, without any warning, or any apparent reason, a line of pigs started to sweep south down Dowling, bellowing "Move on, move on!" and beating and arresting everyone they could get their hands on.

Police arrested more than 50 people, all black except for Gardner, who said he was grabbed by the hair, jabbed in the head with a rifle butt, handcuffed, and thrown into a waiting paddy wagon.

All those arrested in this sweep were charged with loitering and failure to move on. Bond is set at $200 apiece. Many still remain in jail.

******

Some 30 People's Party members and supporters, including a number of *Space City!* people, arrived at Ben Taub Hospital to ensure that Carl and the others received adequate treatment. A large contingent of police was also there to ensure that there would be no trouble when Carl died.

Besides Carl, Bartee Haile, Johnny Coward, Fred Sparkman, and Gregory Clarke had been admitted to Ben Taub. Since then we have learned that other injured were admitted to other hospitals.

Bartee was charged Tuesday, July 28, with assault and attempted murder, while he was still recuperating from the gunshot wound.

The scene at Ben Taub was tense. We were worried, angry and confused. Some of us spent hours trying to get a good, cool doctor to come to the hospital, declare he was Carl's doctor, and be admitted to surgery where he could keep an eye on the operation.

We put a call in to Switchboard at the *Space City!* office and learned that pig cars had virtually surrounded the place. Anyone coming from or going to the office was stopped and questioned.

The regular pigs at the hospital, we understand, had been talking and joking for two or three days prior to the shooting about how they were looking forward to busting up Dowling street.

Carl's surgery was guarded by heavily armed police who, we have been told, exchanged hearty pats on the back after it was all over.

Carl died shortly before 3 a.m. -30-

Photo: December 23, 1970.

Houston Police Harass Hampton Free Clinic

Victoria Smith • December 23, 1970

The Carl B. Hampton Free Clinic recently opened for inoculations at 2828 Dowling St. And it looks as though the pigs are attempting to keep the community away, and, in fact, to prevent the clinic from opening at all.

Police continually harassed people working on the clinic throughout all the months of building. Folks coming or going to clinic meetings were frequently stopped, searched, questioned and ticketed.

But the police seem to be taking the whole thing a little more seriously now that it looks like the clinic

is definitely going to open. After all, the clinic is designed to help meet some of the health care needs of poor people of all races, and it is free.

Only hours after the rally and celebration at the clinic on Thursday, Dec. 17, Tanganyika Hill and Sophie Powell, both members of People's Party II, were busted on McIlhenny St., just off Dowling, on charges of prostitution. They were on their way home from dinner around 9 p.m. when the pigs pulled up and asked Tanganyika how many times she'd been to jail. She answered, "Three." "Well, we're going to make it a fourth time," the arresting officer said.

The sisters were taken down to city jail and held over night while the pigs ran a "check" on them.

Prostitution? Well, one cop at the station testified to the transparency of that charge. "She's no prostitute," he said when he saw Tanganyika (who incidentally is Minister of Finance of PPM), "She's a member of the People Party Number Two."

(A happier note. When friends went down to bail out Tanganyika, there was a mix-up in names and to their surprise, they ended up bailing out a white woman charged with prostitution, instead of Tanganyika. The woman was very disappointed when she found that there had been a mistake and she would have to return to jail. So the folks paid her bail anyway, took her home with them and had a good rap. Power to the prisoners!)

Anyway, the attorney for Tanganyika and Sophie was finally able to bail them out at noon the day after the bust.

Tanganyika, who said that the pigs threatened her life, claims that she will fight the charge in court in hopes of alleviating some of the harassment.

Friday night, December 18, was very tense along Dowling St. Some white sisters who had come to pick Tanganyika up for a meeting were questioned and intimidated by several patrolmen outside the People's Party II headquarters.

Four patrolmen followed close on the heels of the sisters as they walked to the door of the headquarters. One of the sisters, oblivious of their presence, leaned her head in the door to warn the residents about the heat. To her uncomfortable surprise, the next thing she heard was a pig saying, "Hey, who do you think you are — Paul Revere?"

Ha, ha, ha.

The pigs then attempted to gain entry into the headquarters to search for narcotics, but Tanganyika informed them that since they had no search warrant they had no business on the property,

Policemen prowled the area, stopping everyone in cars.

and goodnight. They didn't press the issue, but left muttering that they'd be back with a warrant.

After that, Dowling St. around the clinic and the People's Party headquarters became a veritable pig-pen. As many as 25 carloads of policemen prowled the area, stopping anyone and everyone in cars, searching them, questioning them. This activity continued well into the night. The following night a shot was fired into the headquarters, but there were no further incidents.

It may well be that the pigs are not up for a major confrontation thing with People's Party and supporters at this time, although we should be careful about trying to second guess them. But their activities Friday night indicate that they're trying to frighten the community away from the clinic, as well as people who come into the area to support the project. -30-

Mickey Leland at MAYO rally, Photo by Cam Duncan. April 11, 1970.

Carl Hampton: One Year Later

Space City! Collective • July 27, 1971

July 26 marks the first anniversary of the death of Carl Hampton.

Carl was a revolutionary, and it is not in sentimental retrospect that we can say he was one of the very few men or women in Houston who could lay legitimate claim to that title.

Nor is it merely that Carl demonstrated his willingness to die for his beliefs that he was a revolutionary. He lived for those beliefs, actively seeking realization of his vision for a better society, a society of peace, love, justice, and freedom from material want. He lived those beliefs 24 hours a day, until he was shot down by Houston police one Sunday night on Dowling St.

Carl was 21, and the chairman of the newly formed People's Party II, a black revolutionary organization which still exists in Houston.

The details of that awful night scarcely need repeating. The rally in front of People's Party headquarters, following more than a week of provocative harassment by the Houston police. The white, non-uniformed men sighted on the roof top of nearby St. John the Baptist church. People's Party members moving cautiously, curiously into the street. Then, gunfire. Bullets raining down from the church top into the street, bouncing off the sidewalks. When it was over, Carl lay dying in the street. Several more, including Bartee Haile and Johnny Coward, were seriously wounded. Police casualties: zero.

And then, as if the gun battle had merely whetted their appetites, the police proceeded to trash the abandoned party headquarters and swept down Dowling St., beating and arresting dozens of innocent black citizens who had the poor judgment to be on the street that night.

The impact of Carl's death on Houstonians was dramatic, inasmuch as impact of any sort is possible in this sluggish sprawl of a city. There were those, of course, who applauded the actions of the police in restoring law and order to the wild and wicked Dowling St. area. And there were those who said nothing, perhaps thought nothing, so accustomed they have become to violence and insanity. But there were good liberals whose eternally bleeding hearts were for once touched

Carl demonstrated his willingness to die for his beliefs.

by terror at the brutal extinction of this young black leader.

There were the youthful suburban heads and the Montrose transplants who, though shocked by the killing, saw the incident as further confirmation of their myopic condemnation of violence and guns, including revolutionary violence and guns for self-defense.

For some Houstonians, Carl's death pointed out, in sharp relief, that we the people are indeed at war with them, the rulers, whether we like the idea or not. And though Carl died in 1970 because he was a black man in America, there is no assurance that some of our lives may be in danger in, say, 1973 — because we are young or long-haired or dope-smoking or peace-loving or because we express dangerous ideas or because we even think of ourselves as radicals or revolutionaries.

And if we are at war, a massive though often invisible war against the destruction of the world's people, their minds and their environment, then we really have little choice but to prepare for that war and fight, ultimately for our collective and individual survivals, in whatever ways we can. If we believe only in passive resistance, then we must act on that belief. If we believe that good living and persuasion will make the revolution, then we must live good and do good talking — and this is not as easy as it might seem. If, like Carl, we believe that building and defending socialist institutions is the way, then we must build and defend.

Carl's death, if it teaches us nothing else, should point out the undeniable truth of our situation — that we are a powerless and insecure people living in imperial America — and that we must act today, tomorrow and for the rest of our lives to change that intolerable situation, never giving in to the tempting cynicism and stupefying despair that characterizes the American culture.

It would be unfair to canonize Carl, or even to present his life as the model for people concerned about change and revolution. Carl was not a saint, but a remarkable young man who made the decision to strike back at a system that was strangling him and people like him. He recognized that he carried an immense responsibility, not only to himself, but to the rest of enslaved humanity. That responsibility is ours, too. -30-

In Black & Brown Communities....
People Beaten, Shot, Killed By Police

Karen Northcott • December 2, 1971

" We render a service to the public. We're all they have." Police Chief Herman Short.

To young and Third World people continual police harassment, surveillance and an atmosphere of violence are neither new nor exceptional. Dissenting organizations and individuals and residents in the black and brown communities have constantly been the victims of violence perpetrated against them by members of the Houston Police Department (HPD).

The service rendered by the HPD to Third World people appears to be an apparent policy of repression and violence. And this service is on the upswing.

In the weeks preceding the November 20 city election and the December 7 runoff the number of arrests, beatings and shootings of blacks and browns has increased. Space City! has learned of six instances of what can only be termed unwarranted shows of force by the men in blue.

On Saturday, November 13, black activist and City Council candidate Ovide Duncantell, 35, of 4102 Rosemont, was involved in what he termed a "frame-up" and what Mayor Louie Welch termed a "politically unfortunate" arrest. (See Space City! Vol III, No. 24.) While driving home from a meeting with campaign volunteers, Duncantell was pulled over by a patrol car and subsequently charged with possession of marijuana, assaulting two police officers, fleeing from the officers, speeding, and not having a valid driving license.

Duncantell and the arresting officers offer differing versions of the arrest.

The officers claim that they noticed a station wagon going 47 miles an hour in a 30 mile per hour zone and that they turned on the patrol car's spotlight, red light, and siren, and used the bullhorn in an effort to get the motorist to stop.

Once they succeeded in getting the car stopped, the motorist shoved Officer P.L. Trumble and then tried to drive away, the officer said.

Mayor Welch called the arrest 'politically unfortunate.'

The policemen said that a scuffle followed during which Duncantell was wrestled to the ground. Trumble said that he ordered the man to get out of the car but his order was ignored.

Trumble's partner, Officer F.C. Miller, attempted to handcuff Duncantell as Trumble radioed for help. Approximately 15 patrol cars came to the rescue.

One of the rescuing officers then found a matchbox of marijuana on the dashboard of Duncantell's car.

Duncantell told Space City! he was beaten with the butt of a flashlight 25 or 30 times by one of the arresting officers. He was later taken to Ben Taub Hospital where he was treated for head abrasions. The left side of his head was swollen, the eye nearly shut. He said the officers' pistols were drawn when they approached him.

Duncantell said that the patrol car had followed him for a number of blocks before the officers made any indication to him that it was a police car. The officers turned on the car's siren and spotlight in a dark, dark section of Riverside and he decided to drive ahead to a better lighted area so, in case anything happened to him, he "could have witnesses."

The officers jumped out of the car, pistols drawn, shouting epithets. Duncantell said that he feared that they were "intending to do bodily injury to me, so I grabbed one to defend myself."

The officers made repeated references to his campaign for a seat on the City Council and his past political activism.

The officers filed five charges against him and Duncantell is contemplating filing suit against them.

Mayor Welch, in his weekly press conference, called the arrest "politically unfortunate," saying that it offered Duncantell the opportunity to charge that his arrest and continued harassment were politically motivated, charges which Welch denied.

On Tuesday, November 16, a local organizer for the Free Angela Davis Committee, Mickey McGuire, was beaten and subsequently arrested for aggravated assault on a police officer by Vice Squad Officer Albert Banks at an Operation Breadbasket benefit. (See *Space City!* Vol III No.25.)

McGuire was taking tickets at the door when two well-dressed black men tried to come through without tickets. He blocked their path and told them they would not be allowed entry without paying.

The officers failed to identify themselves as policemen (it is a policy to let officers in free) and began to order McGuire around, calling him "boy" and "nigger." A scuffle followed during which McGuire was wrestled to the ground, dragged to the patrol car (dropped several times enroute) handcuffed, and tossed into the patrol car. McGuire told *Space City!* that while he was handcuffed one of the policemen picked him up by the throat to throw him into the car.

> **The officers failed to identify themselves as policemen.**

McGuire was taken to the downtown station where he claims he was again beaten by the arresting officers plus some others.

He was eventually taken to Ben Taub Hospital where he saw a throat specialist who worked on him for four hours. He was then taken back to the city jail and almost immediately transferred to the county jail. McGuire was released some 20 hours after his arrest. He said that the officers who processed him singled him out as "a militant" and wanted him to say that he "loved the police" before they would release him.

McGuire was charged with aggravated assault on a police officer, beaten during the arrest and at the station.

On Saturday, November 20, James Oiler and Roger Edwards were stopped in the 3300 block of Beulah for a license check by Officer C.R. Herman; Oiler was later charged with robbery by assault and possession of a matchbox of marijuana.

Officer Herman said that he smelled the odor of marijuana as he approached the car. As he tried to handcuff Roger Edwards, 23, of 3400 Corinth, both men jumped on him, attacked him, and beat him to the ground according to Herman. Oiler supposedly managed to take away the officer's pistol and aimed it at him for several minutes.

Herman said that he was retreating towards his car when he ducked behind another car and pulled a second pistol. "One of them was trying to get the safety off, so I opened up on him," Herman said. Oiler suffered superficial head wounds.

The right front tire of the automobile was shot out and the two men and an unidentified woman managed to get away. They abandoned the car a few blocks away and Oiler was captured and two others escaped, taking Herman's pistol, the officer charged.

One man, who was charged with aggravated assault on an officer and possession, was shot in the arrest.

On Sunday morning, November 20, an unidentified Harris County constable on horseback was involved in some sort of incident with a black youth in the vicinity of Kewanee Street. No one was charged with any offense.

Later that afternoon in the same area Albert Blaine Davis and Nelson Miller were involved in a confrontation with Officers C.R. Herman and A.M. Baimonte and Davis was later charged with two counts of aggravated assault on a police officer.

Officers Herman and Baimonte were in the 4200 block of Kewanee looking for a pistol Officer Herman had lost the night before in an incident involving James Oiler and Roger Edwards.

While searching for the gun, an unidentified man (who witnesses reported to *Space City!* was the constable on horseback who was involved in a scrape earlier that morning) approached one of the policemen and told of being attacked by a youth, later identified as Albert Blaine Davis, 19, of 4122 Alvin.

Officer Baimonte claims that he went up to Davis and requested that he identify himself. Davis refused and became abusive, according to the policeman.

An angry crowd of 100 people gathered around Davis and the two officers.

Ad: July 6, 1972.

The officers claim Davis struck Baimonte across the neck and struggled with both of them. During the melee Davis was shot once in the side and Nelson was injured slightly.

Police accounts vary as to who actually shot the two youths. Baimonte said an unidentified youth grabbed the gun away from him and tried to run away, at which point Baimonte grabbed the pistol back and it fired as he turned to help handcuff Davis.

Herman said Davis was the youth who grabbed the gun just before it fired.

Two youths injured, one charged with two counts of aggravated assault on a police officer.

On Tuesday, November 23, Officers J.M. Hinton and H.L. Kuykendall arrested Richard Rincon, 45, and Louis Rincon, 36, for aggravated assault on a police officer.

Officers Hinton and Kuykendall claim they followed Richard Rincon to his house after noticing his car was weaving. The officers said Richard stopped at 7719 Canal and ran toward the house.

Cover: December 20, 1969.

Hinton said he struggled with Richard at the gate and then they fell onto the porch. As they were struggling, two women and a man ran onto the porch from the house and joined the struggle, according to Hinton.

The officers said Richard struck Hinton and Louis struck Hinton in the cheek. Hinton said he ran from the porch, leaving Kuykendall with the struggling family, and put out an "assist to officer" call. He further claims that he waved down a passing patrol car and they assisted in the arrest of the two brothers.

The Rincon family's version of the arrests differs from that of the police.

Eleanor Rincon, Richard's wife, and Juanita Rincon, 68, Richard's mother, claim that they were on the porch waiting for Richard to return when Richard drove up to the house, and was followed by an officer who struck Richard from behind as he was walking up to the porch.

The women claim the officers began to shove them at which point Louis Rincon ran to the porch. Juanita Rincon said Louis was merely trying to protect her when the officers struck him. They also said Richard never struck either officer; that he was attempting to protect himself by covering his face and head with his hands.

The official police version is somewhat garbled.

The record shows no call to assist an officer. Hinton later told a *Chronicle* reporter that he "did not get to make" the assist call because he saw the other patrol car approaching and he waved them down. He also claimed the women were not on the porch when he arrived.

Kuykendall said he didn't know the whereabouts of Hinton when the second patrol car arrived.

Officers R.L. Starbuck and W.L. Fielder reported they were cruising in their car when they heard a disturbance and drove to it. They said they were not flagged down by Hinton. They said they "saw two policemen struggling with two women and two men when they drove up."

State Representative Lauro Cruz has asked Governor Preston Smith to investigate the incident. "It is the epitome of disgust when the Police Department has to beat up on a 68-year old grandmother and assault a man in his own yard.

"If the Police Department can explain to me why force was used with this old lady, it should be forthcoming immediately," he said.

Two men charged with aggravated assault, an entire family beaten, including a 68-year-old grandmother.

On Thursday, November 25, Daniel Moreno was killed by police answering a call about a suspicious man.

Officers W.D. Simmons and F.C. Dodd fatally shot Daniel Moreno, 27, of 3724 Rupert, who they say drew a pistol on them as they attempted to question him.

The officers were called to the 5100 block of Dabney by Rev. Ivan Turic, 30, of St. Francis Assissi Church, to investigate a suspicious man watching children from the bushes in front of the church.

The officers said they drove alongside Moreno as he drew what appeared to be a .45 caliber pistol. They said they shouted for him to drop the weapon, but he leveled the gun at them.

Dodd said he fired one shot at him and Simmons fired two shots at Moreno because he was still holding the gun on them.

Witnesses substantiate the fact that Moreno was holding a gun on the officers; it was a B.B. gun. Two witnesses said, however, that Moreno dropped the gun before the final two shots were fired.

"The man dropped the gun and staggered towards the police car and then several more shots were fired," said James Prichard, 5818 Hickman.

It has not been determined which officer's shot killed Moreno.

As in all cases involving the use of excessive force or police brutality, it's the Man's word against the word of the victim. The police in all of the above cases claim they were merely defending themselves against assault.

Assistant District Attorney Bob Bennet remarked during the Bartee Haile trial (arising out of the Dowling Street incident which left Carl Hampton, chairman of Peoples Party II dead) that "You've got to have hard aggressive individuals in the police department. It takes a special kind of individual, a special kind of man to devote his life to this."

The members of the Houston Police Department are the kind of men that Herman Short can be proud of. They are, to say the least, hard, aggressive and devoted. Devoted to a rigid policy of repression and violence against those they consider a threat. -30-

Art: Jim Franklin, August 10, 1971.

Space City!
Culture

Cover: Art by Bill Narum, June 29, 1971.

Arts and
Culture

Cover: Art by Kerry Fitzgerald, October 17, 1970.

Janis

Jeff Shero • October 17, 1970

Time keeps moving on
Friends they turn away
I keep moving on
But I never find out why
I keep pushing so hard that
Baby I keep trying to make it right
Through another lonely day.
Oh Why ?

Kosmic Blues
Janis Joplin

Every time Janis sang in person, she shone with an incandescent, fixating vulnerability. It wasn't that she had more talent than Mama Cass, Grace Slick, or even Tracy Nelson, but that each time she pushed beyond the limit, giving so much of herself away that each concert you knew she was closer to the end. She never sang; she twisted and contorted words into moans, pleas and cries of sadness, desperation, loneliness, and sexual release. It was her only way to crash through the barriers created by the big business rock industry and touch people.

Janis was on one long, careening roller coaster ride which began in Port Arthur and ended in a lonely Hollywood motel room. She was the Queen of Rock, desired by thousands of men, yet her last moments were spent alone with a blood-tipped syringe which had spurted a death dosage of heroin into her veins. She had no lover to say goodby. It was 12 hours before she was missed and somebody wondered where she'd gone.

Heroin finished Janis, but she was slowly consumed by Amerika in much the same way as her predecessors, Billie Holliday and Bessie Smith. Bessie Smith bled to death after a car wreck when a hospital refused to admit her because she was black. Billie Holliday, trying to live a black life with dignity, sought escape from her blues in junk until her body collapsed.

Janis grew up in an oil town that was interested in making money and owning things. Janis, who was sensitive and didn't hate blacks, never fit in. Growing up in Port Arthur, in a fifties white culture which tuned-in on Paul Anka, Rick Nelson, Pat Boone, and a catty high school culture which didn't have much room for bright

> **Janis was on one long, careening roller coaster ride.**

and plain-looking girls, was like drowning in a pool of alienation. She turned to black culture and its blues roots to survive honkey society. Looking back she said, "You don't have to be black to have the blues. You just have to suffer."

Port Arthur produced the lonely blues, the blues when you don't have anyone to share your feelings with. You learn to act tough, so others don't see the pain and take advantage of the weakness. But now freak culture has spread across Amerika, and dropouts and rebels dwell even in towns like Port Arthur. Unlike in the fifties, people don't grow up alone. They have sisters and brothers and communities to escape to. Janis was a product of an earlier time. She was loved as an outrageous and gutsy rebel by her audiences, but she was a whiskey-drinking rock star in an acid generation, and she never felt part of a new freak generation of people.

The New York and San Francisco rock Jet Set didn't help, with its phony, under-assistant-west-coast-promotion men, and rock star parasites and groupies, who hang around the hotels and clubs, fawning and telling lies and hoping to steal a little piece of a star's soul. Janis sang:

I guess I'm just like a turtle that's
hiden' underneath its hardness shell
Oh — Oh yeah like a turtle
hiden' underneath its hardness shell
But you know I'm very well protected
I know this goddamn life too well.

Turtle Blues
Janis Joplin

The first time I saw Janis sing in New York was at a special-invitation opening of a now-defunct rock club. Martin Luther King had been assassinated a few days before, and though Buddy Guy was being introduced that evening, Janis did a few songs. She started with "Summertime," as a tribute to King, and sang it unlike ever before. Her phrasing transformed that old standard into a soaring spiritual of resurrection and hope. Her voice reached places I never heard it find again. The underground press people present were moved. Meanwhile, the record company executives swizzled their scotches, munched their hor d'ouvres, and discussed business, while the rock parasites paraded their rumors and gossip.

> Once I had a daddy
> Said he'd give me everything in sight
> Yes, he did
> So I said, honey,
> I want the sunshine
> And take the stars out of the night.

Turtle Blues
Janis Joplin

Each time I saw Janis after that she seemed a little more exhausted, and though she would deny it with the passion of someone who recognized the Truth, her voice seemed a little more strained and limited in range. At those parties there always seemed to be too much liquor, too many photographers, and too many people who needed to live off other people's energy. In New York, Janis passed through a glittering wasteland, often a bottle of Southern Comfort her best friend.

Her voice reached places I never heard it find again.

One night one of her closer girl friends told me Janis was shooting junk. And with that infectious detachment common to New York, we discussed Methadone, and apomorphine treatments in London, and the spread of heroin in general. The average life expectancy of a person from the first time they shoot junk is five years. But nobody was close enough to Janis to say, "goddamn, you're killing yourself!" So the conversation ended with a cool and false knowledgeability — Janis obviously would have the money and connections to score good junk and could live for 20 years we concluded. The fact that she was going to die in less than two years somehow got erased in a stupid, jaded hip optimism.

As time passed Janis began experimenting musically, first with the Kosmic Blues Band, later with the Full Tilt Boogie Band, which she was recording with at the time of her death. Things seemed to be getting together. For her *Kosmic Blues* album she'd written:

> Honey, I love to go to parties
> And I like to have a good time
> But it begins to pale after a while
> Honey, I start lookin' to find
> One good man.
>
> I don't want much out of life
> I never wanted a mansion in the South
> I just wanted to find someone sincere
> Who'd treat me like he talks
> One good man
> Oh, honey, don't you know I've been lookin'
> One good man, oh, ain't much
> Honey much, it's only everything.

One Good Man
Janis Joplin

But more recently she seemed to have accepted her life and begun thinking about her roots. In the October issue of *Circus* magazine she said,

> I've given everything up for music. Music, that's what I live for. I'm on the road most of the time. I give up everything for that chance of being up there performing on that stage. I give up the chance of having an old man. I have a beautiful new home near San Francisco, but I spend most of my life in hotel rooms and planes. I have friends I hardly ever get to see. And all I get is

being insulted by waitresses and hotel clerks. Why do I do it? For those three or four hours a week I spend on stage.

At the same time, she also said,

Eighteen months ago I really had the Kosmic Blues. I really had them bad. But it's a matter of accepting things. Accept things and life doesn't seem so bad. You've got to realize that you'll never have as much as you want, and that when you die, you'll be alone — everyone is.

Not long ago Janis returned to Port Arthur for the tenth anniversary reunion of her high school graduating class. Despite reports in the local press which made her seem spiteful towards the kind of people who used to ignore her and are now plumbers in Port Arthur, people present say she didn't play that celebrity role. Instead she tried to be friendly and unassuming and fit in with the group. One girl in her class said, "It was like it mattered to her what we thought after all these years. It seemed like she remembered her high school days and wanted to be accepted."

Janis told one Houston reporter that when she was in high school people threw books at her. Later, when one of her Port Arthur friends asked why she'd said something that wasn't true, Janis replied, "I know it wasn't true. It was the only way I could explain the hurt I felt." During her visit to Port Arthur it was as if she was trying to find some substance in the people and relationships that she had missed as a touring rock star.

At the University of Texas Janis had hung out with the folk-singing crowd in 1960 and '61. She was enough of an oddity at the time to be featured in *The Daily Texan* in an article titled "She Dares to be Different." She was the folk-singing predecessor to the later Chuckwagon freak scene. Hanging around, she'd sometimes show up at the weekly folk-singing session in the Union which featured such local standouts as Kerry Rush and John Clay, or she'd wind up at Kenneth Threadgill's tavern north of town, working with Powell St. John, Threadgill and others.

This summer a Jubilee celebration was organized in honor of Threadgill, a 60-year-old country folksinger and noted proprietor of a tavern housed in an old gas station. Mance Lipscomb up from Navasota, and all the local musicians as well as an audience of freaks and country people, were on hand for the benefit. Then miraculously Janis appeared. She had heard of the get-together while in Hawaii, hopped aboard a plane and flew to Austin.

She came in by herself and capped the evening. On stage with her own guitar as accompaniment, she apologized to the crowd, "I never did learn to play this thing very good," and then belted out a few songs. To Threadgill who was also on the stage she announced, "I've brought you just what you've always needed — a good lay." Then she took the lei off her neck and put it on Threadgill with a kiss. Everyone was happy, and in Austin Janis was something more than a distant rock celebrity. Maybe Janis had a home.

Just as life may have been settling down and her music with the Full Tilt Boogie Band taking an exploratory country-blues-rock turn, the junk caught up with her and she died. Her ashes now are drifting in the Pacific off California. Her energy and her blues have touched all of us, and we will carry that part of her into the future. But as she herself said:

She seemed to have accepted her life and begun thinking about her roots.

Don't expect any answers dear
For I know they don't come with age.

Kosmic Blues
Janis Joplin

-30-

Two Years in Space (City!)

John Lomax III

Space City! was my rocket to 50 years in music journalism, artist management and distributing careers. The tiny underground paper opened a door for me in Nashville and further musical adventures in the U.S., Europe, and Australia.

The publication was starting its third year when I came on board in January 1971. I had returned to Houston to work at the downtown location of the Public Library as a Reference and Young Adult librarian.

I came to *Space City!* sporting a dossier that included a few articles for the UT student paper, *The Daily Texan*, a Blind Willie Johnson liner note project my dad passed to me, and a piece in (then) influential rock magazine *Creem*. Despite these puny accomplishments, Thorne and the Collective believed in me. They turned me loose to present my views of the music and entertainment worlds. I rocked, railed, and raved from then until *Space City!* crashed late in 1972.

It's clear to me that if I did not have my two years of *Space City!* clips I would never have landed a job as a publicist in Nashville for future Country Music Hall of Fame inductee "Cowboy" Jack Clement. That allowed me to continue writing about music and musicians.

And had I not moved to Nashville I would never have launched an artist management career in 1976. Twenty years later those experiences enabled me to create a specialty music distributing operation that became Nashville's top independent exporter of CDs, DVDs, and LPs.

All of those endeavors earned me the coveted Jo Walker-Meador International Achievement Award in 2010. The award is presented by the Country Music Association; to date only 24 people have ever won it.

Space City! was my launching pad.

Space City! thus was my launching pad and for that I am forever grateful.

I debuted on the paper's pages with a review of an album by enduring Afro-rock band Osibisa, awarding them a grade of 90. Back then Robert Christgau's "Consumer Guide," published weekly in the *Village Voice*, was the gold standard for record reviewers. He critiqued the new albums with a school grading scale: A+, A, A-, B+, etc. down to F. I felt 13 slots would be too limiting so I adopted a straight 1-100 grading scheme for the weekly column that I dubbed "Platter Chatter."

No release ever merited 100, nor did any get a zero. I gave ZZ Top's *Rio Grande Mud*, which I still have, a 98.5, my highest scorer, just ahead of the 97s awarded to the Allman Brothers, Tim Buckley, the Dillards, English "space rockers" Hawkwind, Jethro Tull, and John McLaughlin's Mahavishnu Orchestra. An album by someone called Screaming Lord Sutch, *The Hands of Jack the Ripper*, which I did not keep, got a 6 to win my biggest dunce cap, beating out the vomitous English Congregation's *Softly Whispering I Love You*.

At the time there was of course no Internet and neither daily newspaper or TV station presented much popular music coverage. At best they'd review the big shows at the Coliseum or Music Hall, but as for local music, club shows, or record reviews — forget it! FM Radio was shaking up those airwaves by playing a broader musical palette, so music lovers were hearing plenty of the new "counterculture" artists that the local print media was ignoring.

"Platter Chatter" and its successor "Rockin' New Mania" delivered verdicts on 255 releases in less than three years. I felt privileged and excited to bring readers news of John Lennon's *Imagine*, David Bowie's *Rise and Fall of Ziggy*

Stardust, Jimi Hendrix's *In The West* and, I believe, the first review to spotlight Don McLean's iconic *American Pie*.

I started out writing only album reviews but soon expanded into concert coverage, then penning features and delivering information about upcoming shows. I aimed to plug the gaps the dailies were overlooking.

For instance we ran a piece on blues Hall of Famer Lightning Hopkins, provided the most thorough coverage of the original Willie Nelson picnic in Dripping Springs, spotlighted the Rolling Stones' Hofheinz Pavilion show and a spectacular Liberty Hall triple bill of Jimmy Reed, Johnny Winter, and Rocky Hill.

"Platter Chatter" was not a particularly stern musical umpire — 43 percent of the 255 titles examined were rated at 90 or higher while only 23 flunked entirely, falling below 70.

I do recall imposing a penalty on John & Yoko's *Sometime in New York City* as I felt Yoko's "singing" pulled the project from a score in the 90s to one well beneath that.

I recruited some sidekicks to add their voices to our coverage, handing out assignments as if I were a big-time, cigar-chomping downtown editor. Scout Schacht (aka Scout Stormcloud) was my most prolific contributor.

Talk about chutzpah! I was asked to review new albums, then I began calling myself the Music Editor, ranging far beyond my original assigned musical territory!

Have to put in a digression here. A couple of decades later my son, John Nova, was hired as Music Editor for the *Houston Press*, in its incarnation as a weekly. He added a new link to a four-generation Lomax literary tradition.

In 1971, my job was unpaid of course but I learned how to hustle free records, promotional pictures, show tickets, and t-shirts from the local record label reps, Henry Withers, Sammy Alfano, and Al Mathias among them. They lived in small apartments and had far more of their albums than they could possibly distribute before the next round of releases arrived. They were happy for someone to haul 'em off.

And haul 'em off I did. When I moved son John Nova with me to Nashville two-and-a-half years later

there were over 2,000 LPs in the trunk, the majority free goods. I still have some of those, though most have been sold or donated to the Country Music Hall of Fame or the Woodson Research Center at Rice University.

I kept my writing centered on the entertainment world and so was not involved in *Space City!*'s political coverage or with news beyond my niche. How I thought I could get away with writing for Houston's most radical publication while simultaneously working for the Houston Public Library and selecting Young Adult books illustrates how naïve I was. There I was toiling away reviewing concerts and discussing the merits of album releases by admitted drug users and others pushing the envelope of contemporary social practices!

I was fired from my city job but, thanks to parental financial support, was able to continue developing as a music journalist.

I was earning a few bucks being a very small-scale pot dealer. I got busted one night with a pound of weed in the car's trunk. By then *Space City!* was gone and soon I was too.

The state of Texas sentenced me to serve five years in Huntsville prison, a circumstance which would not benefit my burgeoning career. My attorney, Michael Hunt, convinced the judge to probate the sentence. A marked man to law enforcement now, I left for Nashville, feeling as if the hellhouds were on my tail.

My writing philosophy was that I'd just start slinging out words and if people complained, then I'd stop. So far, 50 years on and a few million words later, no one has. I did have one guy call me a "turd merchant" for what he felt was a slam of Ricky Skaggs' religious beliefs, but the comment was actually written by someone else. Besides that, being able to sell turds would be a singular achievement.

Space City! started me on the writer's path, a journey which now encompasses hundreds of columns, reviews, and features published on four continents. My books include *For the Sake of the Song: The Townes Van Zandt Songbook*, a collaboration with my late brother Joe, also a *Space City!* contributor. I wrote *Nashville: Music City U.S.A* in 1986 and *Red Desert Sky*, a biography of Kasey Chambers, in 2001.

My *Space City!* work brought me to Nashville and there I began managing artists such as Van Zan-

My job was unpaid of course but I learned how to hustle free records.

dt, Rocky Hill, Steve Earle, "America's Dulcimer Champion" David Schnaufer, The Cactus Brothers, line-dance princess Kimber Clayton, Texas singer-songwriter Sunny Sweeney, and the outrageous Manhattan performer, Tammy Faye Starlite.

And *Space City!* also put me on a path which developed into a third career as an exporter of hard-to-find musical releases. Roots Music Exporters, begun in 1996 and lasting until March, 2021, when stREAMING ate it, was the most profitable of my music biz forays, earning me at least a million dollars over that 25 year span. We shipped about 750,000 CDs, DVDs, and LPs to importers in Europe, Australia, and Asia. And that spun off a related satellite enterprise in 2011, an ongoing Amazon Marketplace operation, Lomax Global Music.

It's said that big trees grow from tiny acorns. The tall tree of my career was the acorn planted, watered, and nourished by *Space City!*, so thank you Thorne and the Collective for all of that.

Nashville
May 2021

John Avery Lomax, John Marable Lomax (aka John Lomax III) , and John Avery Lomax Jr., Houston, Texas. Photo: Margaret "Mimi" Lomax, 1947.

The Lomax Legacy

My grandfather John Avery Lomax's 1910 publication, *Cowboy Songs and Other Frontier Ballads*, began a family musical tradition enduring 111 years and three generations. He and younger son Alan wrote numerous books and began the Library of Congress Library of Recorded Sound, collecting over 17,000 songs and stories.

John Avery Lomax Jr., my dad, was a land developer who sang professionally, co-founded the Houston Folklore Society (1951) and managed the career of legendary bluesman, "Lightning" Hopkins.

Bess Lomax Hawes, co-writer of the Kingston Trio hit, "M.T.A." directed the folk grant program for the National Endowment for the Arts for decades and was a Presidential Medal of Arts recipient, as was her brother, Alan.

My brother, Joe Lomax, grandson of John Avery Sr., was a noted Houston author, photographer, and founder of Wings Press. He also created the TV documentary, "Reach for the Stars."

John Nova Lomax, great grandson of John Avery and my son, has written two books, was Music Editor for the *Houston Press*, a Senior Editor for *Texas Monthly*, and now writes for *Texas Highways* magazine.

For more information go to www.culturalequity.org.

— John Lomax III (aka John M. Lomax)

Rolling Stones. Photo by John M. Lomax.

Stones: Liquid Raunch

John M. Lomax • June 29, 1972

The world-famous Rolling Stones, generally acknowledged to be the greatest rock and roll band around, paid two Sunday visits to Hofheinz Pavilion June 27. Eighty-one persons were arrested for various absurd infractions of Texas' equally ridiculous laws. The concerts were also dampened considerably by the unexpected absence of Stevie Wonder, said to be caused by the nervous breakdow of his drummer. Bidy [Lomax] was backstage before the first show and offered to obtain the capable services of Frank Beard, ZZ Tops' drummer, but this offer was rebuffed.

The Dorothy Norwood Singers, an Atlanta gospel group, filled in for the missing Wonder and were not exactly what the crowd had come to see. They played very well — an eight-piece group with organ, bass, drums, guitar, tambourine, and three girl singers — presenting a program of religious numbers like "I'm So Glad," "Just the Two of Us," and concluding with a rousing version of "When the Saints Go Marching In."

After about 30 minutes the Stones came onto a stage raised about seven feet above ground with two long banks of colored spots hung overhead and behind, and with major sets of amps slung high on two 20-foot towers to the right and left of the stage. These tactics afforded maximum visual exposure to the crowd — at least those fortunate enough to be in clear areas.

Unfortunately for many, the hall was sold to capacity and many folks wound up behind the stage in seats perfect for a basketball game but with a rather pitiful view of the backside of the Stones amps.

Suddenly, there they were. The real, live Rolling Stones. Plus, Nicky Hopkins on keyboards and Texans Bobby Keys and Jim Price on assorted horns — quite professional, but too brief. The not-so-young machos laid about 16 songs on us at the 9 p.m. show, were on stage around one-and-a-half hours and left the crowd begging for more. But there were no encores from this band and the crowd filed out of the hall at 11:35 p.m. feeling partially fulfilled, but wishing for more. Indeed, when you have waited six years for a return concert, you have the right to at least ask for more.

Due to occurrences of violence at concerts in Vancouver, San Diego, and Tucson, it was feared riots would develop here. So, Herman Short dispatched 112 of his finest blue boys to prevent a repetition in Houston. Nothing much developed during the afternoon show, but by nightfall a hastily instituted no camera/no tape recorder edict was introduced, giving the cops an excuse to hassle people, look in purses, and engage in general harassments which resulted in beefed-up arrest figures.

Twenty-five were busted for marijuana and other drug offenses, many arising from seemingly illegal searches of purses, pockets, and briefcases. Of course, these arrests won't stand up in court for a minute; the victims, however, missed the concert, spent time in jail, and are out the mandatory $300-$2,500 it will cost them to hire lawyers to extricate themselves.

The cops were so frustrated with the lack of anything resembling provocation that they were busting folks for jaywalking across Cullen to get into the Pavilion. Police at rock concerts are like warts on your hand; no one wants them, they just appear.

Mick led the boys as only he can; it has been said that the Stones are a top-flight group, but that it is Jagger who lifts them into the top position in such a competitive industry. I think that argument gives far too little credit to Keith Richards and Mick Taylor, who are two of the finest electric guitarists to be found anywhere and it also ignores Charlie Watts and Bill Wyman, two phlegmatic chaps who lay down the solid rhythm that allows the rest of the group to freelance. All eight of the musicians are excellent and somehow like a winning athletic team — the whole is greater than the sum of their parts.

And if Mick baby isn't as superb a physical specimen as I've ever seen … twisting, spinning, dropping, jumping, and throwing us a hip with the coordination of a young leopard; indeed, his dad was a physical education instructor. He led the other seven through the show, beginning with "Brown Sugar" and ending in a shower of popcorn from the ceiling during the final throes of "Street Fighting Man."

In between, they did "Rocks Off," "Happy" "Tumbling Dice," and "Sweet Virginia" from the new album, *Exile on Main Street*, to go with older tunes such as "Gimme Shelter," "You Can't Always Get What You Want," "Midnight Rambler," "Jumping Jack Flash," and "Johnny B. Goode." And a few more. All done in a very businesslike yet infec-

Mick was twisting, spinning, dropping, jumping, and throwing us a hip.

tious manner with Mick complimenting the crowd often, at one point stating:

You're a good crowd here in Houston. Should be in church, though.

Where did he think we were?

He closed by giving three deep bows to the crowd and flinging armfuls of red roses to the folks in the floor chairs. Through it all the Stones' liquid raunch — patented and unequalled — was laid down beautifully. The sound system was loud yet not distorted and Chip Monch's ingenious lighting set-up at times allowed me to use camera exposures as brief as one-sixtieth of a second. You see, we were tipped to the camera ban before reaching the gates and secreted them on our persons. As Rex wryly remarked: "Well, that's just one more rule we'll get to break."

Ace Pacifica reporter Scoop Sweeney, covering the scene outside, wasn't so lucky; he was rudely relieved of his tape cassette by Feyline thugs and Houston cops, because what he was recording would spread "bad publicity." Barry Fey had recruited a scurvy band of brute enforcers to dissuade anyone foolish enough to try to bend the rules, stand in their chairs, or otherwise overstep the prescribed limits of enjoyment.

Maybe this dampened the enthusiasm, or maybe it was the lack of a sizeable crowd of blacks, but this concert was much more subdued than Sly's show where the entire stadium — full of people — were on their feet boogieing, most atop their chairs. Things did get a little looser toward the end, but it was, all in all, a relatively quiet concert, marked more by paranoia and apprehension than unrestrained joy.

The Stones did not play as long as groups like the Allman Brothers, Jethro Tull, Led Zeppelin, and The Who, all of whom like to put on two hour-plus sets. And to the Grateful Dead, 1 1/2 hours would be but a warmup. We got what they gave, though, like it or not; perhaps it will be less than six years before their next time here.

Are they the greatest rock 'n roll band in the world? That's up to you. They play straight ahead hard-ass music perhaps better than anyone else. I still prefer the old Grateful Dead lineup, back in the days when they were heavily into acid and when their music was so full of magic.

Are the Stones a symbol of death? No. That music brought vibrant life to over 20,000 people Sunday; they have caused innumerable unwanted pregnancies, and given anthems to an entire generation. Shucks, even Truman Capote was in Houston for the event. -30-

Lightning Hopkins

John M. Lomax • June 19, 1969

We live in an age of technology. We are filed by number and trained in specialties. Our grocery stores used to carry four varieties of cheese; some now stock over 70. We are living longer and more comfortably, working less and in better conditions. We are so far advanced we can quibble over the legal problems of heart transplants and look forward to color TV shots of the first moon voyage to break the summer rerun monotony.

Our music tastes in 10 years have advanced from saccharine ballads to rock-and-roll to folk to psychedelic to a current craze of country rock or "rockabilly." Rock and roll is dead but by its death we have folk-rock, acid rock, country rock, jazz-rock, hard rock, shlock-rock, blues-rock, psychedelic rock, shock-rock, and rock theatre.

All these dialects of rock employ electricity, electronics in some cases, and a cast of literally dozens of people to produce and market their recorded work. These gems are dug up and out of the musicians and doled out to the consumer on an annual or semi-annual basis. The purveyors of this product claim their "property" has "soul," then they tell us what "soul" is.

Blues is simply one man singing alone. Blues is your feelings, your emotions, your fears. Blues jump from your mind and soul. Blues authorities, performers, and hangers-on currently are engaging in fierce debate over the vital question of whether or not blues can be sung by the white man. Big deal. Blues can be sung, talked, heard, or felt by anyone.

The mass media blues of the Supremes — Aretha Franklin, Otis Redding, Janis Joplin, or Lou Rawls — is a lot different from the blues of Sam "Lightning" Hopkins who has been called "the last of the great blues artists." Does he appear on national TV? Does he sell out the coliseum, do his records earn million-seller certificates? Of course not. But he is authentic, vibrant, and enormously talented at the art he has made into his life's work.

Some sources say Sam was born in 1911, others say 1912, but all agree that to be emerging into manhood in 1929 was no easy task. Sam grew up in and around Centerville, Texas. He remembers first playing a guitar (homemade from a cigar box) before his ninth year. He also recalls going to work in the cotton fields around his tenth year. Sam left home before he turned 21, working where he could, farm-

Lightning Hopkins. Photo by John M. Lomax, June 19, 1969.

ing some and drifting. He had a period of gambling and drinking, but always had a guitar of some kind with him.

As the years wore on, Sam began to play and sing for pay in roadhouses throughout East Texas. He moved here in 1939 or '40 and soon acquired a local following large enough to aid him in first being recorded exactly 25 years ago. Since then, he has been recorded countless times, had over 40 albums on many different labels, and appeared all over Europe and America.

He has been honored in Washington, D.C., and inspired encores in Carnegie Hall. He was a subject of two recent films, one for HemisFair and the other, an hour-long, color documentary which hopefully will be seen on TV across the continent. He has influenced and interested people such as Bob Dylan, Leonard Cohen, Ringo Starr, Taj Mahal, Muddy Waters, Townes Van Zandt, and countless others.

Sam has appeared in Dowling bars, at the Ashgrove and Village Gate, at Newport and in psychedelic dance concerts.

His fans range from "old-time" Negro Texans through the "turned-on young set" to jazz critics and sociologists. At this stage in his career, he has become a legend of blues, of one man's voice among the many.

In concert Sam is alive with feeling. He plays his guitar with 50 hard years of practice behind him. He can play it with one hand, with a can opener, coke bottle, or knife blade. He can strum his instrument with patient care or he can pick it, bend it, and shape it into producing the sounds of pain, of the joy of the life he has led and is now singing. He tells us of lost women, of feeling down, of his everyday experiences.

He has a remarkable ability to improvise rhyming, multi-verse songs about his everyday experiences. His response upon hearing about the Friendship 7 was an instant ballad about the astronauts.

On the plane to Washington, D.C., for the Smithsonian Institute Festival last July, one of the engines went out. Af-

Ad: May 11, 1971.

ter being assured that the remaining three jets were sufficient, Sam got his guitar from the rack above and broke into song.

Lightning says, "Blues is just a feeling — happy or sad. Mostly about troubles … Get to thinking about a subject and words come up."

Lightning has written many, many songs. Such as "Short-Haired Woman," "Mister Charley," and "Take Me Back." He sings these as well as classics such as "Trouble in Mind," "Corinna, Corinna," and "Got My Mo-Jo Working."

Lightning is seldom seen without his sunglasses. He speaks in a low, gravelly tone, much like his singing voice. There's nothing "just that simple" to Lightning. He answers questions with examples and rambling anecdotal stories:

"Where do all the colored people hang out around here? See that tree over there. The last one we hung was on that big limb on the right..."

"I'm living as good as I want to," says Lightning. "I love everybody who walks on God's ground. I like Houston."

"I live here because the people treat me nicest."

Sam is now nearing 60. He is living comfortably but the hard East Texas years have taken their toll. He won't be around forever, there will come a day when he will be discussed in the past tense and when his records will be regarded as collectors' items.

He will be playing in and around Houston for some time to come so if anyone wants a living definition of the blues, of "Soul," and of life, they should see him play and sing. If you are lucky, Billy Bizor may be around to accompany on harmonica for a few numbers. Then you can go home and bury your head in the sand of the latest super soul sensation that's sweeping the nation. Some art is timeless.

"Tradition such as the blues is perpetuated not by attempts to emulate and preserve but through growth and contribution of many egos." Art— John A. Lomax Jr.

-30-

Big Mama Thornton at Liberty Hall, Photo by Sue Mithun, May 18,1971.

Velvet Underground at Liberty Hall

John M. Lomax • August 24, 1971

Hard rock returned to Liberty Hall last weekend (August 20-21) with the Velvet Underground. They stepped from the vinyl of four albums onto the stage to lay down their brand of pure, hard rock. Playing to a packed house they brought a new dimension to the local music scene.

As you know, their sound is definitely an acquired taste. No group around plays rock quite so hard. They have never been the success their stature entitles them to, mainly due to inept handling by MGM, their first label. They lay down a brisk, gritty style of raunch uniquely their own. There is an urgency to the sound as they hit hard and insistent — like a piledriver. The music slashes and rips into you.

Prior to the Airplane, Cream, the Dead or Hendrix, the Velvet were performing at Andy Warhol's Exploding Plastic Inevitable. They pioneered the "total environment" form appearing in front and inside a mixed-media light show.

The hypnotic *Velvet Underground and Nico* was released and was completely stunning. Their initial cut "Heroin" on the album was a seven-minute interlude into dope addiction. All the mystery, the evil pouring out — a stark reminder of the uselessness of a dope-hell. Three albums have followed; the last, *Loaded*, came out last winter on Atco's Cotillion label.

Lou Reed has tired and left the band to write a novel. Doug Yule now plays lead and sings. Maureen Tucker drums sparingly yet with force and inventiveness. Sterling Morrison on rhythm utilizes a stutter-step method around surging tempos which send the flow outward unevenly. Walter Powers, the bass, is able to roam a bit more freely because of the solid drumming.

They opened the first set with "Waiting for my Man." As Doug said, "We're the Velvet Underground, love it or leave it." If anybody did take off, they missed a chance to drive the AM crud soft-rock insipid strains from their minds like sand before the sea.

Waiting for my man,
26 dollars in my hand

They lay down a brisk, gritty style of raunch uniquely their own.

first thing that you learn is that you always gotta wait

They breezed through "Cool It Down, Mean Old Man," with a staccato high-hat rhythm, a surging tune with alternative blasts and caresses from the strings. "Some Kind of Love" followed, with Doug snapping on and off earth with brief buzzing breaks as their frenzy was under total control. Without Lou the group is more balanced; they work harder around their basic breathless framework.

By now the crowd was already asking for them to play "Heroin," but Doug said, "We might do 'Sister Ray' later; Heroin's too much in the air these days. Ever since Methadone."

Surprisingly the — as Marge Crumbaker [of the *Houston Post*] says — "mysterious" Velvets are friendly and very approachable backstage. Maureen

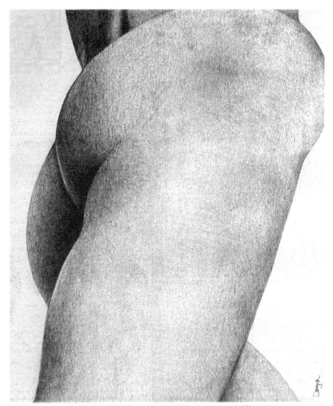

AUGUST 20 & 21 the VELVET UNDERGROUND LIBERTY HALL 1610 CHENEVERT 225 4250
Presented by the Southern Voice
TICKETS: BUDGET TAPES ON WESTHEIMER   2.50 ADVANCE - 3.50 AT DOOR   TWO SHOWS   8:00 PM no age limit   11:00 PM over 21 only

Ad: August 17, 1971.

has a 13-month-old baby, Doug likes to talk about Hofheinz, the LBJ Library, and Preston's play in defying Nixon.

Sterling talks of pro football, the winter they spent skiing daily in Vermont, and the loss of his vintage record collection.

"I had so many albums, they had to break in three separate times to steal them all."

"I really liked it at Max's. We were the backroom boys. I mean we played there and I went every night for years. I was there 10 days after he opened so we just kind of became his band."

Andy Warhol?

"We still see him often. He's very kind."

I saw you moving around on your solos.

"That's because I was staggering."

The second set opened with "White Light, White Heat." Beer and wine were now being freely dispensed. The crowd had grown and loosened up considerably. Five minutes of "White Light" — then "in the same vein..." — "Waiting for my Man." They were really burning as the eager crowd screamed approval.

This set was much more raucous as the Velvets warmed to the task; opening up some, they presented songs from all the records. They kept the crowd with them all the way.

> **I pounded my pen in time with the beat so hard it broke.**

Sustained applause brought the encore — "Heroin." They finished off then, saying they couldn't follow that. Only two or three groups in the world could. I pounded my pen in time with the beat so hard it broke. A landmark performance from an outstanding band.

Liberty Hall pulled a real coup in landing the Velvet Underground. They follow strength with strength bringing in Freddie King this weekend. Then the Flaming Groovies on September 3-4. John Baldry on the 10th and 11th. Wishbone Ash will perform on the 8th and 9th. And then Atomic Rooster comes in the 17th and 18th.

An outrageous lineup and one meriting full support. -30-

Ad: August 28, 1969.

Dripping Springs Reunion

John M. Lomax • April 6, 1972

D RIPPING SPRINGS, Texas — Three weeks back — and three years after Woodstock — Bidy and I went to the Dripping Springs Reunion. It was held in a masochist's dream spot — a pit of dust, dirt, and rocks 29 miles west of Austin on a 7,000 acre ranch the promoters had shrewdly retained for a mere $42,000 — a rental fee possibly less than the current market price for barren scrub brush land in central Texas.

The four thirtyish Dallas promoters bandied figures about — like 60,000 per day for the largest C&W festival ever. More pragmatic planners, however, had prepared facilities and security for 26,000 per day, in accordance with the newly passed Texas Mass Gathering Act which covers events lasting longer than 12 hours or with crowds above 6,000.

So they cleared the fest through state, county, and local channels; spent an estimated million dollars preparing the roads from the paved local byways to the site, securing top talent, erecting a giant permanent wooden stage slanted like a gaping mouth (probably being used right now as a podium from which to address the area's cattle); fenced everything either in or out; hauled in 200 portable crappers, drinking fountains, and concessions, and eagerly awaited the redneck dollars to come pouring in.

Everything was handled professionally save for the advertising, which at times seemed to depend on osmosis, rumor, and a whisper campaign; no discounts were offered to students or the military on the $26 total tab or the $10 single day tariff. A big press party was thrown the night before in Austin, but by then it was a mite late for the journalists to spread the word. Sure did enjoy the free beer and barbecue, though.

The highlight of the bash for me was a trip to the restroom which I shared with James Street and Pete Lammons, two

Bill Monroe is rightly known as the father of bluegrass.

of the University of Texas football team's oldies but goldies. The lads were discussing a date Pete had gotten James in New York with a young woman who had failed to come across with the poozle sandwich James had been promised. I haven't heard such vulgar, unintelligible gibberish from the most zitzed out A-head; the entire conversation consisted of the following words:

"Shit, Pete, she fuckin' didn't fuck me you s.o.b."

"Fuck James, it's not my fuckin' fault you didn't get any fuckin' pussy goddam it you fucker."

St. Patrick's Day was Day 1, and we motored out before the 1 p.m. start to watch the last-minute preparations and to avoid the crowds. Today was bluegrass day with an all-star lineup of chaps like Don Reno & the Tennessee Cutups, James Monroe and the Bluegrass Boys, Lester Flatt, Jim and Jesse McReynolds, Jimmie Martin, and the Earl Scruggs Revue — all of whom have been "into" the form for at least 20 years. The style itself originally featured a quintet, consisting of acoustic guitar, fiddle, banjo, mandolin, and string bass, but has changed over the years to accommodate electricity, and in some cases, drums. In the hands of skilled masters such as these men bluegrass becomes a musical form every bit as interesting and exciting as the best of psychedelic rock.

After all the early afternoon acts had performed, 18 of the best pickers came back onstage for a jam session with three fiddlers, three banjos, guitars, mandolins, dobros, and drums. All the men on stage had at one time been members of Bill Monroe's group. He is rightly known as the father of bluegrass, spawning so many of the top talents in the field that his name has become synonymous with the style.

As darkness descended, Charlie Rich, a very classy incredibly overlooked singer/writer/pianist, loped out for his turn. The only jazz of the weekend twinkled out of his keys mainly

in tight duets with his electric bass. A long time ago Charlie had a hit with "Lonely Weekends."

> Well I make it all right
> from Monday mornin' to Friday night
> But ooooooohhhh those lonely weekends

Every event has its climax, and at Dripping Springs it was the Earl Scruggs Revue consisting of Earl, three of his sons, fiddler Vassar Clements, Jody Maphis on drums, Josh Graves' dobro, and Bob Wilson at the ivory 88's. Five longhairs, dapper Earl, Vasser, the image of a linebacker, and Josh in green/black iridescent splendor matched only by the singing ranger Hank Snow's hot pink suit with silver sequins, set off with copious amounts of glitter. To say Scruggs' band plays bluegrass is to call the Grateful Dead a rock group. The comparison fits, Jerry Garcia came to rock through bluegrass; to study the form without coming across Earl Scruggs would be to study sex research methodology and ignore Alfred Kinsey. And would it be too far-fetched to suggest that Earl's sons are quite familiar with the work of the Dead?

The instrumental lineup consists of a frontline unequaled in popular music — Earl's banjo, Vasser's fiddle, the talking dobro in Josh's capable hands, an elite corps of offspring who literally learned from the masters. I also noted the unexpected presence of young freaks in the backup portions of the bands. This age span gives the groups a 40-year variation and allows them to combine experience and exuberance, something found in no rock group except for Spirit, whose drummer is 50.

It would be futile to try to give a rundown on each performance but you may be interested to know that the following stars performed at Dripping Springs: Roger Miller, Waylon Jennings (Buddy Holly's bass player), Sonny James, Loretta Lynn, Kris Kristofferson, Charlie Walker, Kenneth Threadgill, Willie Nelson, Tom T. Hall, and Buck Owens. The combined attendance for the festival's last two days was 20,000 or so — a far cry from expectations.

Since the promoters cleared the area after each day's activities, there was no overnight camping or resultant feelings of community. Those who did come put up with a few minor hassles, like sitting either in the dirt or on rocks since the seating area was as comfortable as a gravel pit. There were no grass or trees to lend comfort or shade in the 90-degree heat. The sponsors had advertised grassy slopes for seating but later found themselves unable to grow anything on the skinned West Texas soil. No one else has been able to grow grass on top of rocks in this baked land where even the cactus has a tough go. If you were shrewd enough to lug in a chair, sunshade and cooler you were faced with a half-mile walk from the parking area to the site. You hauled in a cooler because Dripping Springs is dry — no beer was sold at the fest. (A rather odd circumstance to be found in the middle of a C&W gathering. And in the heart of the country of 1,100 springs as well!)

There were no births, deaths, fights, or public displays of affection. Winner of best song title was Jimmie Martin with his offering of "I Wish I was Sixteen Again and Knew What I Know Now." So many armed guards were present, either on foot or atop a horse with a walkie-talkie, that a determined smoker of the devil weed had no choice at all save for locked seclusion in a Port-A-Can, certainly not the weedhead's idea of smoker's paradise.

Next year they may have the Reunion in the Dome: now won't that be a country setting? In view of the Harlingen fiasco last week, it is obvious that the laws regarding music festivals are selectively enforced. The C&W crowd had its chance and it muffed it: how about letting the kids have a rock festival now? Oh, I almost forgot, they would have too much fun. If there is anything going on where the young have a good time then our discipline-enforce-punish-work-consume-oriented society gets stirred up enough to pass some new laws to prevent people from enjoying themselves and their bodies.

Laugh and sing now before it's illegal. -30-

Dripping Springs Reunion. Photos by John M. Lomax.

Special Report: Celebration of Life

Jim Shannon • July 6, 1971

POINT COUPEE PARISH, Louisiana — It went like this. Two years ago, Peter Fonda and Dennis Hopper were making a movie about Amerika, and picked Point Coupee Parish, Louisiana, as the site of the resultant *Easy Rider* massacre. Scared rural people rudely murder two psychedelic bikers; an alcoholic lawyer along for the ride is killed with an axe.

The last week of June 1971, promoters staged a "Celebration of Life" rock festival, and chose Point Coupee Parish, Louisiana, as the site. Between 50-75,000 young people from all over the country gathered on a grassy peninsula to experience what was advertised as "eight days in the country at the time of the solstice." To aid their enjoyment of the country, the promoters agreed to provide some 45 rock bands and a circus carnival, in exchange for $28 from each festival goer, or $30 at the gate, if you neglected to buy in advance.

The festival was originally advertised to be held on an island, but promoters turned inland due to legal hassles. Point Coupee Parish was an alternate site pressed into service less than a week before the scheduled opening of the event. Local authorities tried to stop the festival and it looked like they were going to succeed, until a federal judge ruled that the festival could go on.

Finally, three days after the festival was supposed to start, the crowd was allowed to enter the site. The delay had slowed the operation down to the point where the stage was not half built and water and sanitation facilities were grossly inadequate. By Wednesday, the situation looked pretty grim. Music and water seemed a long way off, and the security force hired by the promoters appeared bent on brutality.

Motorcycle gangs from all over the South were there to make sure the freaks didn't step out of line. They carried large wooden clubs and were eager to use them. Some victims required hospitalization, and many more were simply bummed out by this senseless violence. The lessons of the past concerning bikers at festivals were ignored by the promoters.

The situation came to a head when local law enforcement officers advised the gangsmen to leave. Faced with machine guns stuck in their guts, they complied. Their parting threats ("We're coming back with a thousand bikers") never materialized.

> **Motorcycle gangs were there to make sure the freaks didn't step out of line.**

Meanwhile, inside the site, camps started springing up: tents, campers, makeshift lean-tos, old parachutes. Modern to primitive, a city was being built. Thousands of people, milling around, smoking dope, swimming naked in the river, waiting for something to happen. Rumors floated around like smoke at a forest fire. "Grand Funk's playin' tonite," or "the Rolling Stones are flying in tonight." Nobody knew anything, everybody knew everything; no one was really sure what was happening, but all agreed: Let it happen!

Slowly but surely, a stage was built, and the P.A. was installed by Thursday night. (A Tuesday storm blew down a tower, seriously injuring two, and setting the construction back a day.) The crowd swelled to over 50,000, every one of them passing through the main gate with ticket in hand. (Many tickets were resold by the bikers, although the promoters' estimate that $200,000 was ripped off seems unlikely.)

At any rate, a lot of money was collected from the crowd that wasn't put back into the festival. Agents from the Internal Revenue Service finally arrived on the site to seize the gate receipts to insure tax payments, but the promoters had split with the loot. Consequently, there wasn't any money to spend on the festival, in spite of the fact that tens upon thousands of people paid good money to get in. This created a lot of problems, and finally resulted in the festival being shut down after Sunday night's concert — only four days after the stage became functional.

* * * * *

I hope the above portion of this report established some sort of idea in your head of the official scene at Celebration. The next part is pretty tricky...

Once they entered the festival site, the celebrators realized that this wasn't going to be all that it was made out to be. The 700-acre site was traversed by a few small dirt roads, and was natural except for a few tents and the scaffolding that marked the beginning of a stage. A dozen Porta-Cans were there for your enjoyment, as well as a water truck. There was no sign of a circus or carnival, save for a lone elephant being led around the grounds by an elderly trainer.

A craft bazaar had been set up on an outer edge of the site, and a lot of people camped out near there, as it was close to the water so necessary for daytime survival. Without a place to swim, the heat would no doubt have taken a much higher toll. The Atchafalaya River runs through Point Cou pee, and has a reputation among area residents as running big and wild. State officials warned of the dangers of the river's swift currents and undertows, but swimmers paid little heed. After all, it was hot as hell and there wasn't much else to do besides get naked and swim.

By Friday afternoon, two young men had drowned. One body was recovered after four days in the water. The word spread. Bummer. Big city flashback: Nameless, faceless death. The white sandy beaches remained full throughout the entire event; if anything, each day won new troops to their ranks.

The county regulars came out to see the "nekkid hippie sunbathers," cruising downstream in their motorboats, coming as close as they dared. Curious fear forced an air of restraint, as being confronted with hundreds of Amerika's children frolicking in the muddy Atchafalaya might very well tend to do.

The county regulars came out to see the 'nekkid hippie sunbathers.'

When the festival site was first announced, there was mutual apprehension from festival-bound youths and the awaiting Parish. As soon as it became apparent that the thing was gonna' happen, tensions generally melted. People could easily see that the freaks were getting a raw deal — having to camp on a gravel road for a week before they finally allowed the festival to begin, all the while holding your ticket that cost you a hard-earned $28 back at the record shop in Baltimore or Detroit or Miami or Houston.

There was no hostility directed at the people — maybe every longhaired beard wearer isn't another Charles Manson. In Morganza, the closest town of any size, we stopped for food at a little cafe called Melancon's. As could be expected, their usual customers were joined by a substantial number of young people who looked like they had just come from a rock festival. The scene right off reminded me of Easy Rider, that cafe scene immediately preceding death. The air was electric, with the freaks and all, and a back wall sported a movie poster: Peter Fonda and Dennis Hopper, *Easy Rider*!

No, it couldn't be — wait, see that framed photo hanging over the center booth, isn't that Captain Amerika and the lady standing there behind the cash register. We turned incredulously to the old woman, scarcely able to open our mouths before she said in a triumphant voice, "That's right, it was right here. As a matter of fact, this gentleman coming up right now was one of the actors."

Through the window we could see a battered Japanese motorcycle (about 350 cc) pulling up, its lone occupant a man in his late 30s, wearing a conservative version of the Easy Rider helmet, blue and white and red, but no stars. Directed over to where we were sitting, he strode up importantly and asked, "You wanta know about the movie?" He responded to our quick nods

A man went looking for America. And couldn't find it anywhere...

"A LYRIC, TRAGIC SONG OF THE ROAD"
—LIFE

"A VIBRANT, BRUTAL VISUAL ESSAY. ONE HELL OF A TRIP!"
—PLAYBOY

{ CANNES FILM FESTIVAL WINNER }
"Best Film By a New Director"

PANDO COMPANY in association with
RAYBERT PRODUCTIONS presents

easy rider PETER FONDA · DENNIS HOPPER JACK NICHOLSON
Written by   Directed by   Produced by   Associate Producer   Executive Producer
PETER FONDA   DENNIS HOPPER   PETER FONDA   WILLIAM HAYWARD   BERT SCHNEIDER   COLOR
DENNIS HOPPER
TERRY SOUTHERN   [R] RESTRICTED — Persons under 16 not admitted, unless accompanied by parent or adult guardian   Released by COLUMBIA PICTURES

delman theatre | 4412 S. Main (opening soon)

Ad: September 12, 1969.

by saying "... Yeah, I'm the one who chopped Jack Nicholson up with an axe."

"Oh, really," was the only response I could weakly muster.

"Actually, that Jack Nicholson is a real nice fellow, me and him hit it off real good. They wanted me to go back to Hollywood to be in the movies. I was sitting over in that booth right over there with the sheriff in the movie, talking about Yankee queers and all — you remember?" he asked.

In unison: "We remember." Finally brave enough to pose a question, I respectfully inquired, "Do you think the film portrayed the people around here in a fair and accurate manner, with the killing and all?"

"Yes," he came back quickly, "I think it is pretty accurate for two years ago. 'Course that was before any of the boys in town had long hair, except for a couple of troublemakers trying to embarrass their parents. That made it a pretty bad thing around here, so two longhairs flying through here ran a good chance of getting shot. It's different today, cause some of the good boys in town are starting to wear their hair long, and everybody knows they're good boys so it's all right. These kids coming through here now are nice and polite just like everybody else, at least 95 percent of 'em are. It's that other five percent that uses narcotics and starts trouble, they're the ones we want to kill."

Equipped with this knowledge, we hurriedly choked down the rest of our food, which was neither better nor worse than that to which we were accustomed, and much cheaper than that on the site. We paused briefly to snap some pictures, and split.

* * * * * *

Our axe murderer's attitudes seemed to be reflected somewhat in the actions of the local police, though their figures on the percentage of troublemakers were a little higher than 5 percent.

At the beginning of the festival, the prevailing mood among the force made up of state police and local sheriffs was one of curious detachment, as they complied with a court order barring the start of Celebration. They didn't seem to really want the thing stopped, they just wanted to go home. They didn't have to get shitty with the people — the bikers were more than capable of doing that.

After the police decided that the brutality of the gangs was too much, they ran them out of the area. They themselves then turned to dogs and horses and shotguns and machine guns and mace and sticks to preserve "order." The scene at the site's only gate was a perpetual bust, as a rowdy crowd of

narcs and uniformed pigs selectively busted and harassed people entering and leaving the site. Many people were arrested (about 170 in all) and most charges were the usual "failure to move on" or "disorderly conduct." One girl was arrested for screaming as her boyfriend or husband or whatever was being savagely beaten. She was charged with "inciting to riot."

Most cops were camera shy and harassed photographers trying to capture the busts on film. I was stopped and had my film seized. It took me a couple of minutes to talk them out of my camera; they gleefully exposed my film and I split, keeping my thoughts to myself.

Space City! photographer Dennis Hunt wasn't nearly so lucky. Astride his bicycle by the gate, he was busily snapping pictures when he was spotted and run down by a pig on horseback. He was then put in a paddy wagon and driven to Lafayette, about 60 miles away. The charge: "resisting arrest." (Also arrested about the same time was a photographer for United Press International.) Hunt's original bail of $3,000 was quickly lowered by a higher judge, and he was released the next day. A trial date has yet to be set.

A lot of Hunt's film was ruined, but some of the remaining shots appear with this story. As you might expect, most of the good stuff was ruined. To finish off a real nightmare story, when he returned for his bike, it had been stolen.

Police roamed the site infrequently, staying mostly around the outer perimeter inside their vehicles looking for naked hippies to ogle. They had an elaborate encampment right outside the gates, equipped with a mobile crime lab and other goodies. There were many reports of pigs confiscating beer from those with a legal right to it (18 and over in Louisiana) to drink for themselves. There are no confirmed reports as to what they did with all the dope they ripped off, and I wouldn't even like to speculate.

In summation, if you stayed well inside the site and didn't take pictures or ask questions at the gate and had some degree of luck, you were generally safe — except from the many narcs circulating among the people, in search of dope.

As far as dope goes, there was plenty. The dope famine has lifted somewhat and lots of good marijuana was going around for what one might expect to pay during a normal season. Hashish and mescaline were plentiful, and beyond that you paid your money and you took your chances. A lot of speedy acid, some poison snuff, animal tranquilizers (PCP) being sold widely as THC (rare substance in chemical form), as well as pills of every variety — ups, downs, pain pills, you name it.

> 'I'm the one who chopped Jack Nicholson up with an axe.'

Death drugs made the scene: ugly smack was occasionally offered by a passing hawker. The heroin epidemic spread to the festival; sooner or later it will directly confront our new culture. For the present at least, it remains in the background.

*****

The promoters knew they couldn't produce what they promised.

That brings us to: the music. Undoubtedly the biggest factor in luring all those people in for such a high price ($28 is a lot to your average freak) was the big name entertainment offered, along with a circus and other goodies. The promoters, despite the slick promises of the advertising, didn't produce, preferring to split with the dough. Anything good about the festival happened because of the people, not the promoters. Here, in pseudo-documentary form, is the story of the great Celebration of Life Music Rip-off.

Ten days before the festival started, the promoters were supposed to pay the groups they had signed 25 percent of the money they would receive for playing, as a guarantee that the thing was still going to happen. This way, if the promoters were to call the thing off, the groups wouldn't lose all the money they could have gotten playing another gig. This protects both the promoter and the group, giving the latter legal recourse on a breach of contract suit, should the group fail to show. All of this isn't particularly groovy, but it happens to be the way the rock and roll business functions at this time. Anyway, 10 days before the festival started there was no confirmed site. The promoters did not pay the 25 percent deposit required by the contracts, so the groups were not obliged to appear.

The promoters decided to do the show anyway, knowing that they would not be able to produce what they had promised. The mass audience was not aware of this, however, and those so inclined packed off for the event.

Thursday night rolled around before the stage was ready. I didn't return to the site until Friday, so I can't guarantee the accuracy of these reports, but I understand that John Sebastian, Chuck Berry, and Eric Burdon played that first night.

One source quoted John Sebastian as saying (predictably) "I just gotta' say one thing: You people are far out!"

Chuck Berry, I am told, was something else. "The high point of the festival – everything from there was downhill." "Berry was fuckin' outasite." "Chuck Berry was damned good." I didn't see him. These people did.

Friday night came and went, and nothing spectacular happened in between.

Only three groups made it up on stage, and they didn't do much for me. Bloodrock opened, and the former Crowd Plus One failed to impress a majority of the crowd. Their popularity seems to be based on little more than hype of the Grand Funk variety: both groups share a common bond, manager Terry Knight. Mediocre at best.

Ad: October 28, 1971.

A new Warner Brothers group followed them, a band called Stoneground (seen here recently with Mother Earth). They were hastily assembled for last summer's Caravan of Love, a rock festival traveling across the country to be filmed for a big-profit movie. They also failed to impress; under different circumstances, I would listen again, but they hardly seemed up to entertaining 50,000 stoned people.

The last group to play Friday was the Amboy Dukes from Detroit. (Some of you might remember them from their Of Our Own gig last fall.) Lead guitarist Ted Nugent played essentially the same freakout and everybody went to sleep.

No groups were able to play during the day. The main stage was set up to run at night, according to the MCs, and a smaller jam stage didn't start functioning until the last day of the festival. As a result, many good groups didn't get a chance to play. The groups that were not widely known that made it to the main stage were able to do so because their record companies paid the promoters money.

ZZ Top, London Records recording artists from Houston, sat backstage for four days and weren't allowed to play. Two other Houston groups were invited to play at the festival, but never played. Saturnalia and Stone Axe both made two trips each to the site, at considerable personal expense, only to find out that it was "no go." Some groups coming from as far away as New York got the same deal. The promoters' bullshit hurt a lot of people.

Just who were these promoters? Steve Kapelow, a real estate heir from New Orleans, was one of the chief men behind the thing. He's sitting down in Jamaica right now, avoiding arrest. John Brower of Toronto, who had previously put on the Strawberry Fields festival, was also involved. I don't know his current location.

The two men who split with the bread were not Brower or Kapelow: they followed their money out of the country. The reason there was no money to spend on the festival was not due to a lack of paying customers; it was apparently decided to protect the investment rather than the people. The reason sanitation facilities were never adequate, or showers ever constructed, or that the water trucks left on Sunday morning, or that free-kitchen supplies had to be begged for from the crowd, was because the money was taken. Cat Stevens and Leon Russell both showed up and soon realized they wouldn't be paid, so they hit the road.

Saturday night rolled around, and the music slate looked somewhat better. A group called Fire & Wind played first; I doubt if they'll ever be heard from again.

Country Joe MacDonald performed and was simply superb. Doing his stand-up guitar and harmonica trip alone on the stage, he reminded me strongly of early sixties folksingers. He wound his way through a number of new originals and old favorites, including "Not-so-Sweet-Lorraine," world famous Country Joe and the Fish tune. He finished up a fine set with the FUCK cheer and the inevitable "Feel-Like-I'm-Fixin'-To-Die-Rag." Just like in Woodstock (sigh).

Next up was Potliquor from nearby Baton Rouge. Some Houston people were familiar with this group from their recent appearances at Of Our Own. Their sound is definitely influenced by the area from whence they arose; their performance was well received. The hit group of the night (and of the festival) was the Chambers Brothers, perhaps the most widely-respected black rock group around today. Their solid repertoire was enhanced by an improved percussion section, with a new drummer and an added conga player (reportedly Richie Havens' ex-conga man). The group came on strong and hard; a fine version of Otis Redding's "I Can't Turn You Loose" was received with standing applause. Forty-five minutes of "Love, Peace & Happi-

Cat Stevens and Leon Russell both showed up and soon realized they wouldn't be paid, so they hit the road.

ness" wasn't far behind; if you've ever heard it you can dig what I'm talking about.

For me, the low point of the set was the first encore. They ran back on stage and announced that they were going to play a new song they had written for the occasion, titled, ironically enough, "Celebration of Life." It sounded like a movie theme song. This was an attempt to raise Woodstock consciousness among an audience bent on having a good time, putting the promoters in a good light for making the thing happen. "Yesterday a young man drowned in the river, but tonight a baby was born. It's a Celebration of Life." Yes, at $28 a shot with few bands or Porta-Cans and not too much to eat or drink — truly a celebration. A celebration of money.

Tony Joe White and a group called Glass Harp also played, but I fell asleep and can offer no report.

Black Oak Arkansas and Jump were the first two groups Sunday, and they bored me to the point I got up and left. Les Moore, a folksinger from New Orleans, was introduced as "A good friend of ours who plays at Andy's on Bourbon Street." He played in a style that somewhat resembled Arlo Guthrie, but was significantly his own. I rather enjoyed his set, although cries of Boogie! were heard during some songs. What really hurt him was the fact that he was brought out for four encores, not by the audience but by the MC.

Lou Weinstock, who was the chief announcer, was really on a groovy trip, man. He made the whole scene just like Woodstock — or at least he tried to live up to the announcers of festivals past. It just didn't work. He would come out of his air-conditioned Winnebago motor home parked backstage, walk up to the mike and proclaim, "We're all here sweating it out with the rest of you people. If you can take it, so can we." Blah-blah-blah. "We're just people like the rest of you. We're really trying to get this thing together." As long as it doesn't mean we have to spend some of the money we took from you.

"There's a dude walking around the audience taking up a collection for the free kitchen. If you people want to eat, let's give them a hand." The promoters couldn't spare any money for the free kitchen; it would hurt concession sales.

As a result, the "free" kitchen was never able to serve anything to any more than a small number of people. "When you really come down to it, we have had a Celebration of Life. Life has its ups and downs, so do we." Ups like 75,000 freaks getting it on together, downs like a small group of businessmen getting it off with a lot of money.

Les Moore and the four encores would be a tough act to follow; you need someone like Melanie. Twilight falls across the land; Melanie walks not far behind. She looked small up on the stage, but when she opened her mouth and sang — wow, no words accurately describe the magic spell she held over the large crowd. A song list wouldn't help much here. If you are turned on to Melanie, my words may seem to be senseless babble. If you have not yet been turned on to Melanie, it is possible that my words may also seem like senseless babble, but Melanie is fine.

You might remember a fellow from the Steve Miller Band of a few years back, a guitar player named Boz Scaggs. He's got a new group together, and they took the stage after Melanie. A brass section, whose arrangements at times reminded me of early Chicago, was interestingly contrasted against the guitar and organ. Scaggs' unusual vocal style reminded you that this was a group with its own identity, not a mixture of old sounds. They played too long, considering the number of groups still left to perform, and were called out for too many encores by the MCs.

From here on out, it all is fuzzy. Scaggs finished about one in the morning and was followed by Delanie & Bonnie & Friends, Stephen Stills, and the Chambers Brothers back for a second night. It was getting near sunrise as the Chambers Brothers finished up, and shortly thereafter I regained consciousness, after a turbulent sleep.

It's A Beautiful Day was scheduled to play next, but two members were going to be late, clearing the stage for one of the rare treats of the festival — the appearance of singer-guitarist Tim Dawe. This fine performer was backed up by Beautiful Day musicians, bassist Mitchell Holman and guitarist Hal Wagenet. The three played electric instruments without a drummer. Most memorable was Dawe's tune "Hotel Ne'er-do-well," about a cat named Junkie John: "When John came into a room, you got the feeling somebody got up and left." Big city blues, blues of a culture infested with killer dope.

The last two groups to play were Beautiful Day and Brownsville Station. Both groups have done concerts in Houston this year that have been reviewed in *Space City!* Their performances differed little from those concert gigs, and have already become irrelevant to me.

Were the people burned? Yes, definitely. With so much offered and so little produced, nobody got what they expected. At the same time, the burn didn't keep anybody from having a good time. Face it, anytime you get that many freaks together for that long, it's going to be some kind of alright. The people were turned on to each other in spite of the promoters. In that lies the best of the festival, and in that lies anything that you can come close to calling a celebration.

Celebration of Life. Photos by Galen Scott, Dennis Hunt, Galen Scott, and Susie LeBlanc, July 6, 1971.

When it was announced Sunday that this would be the last day of the festival, there was no uproar. "We ran out of money," was the feeble explanation from the stage. "We ran out with the money" would have been more like it.

I'll close with some memorable quotes.

> We have great sympathy for the young people who have paid to attend this festival. They have been exploited by promoters of a multi-million dollar enterprise, who had no site or permit when tickets were sold … The Almighty dollar prevails. The situation is out of our hands.
> — *Statement from Point Coupee Parish Police Jury on the Celebration of Life.*

And finally, from the promoters' pre-festival hype:

> Keep the faith, baby, and dig a different kind of vacation.

B.B. King, the Beach Boys, Ballin' Jack, Alex Taylor, Canned Heat, the Flying Burrito Brothers, Ike & Tina Turner, John Lee Hooker, Kate Taylor, Miles Davis, Pink Floyd, Ravi Shankar, Richie Havens, Roland Kirk, Taj Mahal, Sly and the Family Stone, Johnny Winter, Edgar Winter's White Trash, Quicksilver Messenger Service, Cat Stevens, Leon Russell.

That's a pretty impressive list. It's also the list of the advertised groups that didn't show. They weren't replaced by other big names. They were primarily responsible for drawing the crowd to the site. Minds no doubt wandered over the list many times before $28 was plunked down for a green piece of paper. -30-

Don McLean Sings 'Tapestry' and Yodels

Scout Schacht • April 13, 1972

Don McLean came to the Music Hall last Sunday night with his banjo and guitar, some old folk songs and some original ones not so famous as "American Pie."

Hearing that song on the radio and hearing it live is the difference between frozen and fresh baked. McLean is a smiling youth who reminds me of Donovan and Arlo Guthrie. The opening number was "Castles in the Air," an expression to get to know the country, from his new album entitled *Tapestry* that someone told me was recorded before American Pie. Many of his songs are beautiful subtle protests that tell us to look at what we are doing to the earth and each other. "Three Flights Up" is a ballad that stresses lack of communication, although we have all the modern means.

He picked up his banjo and played "Old Joe Clark" and woke everybody up on the second row. The audience was very receptive to Don and he got us to sing "What the Lord Has Done For Me." "Tapestry," the title song, was next, and it's one of the best songs/poems I've heard lately:

> You're now just a stagnant and
>   rancid disgrace
>
> That is rapidly drowning the whole
>   human race
>
> Every fish that swims silent every
>   bird that flies freely

> Every doe that steps softly every
>   crisp leaf that falls
>
> All the flowers that grow on this
>   colorful tapestry
>
> Somehow they know that if man is
>   allowed to destroy all we need
>
> He will soon have to pay with his
>   life for his greed

Danny says that Don McLean reminds him of a young more morose Pete Seeger. Pete Seeger says that "Don is a normal, talented, unpretentious, nervous, relaxed musician trying to use his songs to help people survive in these perilous times. I got to know him best as a volunteer crewman aboard the Sloop Clearwater in 1969. Hauling on ropes by day, singing every evening at a different post and every morning up early to scrub decks and raise the sail."

Don ended up his set with "T for Texas" (he really yodels), a song about the Texas rivers, and an "American Pie" sing-along. Took an encore singing "Worried Man Blues," and said he'd be back. He seemed to like us as much as we liked him. Catch his set sometime. -30-

[Scout later wrote under the byline "Scout Stoumen Reed."]

Art: Kerry Fitzgerald, September 12,1969.

Tary Owens, who wrote about music for *Space City!* and for a time served as the paper's music editor, became a celebrated music historian, archivist, and producer and was himself a musician. Owens received a Lomax Foundation grant (See *Space City!* music critic John Lomax elsewhere on these pages) to research and record roots musicians in Central Texas. His field recordings are archived at the Briscoe Center for American History at the University of Texas. According to the Texas State Historical Association, "Owens not only documented the music of [historically important] artists, but also helped revive their performing careers…"

Tary Owens is in the *Austin Chronicle*'s Texas Music Hall of Fame and was one of the first 10 inductees into the Austin Music Memorial, recognizing individuals "who have made important contributions to the development of music in Austin." Tary Owens died of cancer on September 21, 2003.

Rockin' with Angela

Tary Owens • July 6, 1972

Back in 1966, when the Texas music revolution was just starting, I played in an Austin band called the Southern Flyers. What we lacked in talent and experience we made up in enthusiasm and became a fairly popular local band. Spurred on by local success, California dreams, and assorted herbs, we decided to move our band to San Francisco and seek our fortune.

After all, several of our Austin friends, such as Janis Joplin, Steve Miller, Powell St. John, and Doug Sahm, had gone to San Francisco and were doing quite well. Why couldn't we do it too? We had a fine woman singer named Angela Strehli, who could wail the blues with the best of them, but the rest of the band was largely inexperienced in rock and roll. Most of us had just traded our acoustic guitars for electricity and just weren't ready for the high-charged competition of San Francisco in 1967.

After three months of starving with no gigs in San Francisco, the Southern Flyers went their separate ways. Angela moved to Los Angeles, started Angela and the Rockets, and began paying her dues.

For the last five years Angela has been playing the circuit between Texas and California, changing musicians, shaping her style, and biding her time. Playing every small club and blues bar between Houston and L.A., she has slowly developed a unique sound, soulful and hard as well as sensual. Today she has emerged as perhaps the best white blues singer since Janis.

Angela has a style all her own; she was greatly influenced by such singers as Big Mama Thornton, Coco Taylor, and Tina Turner, but she has nurtured a distinctive sound and has avoided falling into anyone else's bag.

Most of the time, Angela's old man, Lewis, works with her, his excellent harmonica adding a superb contrast to her voice. Lately, though, Lewis has been working with the Austin blues group, Storm, while Angela has been singing mostly with soul bands such as James Polk and the Brothers. This weekend they will be back together again as Angela and the Rockets play at Miss Irene's, Friday through Sunday.

> ## She could wail the blues with the best of them.

Miss Irene's has recently reopened under the management of Rocky Hill and Dale Sofar of the Old Quarter. They promise to present the best of the blues every week, following the tradition set by Miss Irene and Clifton Chenier in 1946.

This weekend is a great one for blues in Houston. In addition to Angela and the Rockets' appearance, Mance Lipscomb will be at the Old Quarter Saturday night, Muddy Waters is at La Bastille, and Rocky Hill will play at Sandee's. It will be possible to get a complete history of the blues and rock and roll this weekend, from the beginnings in the Delta and Brazos River bottoms to the sounds of today.

Last week I said that rock and roll is not dead and you could prove it by attending some of the shows in town recently. Well, this is The Blues Are Alive and Well Week in Houston. Get up off of your apathy and go to any of these shows and catch some of the real excitement of the blues. Mance Lipscomb is 77 years old this year and still going strong; Angela is only a baby in her twenties, but she is one of the sexiest, most real female singers around — a natural-born blues singer. Don't let her get away without catching her act.
-30-

The Band. Art by Kerry Fitzgerald, November 22, 1969.

Rocky Hill: Stirring Up the Ghosts

Tary Owens • May 4, 1972

The Rocky Hill Band, at the Old Quarter and Irene's Club, April 21, 22, 23.

Last Friday and Saturday night the Old Quarter was packed with ghosts; the ghosts of dead but not forgotten bluesmen, resurrected through the guitar and voice of Rocky Hill.

Rocky has been around a long time, playing professionally since his early teens. In his first bands with his brother Dusty (now with ZZ Top), Rocky played rock 'n roll music — with large doses of blues and country music thrown in.

His first influence was Jimmy Reed. Soon he was playing the music of his biggest hero, the legendary Eddie Cochran of "Summertime Blues," "Sittin' in the Balcony" and "Somethin' Else" fame. When he gets drunk Rocky will tell you that that's where he's coming from, that all of his music and much of his personal attitude is a continuance of the spirit of Eddie Cochran.

Later on, Rocky was affected more and more by blues and he played with Freddy King. In the early 1960s, the Beatles and Stones became a major influence and Rocky's band was called The Warlocks. Later it became The American Blues with Rocky on guitar and vocals, Dusty on bass and vocals and Frank Beard on drums. They worked around Dallas and Fort Worth, mostly at the Cellar, playing their own music as well as Dylan, the Beatles, the Stones, the blues, psychedelic music and, of course, Eddie Cochran.

They began to attract a large following. They dyed their hair blue for publicity, becoming even more popular and more freaky. In 1967, they played the Fillmore West, backing Freddie King, and later, made a couple of albums of their own. But the craziness and drugs caught up with Rocky, and he ended up in a mental hospital.

After his release, Rocky found he had forgotten how to play the guitar (shock treatments do weird things to your memory) and began the long, painful task of learning to play all over again. Meanwhile, Dusty and Frank began playing with Billy Gibbons in ZZ Top and became rock 'n roll stars, at least in the Texas scene.

It's taken Rocky more time, but in the end it all may be worth it.

In his process of relearning, Rocky moved away from the Clapton-Hendrix mold of psychedelic rock and became immersed in the blues. He began playing the music of the blues masters: Robert Johnson, Elmore James, Muddy Waters, Freddie King, Otis Rush, Albert Collins, B.B. and Albert King. And in the process, he absorbed much of their spirit as well.

Rocky served an apprenticeship as Lightnin' Hopkins' bass player and then began moving out on his own again, playing solo at the Old Quarter, then sitting in with Zydeco accordionist Willie Stout at Irene's Club. He formed a new band and began working again, taking small jobs around Houston.

His current band consists of Keith Ferguson on bass and Randy "Turtle" DeHart on drums. Keith is a master of the blues bass as well as an informed student and collector of blues records; his driving steady bass is a perfect foil for Rocky's guitar, and his knowledge has helped broaden Rocky's perspective. Turtle, a veteran of several Dallas bands, provides a solid and funky simple beat, and although he occasionally falters, he is able to keep everything together and moving.

Ad: July 6, 1972.

At first, Rocky's playing was erratic; sometimes he could be playing like one of the best and then descend into a flailing monologue of musical nonsense. But this inconsistency has now passed and Rocky has become the peer of Johnny Winter and the late Duane Allman, the only white musicians to become true masters of the blues. Except for Duane and Johnny I can think of no white guitarists who can touch Rocky in the blues idiom. He has his own style now, and when he plays you hear not only echos of every bluesman of the past, but Rocky's own distinct voice and an intimation of the future of the blues.

At the Old Quarter last Friday, things took on a new dimension; Keith had injured his arm and was unable to play, so Rocky's brother Dusty, on vacation from ZZ Top, filled in on bass. Completing the American Blues revival, Frank Beard sat in occasionally on drums.

The Old Quarter was filled with old friends and new expectant fans; they weren't disappointed.

Rocky and his friends played the gamut of their experience, and never has the Old Quarter seen such strong spirits of the past mixed with the electricity of the present. Robert Johnson was there with his slide,

playing "The Preachin' Blues"; so was Elmore James ("When things go wrong, so wrong with you, it hurts me too."); and Eddie Cochran ("She's alright man, she's somethin' else.").

All of the spirits weren't from the dead: Muddy Waters was in attendance; so were Otis Rush, Buddy Guy, Albert King and Albert Collins. But the strongest voice was that of Rocky Hill, finally attaining his place as a major blues man able to stand with the others, regardless of color.

Late Saturday night Dusty joined Rocky on vocals and they completed the circle, bringing back the rock 'n roll hits of their early days, with "Mockingbird," "Lucille," and the Coasters' "Youngblood."

The crowd loved it. They finished with an ironic version of Dylan's "All along the Watchtower."

Sunday night the party moved over to Irene's, the Fourth Ward club where Rocky first introduced his blues band. Irene's Club has been open for over 20 years. The audience is mostly country people from Louisiana, weaned on Clifton Chenier, Lightnin' Hopkins, Willie Stout and Spider Kilpatrick. Now they love Rocky Hill, and Irene's rocks so hard the building shakes with their dancing. -30-

Ad: Art by Kerry Fitzgerald
December 20, 1969.

Big Joe Williams at the Victory Grill in East Austin.
Photo by Burton Wilson from Burton's Book of the Blues, *June 22, 1972.*

Burton's Book of the Blues

Tary Owens • June 22, 1972

Burton's Book of the Blues *by Burton Wilson, with an introduction by Chet Flippo. Speleo Press, Austin.*

Burton Wilson's long-awaited *Book of the Blues* is now out. For the last 10 years Burton has been photographing Texas musicians and his book is as close as you can get to a history of the Texas music scene. More than anything else the book is an excellent chronicle of the Austin scene, how it started, and where it went.

The photographs are fine; they capture the spirit of the '60s as well as anything I can recall. Between 1963 and the present an amazing array of Texas musicians have made Austin their home, or at least their stopping-off place.

Included in Burton's collection are many of the greats of the blues and rock world: Janis Joplin, Muddy Waters, Jimmy Reed, Big Joe Williams, Johnny and Edgar Winter, Freddy King, Otis Spann, Steve Miller, Mance Lipscomb, Robert Shaw, Jerry Garcia, Taj Mahal; the list could go on indefinitely. But the most important aspect of the book is

the accurate representation of a scene; some of the groups are little-known, nationally, and some seem to have little to do with the blues, but all were essential parts of a music phenomenon that grew from a converted gas station to Madison Square Garden.

The book begins with a photo of Janis, who lived in Austin off and on for several years. She began her musical career in Austin in 1962, playing with Lannie Wiggins and Powell St. John in the Waller Creek Boys. Lannie played guitar and banjo, Powell played harp and Janis played autoharp. They all sang, but Janis carried most of the tunes.

They played what was then referred to as folk music, which included Appalachian ballads, the blues, jug band songs, bluegrass and country music, as well as contemporary songs. Included in their repertoire were songs from Woody Guthrie, Lead Belly, Blind Lemon Jefferson, Bessie Smith, the Memphis Jugband, Hank Williams, Bill Monroe, Jimmy Rodgers, and occasionally Bob Dylan or some of their own songs. From this same musical background grew most of the best musicians and singers of the era.

The second photograph is of Kenneth Threadgill, the father of the Austin music scene. Kenneth sings Jimmy Rodgers songs, perhaps better than Jimmy Rodgers did.

His voice is funky yet true, and when he yodels it's like a bell. It was in Kenneth Threadgill's bar on North Lamar that Janis first sang in public and where a whole school of musicians developed. You can still hear Mr. Threadgill sing and sell Lone Star Beer in Austin.

Mance Lipscomb, pictured next, has influenced more musicians than anyone in Texas I can think of; he has been here since the beginning and after more than 100 performances in Austin, still comes back, playing like an 18-year-old and belying his 77 years.

From Threadgill's bar and folk music the Austin scene moved to rock in the mid-60s. The Thirteenth Floor Elevators were among the first acid-rock bands in the country and were the focal point of Texas music for several years. The Elevators preceded Burton's career as a photographer so they are not pictured, but the Conqueroo, who inherited the Elevators' following, are featured prominently.

Other early Texas bands that helped start a revolution were the aforementioned Conqueroo (who were originally a jug band called St. John and the Conqueroo), Shiva's Headband, The Sunnyland Special featuring Angela Strehli, The Southern Flyers, later known as Pure Funk, The Wigs, Jerry Jeff Walker, and Kenneth Threadgill's band, The Hootenanny Hoots.

Some of the blues masters of the Austin area who influenced these bands were Robert Shaw, the king of the barrelhouse piano; Grey Ghost, not pictured; and Teodar Jackson, a fantastic blues fiddler who taught and inspired Spencer Perskin of Shiva's Headband.

(Teodar, pronounced "T Holy," died in 1965 and although he is not pictured, a benefit for him was the first musical event that brought together all the disparate parts of the Austin scene from country, to folk, to blues to rock and featured Austin's first light show. It was at this concert that Janis earned her first standing ovation and rave reviews, some six months before she joined Big Brother and the Holding Company.)

In 1966 and 1967 there was a mass exodus of musicians from Austin to San Francisco. On the West Coast, musicians from all over Texas formed groups and many became nationally known rock and roll stars.

Burton Wilson made several trips to California and photographed many of the members of the Texas musical clan. Among the Texas-California transplants pictured in his book are Mother Earth, with Powell St. John and Tracy Nelson, The Steve Miller Band, Johnny Winter, Freddie King, Cross Country, Pure Funk, Mike Murphy, Boz Scaggs, and The Angel Band (later known as Free Chicken) which featured Powell St. John, Charlie Prichard and Bob Brown, and with whom I had the pleasure of playing bass.

More recently there has been a second wave of bands from Texas who worked the Vulcan Gas Company and later the Armadillo World Headquarters. Among these groups are The Hub City Movers, Greezy Wheels, Krackerjack, ZZ Top (now a national success), and The Brothers.

'Burton's Book of the Blues' is the best chronicle we have.

Finally, Burton's book includes many artists who were not from Texas but passed through and left their mark on Austin's music. Some of them are Big Joe Williams, Muddy Waters, James Cotton, Jimmy Reed, Otis Spann, Doug Kershaw, Fats Domino, Taj Mahal, Earl Scruggs, and from India, the L.D.M. Spiritual Group.

Burton's book, although fantastic, has some important omissions. Doug Sahm and the Sir Douglas Quintet, White Trash, Rocky Hill, Guy Clark, Townes Van Zandt, Hop Wilson, Storm, Jimmy Vaughn, Freda and the Firedogs, Martin Fiero, Bobby Doyle, Big Martha Turner, Wayne Talbot, Freddy Fender, Jerry Fischer, Don Sanders, Rat Creek, Albert Collins, Red Angel, Clifton Chenier, Fred McClain, Minor Wilson (Burton's son), Charlie Mingus, Ornette Colman, Bobby Blue Bland, Buddy Holly, Little Son Jackson, Black Ace, Kris Kristoferson, Joe Tex, and John Clay are a few of the fine Texas musicians who will be featured in Burton's next book.

Until the sequel appears, *Burton's Book of the Blues* is the best chronicle we have.

Texas has produced, and continues to produce, a rare breed of music, with deep roots in country music, the blues, church music, soul, Cajun, Mexican, jazz, and rock and roll. Only in Texas can you find musicians who can play in any of these styles comfortably and without prejudice.

This unique background has produced many of the greats of country music, blues, and rock and roll. Nowhere else can you find such an array of greatness and variety. *Burton's Book of the Blues* is easily the most important book to be published on Texas music, and, perhaps, the most significant era of rock and roll history. It will soon be a collectors' item and even though it costs $5, *Burton's Book of the Blues* is a true bargain. -30-

Space City! and Our Cultural History

Gary Chason

My mother's maiden name was Allen. I was told from an early age that I was a descendant of the Allen brothers, who founded the city of Houston. Aunt Myrtle hoped that I would grow up to be a lawyer and take back the estate that Jesse Jones allegedly stole from the family. My passion however was theater not law so no such lawsuit ever transpired. But I have always had a deep attachment to the city, which is where I currently reside and where I have spent most of my life.

I did spend an uneventful year in New York City in 1969 where I had hoped to pursue my passion for experimental theater in the Off-Off Broadway scene. But, impatient at the absence of directing opportunities there, I figured, "What difference does geography make?" — and moved back to Houston in 1969, where there were more available theaters than eager directors. I didn't need New York to do my work.

Everything seemed new in Houston when I arrived, a city bursting with possibility, recognizing no boundaries, enthusiastically embracing the future. Even gravity was not strong enough to hold us down in Houston, our NASA having just put men on the moon. "One small step for a man, one giant leap for mankind," said the Houstonian as he made the first footprint on the lunar surface. My radical friends who had started the underground newspaper in Austin, *The Rag*, had started another one in Houston, unsurprisingly named *Space City News*. (A legal issue forced them to change the name to *Space City!*) I fell right in with them and felt totally at home.

I wrote film criticism for the paper as I had done for *The Rag* and dove headlong into the local theater scene.

I got a job teaching children at the Alley Theater's Merry-Go-Round School, for which I cut my hair, then got on with challenging the powers at the stone fortress downtown that was the new Alley. I formed Houston Laboratory Theater and produced/directed a machine age Romeo/Juliet at the Jewish Community Center's superb theater, a space that was hungry for somebody like me. Before the show even opened,

> ## I didn't need New York to do my work.

Robert Altman and MGM came to town to make a movie in the Astrodome – the Eighth Wonder of the World, as they called it. I got hired as their Location Casting Director and was launched onto a career in motion pictures that extends to this day.

In my field, theater, so much new stuff was happening that it's easy to forget. Theater Under the Stars was founded and began producing professional musicals in Miller Outdoor Theater for free. A brilliant theater artist, C.C. Courtney, hit town, using the memorable Liberty Hall as his home theater. His first production, "The Earl of Ruston," was a startling, fascinating musical which went on to New York. And he followed that with a Liberty Hall production of "One Flew Over the Cuckoo's Nest," which became the longest running stage show in Houston and probably still holds the record. Then came his less successful but still amazing musical, "Ripped and Wrinkled."

Phil Oesterman created a theater and produced shows for many years. I even got into the action with a highly successful production of Michael McClure's *The Beard* in an art gallery on Alabama Street. Equinox Theater was founded and brought cutting edge material to their venue on Washington Avenue, including two of my original plays, *Charlie's Ear* and *Denizens*.

Mike Condray and associates brought the top musical artists in blues and rock to Liberty Hall for very reasonable prices. Billy Gibbons and Dusty Hill were in the early stages of creating ZZ Top; they're still packing huge venues to enthusiastic audiences. Houston has always been home for many Black musicians, Lightnin' Hopkins being the best-known in that period.

I was part of "the Movement": *Space City!*, its content and the socially-conscious activities it organized created a purpose to which we were all committed. Equality: especially as it pertained to racial and ethnic minorities. Women's rights: the glass ceiling, though still a factor, was being shattered regularly. Now, women are more empowered than they have been in my lifetime with more to come. And their influence in everything, especially politics, is deeply needed.

As we look back after 50 years, even Secretary of Defense Robert McNamara admitted that the War in Vietnam was unjustified, just plain wrong! Gay rights and even gay marriage have become widely accepted. Marijuana is becoming legal in more states every day. Civil rights for persons of color, though still a long way from being complete, are much further along, even to the point of our having had a Black president and now an ethnically diverse woman as vice president. Women's rights have progressed. The "Me Too" movement has put many reprehensible men in jail and opened a lot of minds to the nonchalant disrespect women have endured for decades. Our democracy is currently under siege. We have to continue to be diligent to protect it.

Space City! provided a hugely important voice for all these issues. There was a burgeoning counterculture in the late Sixties, early seventies, and the newspaper expressed it to the community.

I was lucky to be writing about the cinema in the early seventies because it was a particularly rich period. I reviewed *Carnal Knowledge*, *The Panic in Needle Park*, and *Midnight Cowboy* among many others. Reading the reviews 50 years later I am filled with pride. They were easily comparable in insight and cogent prose with those from any other news publication, anywhere. It's something that can be said about the high level of journalism that *Space City!* produced across the board. Unlike the publications that put out "straight" journalism, we were in touch with the zeitgeist, much hipper than they ever were or ever could have been.

Space City! was founded with a clear vision of the future, an accurate notion of the city's culture and identity, without which Houston would have been greatly impoverished. And now our newspaper is an important historical document. It's what happens when 50 years later you are discovered to have been right all along. We were on the right side of history. (And we still are.)

Houston
April 2021

Gary Chason was like a brother to me. He was my dear friend and colleague from the early Sixties on through the decades. I worked with him in theater, as an actor and as associate producer of his memorable and provocative Houston production of beat poet Michael McClure's *The Beard*. And Gary was an important contributor to our underground papers, *The Rag* in Austin and *Space City!* in Houston.

Gary was a stage and screen producer and director; much of his work was avant garde, existential, and edgy. He was also a wonderful character actor and an acting coach and mentor to many. He gained a measure of fame as a casting director and dialogue/dialect coach for major studio directors like Robert Altman, Peter Bogdanovich, and Louis Malle, doing the location casting for films like *Brewster McCloud*, *The Last Picture Show*, and *Pretty Baby*. He was also an activist, opposing the Vietnam War, and co-founder of the Sexual Freedom League at UT in Austin in 1966.

Gary Chason died unexpectedly on Sunday, April 18, 2021, four days after he submitted his contribution to this book: the accompanying essay about his personal travels through the worlds of film, theater, and social activism, and as a film and arts critic for *Space City!*

— *Thorne Dreyer*

Ad: May 9, 1970.

Fantastic Realist at St. Thomas

Gary Chason • November 22, 1969

Man's environment once was defined by topographical configuration, meteorological conditions, the orbit and spin of the earth — things that existed long before man evolved. There was a natural balance between these elements such that life was possible, but from that very life emerged a new element, man-made, to intrude upon that balance and change it — technology.

Technology is not unnatural, since it was a logical development of man's intelligence, and man's intelligence was the product of natural evolution. But technology has by now so affected the natural balance that life sustaining environment, the ecological balance, is being destroyed.

The extinguishing of this phenomenon of life on this planet, surely a rarity in a universe of planets as barren as the moon, looms as the overwhelming tragedy of our age, and perhaps the interplanetary, or even intergalactic, catastrophe of this millennium. Since the perpetrator of this all-too-likely disaster is a conscious being and thus has foreknowledge of his own imminent doom, the tragedy is all the more profound.

Paul Van Hoeydonk, sculptor, is a prophet of this possible doom. The show of his work, "Spaced Out," which is at the Contemporary Arts Museum, University of St. Thomas, focuses on one particular phase of the technological environment, space technology. It is a good aesthetic choice since a totally technological environment is a prerequisite for exploration of space and a totally technological environment is the best milieu from which to draw to make his points. Van Hoeydonk demonstrates to us the danger we are in now by showing us the future result of present trends. Underneath his clinical examination, there is a strong tone of fear — fear of future technology, terror at the speculation of biological life in a technological world.

He has a new word for man in this kind of environment, CYB-Homo Cyberneticus — which makes the human form seem merely humanoid. A species insane enough to toy with its own destruction does not deserve the purity that the term "human" connotes. He corroborates his term by painting all his humanoid figures stark white, conferring upon them a "sense of remoteness, mystery and tranquility. . .turning them from earthly into celestial pawns," as the notes for the show appropriately state.

Instead of dealing with the entire human body, he concentrates on specific parts of it, amputating them to illustrate that all media, in the anthropomorphic sense, are amputations of physical faculties. I was struck immediately by two heads, sprouting ganglia of wires and electronic apparati. In a sculpture titled "The Take-off," there were four seated torsos (the part of the body most affected by the rigors of blast-off); poised for the jolt, one with his hand on the lever.

A sculpture entitled "Great Mutants with Gun" is most aptly commented upon by Jan van der Marck in the notes. "The 'mutants,' space-age babies whose chromosomes have been altered by radiation, engage in unchildlike activities like manning cannons, steering vehicles, and operating mechanical devices. It is a frightening glimpse into a future world populated by precocious minds imprisoned in retarded bodies condemned to control, maintain, and defend an automated but always capricious environment."

Art: Paul Van Hoeydonk, November 22, 1969.

Van Hoeydonk has constructed a series of "Cities of the Future" out of nuts and bolts and other mechanical paraphernalia. They are sterile, hermetically sealed by blue-tinted plastic, and have more the look of factories than dwellings. It is interesting how Van Hoeydonk makes the microcosm, nuts and bolts, recapitulate and comment upon the macrocosm, a city, in which nuts and bolts are among the smallest units.

If I have a quarrel with the show, it is that Van Hoeydonk does not always thoroughly examine the way in which technology is an extension of brain and body. For example, in dealing with CYB feet, he does not explore at all the fact that feet are primarily media of transportation. Their function is more mechanical than electronic, which Van Hoeydonk fails to demonstrate.

For materials, Van Hoeydonk raids supermarkets and hardware stores, working all manner of modern gadgetry into the context of his sculpture. He is an archeologist of the future, commenting upon the present, and using the gadgets of today. Paint, canvas, marble, and clay have little to do with the world we live in, but plastic, chrome, levers, gears, wires, transistors, and such are everywhere.

Van Hoeydonk does not consider himself a surrealist, but prefers the term "fantastic realist." He is making an honest, unflinching projection into the future, and what he sees is not altogether good.

It is way past time for this "progress"-happy culture to have some of the insights, the visions, that Paul Van Hoeydonk has had. If enough people would reach his level of consciousness, the cosmic crime that we humans are about to commit may not come to pass after all.

****

At first appraisal. Van Hoeydonk's interest in future technological tragedy seems to arise from morbid curiosity; it's as if he were titillated by his own death wish.

But his fascination is a valid one. There is a good side to technology, otherwise it wouldn't be so extensively used by mankind. Technology, correctly applied, can be a basic tool for our future emancipation — easing pain, reducing or eliminating work.

It's this two-sided nature of technology that Van Hoeydonk is sensitive to, and it is the complex source from which he draws his tragedy. -30-

Midnight Cowboy

Gary Chason • September 12, 1969

Director John Schlesinger, in his latest effort, *Midnight Cowboy*, develops a grotesque counterpoint between the fantasies of our civilization (given to us, as he sees it, mainly by Madison Avenue via the media) and the ugly reality of urban blight, of human industrial waste, hidden, like dirty underwear, in the back closets of our cities. The film already has many of the earmarks of a cult piece along the lines of *The Graduate* and *2001*.

The story revolves around Joe Buck, a young West Texas drugstore cowboy who goes to New York City to make his fortune as a hustler. He is a victim of the classic male delusion of super-masculinity, fully believing that those horny New York women will gladly pay for his stud services. In reality of course, he is a naive hick, so kind-hearted that he is a sure patsy.

His trip is an almost archetypal odyssey in our culture, and although his naivete seems humorously pathetic, it is impossible for anyone, no matter how sophisticated, to be prepared for New York. The experience is universally shocking.

Joe ends up the victim in his first three attempts to ply the hustling trade: first by a deteriorating blonde who takes a twenty from him to assuage the insult she feels at being asked for money; for another twenty by Ratso Rizzo who, on the pretext of sending Joe to an agent to more effectively handle his services, sends him to a decrepit old homosexual with some weird religious hang-up; and finally, when Joe has reached the terminal stages of desperation (he's lost his money, possessions, and hotel room) by a young gay student who is unable to pay for an encounter in a 42nd street movie house.

When Joe finally scores with a girl from a Warhol-freak party — when it looks as if he has found a niche, an identity — he finds that he can't get it up. "That's the first goddamn time the thing ever quit on me," he says in his humiliation.

He does succeed with the girl after a while, but his success as a hustler is only momentary. In the end, circumstances force him to violence. Such a development is all too familiar these days.

After being swindled by Ratso, Joe develops a close relationship with him. Ratso, being street-wise, is just the kind of friend Joe needs; they decide that Ratso will manage Joe's career. Ratso, a cripple rapidly succumbing to the harsh street life, needs Joe's strength and vitality. Their relationship is not just of the brains-brawn variety however. Both of them are outcasts, living a lonely existence on the blurred fringes of a society that doesn't even recognize their existence, much less their needs. Each is the only real friend the other has.

They both feel that there must be something better than washing dishes in a small Texas cafe or shining shoes in a New York subway station, and they are willing to make the sacrifices necessary to find that something. They have the guts to say "no" to a society that had long before said "no" to them, and in so doing acquire a heroic dimension. That they choose to hustle on the street is not surprising — Ratso never fails to check pay telephones for change left behind. And if you think them lazy to make such a choice, try it yourself sometime. It's a lot easier to work! It may be that one can choose to die slow or fast in this society; their choice is the latter.

Both of them fall victim to the fast-buck fantasy so prevalent in our culture, however. They aren't quite able to break completely away from the society to find an alternate lifestyle, so they are crushed before they have any real hope of finding whatever it was they were after.

It is hard to imagine the acting being any better. Jon Voight plays Joe Buck with telling authenticity. Voight, who is from New Jersey, reportedly drove his friends and co-workers nearly insane by playing tapes of West Texas accents over and over and over. But the work paid off with an excellent character study, demonstrating Voight's sensitive insight as well as his highly developed craft.

Dustin Hoffman portrays Ratso Rizzo brilliantly, never once sinking to the cliches such a part offers up to an actor. Hoffman should get some kind of off-screen award, too, for being consistently his own man, shunning the tinsel of the Hollywood Star Game, even when it is pushed at him by great hordes of *Graduate* admirers.

Marshall McLuhan once said that if you want to learn something about the sea, don't ask a fish. What he is saying is that we're so accustomed to the phenomena of our environment that we don't take too much notice of them. Schlesinger proves this thesis in *Midnight Cowboy*. Being British, he notices all sorts of things about Texas, New York, and Florida that you and I wouldn't.

He brings these phenomena into sharp focus, showing us the what and how of our environment in a manner that is both familiar and fresh. The film is in many ways a landscape piece, focusing on countryside, buildings, highways,

people, radio and TV shows, and billboards, billboards, billboards. We see how cogently various locales are defined by juxtaposition of these elements.

Schlesinger's hand, and to no small extent that of James Leo Herlihy who wrote the novel, is most evident in illustrating the discrepancy between the fantasy and the reality of American life — and thus the hypocrisy of our society.

The notion that most of the fantasy is handed down by Madison Avenue is everywhere in evidence in the film. The fantasy is of a beautiful world, in which you can be somebody extra-special — by taking a few simple steps (buying the merchandise) you can have all the sexual attractiveness, the wealth, the health, the happiness you desire. Dylan said it best with these words:

> Advertising signs that con
> you into thinking you're the one
> that can do what's never been done
> that can win what's never been won
> meantime life outside goes on all around you.

Joe and Ratso, desperately hungry, walk past a sign that advertises steak on every Braniff flight; a man passed out is stepped over and ignored by passersby (he could have been dying you know), right in front of Tiffany's on fashionable Fifth Avenue: these are the kind of things that tell the story of our society's hypocrisy, and Schlesinger's emphasis of them is very to the point. -30-

> **It is hard to imagine the acting being any better.**

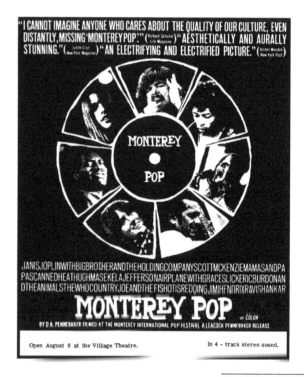

Ad: July 17, 1969.

Ad: September 7, 1971.

Ratting Up: The Panic in Needle Park

Gary Chason • August 17, 1971

The Panic in Needle Park starring Al Pacino and Kitty Winn; screenplay by Joan Didion and John Gregory Dunne; directed by Jerry Schatzberg; playing at the Windsor.

Just the title, *The Panic in Needle Park*, suggests that the film is about hard drugs and the people who use them. "Needle Park" is the slang name for Sherman Square, a small hunk of grimy concrete and dingy benches at Broadway and 72nd Street in New York City. It is inhabited by the world's highest concentration of junkies. A "panic" occurs when the supply of heroin runs out.

As you would expect, the picture makes a statement about the evils of heroin. But fortunately, that statement is strictly a by-product of the story itself. There is never any attempt to manipulate the situation, to propagandize. No, this is a highly (frighteningly) realistic portrait of life in Needle Park for an attractive, likeable couple. Because of the film's tenacious honesty, the statement is all the more powerful.

The AMA and all the other hypocrites who make dishonest, propagandist TV commercials about drugs should be forced to see this film, chained in their seats with their eyes propped open with toothpicks if necessary. It should be required viewing at every high school in the country. However, due to the short-sighted ignorance of some of the fucked-up creeps who sanctimoniously pretend to run our society, young people are restricted from seeing this picture. It's rated R.

Please excuse my outburst of hyperbole, but this subject happens to be one of my pet peeves. Back to the review.

Husband and wife team of Joan Didion and John Gregory Dunne have created a masterful screenplay. It is intelligent, fair, and shows a considerable knowledge of the New York smack scene.

Helen, played by Kitty Winn, falls in love with Bobby, played by Al Pacino. She's from Fort Wayne, Indiana, and like so many others, has come to New York in search of the exciting life. He is a native: street wise, aggressive, very hip, but still very personable.

In the beginning, he sells grass in the Village. But gradually he gets into heroin, pushing and using. He very confidently starts out just "chipping" — using occasionally without getting hooked. But it isn't long until he and Helen both have a habit.

When Bobby gets busted attempting to rob a store with his brother Frank and has to spend time in jail, Helen turns to hooking to support her growing habit. When Bobby gets out, he is upset at this development, but soon grows accustomed to letting her "feed his arm."

Bobby unexpectedly gets a big break: he is employed as a pusher by Santo, an extremely big operator and a very heavy dude. Helen, meanwhile, gets busted for pushing pills to minors.

Hotch, the local narc, offers to fix it for her. In return, she has to rat on Bobby, who in turn will rat on Santo, Hotch's real target.

Helen balks, offering to rat on any number of other friends. Hotch replies, "you rat up, never down." It is at this point that we see how deeply the police are into the whole ugly game. The situation is rotten from bottom to top, without relief.

Helen, faced with a sentence of one to three years, finally does rat on her lover. It infuriates Bobby, naturally, but then that's the way the game is played. In the end the two are back together again, going on to who knows what.

Director Jerry Schatzberg's presentation of the junkie scene is so accurate I found myself involuntarily remembering some of the more unpleasant aspects of my stay in New York. I have strange respect for junkies. They have that jaded look about their eyes that seems to indicate that they know something that you don't. There must be some tremendous pleasure in using skag that makes up, at least partially, for the horrible lifestyle it imposes on an addict.

Junkies have a strange and perverse camaraderie that excludes everyone else. We are all squares to them. Also, you get the impression that your possessions, and even your life, are meaningless to a junkie compared to a fix. (My New York apartment was ripped off twice, rather thoroughly, by skag freaks, and the next occupants, some friends, were mugged in the hall.)

This super-hip ultra-cool quality, which is impressive to many people (even intelligent ones like

> It is hard to imagine the acting being any better.

William Burroughs), is captured remarkably by Schatzberg's camera. The picture is so unbiased, in fact, that I don't believe a junkie would have any objection to it. He would probably consider it a put down of narcs, which on one level it definitely is.

The casting, by Marion Dougherty, is fantastic. Every character is exactly right. The acting is of the very highest quality. Al Pacino and Kitty Winn are right on the button at all times. Kitty Winn won the Grande Prix for acting at Cannes for this performance, and very deservedly.

Part of the acting assignment was actually to shoot up, not with real junk of course. But Pacino, Winn, and numerous other actors really did stick those awful needles into their veins, often in graphic close-up. It's more than I would be able to do, I believe. -30-

Cover: Art by Don Snell, January 20, 1972.

Straw Dogs

John Goodwin • December 30, 1971

Sam Peckinpah's *Straw Dogs*, currently playing at the Gaylynn Terrace and Village theatres, invests the medium of film with the real proportions of myth.

To an audience already shock-stoned from the magical mystical flickers on the screen, it is a devastating demonstration of the potency of the movies. Besides being a really shattering experience that can leave you shaky for days, it is a great film, an American classic, a quintessential pageant of frontier justice.

The "American myth," the whole system of values created from the conquest of the frontier, is reflected in the entire history of Hollywood and the silver screen, a medium perfectly suited to act as a metaphor for the magic of the unknown, the escape from the known, the celebration of our spectacular vitality, our awesome progress, our unquestionable moral vision.

The movies have created a parallel mythology made up of enlarged heroes and archetypal situations that demonstrate an archetypal moral vision. In *Straw Dogs*, Peckinpah purifies the classical aspects of the American film mythology with an invocation of the paradoxes, the savagery, the opportunistic greed, the thirst for power, the competitive sexuality that compose the unexposed underside of the American dream. The picture is such a meticulous and violent destruction of the barrier our dream has built between enlightenment and brutality, that our salvation and our damnation appear in a state of perfect eclipse.

Peckinpah is so electrifying in his total mastery of every aspect of the film, so uncompromisingly ruthless with the ear, the eye, the mind, that he achieves the unforgettably real effect of catharsis. From the classical formulas and familiar devices that the film has made so recognizable, Peckinpah has distilled an ephemeral tragedy of nihilism and violence. There is a beauty in the memory of the film comparable to that in the elegant and intellectual barbarism of Jacobean tragedy, an afterimage that reveals our innocence to be as inevitable and as useless as our guilt in the pursuit of our dreams.

In simplest terms, *Straw Dogs* is about freedom, security, barriers, and threat. David, a young American mathematician, comes to a remote Cornwall village that is his wife Amy's former home, to the house of her dead father, to get away from the past, to find peace and presumably security.

From the opening of the film, the power of the threat begins to be felt, primarily in the guise of three beautifully villainous hired men who are leering, animal, potent, and moronic. Perched like waiting vultures on the roof of the garage they are building for the couple, they insult David, manage to enter the house to kill Amy's cat, and prove their ability to force their way into his terrain. Finally they draw David out of the house on a ridiculous snipe hunt in order to rape Amy.

> **Peckinpah is electrifying in his total mastery of every aspect of the film.**

Peckinpah's treatment of the whole exposition and development is flawless: an opening overhead shot of children playing in an old graveyard; a scene with David in the village pub in which Peckinpah creates a saloon world of power games and the understood threat of violent retribution. The generation of suspense and tension through the development of the relationship of David and Amy, in chilling commonplace situations, in the effect the threat begins to work on both of them, in the alarming way they both contribute to their own vulnerability.

During the whole first half of the film Peckinpah practices a mean game of deception by balancing two distracting lines of development simultaneously. In one he makes David and Amy appear completely overpowered by the thorough, aggressive villainy of their assailants. In the other, he creates a stratified social order which necessitates for David and Amy an ordeal of adjustment. The threat of the outside is seen in terms of such premeditated and needless aggression that we do not realize fully the implications of the passive aggressive games that the couple practices upon one another and upon the intruders.

At the church gathering which Peckinpah provides as the transition into the film's violent finale, Peckinpah creates the atmosphere of a darkening carnal fairground, a world in which goodness is protected by the Devil. In a bizarre sequence of events, David spurns the obvious invitation of an aroused teenage girl; in retaliation she turns her attention to Harry Niles, the town deviant, who innocently murders her. Guilt ridden, humiliated by the rantings of the hired men who are present at the gathering, David and Amy leave early and, on the road back to the farmhouse, hit Harry Niles who runs in front of their car. David decides to take the injured man back to their house until the authorities arrive.

What follows is a siege by the mob on David's territory and a harrowing demonstration of rational savagery that composes the longest and most incisive study in violence the screen has seen, surpassing even Peckinpah's previous violent vision in *The Wild Bunch*.

The cast is beyond reproach. It is to Peckinpah's credit and no insult to Hoffman that for the first time in his career a Dustin Hoffman film has been better than his performance. Hoffman is nevertheless perfection is his delineation of a contemporary hero who is both a defensive intellectual and a rational savage. Even more impressive in many ways is Susan George as Amy, a definitive portrait of shrewd sexuality and self-protective hysteria. The role is more than simply difficult; it is the sort of role that Natalie Wood or some such minimal talent has often torn a passion to tatters in executing. Susan George, however, possesses a sure control of film dynamics that makes her both a star and an actress with the same luminous presence of a Julie Christie or Susannah York. In the rape seduction scene in the first part of the film, she is an unforgettable factor in the most unforgettably carnal scene I can remember.

The rest of the cast combine perfect casting, archetypal film presence, and flawless acting. Particularly memorable are David Warner who played Harry Niles without credit or pay, managing to make the only innocence in the film appear both appealing and sadly repellent. The hired hands (the names of the actors I unfortunately did not catch; I'll try to correct that omission in a future column for they deserve individual attention) create a rich panorama of decadent viciousness. Nor can I resist mentioning another anonymous (to me) actor who plays the minister with an oily David Frost charm that is an invitation to blasphemy.

American film critics have been wary about giving Peckinpah too much credit. It seems that many would prefer not to call attention to what he is doing in motion pictures, or that they don't fully understand the mingled complexity and economy of his commercial approach. That a major periodical reviewer would begin his review of the film with the Cassandra-like premonition that *Straw Dogs* is probably the best film Peckinpah will ever make (in so many words) suggests the same kind of indirect abuse that has been practiced upon the few giants of

American film, notably Orson Welles when he made a rather undeniable and disturbing film back in 1941.

Hopefully, American filmmakers today are not so vulnerable to the snobbish, power-oriented press of their countrymen. It would seem not. Kubrick and Lester have done most of their best work away from America, and this, Peckinpah's best film and conceivably the best "western" ever made, was made in contemporary England. He has crossed the boundaries of nationality and genre into the frontiers of universal myth. And in doing so, has moved into the front ranks of world film directors — combining abilities rarely found in a single director.

He can tell a story; he can make images and sounds and actions work together with economy and intelligence; he can make commercialism and artistry inseparable. And in a relatively short career, he has made three films that at worst can certainly not be dismissed. *Ride The High Country*, *The Wild Bunch*, *The Ballad of Cable Hogue*. And he has made *Straw Dogs*. **-30-**

> ## He can make images and sounds and actions work together with economy and intelligence.

Death in Venice

John Goodwin • September 28, 1971

Death in Venice *produced and directed by Luchino Visconti; screenplay by Luchino Visconti and Nicola Badalucco based upon the novel by Thomas Mann; photography by Pasquale de Santis; film editing by Ruggero Mastroianni; costume design by Piero Tosi; starring Dirk Bogarde; at the Gaylynn Theatre, Rated GP.*

Thomas Mann's fragile and ironic masterpiece *Death In Venice* seems hardly a likely choice for a film adaptation. There is little action in the story, a minimum of dialogue, a solitary central character who is developed in the novella by an omniscient third person narrator, a great deal of wry humor which is sacrificed even by translation from the original German, and an entire section of narrative devoted to a discussion of the artistic development of the central figure, Gustave Aschenbach — an element essential to the understanding of the work as a whole but for which there is no easy cinematic equivalent.

In addition, much of what makes Mann's work a masterpiece is the sensitivity with which he leaves things unsaid. Beyond the overwhelming technical obstacles in adaptation alone, there are inherent obstacles in virtually every aspect of mood, emphasis, characterization, and motivation which, if not solved with the perfect balance of intelligence and inspiration could only result in banality and pretentiousness.

Luchino Visconti has prevented that with perfect balance in his film of *Death in Venice* currently on view at the Gaylynn. It is as overpoweringly beautiful as it is difficult to conceive of, as rich and delicate a creation as the novella, and the finest translation from print to film in the recent history of the movies.

The screenplay, a collaboration of Visconti and Nicola Badalucco, who co-authored the screenplay of *The Damned* as well, is a meticulous balance of literal fidelity and brilliant imagination. Beginning with Aschenbach's arrival, the film manages to include almost every incident, every image, every moment from the story that traces the artist's spiritual disintegration and death. Almost every diversion from the source manages brilliantly to preserve the spirit of the original and at the same time maintain its authority as a

It is the finest translation from print to film in recent history.

film experience. Visconti and Badalucco have made Aschenbach a composer in the motion picture rather than a writer as he is in the novella, and they have introduced the contribution of Gustave Mahler (a contemporary of Mann), employing his music in the scoring of the film and investing a feeling of his presence in the character of Aschenbach as well as a kind of spiritual collaboration in the whole of the film.

The choice is a brilliant one.

The story of the film — for those unfamiliar with the novella — concerns an aging German composer who, some 10 years after the turn of the century, comes to Venice for uncertain reasons, and falls in love with a beautiful Polish boy named Tadzio, who from a distance consumes him with a passionate fascination which he cannot resist. At the end he dies while sitting in a beach chair watching his beloved wade out into the sea.

In terms of action there is really little else, but Visconti has enriched every moment, every detail, every nuance in the elusive story and created a sensitive and passionate portrait of love and death in a diseased and contradictory city. Even more to his credit is his enormous skill in delivering the sharp irony of the work. He has made Aschenbach repeatedly aware of the absurdity of his obsessions and their strange effect on the whole direction of his life which had previously been characterized by discipline, reason, and the most irreproachable standards of art and personal behavior.

The inescapable irony of Venice itself with its elegant Hotel des Bains at the center of Aschenbach's life — the absurd self-important manager, the rows of beautiful painted beach stalls, the elaborate finery of Europe's first class tourists on parade — while outside the streets are being washed with milky stinking disinfectant, belongings of cholera victims burn in piles in doorways, and an atmosphere of doom encircles a palace of formal and uncomfortable leisure.

The first part of the film slowly, solemnly presents a vision of Venice and of Aschenbach the man and the artist. There is little dialogue, very little happens. Pasquale de Santis' extraordinary camerawork describes in fluid, elliptical strokes the magnificence, the age of Venice; moves through the hours of the days, watches the dark waters of the canals, the colfin-like gondolas; and then changes its rhythm and intrudes upon Aschenbach, recording private gestures, thoughts, mannerisms, fragments of personal routine, personal fears that tell more and differently than words.

The scene where Aschenbach first sees Tadzio is magnificent — a sentimental chamber orchestra playing a Lehar waltz sentimentally; Ascbenbach disgusted with the old newspaper he is glancing at and the bad taste of the music, gazes slowly around the elegant room, repeatedly returning to look at the beautiful boy with the long golden hair and the enigmatic smile until he has forgotten the music, the newspaper, all else. The scene takes several minutes, the pace is full of ironic and delicious intricacy. From here the film swells with the headlines of Aschenbach's first-felt passions, the fascination of watching all of the fine details of a secret and inconceivable experience.

Later Aschenbach suddenly decides to leave Venice, makes a fetish of having privately said his farewell to the boy, and in one of the finest sequences in the film we watch him glide through Venice in a gondola, silently relishing the bittersweet agony of his departure. In the train station he seizes upon an error in the delivery of his trunk as a justifiable excuse for remaining in Venice and his anticlimactic and triumphant return perfectly completes the sequence that had begun with his departure.

The rhythm changes once again and concentrates upon the further fascinations of Aschenbach with Tadzio, with the plague that is enclosing the city, and with his own fears of age, death, and insignificance. The last scene watches a painted, pretentiously vain old man dying in a beach chair, the black lacquer on his hair streaming from underneath his straw hat, watching the boy motion ambiguously to him from the sea.

From the Venice sequence of Mann's story Visconti and his collaborators have altered little of Mann's story — they have managed to enrich the sensuality of it and execute it with academic integrity and cinematic brilliance. The only addition of any consequence is a droll scene with a prostitute which may strike some as an unnecessary sensational device directed toward adding a little heterosexual interest to the film. It seems to me that such an exquisite touch of bitter social comedy underlines deftly Visconti's unques-

The last scene watches a painted, pretentiously vain old man dying in a beach chair.

tionable understanding of the work. Aschenbach does not shudder in the doorway before leaving hurriedly because of a frustrated homosexual condition. It is the utter banality and conventionality of such an arrangement, its tasteless theatrics, that he compares with the spirituality of his passion.

The first part of the novella — the biography of the artist, selected details about his past, and his life in Munich appear in the film in a series of flashbacks — thoughts, memories, dreams. Arguments with a younger artist (suggested by a figure that is not developed as a character in the book) about the purposes of art and the identity of the artist, memories of his wife and child and of the child's death, fears of his own failure seen through a concert where he is jeered — the scenes serve economically to provide insight into the ambiguities of the man, the significance of his stay in Venice, his fears of age, of death, that his career and his beliefs have been a lie. They are the most superficial and contrived parts of the film but they contribute a great deal to the whole that is necessary, and if there are moments that are overstated and incline towards melodrama, the real feeling and incisive perception of the rest of the film is more than enough to make up for them.

Dirk Bogarde, in the incredibly difficult role of the composer, insures the validity of Visconti's concept of the work. Mirrored in his smallest gestures, mannerisms — the reading of a single word, the execution of the simplest notion, are the dreams and stories and thoughts of a complex, petty, proud, vulnerable, brilliant man. It is an unforgettable piece of acting — without Bogard's intelligence, his craftsmanship, his phenomenal sensitivity, these same qualities in the other makers of the film might never have been known. In other roles Visconti has cast perfectly, particularly in his choice of young Scandinavian Bjorn Andresen as Tadzio, who possesses the same beauty, the same ambiguity, the same fragility that Mann wrote about.

Editing is by Ruggero Mastroianni. The costumes were designed by Piero Tosi. They deserve something in the way of special thanks.

Death in Venice received the Grand Prix at the 1971 Cannes Film Festival. It is a significant film, an unusual one, demanding and severe. It vividly recreates a dying time and place with fascinating complexity, but, more than that, it produces a sense of euphoric fascination with passion and death that becomes inexplicably spiritual. **-30-**

Community
Building

Cover: Photo by G. Emerson Brant, June 15, 1972.

Of Our Own

Sherwood Bishop

On June 25, 1970, a concert (Traffic, Mountain, and Mott the Hoople) at Hofheinz Pavilion on the University of Houston campus turned into a near riot when hundreds of fans, angered at the high ticket prices, stormed the pavilion doors and caused major damage.

In the July 4 issue of *Space City!*, in "Traffic Jam at Hayes Pavilion: Up Against the Wall Culture Vultures," Dennis Fitzgerald wrote:

> Something that ought to be ours — everyone's — is owned and sold by a few people. Rock music, like the rest of our culture, grows from a million roots. In the places where it seems to reach its fullest expression, it is bought (placed under contract) and sold like underwear at Sears... People here suffer from a sort of inverse provincialism. They'll pay absurd prices (or riot) to hear most any big national name but will hardly drive around the corner to support local groups, which may often be just as good (or at least deserve the chance to become so). That means that unless you can bring in the stars every weekend (which nobody can pull off), you can't afford to keep a big enough place to pull in name groups any weekend. Which leaves the control in the hands of big promoters who can afford once-a-month rip-offs at Hayes (Hofheinz) or the Coliseum.

Fitzgerald further wrote:

> We need to regain control of our culture. Liberate the Pavilion (or get our own place)... A place of our own would mean that we would have to pay bands, rent, utilities, some advertising, reasonable salaries to people to manage the place and a few other things like that. But if people supported the place consistently, we wouldn't need to pay the prices we do now; we could be flex-

ible in admitting people for little or no money (maybe in exchange for work or other commodities); and we wouldn't need an armed guard to protect us from ourselves.

In the July 18 *Space City!*, Richard Ames, co-producer of the ill-fated concert, blasted the fans for their violence, and Fitzgerald as a "reckless, shallow and obviously neophyte writer." However, Bill Metzler, a musician and *Space City!* staff member, visited Ames in his office. Metzler knew that Ames Productions was stuck with a $1,250 per month lease on another venue, the Catacombs, which had closed earlier that year after chronically losing money.

After extensive, and somewhat miraculous negotiations, an agreement was reached between Ames and representatives of Houston's alternative community.

In the August 1 *Space City!*, Ames wrote:

> There is need for a place here for the professional presentation of local rock talent at a reasonable price and in an atmosphere that allows for audience appreciation and communication and is free from commercial exploitation by any person or organization. Such a place should be organized and operated on a nonprofit basis by people directly concerned with the local hip community.

Ames Productions agreed to allow the Catacombs building to be the home of a new non-profit. The venue, which was named "Of Our Own," would be administered by a nine-member Management Committee that included Ames, Metzler, and Fitzgerald. After expenses were paid, any remaining funds would be distributed to community organizations chosen by the Committee. Ticket prices would be $2 on weekends and $1 on weeknights.

Paying the expenses would be a formidable challenge. In the Sept. 5 issue of *Space City!*, Fitzgerald wrote:

If we can get minimally 500-600 people a weekend to pay $2 each to hear good music in a really free atmosphere, that brings in enough bread to keep the place going. That much money will pay rent, utilities, band costs, subsistence salary for one or two people, and incidentals. We could stay alive. That means we've not only got a place to make music in our own way, we've also got a place to show films, to do theater, to hold rallies and benefits —in short, to experiment with.

A series of town hall meetings was held, a manager, Mike Harvey, was hired, and Of Our Own held its first concerts, with Saturnalia and Shiva's Head Band, on Friday and Saturday, August 15 and 16, 1970.

Of Our Own was very successful, sometimes. A concert in May 1971 attracted 1,400 customers. There were also numerous benefit concerts held to raise funds for community non-profits, including *Space City!*.

However, the impact of what Dennis Fitzgerald had called "inverse provincialism" was a chronic problem, especially because other Houston venues lowered their ticket prices in response to Of Our Own's challenge.

Of Our Own wasn't air conditioned until July 1971. Houston's heat and humidity had sometimes driven fans from the building. Unfortunately, the air conditioning increased the overhead. Even when there were only a few customers, the entire building had to be cooled. A weeknight crowd of 50 would require almost as much overhead as a weekend crowd of 500.

Many concerts only drew 100-200 people. Of Our Own didn't sell beer or other alcohol, so teenagers were allowed. It had a loyal but small teen audience, but the lack of alcohol sales hurt its bottom line. As Dennis Fitzgerald had predicted, getting large crowds was a challenge. The big venues, which could hold 5,000 or more people, and which were only open on weekends, would bring in world famous bands, and most people would choose to see them.

Besides being a venue for concerts to raise funds for nonprofits, and a place where teens could hang out and hear live music, Of Our Own provided other community benefits, such as being a meeting place for community groups. However, it didn't receive income from those activities.

Of Our Own held its final concert on Oct. 9, 1971. Tim Leatherwood, the venue's last manager was quoted in the Oct. 11, 1971 issue of the *Houston Chronicle*: "It was costing us $1,400 a month just for the rent… That doesn't include utilities or other kinds of overhead. We had to gross $6,000 a month just to break even, and there was no way."

San Marcos, Texas
June 2021

SCHEDULE

Nov. 25 – FREE JAM
Nov. 26 – RED COYOTE HONKY TONK HOE
                DOWN AND HOWL IN. 4 pm to 1 am
                FREE.
Nov. 27 – HI SKOOL RIGHTS CONF. – 4 pm
Nov. 28-29 – MC5, LA PAZ & LORIEN – ($2.50)
Dec. 5 – FREE JAM
Dec. 11-12 – DENIM & GINGER VALLEY
New Years Eve – SHIVAS HEAD BAND

UNIVERSITY
AT KIRBY

Ad. November 26, 1970.

Art: Kerry Fitzgerald, July 4,1970.

Culture Vultures:
Traffic Jam at Hayes Pavilion

Dennis Fitzgerald • July 4, 1970

Traffic tickets were selling for $6.50 a head at Hayes (nee Hofheinz) Pavilion last Thursday night. And a lot of people were translating their indignation into action: a message for local promoters. University of Houston Security Chief Larry (Fuzz) Foltz was shaking his head the next morning, assaying a formidable stack of "Please Call" notes. He predicted that Traffic would be the beginning of the end for Hayes Pavilion concerts (Creedence is still scheduled for that location later this month). When I arrived 30 minutes early, bundle of *Space City!*'s under my arm, a crowd of several thousand was milling around in front, waiting for the doors to open. The scene was low key, stoned, meeting friends unmet since the last concert.

Shortly after 8 p.m. they began letting in ticket holders. Almost immediately you could see this wasn't going to be a concert like other concerts. There are always a few penniless malcontents hassling to get in free. But this night there were more than a few and they were being uncommonly aggressive. One source of anger was that there were no low-priced tickets being sold, $6.50 seats only.

Within a half hour the lines had formed. The doors were shut and locked. Outside a thousand people (of whom maybe a tenth had tickets) were pushing and chanting, demanding to be let in.

It was often like the spirit generated by a hard fought football game. The people were digging on each other and on this sudden solidarity. It was fun. The cause was clearly just: all the money that was to be made had already been made; inside there were still many empty seats; and outside there were people who wanted in. But such logic runs counter to a promoter's ethic, so the doors had to be defended.

It worked like this. A couple of sympathetic ticket holders would squeeze to the front, flashing their purchased legitimacy through the glass doors to the cops inside. A door would be cracked open to admit the fortunate pair. Instantly a tug of war would ensue, the crowd attempting to hold the door and rush through the breach, the cops attempting to repel the invaders.

Maybe that makes it sound too casual. It wasn't. There were more than a few scuffles — there was some hard fighting done to crash those doors.

One incident: a door was opened for a ticketholder, who entered walking, then turned back quickly and opened suddenly three, four doors.

The crowd surged forward. Hundreds of bodies pushing. Forcing their collective weight against the bodies before them. The people in front twisting, swinging at the cops, while dozens of other people poured in around them.

Just when it seemed that the cops couldn't hold back the crowd any longer, a dozen reinforcements arrived and regained control of the doors. (The concentration of force on those few doors was at the same time an advantage and the decisive handicap: a limited objective easily won and easily lost.)

The people would have won anyway, but for the mace. At least twice (once to my very personal knowledge) the cops used mace on the crowd. That cooled it quick. Everyone fell back, eyes and noses burning, kicking at the apparently unbreakable doors. People regrouped quickly, but the advantage was lost.

For the rest of the evening, bitter at that defeat, people were less restrained in their actions towards the cops. The race was a formal notice of escalation. Every door opening elicited a barrage of whatever debris people could lay their hands on. People were fighting for something they felt was theirs: the music, the right to be together inside that building. Two or three times sizable numbers of people made it through the double set of doors, running and swinging. A few were caught and returned to the battle outside. Most

There was some hard fighting done to crash those doors.

who made it all the way in stayed there, some continuing the fight to open more doors.

As the hours passed, the battle surged and waned. It was always a game, but it grew increasingly more serious. Towards the end, lots of people were smoking dope openly, even tauntingly, in front of the cops. There was that much togetherness; people knew the cops couldn't bust anyone. By 10 p.m. about the only people flashing peace symbols were the promoters. The people responded with the finger, the fist, and an occasional Dixie cup packed with ice.

Inside, people were running defense for hotly pursued gate crashers. One UH security pig, who has revealed his disproportionate sense of duty in the past, drew his gun on a circle of about 40 people coming to the aid of a freebie.

Back outside a city whirlypig circled ominously overhead, and a dozen patrol cars waited by the sidewalk.

As Traffic began their second number, the promoters relented, and the crowd surged in, cheering, fists high. There was a roar of welcome and victory from the nearest sections of the auditorium, but probably most of the people inside had little or no idea of what had been happening for three hours outside.

Sadly, Traffic without Dave Mason wasn't worth the effort. After a taste of their thing many folks left. Mountain's performance (so I'm told) was by far the evening's high point. But the effort was worth the effort — and may be significant if the University of Houston is indeed to be closed to rock concerts now.

Concerts in Houston have become increasingly a time for energy outpourings, for kicking out the jams. But promoters and people who own things want concerts to be shows where other people pay for their tickets, stay in their seats, and applaud and go home quietly at the end. That just ain't gonna work.

The dilemma is identical to the other problems we face in this country. Something that ought to be ours — everyone's — is owned and sold by a few people. Rock music, like the rest of our culture, grows from a million roots. In the places where it seems to reach its fullest expression, it is bought (placed under contract) and sold like underwear at Sears. This process commercializes and isolates the bands, the music and the "audience" (who would ideally be participants in the music, not merely spectators).

People here suffer from a sort of inverse provincialism. They'll pay absurd prices (or riot) to hear most any big national name, but will hardly drive around the corner to support local groups which may often be just as good (or at least deserve the chance to become so).

That means that unless you can bring in the stars every weekend (which nobody can pull off), you can't afford to keep a big enough place to pull in name groups any weekend. Which leaves the control in the hands of big promoters who can afford once a month rip-offs at Hayes (Hofheinz) or the Colliseum.

A place of our own would mean that we would have to pay bands, rent, utilities, some advertising, reasonable salaries to people to manage the place and a few other things like that. But if people supported the place consistently, we wouldn't need to pay the

We need to regain control of our culture.

prices we do now; we could be flexible in admitting people for little or no money (maybe in exchange for work or other commodities); and we wouldn't need an armed guard to protect us from ourselves.

That's all gonna mean people getting their shit together, giving as well as taking. The Switchboard is starting this week. A good project might be to use them to place interested people in touch with one another towards the end of getting a place of our own.

We need to regain control of our culture. Liberate the Pavilion (or get our own place). Support our local bands, who now most often find their subsistance and sympathy in the arms of a buck-hungry agent. Don't watch the world, build it. Create what needs to be created; destroy the old forms which restrict us. Now, because tomorrow they may have you under contract. Do it! -30-

Jan.14,15,&16

LITTLE FEAT

(former members of the Mothers of Invention & the Fraternity of Man) with KUBA $2!!! and BRUISER BARTON

Jan.22 & 23

SKYROCKET   with LA PAZ
8:00pm $1 (cheap)

OF OUR OWN

UNIVERSITY & KIRBY

—COMING— Captain Beefheart & his Magic Band with Ry Cooder Feb.19 $3.00

Ad: January 16, 1971.

A Place of Our Own:
An Exchange Between Promoter Richard Ames and Space City!'s Dennis Fitzgerald

August 1, 1970

ames sez:

For the last month there has been a constant current of expressions from all levels of the Houston community regarding the present status of rock music presentations here and its relation to those who view it as a very important communication media to the "hip community" here as well as many other persons and organizations.

Most of the expressions have been destructive or critical in content and we at Ames Productions have contributed in that vein as much or more than any other person or organization. All have recognized faults and inadequacies on all sides and have gone to considerable effort to express such. The analysis of the entire situation here has now run its full course. The destructive and critical phase must now yield to a movement of constructive and sincere expressions and action, which is important if anything of change and betterment is to be achieved now.

In careful study of the presentation of local and national rock talent here, both in clubs and concerts, and the recognition of rock as a definite media of communication and the desire by some to organize, develop and enlarge an entire local rock culture-oriented community of people here, I have come to a few basic thoughts that we consider an immediate need and necessity here:

1. The hip community needs to organize an effective means of expressing the views of all the people here that can be effective in seeing that they have a say over the manner and cost of the music and other related entertainment that is presented in Houston and aimed specifically for their patronage and consumption.

2. There is need for a place here for the professional presentation of local rock talent at a reasonable price and in an atmosphere that allows for audience appreciation and communication and is free from commercial exploitation by any person or organization. Such a place should be organized and operated on a nonprofit basis by people directly concerned with the local hip community.

3. A portion of the money paid by the people here to see and enjoy rock music should be put back into community efforts and projects that are operated for their use and benefit and are nonprofit in nature. This should be required of concert productions as well as any locally operated regular presentations of such music.

These ideas were developed after several initial "discussion" meetings between myself and Bob Cope representing Ames Productions and Bill Metzler, who originally contacted me on the premise of what might be done regarding the local rock situation and who served as an important catalyst to the entire effort of all of us to come up with ideas and contributions toward a real community operated project. Other people who have participated to one extent or another in these discussions are the people listed below as the Management Committee.

Basically, we have come to some definite decisions and commitments which we feel can be the beginning for realization of the objectives mentioned earlier.

Our firm commitments are as follows:

1. The new Catacombs at University and Kirby, which we own the lease on and operated until its closing in the early spring, will be reopened, renamed, and available for the use and benefit of all the people and organizations within Houston's hip community and will be operated and supervised by a management committee consisting of community people and our representative on a totally nonprofit basis.

The monthly lease charges are presently $1,250, and we are attempting to have that lowered. Utilities and any maintenance or repair work requested by the management committee will

> **Most of the expressions have been destructive or critical in content.**

be the only funds directed to Ames Productions from any receipts taken in at any scheduled event in the building.

2. All funds, other than the rent, utility, and maintenance reimbursement, will be placed in a special bank account for the sole distribution to and use of the various local community projects or to individual people in the community in need of such assistance. Any distribution of this money will be by a majority vote of the member management committee that will oversee the entire use and operation of the facility. Other than myself as one member of this committee, no other agent or employee of mine will serve on the management committee, and we have no final vote or consent to provision whatsoever. The entire membership of this committee is listed below.

All records and distributions of the operation and the fund will be kept current and will be available for audit as may be requested by any concerned party.

3. The name selected by those organizing the project is "Of Our Own" and will be the new name for the facility. The name has been the theme of people who have been working for many months toward this type of community project.

4. "Of Our Own" will be operated on a seven-day schedule generally as follows:

Monday and Thursday — Open nights. Any type activity may be scheduled; if none is set, then it will not be open on those nights.

Tuesday — Auditions. Groups or individuals will perform and will be paid for performance. Open to the public from 8-12 A.M. and a $1 donation will be charged.

Wednesday — Open Forum — This will be a town hall type meeting or discussion session open to the public. Any individual or group may present any plans, activities, or other matters to those in attendance. The only restriction on any speaker or group is that they conduct their activities within the law and

notify the management committee of their desire to make a presentation.

Friday and Saturday — Open to public from 8 p.m. - 2 a.m. Rock music presented each night featuring local and regional individuals and groups. $2 donations each night. If a nationally known act is scheduled by the management committee, a slightly higher donation may be requested.

The Management Committee as initially organized, is as follows:

R.C. Ames — Ames Productions
Dennis Fitzgerald — *Space City!*
Bill Metzler — Musician
Linda Eubanks — Food Club
Mike Harvey — formerly of Love Street
John Bartlett — Good Relations
Vicki Moreland — Inlet
Mike Dunham — Sonic Productions
George Banks — formerly of the Family Hand

These projects have been sincerely undertaken to benefit the Houston community.

With the above in motion, we are planning on an opening within the next two to three weeks. I have set no timetable or trial period as far as acceptance and attendance by the public, but we all agree that within several months we should have a good idea of the people's attitude toward this project.

Additionally, we are now working on an idea toward a Promoters-People agreement regarding any future rock concerts that may be held in Houston. Such an agreement would set a fair-to-all price range on tickets and would cover other matters regarding the manner of presentation of these acts and what is expected of the Houston audience who attend the events.

Upon completion of such a set of standards, it will be presented to all promoters and the public. It is hoped that it will be broad and fair enough for all to accept and abide by. Such a cooperative effort can be an important step in bringing about a new mutually beneficial relationship between area concert promoters and the public that patronizes their events.

It should be obvious that these projects have been sincerely undertaken to directly benefit the Houston community, and, in turn, are going to require the full support of the people here if they are to develop and survive at all.

If these projects are faced with the past Houston apathy and indifference, then a lot of effort on your behalf by sincere and dedicated people will be in vain.

mana ger's re port

This is your OF OUR OWN manager reporting in with the bi-weekly Of Our Own manager's report. Things *are* happening.

The board met Wednesday and got a lot done, mainly setting up committees of volunteers with board members as chairmen. The purpose of this was to get our shit together and to involve more people in the actual operation of Of Our Own. We also promised ourselves that any board member who didn't work would get canned. Anyone wanting to get into what we're doing come to Town Hall Tuesday at 8 p.m.

Last week's Town Hall was pretty far out, too. The few people that come each week are really getting into it. These people are the real core of Of Our Own.

So much for the human side. Here's the facts and figures on how we did during the last two weeks.

       October 2 & 3
       Headstone & Rabbit
Attendance . . . . .App. 400 people
Total Gate $800
Total Expenses . . . . . .$550 (including $400 for Roky Ericson)
Total Profit $250

       October 9 & 10
       Josefus, Wolfgang, Boot Hill
Attendance . . . . .App. 700 people
Total Gate $1300
Total Expenses . . . . . .$ 820
Total Profit $480

As you can see, things are getting better all the time. Get involved with Of Our Own. It's your place.

                                                                — Mike

---

Report: October 17, 1970.

We are pleased to be able to contribute our part in this project and certainly the contributions, suggestions and ideas of others are welcome and needed.

—*Richard C. Ames*

in reply to which we sez:

Directions: before proceeding further, read the letter from Richard Ames (presumably somewhere on this same page).

Okay, now ask yourself, "Why would a promoter who has the reputation of being one of the most piggish of his species, suddenly turn around and offer to underwrite a hip community center, controlled by the community, all profits to be returned to the community, etc. etc.?"

Well, there don't seem to be any completely satisfactory answers. There are, however, several worthwhile guesses.

1. There's been a lot of stuff coming down around concert prices, etc. lately, and Ames is scared and/or thinks he sees a way to divert all the energy.

2. Ames has the lease on the Catacombs and is putting out $1,250 a month while the place stands empty. He figures that, where his own management couldn't make the club work, a community effort might pay for the building. In any case, he has nothing to lose there in dollars and cents.

3. At the same time that he is recouping at least some of his financial loss, he is receiving a PR bonus which transforms Ames Productions from a "culture vulture" into a people's promoter, an image other promoters will have a great deal of trouble matching.

4. The other side to Ames Productions is Ames Agency which managed local bands until recently when there ceased being anything to manage them into. Of Our Own will provide the means for revitalizing local talent, and will also give Ames an inside track for signing that talent. You know, all of that stuff could almost make him THE Houston promoter.

Anyway, that's our estimation of what Ames stands to gain by the deal. For him, this is a business proposition, a fact all of us should keep foremost in our idealistic little minds.

An aside for the people who object to the all-pervading cynicism of this article: Richard Ames has never been a member of the Houston hip community, but rather has related to it most often in an exploitative manner. Until his words are matched by substantial and continued actions, it seems naive or dishonest to view his offer with anything other than frankly open distrust.

On the other hand, if Ames follows through on the agreement, and if we can get ourselves fairly together, there should be sufficient advantages for us, too.

Sometimes, you just might find, you get what you need.

We definitely need a place where we can come together in large numbers without being intimidated. We need to do this in order to formulate a sense of our own identity and of our proper struggle.

A place of our own we can structure around our own needs. A place of our own can be turned to any cultural or organizational use we want: movies, rock, theater, speakers, rallies, classes, community meetings. We can do free things when we want to and low admission or donation things when we have to.

And if we support it in sufficient numbers, we can concentrate enough skills and bread to build and sustain critical survival institutions: Switchboard, Inlet, medical centers, day care centers, schools, food co-ops, free stores, mechanics' co-ops, artists' co-ops, breakfast programs. We can teach each other, and we can learn from each other.

One of the major stumbling blocks in this deal is the concept of community control. The "Management Committee" doesn't really represent much more than the people who are on it. It's simply a group of people who were collected because they had a variety of skills and contacts. Ideally, this is only a temporary group, and ways will soon be found to define exactly what it is that such a group should do and to democratize the whole situation. [Cautionary advice: Sometimes when the State don't wither away exactly like it oughta, a little push by the people can help things along.]

One thing for sure: this ain't the revolution. This is a business arrangement with a man who calls himself a Nixon Republican. You can't always get what you want, but... sometimes, you just might find, you get what you need. Dig It!

—*Dennis Fitzgerald*

Community Building

Alice Embree

Space City News (later *Space City!*) set up shop at 1217 Wichita Street in Houston, and the space became a launching pad for an alternative community that Sherwood Bishop has described in a section about the paper's origin, on page 14. In April 2021, A.J. Montrose shared a memory about his own experience:

> *Space City News* was the portal, the entry for so many people that led to so many memorable experiences. For me, the discovery of a lifetime was a wacky, glued-together clan of do-gooders who cobbled together an entity called Houston Switchboard, which was housed, where else, at *Space City News*.

The newspaper was a portal, not only for Houston Switchboard, but for community building, allowing space for draft counseling, drug counseling, a germinating food cooperative, and a Liberation Library, as well as a space to mentor high school reporters and develop a free school called the University of Thought. Articles in this section capture several community ventures in their early days.

Austin
June 2021

Art: Kerry Fitzgerald, December 17, 1970

Switchboard

Space City! Staff • June 20, 1970

The Houston Switchboard, everyone's communications center — and information clearinghouse. Starting soon, with your help. This is what we'll do!

Crisis Center:

Often, a person has an overwhelming problem or emergency and doesn't know where to turn. The people at Switchboard try to respond in a human non-hysterical way to people in any kind of crisis.

Rap Exchange:

A rap exchange is a person who enjoys talking to people. If you feel like talking to someone, call the Switchboard: We'll be happy to turn you on to someone. If you would like to be listed on our rap exchange, call the Switchboard, tell us about yourself and what you enjoy talking about. You can limit your involvement as to time, area of interest, ages, or in any way you wish.

Buy and Sell File:

Many young people are looking for full-time or part-time work. Switchboard will try to keep a list of all kinds of jobs. If you wish to offer work, please call. Switchboard is also a good place to list unusual jobs and one-day odd jobs.

Message Service:

Runaways — Parents who wish to get a message to their son or daughter may leave it at Switchboard. Names of all people who have messages here are listed biweekly in *Space City!*. We guarantee runaways and missing persons that we will not inform anyone whether a message has been picked up; therefore runaway youths can feel free to check with us for messages without feeling that our service is a trap to have them arrested or returned home against their will.

General: Switchboard is a message service through which anyone may leave a message for anyone else. This service is directed toward people who have no other means to receive a message.

Transportation File:

A connection of rides and riders.

Other Things Switchboard Hopes to Do:

Legal Aid
Pregnancy Help
Entertainment File
Housing File
Crash Pads
Medical Aid File

But we need much help to get it going. We need money to pay for the phone bill and the cost of informational leaflets. We need office equipment, filing cabinets, etc. And most of all, we need people: doctors, lawyers, specialists, people to rap, people to help us at the Switchboard. Because this is a community project, not a personal one. The Switchboard is here to bring the community of Houston together again and to let people help each other.

Donations can be sent to:
Houston Switchboard
1217 Wichita
Houston, Texas 77004

There will be a meeting of all the people interested in helping to make the Switchboard work at 7:30 p.m. Monday June 22, at *Space City!*, 1217 Wichita. If you miss the meeting and want to help, call 526-6257 and let us know that you exist. -30-

Art: Kerry Fitzgerald, December 23, 1970.

Library for the Left

Doyle Niemann • October 17, 1970

One of the most common claims against the Left today is that it has no theory, analysis, or program sophisticated enough to deal with contemporary Amerikan reality. This is not exactly true. While the Left has not yet developed a complete analysis of our society — which is not surprising considering it is still relatively young (SDS was only formed in 1962) — it has gone a long way towards defining some of the contours of that analysis and program. The problem is that much of this work is not generally available to people. It is in a variety of pamphlets, papers, and a few books. None of this material is readily available in bookstores, libraries, or the mass media.

To help alleviate this problem a few of us at *Space City!* would like to set up the Liberation Library. *Space City!* has donated us a room in their office — 1217 Wichita. We already have a great deal of material to put in the library — the personal libraries of a few of us, plus all that *Space City!* regularly gets in exchanges with other papers. This gives us good material on what people around the country are doing and thinking right now, plus some stuff of a more general theoretical and analytical nature.

We'd like for the library to serve as both a resource center for the movement, where people can find out information they need to know and can improve their own understanding of Amerikan reality, and as a place where people who are new to the movement can find out a little of what it is about. We'd like for it to be a nice comfortable place where people can sit around and read and rap.

One other thing that we would like to do, providing we can get some financial support, is to set up a literature store and maybe a bookstore. There is a fantastic amount of material in pamphlet form which is relatively cheap and also quite good, but it is simply unavailable in Houston at the present moment. We would like to be able to order some of this and to have it around for people to buy. We might even be able to get to the point where we can print some of our own material.

But if all of this is to come off we are going to need a lot of help and assistance. *Space City!* has given us a nice comfortable room (with a fireplace even), but we have absolutely no furniture at the moment. We need easy chairs, couches, desks or tables, lights, and hopefully a real rug. We also are going to need lumber to build shelves and other furnishings as well as file cabinets to put all our stuff in.

Our most pressing need, however, is that perennial one of MONEY. In addition to needing money just to get the library operating, we also need money to make it a real library. Right now we are getting a lot of material through the personal subscriptions of some of us setting up the library. That cannot continue since none of us have any more money. Our subscriptions are expiring.

Right now, for instance, our subscriptions to *Liberation, Hard Times, The Militant, International Socialist Review, Women: A Journal of Liberation, New Left Review, Socialist Revolution* (see review this issue), *The Black Scholar*, the index of radical publications of the Radical Research Center, and about 10 other publications are all up for grabs.

We also are going to need money to subscribe to new publications and to keep up to date with all the pamphlets, books and papers that are coming out everyday. Certainly we are going to need some substantial amounts of money before we could ever set up a real literature or bookstore.

But money is not our only need, we would gladly accept donations of books and literature which would be useful for the library to have. Of particular interest here are things which would be useful for power structure research as well as material from or about the ear-

a library for the left

Art: Skip Williamson, October 17, 1970.

lier periods of leftist activity in this country. If you don't want to just give us money, we would accept contributions for a specific publication or book.

Finally, and perhaps most important, we are going to need people who would be interested in working with the library. The more people we can involve in setting up and operating the library the better it will be. We really want it to be a community thing.

If you would like to help, give money, donate furniture or materials please contact Doyle Niemann in the *Space City!* office at 1217 Wichita, 526-6257

Power to the People -30-

University of Thought

Richard Turner • October 17, 1970

Well, folks, the University of Thought has done it again. The fall semester started on October 5, and everything is working out as well as can be expected with, of course, the normal hassles. We opened with about 100 courses which are being taught by graduate students, professors, and people from the community. At the moment, we've got some 2,000 people of all ages participating in the program.

All of the classes are free, and everyone is welcome. Each class meets 10 times — once a week for an hour and a half. We try to offer any class which is wanted by the community. If you want a class offered, let us know. If you can't teach the class yourself, we'll try and find a teacher. We'll listen to anyone who wants to talk to us.

We've got a long way to go until we can establish ourselves, but we're gettin' there. If you're interested in more information, or just want to talk about free education, give us a call at 526-7743 or 526-1829. Remember, education is an infinite process which is still to be explored. -30-

Community Bread

December 12, 1970

If you're paying high prices for food, and are tired of the impersonal atmosphere of established grocery stores, you need The Incorporated Community Bread (formerly Houston Food Co-op) — and Bread wants you.

The Incorporated Community Bread provides a nonprofit service of household products and food distribution to its members. Prices are wholesale and below, much cheaper than your present grocery store. And Bread is community, brotherhood/sisterhood and involvement. Bread is a cooperative venture.

Bread has eggs, milk, cheese, yogurt, real bread (including organic), fresh fruits, fresh vegetables, canned goods, pet foods, paper products, a small selection of packaged meats, and numerous other food and household products, including cat litter! We are also looking toward ecology-minded products and more organic and health foods.

Bread is presently open Sundays, from 1 to 6 p.m. Members of Bread work in the store to keep expenses down and create a feeling of community.

Membership in the co-op costs $5 with monthly dues of $1 to meet expenses. We do not make a profit.

So, if you would like to work with your brothers and sisters for cheaper food and good times, call Switchboard (526-3666) for our number. The Incorporated Community Bread is presently located behind Texas Art Supply, off Montrose near Westheimer.

Switchboard has just moved into its own house — along with the Red Coyote Tribe. Our new address is 2701 Albany (corner of Albany and Dennis). Also, due to technical difficulties with "Ma Bell," we have a new phone number: 526-3666.

We have a lot of space around our new house and we've been working on ideas on what to do with it. Ideas like a free store, day care center or a crash pad. Things like these are good and they are needed and it's going to take interested people to make them real. It takes people willing to contribute either time, money, materials, or all three. With your resources and your continued interest we can keep what we have and make what we need. If you can contribute time, money or materials (anything), please contact Switchboard. -30-

Inlet Lives

May 25, 1971

Those of you new to Houston may not know yet of a place that's been open here nearly a year. Inlet — the drug crisis house at 708 Hyde Park (near Montrose-Westheimer). It's a place to come to at any time day or night to get help with drug-related problems. It's a house, not an office, opened by some Houston freaks who know the answers to your questions because they have been there themselves.

They need people who know their drugs.

They don't keep any records or even care what name you give them (as long as you use the same name each time you go over there!). No heat, no hassles, just help. For freak-outs, overdoses, help for those who want to quit being strung out (and for mamas who are worried about their darlings getting hurt by that nasty marijuana...), lifestyle counseling, friendly help, warm vibes, and caring.

Inlet people do not get paid for their time; you do not get charged (though they have never been known to turn down a donation. . .). The house is run as a collective, staffed by a crew of assorted volunteers, and kept alive by community support. It is your drug crisis center. They pay their bills with donations, begging, returning coke bottles, etc. (i.e., money is hard to come by).

To help get more bread, they are having a benefit at Of Our Own in the Village on June 7. Performances by name groups such as Don Sanders, Pelican, One Human Family, Sweetpeter, and Inlet's Own Scott Henderson. Come and enjoy the music — Monday nite June 7, 8 p.m. — for the whole evening just a $1 donation (or more if you love them. . .).

Inlet also needs the usual help in the form of furniture, air conditioners, food, linen, people, and money, etc. Inlet is a community-run thing — of, by, and for the people. If you want to help out, come by or call 526-7925. But only if you are responsible enough to dig what they're doing and willing to help, not drag them down by freeloading, and only if you know the drug scene from the inside. They need people who know their drugs, and don't have to be explained to about what LSD is.

We have had several calls lately about THC (tetra-hydrocannabinol). Without going into boring details, this is a chemical that is an attempt to synthesize what is in the marijuana that gets you high. It is expensive, usually $15 to $20 per cap. Someone in this fair city is supposedly selling THC at $2.50 a cap, and unless (s)he is amazingly charitable and taking a huge loss, (s)he is ripping you off. We have found that usually people sell pig tranquilizers, yes animal stuff, and call it THC. At least two people have called over the weekend to say they tried some of the $2.50 caps and got super-sick; one guy had convulsions. Do what you want, but we thought we'd tell you. -30-

Space City!
Power Structure

VOLUME II/NUMBER 22/APRIL 27, 1971/HOUSTON, TEXAS/(713) 526-6257
NOW WEEKLY

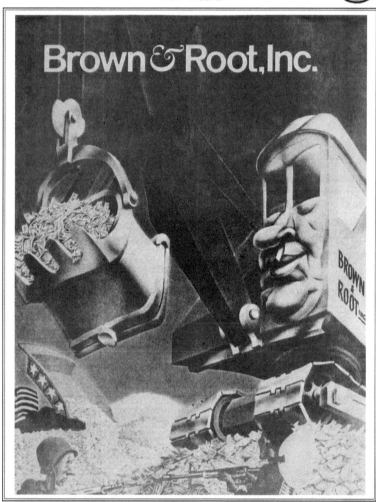

Cover: April 27, 1971.

Space City! And Houston's Power Structure

Cam Duncan

In its first "Letter from the Collective," published in the July 4, 1969 issue, the Collective wrote: "According to the *Peninsula Observer* in Palo Alto CA, 'The major service a paper can do for the movement community is to organize and publish power structure research and analysis.' ... How can we better service the movement? Let's talk about it."

Space City! was born at a time when there was growing awareness in the underground and Left press of research on urban "power elites" — wealthy families and businesses who wield power through their support of foundations, commissions, universities, and the mass media. Papers like the *Berkeley Barb*, Atlanta's *Great Speckled Bird*, and *NOLA Express* in New Orleans educated their communities by exposing the dangerous concentration of power and wealth in their upper classes. *Space City!*, in the belly of one of the richest oil-based cities in the nation, was part of this effort to expose the many ways ruling elites control economic and political decision-making.

The *Space City!* staff was motivated in part by writers like William Domhoff, whose 1967 book *Who Rules America?* argued that municipal power is wielded not directly by the wealthy class as a whole but through a range of megacorporations, banks, media, and institutions whose interests are united in a pro-growth coalition. Their unity is reinforced by the fact that the pro-growth landed interests soon attract a set of organized opponents, often neighborhoods, environmentalists, university students and Left activists.

> **'Space City!' is in the belly of one of the richest oil-based cities in the nation.**

Who Owns the Media?

With this power elite framework, *Space City!*'s coverage of Houston's ruling structures began with two articles on ownership of the largest radio and TV stations: "Who Owns the Media" in Houston. The first story appeared opposite a piece on the recent history of the underground and radical press. On the role of commercial media wielded by the overseers of the city's economy, the authors wrote:

> We set out to uncover Houston's media barons and to discover how they operate. Wealthy Houstonians built up the first radio and TV stations during the 30s, 40s, and early 50s.... Although a few of the more powerful local baronies, such as the Hobby family, have retained their broadcasting holdings, most of Houston's radio and TV stations are now controlled by absentee owners, often national powers through media conglomerates.
>
> If we want to change the world we must take control away from those who are now defining our environment; that is, we must make another environment possible. We must get to the media.

The Jones Empire

In the following issue, Dennis Fitzgerald, Jeff Shapiro, and Sue Mithun wrote an analysis in a pull-out section that no one had published before about Houston's power elite — "Houston Endowment: Blessed Are the Tax Exempt." The section focused on the fortune and influence of "Mr. Houston," Jesse H. Jones.

Art: July 17, 1969

The section's first piece discussed the Houston Endowment, "the greedy ghost of Jesse Jones," described also as "the largest single corporate force" in the city of Houston. One of the authors, Jeff Shapiro, recalls that the Endowment expose was a "seismic" story for Houston. Few people knew about it. Despite its vast financial and political power, the Endowment had never been investigated or written about before in any Houston newspaper. At least, not until *Space City!* showed up.

A second piece on the Jones Empire — excerpted here — covered Jones's purchase in 1910 of part interest in the *Houston Chronicle*, now the city's paper of record. In the 1930s, the *Chronicle* extended Jones's real estate empire by buying TV and radio stations. At Jesse Jones's death in 1956, his assets in media, banking, and 40 office buildings came under the control of the Endowment — today the second-largest private foundation in the city ranked by total giving — and its president, his nephew John T. Jones, Jr. This kept the empire within one of Houston's most powerful ruling families.

Karolyn Kendrick launched the paper's coverage of the city's powerful politicians with an insightful article in the July 17, 1969 issue titled "Welch: A Profile of Power." Louie Welch served as Mayor of Houston from 1963 until 1974. Kendrick focused on Welch's skillful control over an ineffective City Council, allowing him to manipulate $15 million in city contracts to fill the pork barrel for his friends, family, and campaign contributors. She highlighted Welch's practice of systematically dividing whites from Blacks — who had no representative on the Council until 1972 — and Houston's highest residential segregation index among major U.S. cities.

University Support of Power Elite

Space City!, along with student contributors, wrote about the close ties between the major universities' governing boards and the local business elite. Jeff Shapiro, Dennis Fitzgerald and Rice student Karolyn Kendrick wrote a special muckraking pullout entitled "Who Rules Rice," inspired by a

> **Rice students had forced the resignation of a president.**

student uprising in response to the Rice Board of Trustees' decision to ban Chicago 8 defendant Abbie Hoffman from speaking on campus in April 1970. Students had demonstrated for two years against CIA and ROTC recruiting on their campus and the University's research contracts with NASA and the Defense Department. The article, reprinted in full in this section, details the trustees' intimate relationship with Houston's financial moguls as well as professors' involvement in counterinsurgency military research funded by the Pentagon.

A related piece in the Rice pullout by David Williams — "Kingdom of Rice: Tear Down the Walls" — enumerates key student demands, including more admissions of minority and female students, student representation on policy-making bodies, abolition of military research, transparency of university financial records, and decent wages for Rice hourly- paid employees. Rice students in February 1969, had forced the resignation of a president appointed by the trustees who failed to consult an advisory board of faculty and students.

Contributor Randy Chapman, a University of Houston undergraduate, researched and wrote — with help from Bill Casper, Gavan Duffy, and Dennis Fitzgerald — a scathing analysis of the corporate business domination of the University. Chapman's critique, "Inside the University of Houston," focused on the Chair of the Board of Regents and founder of one of Houston's two largest law firms who, when asked his opinion of the Student Senate vote to close the university for one day in honor of the students killed at Kent State, responded, "I think our public is disgusted with the students…the Board has a difficult time raising money, students should act responsibly."

The article, subtitled "A Microcosm of Society," described UH as "controlled by the same class of persons who influence our national policies and priorities." It highlighted the University's racist and sexist foundations, including the administration's refusal to fund the Black Student

Art: July 17, 1969.

Art: Kerry Fitgerald, July 17, 1969.

Union and the defunding of a Save our Students program that provided tutoring services.

The UH ruling Regents and administration were composed, like the city's business barons, almost exclusively of white males. A centerfold spread, reprinted in this section, graphically detailed the myriad links between each member of the Board of Regents and key sectors of the corporate community — the largest banks and finance, insurance, law firms, and construction. The web of interlocking relationships revealed how nine Regents influenced and manipulated the university's public funds for their private benefit.

Brown & Root Conglomerate

One of the key pillars of the Houston business establishment is the giant construction engineering firm Brown & Root, now known as Kellogg Brown & Root. KBR built about 95 percent of the infrastructure needed by the U.S. Army during the Vietnam War, including ships and military bases. Victoria Smith and Jeff Shapiro authored a devastating eight-page spread on the history and power of the second largest contractor in the world at the time, "Brown & Root: How to Build an Empire." The article was prompted by the revelation in February 1971, that the firm had received a Defense Department contract to upgrade a secluded

> **The company used its corrupt role as Johnson's personal vehicle to power.**

group of prisons called the "tiger cages" on Con Son Island which the U.S. military used to confine South Vietnamese political prisoners.

The authors tell the story of how the KBR combine grew from building roads in central Texas in the 1920s to become a key corporate supporter of the political career of Lyndon B. Johnson, helping him win election to the U.S. Senate in 1948 after a fraudulent primary. The company used its corrupt role as Johnson's personal vehicle to power and thereby became a new player in the oil and gas industry. The story details KBR's remarkable power over the Texas legislature, its success in banning the "closed shop" labor organizing protection in Texas, and its resistance to attempts to unionize KBR workers.

Smith and Shapiro conclude by putting the company's mega-power in political perspective: "We think Americans should study corporations like Brown & Root because they generate the breathtaking power that is largely responsible for the sorry state America and the world is currently in."

Santa Fe, New Mexico
June 2021

Houston Endowment:
Blessed Are the Tax Exempt

Dennis Fitzgerald, Jeff Shapiro and Sue Mithun • September 27, 1969

The Houston Endowment is the greedy ghost of Jesse Jones.

The foundation was described in a 1966 *Atlantic Monthly* article as "the largest single corporate force" in the city of Houston. Through the Endowment's ownership of communications media, its board of trustees has played a powerful role in shaping the political and social consciousness of this city. Today it remains as guardian and executor of the Jesse H. Jones financial empire.

Yet it is doubtful that one Houstonian in 10 is aware of the Endowment, or would even recognize the name of its President, Joseph Howard Creekmore.

Houston Endowment Inc. was established on September 25, 1937, by the late Jesse H. Jones and his wife Mary Gibbs Jones as a "nonprofit, philanthropic corporation." According to its charter: "The purpose for which this corporation is formed is the support of any charitable, educational, or religious undertaking."

The initial capitalization of the Endowment was a gift from Jones in the amount of $1,050,000. Estimates of its worth today range as high as $500 million. Not a bad record for a nonprofit corporation.

Administering the Endowment in its continuing quest for nonprofits is a six-member, self-perpetuating Board of Trustees. Self-perpetuating means that upon the death or resignation of any member, the remaining trustees are empowered to replenish their own ranks. The directors of the Endowment are accountable to no constituency or body of stockholders, but only to their own consciences and the rather lax guidelines which the Treasury Department has seen fit to set out for the operation of such enterprises.

Among its holdings, the Endowment counts "substantial" interests in about 100 corporations, with a majority interest in perhaps a dozen. It owns hotels, downtown office buildings, city real estate, ranch land, oil royalties, blue chip stocks, a lumber company, a newspaper, and perhaps not even the specter of Jesse Jones knows what else. A 1956 article in the *Houston Post* devoted several columns to listing the Endowment's holdings but admitted that "there may be properties even in Houston that the reporter missed."

The *Houston Chronicle* is 100 percent owned by the Endowment and J. Howard Creekmore, publisher, sits atop the masthead as demonstration of at least one man who has kept up with the Joneses.

The Magic Kingdom

But what is this Endowment, which does not pay federal taxes but controls an empire, which disburses thousands of dollars to charity but accumulates in the best snowball (snow job?) fashion millions in assets?

Houston Endowment exists in that shadowy economic sphere known as The Magic Kingdom of Tax-Exempt Foundations and Charitable Trusts. This kingdom was established by subscribers to the Order of the Great Capitalist Tax Dodge (among whom there were Fords and Mellons and Dukes and Rockefellers and Carnegies and innumerable other princely figures), and the guiding motto of this kingdom is: "Them that knows best how to get it, knows best how to give it."

> ## The Endowment counts 'substantial' interests in about 100 corporations.

Art: September 27, 1969.

Cover Art by Kerry Fitzgerald, September 27, 1969.

Since 1961 Rep. Wright Patman, a crusty old East Texas Populist, has been sweeping foundation dirt out from under fancy corporate rugs all over the country. And some of the conclusions reached by his House subcommittee on Foundations bear reprinting here.

From Patman's opening statements prior to testimony before the Subcommittee, July 21, 1964:

> The continuing huge purchases of common stocks by foundations are signaling a change in the location of the economic power in this country. This is a force that can affect the course of our national economy. The power will, in reality, rest in the hands of a relatively small group — the foundation managers.
>
> ....substantial parts of the great fortunes of those who have profited from the enormous expansion of American industry have found their way into tax-exempt foundations. These foundations have already passed and will continue to pass — by right of inheritance — to the control of heirs or their trustees.
>
> ....More and more, the 'cream' is slipping out of our tax system as the great fortunes go into tax exempt foundations. Thus, the "skim milk" incomes of average, hardworking families must shoulder an increasing part of the tax burden, both Federal and State.

Defenders of the tax-free foundation concept come on with all sorts of high-minded, socially-responsible type arguments. Playing upon the fears that grip Everyman as he sees the American Dream slipping into nightmarishness, the foundation proponents cite the relative ease with which the private sector may rush out applying bandages to broken social schemes, feeding and housing the indigent, uplifting downsliding cultural programs, funding education for the uneducated, etc. etc.

In short, the foundations are to do what the government cannot do (because of bureaucratic red tape or unenlightened priorities) or will not do (because of timidity before the electorate or unenlightened priorities).

It's an interesting argument, part of the way. The government, they say, is increasingly unable to meet the needs of the people. So far, so good.

Now we have Vietnam, spiraling inflation, middle class alienation, lower class rebelliousness, rising prime interest rates, commies on the campus and Spiro Agnew on the back steps of the White House — and all the government knows to do is bring out more guns. So?

So now the Sons and Daughters of the American (Industrial) Revolution intend to step in and help straighten things out. Which is where the argument stops being interesting.

Moral: a tax-exempt butcher does not a veterinarian make.

An examination of typical foundations' appropriations reveals that either "Them that knows best how to get it, don't know at all how best to give it," or else they do know and won't. Same difference. Moral: a tax-exempt butcher does not a veterinarian make.

Another question altogether is the "rightness" of the power they exercise. Even if some foundation made nothing but the highest and noblest appropriations, what "right" would it have to do so? That is, just because some guy has a bundle of money, where does he get off deciding that rather than pay taxes, he'll spread the loot around his way and get a bunch of buildings named after himself in the process? (Of course, this does not suggest that tax monies are actually allocated democratically.)

But we're falling a good ways far from the truth if we accept the assumption that the foundations' *raison d'etre* is really to hand out free money.

The trustees and directors of the Endowment, for instance are businessmen, not Boy Scouts. From 1961 to 1967 the Endowment doled out about $17.9 million for grants, scholarships and other "good causes"(more on this later). But – though doubtless they were working night and day at the business of giving — somehow the trustees fell behind: Endowment assets for that same period (by Endowment records) rose from 77.6 million to $167.2 million. Final score: Endowment $95 million. Philanthropy $18 million.

If, as a sort of comparison, we use another set of disbursement figures drawn from a current series in the Endowment's own *Chronicle* — we find an amazing circumstance. Jacqueline Onassis is capable of consuming it faster than the six trustees of the Houston Endowment can shovel it out! (The *Chronicle* claims that Mrs. Onassis and her husband, Aristotle, spent between $15 and $20 million last year.)

Which seems to call for a closer look at those trustees.

All six of the current Endowment trustees are related to Jesse Jones by blood, marriage, or former business association. They are J. Howard Creekmore, 64, president-treasurer, as well as vice president and director of Bankers Mortgage, director of Texas National Bank of Commerce (TNBC), and former director of C&I Life Insurance Co., who first joined Jones in 1926 as a bookkeeper for Bankers Mortgage; J.H. Garrett, 70, vice president, also former senior vice president of TNBC, nephew and former employee of Jones; and W.W. Moore, 84, vice president, also president of Bankers Mortgage, a rancher with land in Jackson and Bastrop Counties, who joined Jones about the same time as Creekmore;

Audrey J. Beck, granddaughter of Jesse's wife by her first marriage, received two-thirds of Mrs. Jones' estate upon her death, at one time owning sizeable acreage of valuable ship channel property under the Beck Cattle and Land Co., though the present status of that property is not clear; John A. Beck, 52, husband of Audrey, also director of Bankers Mortgage, director of TNBC, an initial backer of Houston Colt .45's; and former co-owner of Bobreck Engineering Co.; H.F. Warren, 68, secretary, was elected to replace John T. Jones after his resignation as trustee; he is also director of Bankers Mortgage, employed by Jones interests since 1929.

These five men and one woman administer the Endowment's holdings — which lie in two principal areas, real estate and stocks and bonds. Because ownership is listed under many different corporations and subsidiaries, a complete account is difficult to obtain — and the worth of such holdings purely a matter of opinion, since no two appraisers will grant the same value to any one piece of property.

The Endowment's 1968 tax return indicated total assets as being $167.2 million. Other informed sources have placed the

Endowment's worth at closer to $500 million. Probably there's no way of estimating a true value — short of actually selling all the properties and counting the money, a method the Endowment would be unlikely to favor.

The following are the major properties of which we were able to establish Endowment ownership:

Real Estate

Downtown (see map) — All or part of 10 city blocks under the name of Houston Endowment or *Houston Chronicle* Publishing Co. This property includes both the land and the buildings mentioned on the map. Total worth (derived from assessed valuation figures and almost certainly too low) is about $30 million.

Up until May, 1968, the Endowment also owned the Gulf Building and that lot; both were sold to American General Insurance Co. The blocks on which Jones Hall and the Alley Theatre now rest were donated to the city in 1962. During the past several years, the Endowment has also sold various other smaller properties in the downtown area.

Ship Channel and Industrial Area — Properties owned under the Endowment, Bankers Mortgage, and the *Chronicle*. Total worth (again from assessed valuation figures) is around $6.1 million. There is another huge section of land, formerly owned by the Beck Cattle and Land Co., for which we were unable to locate the present ownership. If that may still be counted among the Jones' holdings, it would double the above worth.

Other miscellaneous Harris County properties belonging to the Endowment might total about $3 million.

Art: Kerry Fitzgerald, September 27, 1969.

It should again be emphasized that the above figures are almost certainly too low. A 1956 article in the *Houston Post* gave estimated values 300 percent higher than these.

Stocks and Bonds

No listing is available save for corporations in which the Endowment owns 5 percent or more stock. Total assets in stocks and bonds listed on 1968 tax return was $117.2 million. Corporations in which 5 percent or more stock is owned (with their estimated market value) are as follows:

- Bankers Mortgage Co. - 98.5 percent ($12.5 million).
- Cherry & Burnett Properties, Inc. - 100 percent ($100,000).
- H&D Corp. - 100 percent ($775,000).
- Jones Lumber Co. - 100 percent ($400,000).
- Park Avenue - 65th Street Corp. - 100 percent ($6 million)
- Realty Management Co. - 100 percent ($70,000).
- 612 Park Ave. Corp. - 100 percent ($245,000).
- Houston Terminal Warehouse & Cold Storage Co. - 70.5 percent ($558,450).
- Ridgeview Land Co. - 72 percent ($23,000).
- Kyle Building Co. - 50 percent ($375,000).
- *Houston Chronicle* Publishing Co. - 100 percent ($35 million).

The stocks in two other major corporations in which they owned over 5 percent were sold last year. A 28 percent controlling interest in Texas National Bank of Commerce was sold in the American General deal for $42.8 million and a 7 percent interest in Bank of Texas was sold to Herman J. Hochman & Co., a Houston investment firm, for $773,000.

Other Endowment assets in the 1968 report — including cash, notes receivable and other investments — total about $44.25 million.

How It Works

So, there are the pieces — or most of them, anyway. But how do they fit together?

Briefly, it looks something like this. Houston's power structure embodies what might be called a "limited pluralism." That's not pluralism in the same sense as defined in anybody's civics textbook; it means only that Houston isn't run by as tight a group as controls, for instance, Dallas or New Orleans. Limited means that although several factions may contend for a larger slice of the pie, nobody wants a different flavor. One group may have its interests

centered in the downtown area, and another may be trying to pull money out towards the Southwest — but both will oppose moves that could threaten their financial empires, like the cutting of the oil depletion allowance.

Along with its capital assets, the Endowment inherited a sort of residual influence from Jesse Jones, a position in the power structure. It is a member of the group which is usually referred to in the newspapers as the "downtown interests." (Another strong member of this group is Gus Wortham's American General Insurance Company, mentioned previously. Wortham was an old business buddy of Jesse Jones, and, as is evident from such in-dealings as the TNBC sale, the malady lingers on.)

Threats to the Endowment's happiness, in addition to Patman, have been the City of Pasadena and, most recently, a developer named Gerald Hines.

Pasadena tried to annex 576 acres of the Endowment's property along the Houston Ship Channel. The foundation balked and got an injunction in court, saying the land is suitable only for agricultural and industrial use and annexation would "seriously

Ad: Bill Narum, November 18, 1971.

injure" its market value. The State Supreme Court disagreed and Pasadena annexed the land this June, adding insult to injury by demanding up to $40,000 it said it lost in taxes during the 10-month-long court fight.

Hines recently proposed an elevated circulatory transit system in the Post Oak-Westheimer shopping complex. At his request, City Council is applying for federal funds to study the idea.

Billed as a possible solution to the city's traffic problems, the circulatory system would enrich the Post Oak-Westheimer merchants — at the expense of downtown interests — by luring shoppers to what is now a bad location on busy freeway and road intersections.

> ## The most visible show of the Endowment's muscle-flexing is its operation of the 'Chronicle.'

Art: September 27, 1969.

The Endowment's influence surely played a part in City Council's delayed approval of Hines' request for federal monies until he had promised to include the downtown area in his study. No mention of the proposal was in the *Chronicle* until the downtown area was included.

The most visible show of the Endowment's muscle-flexing is its operation of the *Chronicle*.

It would be repetitive here to go into a lengthy discussion of the *Chronicle*'s influence in Houston politics (see that article elsewhere in this issue), but one should note the very demonstrable conflict of interest between the direction of a large financial enterprise and the publishing of a powerful daily newspaper. Though such situations are not unusual in this day of communications empires, their existence reduces to an obvious sham the "free" press's claim to objective and disinterested news.

Apparently, however, even the Endowment isn't too comfortable about its ownership of the paper. Treasury Department officials will please note the following:

The *Chronicle* is a political organ. It endorses and opposes candidates for public office. It editorializes on bond elections, Vietnam, inflation, government policies — in short, all the things every newspaper talks about.

It seems *Chronicle* publisher and Endowment president Creekmore does not read his own paper.

The following questions appear on the Endowment's 1969 990-A tax form:

> 12. Have you during the year advocated or opposed (including the publishing or distributing of statements) any national, state, or local legislation? The Endowment answers "no."

> 13. Have you during the year participated in, or intervened in (including the publishing or distributing of statements) any political campaign on behalf of or in opposition to any candidate for public office? The Endowment answers "no."

Selling Out

Foundation power is not quite as safe a game as it used to be. Since Rep. Patman began eyeing around in 1961, the Endowment has been making moves to divest itself of too controversial holdings.

In 1964 the Endowment's C&I Life Insurance Company was merged into American General Insurance Company (the Endowment retaining ownership of the C&I building, however).

In 1965, the *Chronicle*, which has controlling interest in the Texas National Bank of Commerce, almost sold the low-profit Rice Hotel properties to John Mecom. But the deal fell through, reportedly because Mecom couldn't raise the cash.

In May 1968, American General cooperated again by picking up the TNBC stock for $42.8 million — and though the trustees must have grieved to see poor Uncle Jesse's bank go, they did have a $34.5 million profit for solace.

The *Chronicle* is still on the market, but only for the right party. "The Endowment has tried to get rid of all of its controversial property," says John T. Jones Jr., nephew of Jesse, and who himself resigned as an Endowment trustee in 1965 in order that he might relieve the foundation of controversial Radio Station KTRH and KTRK-TV. But, continues John, the man who eventually buys the *Chronicle* "must be a Texan." Who presumably will continue in the understanding that the Emperor is never naked.

One needn't be much impressed, however, by the Endowment's facelifting program. Equally as significant as its sale of "controversial" holdings is its choice of purchasers. The Endowment is taking great care that no liberal Yankee corporate-baggers be let in the back door to Houston's establishment.

Income from the sale of such properties as those above has been reinvested, primarily in less obtrusive stocks and bonds.

Holdings are sold, but only to the "right" people. By such incestuous transactions as the TNBC sale, loss of ownership doesn't necessarily mean loss of power. Common purpose imposes common needs and in that situation a telephone call may work as well as stock certificates in the vault.

One last point: the Endowment's "philanthropy." After all, they did give away almost $4 million last year, and — what did we say? — $18 million during 1961-67.

Let's look at 1968 as an example. Of that $4 million, two grants consumed over half: $667,635 to Houston Baptist College and $1,732,841.42 (!) to Texas Wesleyan College in Fort Worth. Can the Endowment ever again find two less

boat-rocking, unprogressive outlets for its money? (Tune in next year.)

The next largest gifts went to the following: Houston Symphony Society ($30,030), Houston Independent School District ($151,750), St. Mary's University in San Antonio ($50,000), University of Texas Law School Foundation ($50,000), Episcopal Theological Seminary of the Southwest in Austin ($30,000), Marian County Hospital District in Jefferson, Texas ($40,000), Houston Legal Foundation ($35,000) and United Fund of Houston ($60,750).

All safe, respectable, unthreatening. None attack in any significant way the real crises in America today. (Indigent families received $6,600 from the Endowment.)

What must be the foundation's true politics are expressed infrequently and subtly. *Danger on the Right*, a book analyzing current right-wing politics, claims the Endowment has given $20,000 in recent years to the National Education Program at Harding College in Arkansas, a tax-free producer of "far-rightist" films and propaganda. Harding received $2,000 from the Endowment in 1968. And Radio Free Europe, long a recipient of C.I.A. funds, consistently receives small gifts from the Endowment.

Can you think of a cheaper way to accumulate $95 million in seven years? -30-

Ad: December 12, 1970.

Houston Chronicle: What Money Can Buy

Cam Duncan • September 27, 1969

In 1968 the *Houston Chronicle* earned $150,000 in dividends for its owners, six trustees of a tax-exempt "charitable" foundation called the Houston Endowment. How did these people come to "own" the *Chronicle*? How important is a single newspaper to the Endowment's power in Houston? In previous articles we have looked at the history and ownership of Houston's radio and television media. We believe that it is important to examine the organic role media plays in capitalism. The following history of Houston's largest newspaper reflects an initial understanding of its function in the Houston environment. We invite readers to respond to the article and to supply us with more information useful in understanding the role of media in Houston.

In 1901, Marcellus E. Foster, then editor of the *Houston Post*, and Charlie Myers, former *Indianapolis Star* circulation employee, had an idea for starting a third paper in Houston to compete with the *Post* and the *Daily Herald*. They and a group of friends raised $25,000 capital and rented a three-story building two blocks from the present *Chronicle* Building.

The rent, $250 a month, was paid by subletting two-thirds of the building. The entrepreneurs bought three typesetting machines and a printing press on credit and began operations.

The *Houston Chronicle* sold 2,000 issues its first day on the street, Oct. 14, 1901. The city's first newspaper was peddled by boys who stood by barrels filled with pennies for change, since few of the 45,000 Houstonians carried pennies then.

By the end of the month, the *Chronicle* had a circulation of almost 4,400. After a year the paper was able to buy out its competitor on the afternoon market, the *Daily Herald*, for $6,000, and rename itself the *Houston Chronicle and Daily Herald*. The latter eventually disappeared from the banner.

In 1904, the *Chronicle* began publishing a Sunday paper and in 1910 occupied its new 10-story building at Texas and Travis. The builder was a rising financier named Jesse Homan Jones, who liked the building so much he moved in as partner of the owner-editor, M.E. Foster.

In its early days, the paper was known as a "crusader," fighting private water service owners who wouldn't raise water pressure, trying to get saloons closed on Sundays during church service hours, and

In its early days, the paper was known as a crusader.

battling to stop gambling on Main Street. The paper even fought the powerful Ku Klux Klan.

In 1926, Foster and Jones, who had by this time made a sizeable fortune in Houston real estate and a reputation in national Democratic Party politics, had a falling out, presumably a political dispute. Jesse found his venture in journalism profitable and perhaps he saw the importance of owning a newspaper to a successful business and political career.

It is said that Jones proposed to name a fixed sum of money which Foster could either pay Jones for his half interest in the paper or could accept from Jones in return for giving up his interest. Foster couldn't raise Jones' stiff price, so he sold his interest to Jones and retired. Later he became editor of the Scripps-Howard paper, the *Houston Press*. Jones became president, publisher, and sole owner of the *Chronicle*.

Jones Spreads Out

During the Depression, Jones was one of the few big-monied magnates who could withstand the pressure of tight money and still continue investing. In other words, he had plenty of cash, and he quickly spread his control over the Houston media. In 1930, the newspaper company received the broadcasting license to Houston's second radio station, KTRH.

At the same time, the owners of the *Houston Post* were in financial difficulty. Generous Jesse bought and held the notes on the *Post*, exercising a real monopoly ownership over news in Houston, until 1939 when the *Post*'s editor (and Jones' close friend), William P. Hobby, bought it back

Before letting go of the *Post*, Jones established in 1937 the Houston Endowment, a tax-free foundation which enabled him to effectively retain control over the income from his valuable assets and at the same time deferred him from paying taxes on his profits. Jones' original gift to the foundation was some $1,050,000, and the original trustees were either Jesse's relatives or close business associates, as they are today.

It's Called Keeping It All in the Family

Jones was clearly not feeling guilty about his monopolization of the media and the rest of Houston's economy. In 1953, the *Chronicle* bought one-third interest in KTRK-TV (Channel 13). Jones then owned the city's biggest newspaper, its most powerful radio station, and held a controlling interest in its second TV station.

Jones named himself board chairman of the Chronicle Publishing Co. in 1950. His nephew, publisher John T. Jones Jr., became president. The nephew took over the paper and became president of the Houston Endowment in 1956, when Jesse Jones died.

In the 1950s the *Chronicle* was an unabashed mouthpiece for the city's aging oligarchy, dull, cliched, and falling behind its competitor, the *Post*. A little-known incident occurring at the end of that decade reflects the tension between the paper's management and its employees resulting from the management's generally reactionary policies.

Guild Election

In 1959 a committee of employees formed to unionize the editorial staff and affiliate with the American Newspaper Guild. The Guild was founded in the 1930s. Most editorial staffs of big city dailies, except in the South, belong to the Guild. Employees of only two Texas papers, one in San Antonio and one in El Paso, are represented by the Guild.

Prior to the election, which was supervised by the

National Labor Relations Board, numerous letters, pleas and threats were delivered to the employees by both the union organizers and the management. The close October 15, 1959 election was initially won by the Guild 54-50, not including five ballots challenged by the union.

The NLRB allowed two of the challenges (one was a blank absentee ballot and the other was the vote of Everett Collier, who had recently been appointed acting managing editor.) The other three ballots, votes of the *Chronicle*'s Washington Bureau correspondents (whom the union claimed were not real *Chronicle* employees since the Bureau itself was on a contract), were against the union and were certified, resulting in a slim Guild victory 54-53.

The *Chronicle* board of directors was shocked, and steadfastly refused to recognize the union. The NLRB then appealed on behalf of the union to the Fifth Circuit District Court in New Orleans, which took its time in making a judgment. The court's verdict, issued two and a half years later, stated that the election was void as a result of a single factual error contained in a letter to the employees from a Guild organizer, in which he described some of the wage benefits contained in a Guild contract in San Antonio.

A reporter who worked for the *Chronicle* at that time told us that, after two years, there had been a large shift in personnel and conditions were more tolerable on the editorial staff, so there was unfortunately no more talk of unionizing. Needless to say, there was no mention of the certification election in the pages of the *Chronicle*.

A *Chronicle* reporter for a few years in the early 1960s, Saul Friedman, commented on the reactionary policies of the 1950s. Under the editor, Emmett Walter, managing editor Roderick Watts, and associate editor Everett Collier, Friedman said that "the *Chronicle* was slightly to the left of Rasputin — and to the right of the *Dallas Morning News*."

Brought in to rejuvenate the paper in 1960 was William P. Steven, an experienced editor who reversed the paper's dying tendencies and began to look at the *Chronicle* as though it were being published for the whole

Art: July 17, 1969.

community. In addition to this heresy, he was pretty "radical" for Houston: he supported higher education, Lyndon Johnson, and civil rights.

Steven recalled to an *Atlantic Monthly* writer his first meeting with publisher John Jones, during which Steven expressed his strong feelings about integration. As Steven remembered it, Jones replied, "The *Chronicle* supports the law of the land. The only trouble I'll have with you is that you may want to talk about it too much."

Steven at once began building the local news staff, which was suffering from inbreeding, age, and low salaries. Top reporters at the *Chronicle* in 1960 were getting $120 a week, and Steven raised their salaries substantially. The *Chronicle* withdrew its support from the conservatives on the school board, pressed for televising of school board proceedings against the bitter opposition of conservatives, and won.

In 1964 the *Chronicle*'s afternoon competition, the Scripps-Howard *Houston Press*, finally gave up and sold its assets to the *Chronicle*, which then became the largest paper in Texas, with 254,000 circulation.

"I've heard the *Chronicle* cussed out at public meetings, at John Birch meetings," Friedman told the *Texas Observer*. "Yet I somehow think that this pressure did not have any real reaction on John Jones. I think it had its reaction on the people who ran Houston Endowment, and this is where the real pressure began to come from — Houston Endowment."

Whatever the precise reason that precipitated the Endowment's anger, it was on September 2, 1965, during the Watts Black rebellion in Los Angeles, that Steven was notified of his dismissal.

J. Hurt Garrett, Endowment trustee and former vice president of the Texas National Bank of Commerce, said of the shake-up: "We didn't like their editorial policy, that's all. I never heard anything but complaints about it... It was all this racial desegregation business. Things were all right in Houston before they came down. But all this racial business — nobody liked it."

In line with "this racial business," *Chronicle* reporter Friedman had spent three months researching a series of articles on the Houston Black community that documented, among other things, the activities of local slum lords and housing authorities. The *Chronicle* refused to print the series. Shortly after Steven's dismissal, Friedman left the paper for more liberal Northern climates.

'I've heard the "Chronicle" cussed out at public meetings, at John Birch meetings.'

When the Endowment fired Steven, it had already accepted John T. Jones' resignation from the board. Jones had stepped down a month earlier to avoid a charge of self-dealing when be bought from the Endowment the *Chronicle*'s radio and TV stations.

There followed a watchful period, during which Collier treaded very conservatively, and the staff watched the sky for bolts from the Enigmatic Endowment. None came.

Oilman John Mecom is a Houstonian whose assets in 1966 were said to be between $400 and $500 million (perhaps on a par with Endowment's holdings).

Mecom was the buyer in the abortive "sale" in early 1966 of the *Chronicle* and other Endowment properties, for a reported $85 million. Had he really bought the properties, Mecom now would own about 10 square blocks of downtown Houston. The package included the paper, the Rice Hotel, the Rice Hotel Garage and Laundry, and Endowment's controlling stock in Texas National Bank of Commerce, the city's second largest bank. The bank stock was estimated to have been worth between $40 and $50 million.

Mecom was elected board chairman and chief executive officer of the bank where he already was a director. He announced that he was retaining the paper's editorial hierarchy and that its policies would not change. Mecom was a Democrat at the time, an ardent supporter of Johnson and Humphrey.

It appeared to all as a real sale, and that's the way the Endowment had announced it in a front-page story. But six months after the announcement Mecom's name simply disappeared from the masthead on the editorial page and now-deceased Jesse Jones' name reappeared.

Reporters read about the non-sale in such papers as the *New York Times* and *Washington Post*. Indeed, some *Chronicle* reporters wrote the stories that appeared elsewhere. But again, no coverage appeared in the pages of the *Chronicle*. If Houstonians depended on their biggest paper, they would not know that the community had undergone a profound change, that "their" leading newspaper, the most prominent Texas representative of that crucial institution of free and independent press, was being bought and sold like an anonymous link in a string of corporate hot dogs.

The most credible explanation for the non-sale was that the Endowment's financial spies learned Mecom was up to his ears in debt, having over-extended his credit, and put it to him in plain words: cash now or no sale. Mecom, of course, could not come up with the cash, even whatever portion the seller was demanding on the spot.

The reason for the sale remains a matter of pure speculation among Houston corporate circles. Why would the Endowment have wanted to dispose of such valuable property in the first place?

The possibility of a conflict of interest was as inherent under Mecom's ownership of the *Chronicle* as it was under its previous owners. But the Endowment had been pursued by the Treasury Department and by Congressman Wright Patman. Patman was digging deeper into the Endowment in 1965, compiling an impressive record of the Endowment's large-scale corporate dealings and its modest indulgence in charity. The foundation was feeling considerable pressure to divest itself of some of its commercial interests, particularly the newspaper, its most obvious political tool. But why did they pick Mecom?

Collier's explanation is: "The trustees of the Houston Endowment were determined to keep these properties in the hands of someone who has the same deep love of this community and the same concepts for its betterment and progress that Jesse Jones had." The trustees no doubt felt they were expressing "the same concepts for its betterment and progress" when they fired Steven for being too liberal and too pro-Negro.....

We have mentioned major incidents of interest to the community which, to preserve the secrecy in the corporate chambers, the *Chronicle* owners did not deem newsworthy. There was also a bitter stockholder struggle in 1965 within the Texas National Bank of Commerce (then owned by the Endowment) which received brief coverage in the Post and, of course, no mention In the *Chronicle*. Earlier, during the period of 1959-60 when downtown department stores and lunch counters were desegregating for the first time, both papers agreed that to avoid a possible white "backlash" they would ignore the issue completely.

And it is well known that both papers operate closely with the mayor's office to determine news coverage in times of possible racial unrest. For example, when Stokely Carmichael spoke at a rally in Houston in 1967, the *Post* wrote three paragraphs on him, and the *Chronicle* carried only a picture buried in the paper's third section.

As for the *Chronicle*'s current editorial policy, the paper is above all else still owned by the Endowment. Although we occasionally get a glimpse of Establishment Liberalism, on its editorial page, such as tepid support of the housing code and increased welfare spending, when the issue hits the rich man's pocketbook (the oil depletion allowance controversy) the paper shows its true colors.

The cooperation between the *Post* and *Chronicle* is not surprising. Both newspapers represent the interests of two families within Houston's ruling class, a small, elite group of corporate businessmen who constitute a kind of "family" themselves. The *Chronicle* is indeed the "family newspaper."

> I regard the publication of a newspaper as a distinct public trust, and one not to be treated lightly or abused for selfish purposes or to gratify selfish whims. A great daily newspaper can remain a power for good only so long as it is uninfluenced by unworthy motives, and unbought by the desire for gain. "The *Chronicle* will always be … a newspaper for all the people, democratic in fact and principle, standing for the greatest good to the greatest number.

— from a *Chronicle* editorial Jesse Jones wrote after buying the newspaper in 1926.
-30-

Ad: December 12, 1970.

Who Rules Rice?

Jeff Shapiro, Dennis Fitzgerald, and Karolyn Kendrick • May 9, 1970

There are certain institutions in which economic — and therefore political — powers meet and work their deeds in what might be moralistically termed financial adultery. Less colorfully, that arrangement is called oligarchy. In one instance, it is called Rice University.

A succinct description of Rice's structure appears in the 1964 Self- Study of Rice University, prepared by the faculty and administration:

> William Marsh Rice University is a non-profit corporation existing under and by virtue of the laws of the State of Texas. . . Its corporate structure is similar at points to a business corporation and at other points it is very dissimilar. . . .it does not have stockholders, does not issue stock, does not operate for a profit and therefore does not declare dividends. . . .provision is made for the appointment of seven Trustees who constitute the governing board, and who must be deemed to be the holders of the corpus of the corporation in trust for its declared purposes.

Rice University and its roughly $175 million in assets (Rice's endowment is the 13th largest of any private university in the country, according to a 1967 Boston Fund report) is controlled totally by a board of seven persons (currently six men and one woman). By virtue of its nonprofit corporate status, Rice is not required to reveal any of its financial records; nor is Rice bound by any responsibility to the public, other than the very broad directives of William Marsh Rice's will and the minimal legal notions of a nonprofit corporation.

The trustees of Rice and their 26 fellows on the Board of Governors represent the elite of Houston's business community. Of those 33 Board members, all but eight hold bank directorates. Six of those eight are oilmen; one is the president of a large dairy company. Only one, the well- known oceanographer and director of the Lamont Geophysical Observatory at Columbia University, W. Maurice Ewing, can claim substantial academic credentials. (And, alas, even

William Marsh Rice came to Texas as a penniless drifter.

Mr. Ewing has been known to sully his record by odd-jobbing for the oil industry.) All of the Board of Governors are wealthy to very-wealthy. All are white. Only one is a woman.

But if the academic character of Rice University appears to be subverted today, there hasn't been much purity lost along the way. Whilst barely an infant, Rice Institute was orphaned by violence and opportunism, a misbegotten institution whose rhetoric has always concealed its intent. An historical digression:

The Butler Did It

William Marsh Rice came to Texas as a penniless drifter and stayed to make his fortune in lumber. In 1891 he founded Rice Institute, and then left the state to live on an entire floor of the Berkshire Hotel in New York City.

Rice's famous eccentricity (a rich man's infirmity; the poor are referred to as "crazy," or worse) is noted by stories about such things as his practice of leaving waiters a pittance after having been served luxurious meals.

At one time Rice decided that bananas would do his faltering digestive tract a good turn. So he ate them in tremendous quantities. Needless to say, a formerly chronic case of dyspepsia worsened so drastically that his physician feared Rice would not survive.

He did survive, but only long enough to be murdered by his valet, who was in league with a New York lawyer, both of whom were determined that the Rice fortune should go to themselves rather than to Rice Institute.

The valet, Charles F. Jones, had no reason to love his employer. Rice believed that someone was trying to poison him, and it was among Jones' duties to sample any food or drink which the philanthropist was to consume. The poisoning actually occurred, but, appropriately, it was Jones himself who did the deed — at first slowly with mercury, and then for the *coup de grace*, with chloroform.

After Rice's death, the treachery was found out. Investigators also discovered numerous forged checks, written to the lawyer, and they exposed as bogus a Rice will, which would have canceled his bequest to

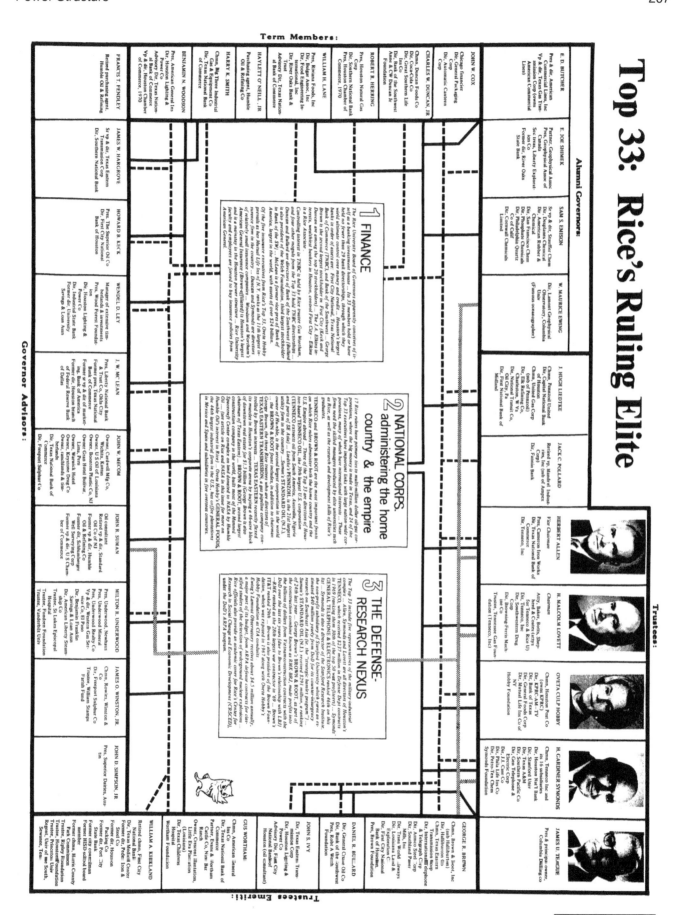

Chart: May 9, 1970.

Rice Institute. Neither of the murderers was convicted, however. The valet was let go immediately. The lawyer, after some extended legal proceedings, was granted unconditional pardon. The eccentric ashes of William Marsh Rice were shipped back to Houston, where they rest today in the center of the Academic Court. And thus began the illustrious history of Rice University.

Upon Rice's death, the Board of Trustees found itself with an estate of about $10 million and with immense freedom in establishing a regional university dedicated to the "Advancement of Literature, Science, and Art," but limited by the will to *white* "boys and girls struggling for a place under the sun."

When expansion of the Board became desirable in 1949, the Trustees, in order to avoid a court battle to change the will, and in order to maintain their exclusive control of university affairs and money, provided for Governors, who serve a term of four years and may be reappointed only by unanimous consent of the Trustees. After serving their terms, the Governors became Governor Advisors. Although the Trustees are appointed for life, they have agreed to retire at the age of 70. Retired trustees are Trustees Emeriti. There are also now seven Term Members, Rice graduates, elected by their fellow alumnae to assist the Board. All together, these groups form the Rice University Board of Governors.

Yet complete control still rests with the seven, self-perpetuating trustees, all members of the corporate business world, who see Rice as one more corporation to administer. Their view of the university pervades the campus world so thoroughly that it has enforced a certain consensus of style upon faculty members and ultimately upon even the majority of the students themselves.

Bankers on the Board

The physical plant of Rice University is easily accessible to anyone who wishes to wander over to the manicured 300-acre campus on South Main Street. But the hows and wherefores of the real decision-making at Rice constitute privileged information. The particulars of Rice's financial operations are among the better kept secrets of that university. So, save for what rumor speaks or what one is lucky enough to stumble onto in a dusty file cabinet, little information is available.

> **The eccentric ashes of William Marsh Rice were shipped back to Houston.**

According to the 1967 Boston Fund report, 61.3 percent of Rice's endowment (or roughly $77,436,000) is invested in common stocks, and 28.3 percent of the endowment (or $35,650,000) is in income-producing real estate and mortgages.

Rice's access to and involvement with Houston's ruling class is typified by its banking connections. The three largest banks in Houston are, by order of their assets, First City National Bank, Texas National Bank of Commerce, and Bank of the Southwest.

Trustee Emeritus George R. Brown is the second largest stockholder in First City National. Governor Advisor Howard B. Keck and Term Member Charles W. Duncan, Jr. are also among the 20 largest stockholders in that bank. Controlling stock in First City National is held by the J.A. Elkins interests. Elkins is a Rice University Associate. (Associates are persons making grants to the University of at least $1,000 per year.) Five Directors of First City National are themselves members or are employed by members of Rice's Board of Governors. Rice directly owns 10,038 shares of the bank's stock.

Controlling interest in Texas National Bank of Commerce is held by Rice Trustee Emeritus Gus S. Wortham. Rice owns an additional 31,551 shares. TNBC Chairman of the Board Ben Taub is a Rice University Associate.

The third largest stockholder in Bank of the Southwest is the Robert A. Welch Foundation, represented on the Rice Board of Governors by Trustee Emeritus Daniel R. Bullard. Term Member Duncan is also a director of Bank of the Southwest and owns considerable stock in the bank. Associate John H. Crooker is a partner in the law firm Fullbright, Crooker, Bates, Freeman and Jaworski, which controls the M.D. Anderson Foundation, which in turn owns controlling interest in Bank of the Southwest.

By the above, it may be seen that Rice is readily assured of whatever assistance and advice is available from Houston banking (which is considerable). Furthermore, as the accompanying chart indicates, Rice's influence extends from banking into virtually every significant aspect of Houston business (and often into national and international business).

In areas where Rice's potential influence is not immediately evident, it may often be easily inferred. For instance, Trustee Mrs. Oveta Culp Hobby may be expected to see that the community image of Rice is protected by the editorial policies of her paper, the *Houston Post*. But the *Chronicle* should not be expected to be much more vigilant. The Houston Endowment, owner of the *Chronicle*, has interlocking interests with many of the members of Rice's Board of Governors (notably Gus Wortham, whose connections with that paper date back to the early business days of *Chronicle* founder Jesse H. Jones).

Suman's ducks

The rulers of Rice may, therefore, presume that the public image of Rice and of themselves will be protected by the press. And, of course, it usually is. Indicting reportage of Rice's elite has normally been limited to such incidents as the *Chronicle* story on former Alumnus Governor John R. Suman, who was charged in November 1960, with possession of illegal ducks. Suman and six other businessmen-hunters were arrested and fined $959 on charges of killing too many ducks on which there was a closed season. At the time Suman was a national trustee of Ducks Unlimited, an organization dedicated to the conservation of waterfowl. Contacted at home, Suman told newsmen that "they promised me there would be no publicity." There wasn't much, but at least no one could accuse the Houston press of trying to hide anything.

Curiously, however, no Houston newspaper discussed the financial advantages of Rice's "desegregation" suit in 1963. No Houston newspaper questioned the motives behind Rice's generous land gift to NASA. No Houston newspaper is so bold as to accuse the Rice trustees of in-dealing. No Houston newspaper has found space to report that a Rice professor is currently doing counterinsurgency research for the Department of Defense. The published word on Rice University is that it is now, as always, an institution dedicated to the "Advancement of Literature, Science, and Art" — with only an occasional dead

No Houston newspaper is so bold as to accuse the Rice Trustees of in-dealing.

duck to mar this lofty ideal. So much for crusading journalism in Big H.

Rice University is a business. Its purpose is the production of excellently trained young administrators and technicians dedicated to the service of advanced industrial capitalism — young workers whose perceptions of the world do not include such phenomena as racism and imperialism. Rice is a cog-maker for the machinery of Amerikan Manifest Destiny.

War Games at Rice

Rice University has consistently denied over the years that it is engaged in activities which could be defined as military research. And. indeed, investigators have been unable to uncover any such projects. But they do exist.

Rice professors are now, and have been for some time, involved in research which will be used directly by such government agencies as the Agency for International Development (AID) to suppress wars of national liberation all over the world.

The reason that previous efforts failed to establish Rice's complicity with the long arm of Amerikan imperialism is that the investigators were looking for napalm and ICBM warheads. They should have paid more attention to projects such as those which study the introduction of tomatoes into the agricultural system of Mexican peasants.

Direct government funding of counterinsurgency research is carried on at Rice at the Center for Re-

Art: Trudy Minkoff, February 14, 1970.

search in Social Change and Economic Development (CRSCED). CRSCED was established in the fall of 1966 with a grant of $440,000 from the Advanced Research Projects Agency (ARPA).

ARPA was established in 1958 under the Eisenhower Administration as an agency specializing in research and development (R&D) for the Pentagon. It wasn't until the Kennedy Administration, however, that ARPA began heavily courting the universities. According to insiders like Roger Hilsman (*To Move a Nation*. Doubleday, 1967), ARPA then began to move away from a dependency on massive military intervention. This trend was hastened by the creation of ARPA's "Project Agile," which represented the thinking of the "Kennedy intellectuals" who sought a political approach to the problem of liberation movements.

There are currently underway at Rice 33 ARPA-funded projects, ranging in content from Prof. D.L. Huddle's "A Cost/Effectiveness Study of Clinical Methods of Birth Control" to Center Director Fred R. von der Mehden's "Development, Insurgency and Political Violence in Southeast Asia."

Counterinsurgency Research

Since Prof. von der Mehden's study is probably the clearest and most direct example of the Center's purposes, we'd like to discuss that at some length. But just so our reference to Mexican tomatoes isn't construed as flippant, we want to quote first from a letter we received from Jim Denney, a 1968 Rice graduate. Jim was employed through the Center as a Research Assistant in Anthropology. His project was Dr. John Ingham's study of personality, motivations for social change, and mechanisms of agricultural innovation in a Mexican peasant village. Excerpts from his letter (which incidentally was rejected for publication by the *Rice Thresher*) follow:

> The Center is and was an obscure institution, even though it holds the largest single block of defense monies in the University.

> When first told of the Department of Defense connections with CRSCED, I was simply amused: how ironic that the DOD should be paying my salary, especially in the light of my political views.

When I asked the director of the center, how "we" could justify accepting defense money, I was told that at least they weren't making bombs with the money and we were putting it to good use. I blindly accepted the explanation. It was only later that ... I began to wonder who should be laughing at whom.

To be specific: the DOD doesn't need to use CRSCED's money for bombs, military "hardware." They have quite enough appropriated as it is. And though the DOD is wasteful, this is not to say that they just *give* their money away. As a matter of fact, I think the DOD knows exactly what it is doing by funding centers like CRSCED.

There are currently underway at Rice 33 ARPA-funded projects.

For, you see, the Defense Department also has a complete philosophy built around the importance of social science to the defense (sic!) of this country. In their parlance, what CRSCED is doing is "software." A complete knowledge of social conditions is required in order to fight successfully in the conditions of modern counter-insurgency warfare.

Some of the first "advisors" in Vietnam were social scientists scoping out the situation. Anthropologists especially have been a big help to our country's noble effort in Southeast Asia.

People may remember Major John A. Dean, head of counterinsurgency operations for the Army, who spoke on the Rice campus. I have been in correspondence with him and want to quote a letter from him!

"All of the topics being studied by the CRSCED relate to counter-insurgency when the Societies under study are those of the Third World. ...

"Your particular project regarding the introduction of tomatoes in a Mexican village has definite applications in economic development and thus counter-insurgency. Many Latin American countries have one crop economies. Fluctuations in the world market price mean fluctuations in the capital available for development. This undermines development planning … In an insurgent situation, the military may be the only government agency capable of carrying out development (esp. in insecure areas). The military unit involved in introducing a new crop must understand the full ramifications (i.e., changes in land use, requirement to additional storage or transportation, etc.)"

So are there no "strings" attached to CRSCED's work? I fail to accept this kind of explanation. I see what counterinsurgency has meant in Vietnam. I have also come to see that making an area, no matter where it is, politically and economically "secure" means making it ripe for United States intrusion into such areas.

The first official publication that appeared from CRSCED's funding was *Detection of Potential Community Violence* written by Dr. Blair Justice. The book is... a study on how to head off rebellion in the ghetto, i.e., how to keep the Blacks repressed. It studies methods of infiltration and subversion of militant groups as well as providing scales for measuring growing anger in the ghetto.

It makes special mention of the TSU "riot." Indeed, Dr. Justice has a very special interest in the incident. It was Dr. Justice who was a prime state witness in the abortive trial of former Rice student Charlie Freeman. I for one am quite sure where Dr. Justice's loyalties lie.

However, it would not be fair to say that most of the CRSCED projects are of the same ilk as Dr. Justice's. In large part, the projects are of legitimate interest to social scientists. They also

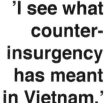

'I see what counter-insurgency has meant in Vietnam.'

continue to be of interest to the Department of Defense. It is this that is the crux of my questioning.

Von der Mehden

Back to Dr. von der Mehden. Remember him? He's Rice's Blair Justice of Southeast Asia.

Dr. von der Mehden occupies the Albert Thomas chair of political science at Rice. That position was established for Rice with a $500,000 gift from Trustee Emeritus George Brown, whose omnipresence at the university would by now begin to be a little boring, if it weren't so frightening.

Von der Mehden's current project is "a comparative study of the relationship of development to political violence in selected countries of Southeast Asia. It is based upon early work (1965-67) in Thailand, library research in the United States, and various studies made by other researchers in Southeast Asia. The Thai, Vietnamese, and Philippine data are in part based upon interviews in insurgent areas or with former in-

surgents done by the principal investigator and others." (From CRSCED's "Final Report of Research Activities," January 30, 1970).

In Thailand, ARPA (the funding agent for CRSCED) runs "Project Agile," the Pentagon's worldwide counterinsurgency research program. According to H.E. Robison, vice-president of the Stanford Research Institute, one of Agile's chief contractors, the project's purpose is "to provide a multi-disciplinary vehicle for research into counter-guerrilla, counterinsurgency, and communications operations in Southeast Asia."

Under Project Agile, ARPA's major research program in Thailand has been drawing on universities, research institutes, and corporations to complement military know-how. Centered around the specially created Joint U.S./Thai Military Research and Development Center (MDRC), the Thailand program began in 1961.

"The primary objective of the ARPA mission in Thailand was, and continues to be R&D (research and development) support of the war in Vietnam — using the relatively similar terrain and physical environment of Thailand to make permissive tests of military hardware under controlled conditions," wrote Michael Getler in the Dec. 19, 1966 *Technology Week*. "However, with the recent increase of guerrilla activity in Thailand, and the mounting interest of the Thai government in improving its ability to cope with this, the joint U.S./Thai R&D group has taken on a new importance."

ARPA's director Charles M. Herzfeld told the House Appropriations Committee in 1966: "Last year ARPA initiated a major R&D program to assist the Royal Thai government and the U.S. Mission in Thailand in their efforts to suppress the growing Communist insurgency in that country's northeast provinces."

Herzfeld defined the significance of this program succinctly at the hearings: "I think to some extent we are breaking ground here for a new way of looking at insurgency, how to stop insurgency while it is small. This is absolutely a major military problem for the United States and it is largely unsolved."

So ARPA's (and von der Mehden's) mission is to save Southeast Asia from the commies, right? Wrong! Their mission is to save Southeast Asia for

Amerika. The State Department's Agency for International Development (AID) explained U.S. objectives in Thailand this way in its 1970 Congressional presentation: "Thailand's importance to the United States lies in its geographic position in Southeast Asia, its key role in the economic and political development of the region, and its close cooperation with the United States."

U.S. investors in Thailand are numerous, though they rank behind our Asian trading partner, Japan. The Chase Manhattan Bank has perhaps been clearest about its interests in Thailand: "Thailand promises to be an excellent investment and sales area for Americans," Chase's Economic Research reported in an April 1, 1969 publication, "if the rebel insurgency can be contained."

> 'Thailand's importance to the United States lies in its geographic position in Southeast Asia.'

Presumably, our point being made, this article could end here. However, it seems important to demonstrate somewhat further that though some of the scientists at Rice may be a bit naive about the potential applications of their CRSCED research (or perhaps they don't care), the directors of the program are in no sense "dupes" of U.S. imperialism.

Von der Mehden, for instance, has been around enough to know what's going on. He is a member of the Southeast Asian Development Advisory Group (SEA DAG), a sort of AID subsidiary, and at least in 1966 was with the Research Division of United States Overseas Missions (USOM), when he wrote a paper for them titled "USOM Programs in Sakol Nakorn." USOM/Thailand and USAID/Thailand are the same mission.

In a 1965 report submitted by the directors of SEADAG it was stated that "a principal task of the Advisory Group is to draw the American university community more integrally and systematically into the activities of the AID."

The report continues:

> It is the opinion of this team and of the Southeast Asian Development Advisory Group in general that no single university is able to provide the range of resources that can be useful either to AID Washington or to any of the overseas missions. The Advisory Group and this team are thus oriented toward the

mobilization of the relevant resources in the total university community rather than toward the selection of specific universities as chosen instruments or backstops.

The authors continue:

USOM wants what has been aptly termed a continuing conversation with the universities, or more accurately with Thai specialists in the universities. . . .There is a desire to know more about the relation between economic development and political stability, or the type of political development that sustains an open society." (Thailand was not, we believe, an open society at the time.) This last sentence is an almost exact description of von der Mehden's project, curiously enough.

One last parting shot at AID. The agency's 1968 pamphlet "The US/AID Program in Thailand" declares in its first paragraph: "The US AID program in Thailand is concentrated upon a single objective: supporting the Royal Thai Government in its efforts to contain, control, and eliminate the Communist insurgency in rural areas."

So the question now remains for the honest social scientist: "Are we to cease research in any area that might be involved some day in counterinsurgency?" The only possible answer, if one chooses sides with the insurgents, or chooses not to choose sides, is yes, we are to cease such research, especially now that AID has so kindly shown that nearly every area of "legitimate" social sciences scholarship is also an area of legitimate counterrevolutionary concern. The day is long past when war criminals were only goose-stepping military chiefs; now they also reside in the offices of "scholarly" universities.

*****

We'd like to acknowledge, in the preparation of this article, a little help from our friends, the good folks at The Pacific Studies Center in East Palo Alto, California. -30-

Kingdom of Rice: Tear Down the Walls!

David Williams • May 9, 1970

Rice University operates under the delusion that it is an isolated and autonomous kingdom. Like all good fairy tale kingdoms, Rice is surrounded by a wall to keep out invaders, and gates that can be closed in case of an attack. In case of siege Rice has its own internal power-generating station, its own telephone system and a post office with a campus mail system. It has its own police force and court system, and the University Charter serves as a constitution.

In keeping with this myth, the rulers of the Kingdom of Rice, the Board of Trustees, announced that on Sunday, April 12, the campus would be "closed." An invasion, led by the notorious revolutionary Abbie Hoffman, was imminent. This edict was laughed at throughout the land by the students, and any semblance of effectiveness was shattered Sunday night when 300 invaders came across the hedges to join the rebellious students in the Abbie Hoffman Free Speech Center.

The Rice students inside the building were caught by surprise. They had talked about things that were going on in Houston, but for a Rice group to actually work with and alongside such groups as MAYO and UH SDS was unprecedented.

The rulers of Rice had called upon their allies, the Houston pigs, who sent carloads of reinforcements for the Rice police force. In addition, there were a lot of Rice jocks and some Louisiana people present. The Rice students decided that it wasn't a good time for a violent confrontation, so we regretfully left our building.

But a transformation had taken place in the Rice community. We can no longer ignore the larger issues that are confronting the Houston community and this nation. The alternatives facing Rice at the moment are 1) active involvement in Houston and the national political scene, or 2) continue as before, implying isolation and a reactionary position in political issues.

For the past two years there has been general discussion of the racist and imperialistic stance of Rice as exemplified by the University's ties to NASA, George Brown (builder of Cam Ranh Bay), ROTC, and NROTC, Rice's token admission of Blacks and Chicanos and women, and the mechanical training of Rice engineers and professionals to fill the existing power structure.

Last year's controversy over the Board of Trustees' selection of Dr. Masterson to be president limited the scope of the Rice movement. The issue was discussed as a purely internal affair. The students and faculty protested the appointment of Masterson as an unprecedented action by the Board of Trustees. Discussion centered on the existing university structure and the academic qualifications of Masterson, without any mention that this was just another case of the Board's exploitation of people, whether students, faculty, construction workers, Vietnamese, Mexicans, or Blacks. People realized that, for the Board, students were niggers, but failed to achieve ideological unity with the other oppressed groups.

LIBERATION NEWS SERVICE

NO.119   NOV. 16 1968   NEW YORK CITY

Ad: July 17, 1969.

The readmission of Charlie Freeman (who was active in the black struggle at TSU) was also regarded as an internal matter. Again, due process was the issue. The "normal channels" had been blocked by intervention of an anonymous person higher up in the administration who nullified the decision of the Committee on Examinations and Standings to readmit Charlie. It wasn't realized that the nature of the intervention was an attempt to keep a dangerous, politicized Black out of the smoothly running Rice machine which feeds directly into the corporate machinery of Houston and the United States.

There was an education campaign on campus throughout last year focusing on ROTC, corporate recruiting, military contracts and the Board's involvement in political and military deals. None of this background was utilized in either the Masterson or Freeman cases. In November of this year students obstructed CIA recruitment activities and two students were put on disciplinary probation. There was no disciplinary action by the administration as long as students kept to on-campus issues (last year), but when students tried to break out of the Rice prison and relate to a national issue, the administration reacted in the traditional Rice isolationist manner.

This spring there was an attempt to burn the NROTC building that resulted in minor damage. A week later, when the Dean of Students refused to allow Abbie Hoffman to speak on campus, his office was gutted by fire. The students kept pushing and the administration backed down. Acting President Vandiver announced that Hoffman could speak on campus and, fearing the reaction of the Board of Trustees, he resigned.

The Board overruled both parts of Vandiver's decision, refused to accept his resignation and announced that the campus would be "closed" on Sunday, April 12, because of threats to the security of the University. The Board claims that these threats came from people outside Rice who threatened to blow up the brick and mortar buildings that the Trustees value so highly. In reality, the Board was trying desperately to hang on to the Rice isolationist myth.

The "closing" of the campus was a farce. Some 300 screaming Houston radicals, the Houston pigs, and the Louisiana KKK demonstrated to the Rice Kingdom that their world is no longer invulnerable. A three-foot hedge is not enough to separate Rice from Houston and the nation. Rice students are demanding that the University's connections with the outside world be openly admitted by the Rice power structure, and that they be strengthened. The following demands have been presented:

1. By 1971-72, 10 percent admission of third world people. By 1972-73 this must be raised to 14 percent with emphasis on Chicano admissions since Chicanos comprise a large minority in the Southwest. Admissions must be reinforced by summer sessions and extensive tutoring for those who need it.

2. A redistribution of power within the university. Students must be adequately represented, with votes, on all policy-making bodies in the university. "Policy" includes budget negotiations and long-range planning.

3. A Bill of Rights for Rice students.

4. University resources must be shared with the community. Free breakfasts, medical clinics, summer programs for the economically disadvantaged must be instituted.

5. Military research and ROTC must be abolished. Furthermore, recruitment by government and corporations must be abolished.

6. All financial records, including the personal finances of Board of Trustees members, must be made public.

7. Within two years, 51 percent of admissions must be women.

8. All policy-making meetings and decisions must be open.

9. Wide-scale curriculum reforms must be made. A lowering of the total course requirement, abolition of distribution requirements combined with a much-improved counseling service are among these reforms.

10. Rice employees must be paid decent wages.

There is a need for Rice to work together with the other groups in the Houston movement. Rice's admission policy should be pressured not only from within, but by the Chicanos, Blacks and women in the Houston community.

The janitorial and maintenance forces at Rice are predominately Mexican-American and Black. Many don't even speak English. They are all referred to as "gnomes" by everybody at Rice. Many of the employees are paid below the national minimum wage. The Rice NROTC program recruits not only from Rice, but also from UH and TSU.

Mrs. Oveta Culp Hobby, one of the Trustees, owns the *Houston Post*. Rice has a Black Studies program in conjunction with other Houston schools, but only graduate students from TSU, UH, and St. Thomas can take the Rice courses in the program. Rice undergraduates can, however, take courses at the other schools, but get no credit for them, presumably because courses at other schools are inferior.

In sum, Rice issues are inextricably bound to the issues that face Houston and the U.S. The time to act together is NOW. -30-

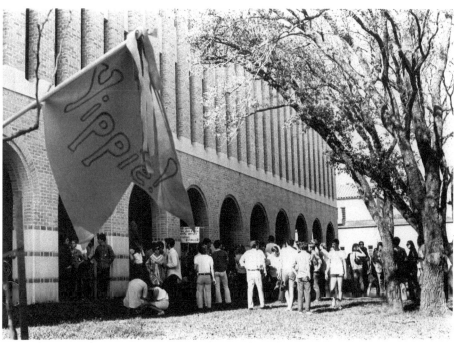

Demonstrators at Rice with Yippie flag.

University of Houston: Microcosm of Society

Randy Chapman • January 30, 1971

A special eight-page section on the University of Houston was researched and written by Randy Chapman with help from Bill Casper, Gavan Duffy and Dennis Fitzgerald.

As a public institution controlled by the same class of persons who influence our national policies and priorities, the University of Houston is but a reflection and not a leader in the fight against social injustices in this society. In fact, the record has shown that University policies have changed only when they were forced to change.

Racism

Nationally, we did not see any move to pass civil rights laws until after massive marches, riots, and property destruction. Likewise with UH. UH did not move to integrate until becoming a state institution in 1963. V.P. McElhinney said he felt the social mores of the day would not have permitted it. The administration did not move to create a Black Studies Department or recruit minority race administrators, faculty, or students until the militant Black student organization Afro-Americans for Black Liberation (AABL) presented a set of demands to the University. Previous "suggestions" by Blacks had been ignored. Hoffman responded to the demands by naming committees. Tension stayed high while committee members talked. Then from the Cougar Den erupted a "mini-riot" in 1969 that involved property destruction in excess of $2,000 to the University Center. The threat of further property destruction gave Hoffman the incentive to act. Chester Branton, a Black, was named to act as an assistant to Vice-President Yardley (Student Life) and a Black Studies Department was created.

Two years later, in 1970, AABL gave up on the University as a "hopelessly racist institution" with "racist foundations which could not be changed." In 1971 the University continues its past policies except for some tokenism; AABL's Demands have been forgotten. An alleged racist coach was never fired. The Black Student Union was never funded. Chester Branton quit,

From the Cougar Den erupted a 'mini-riot' in 1969 that involved property destruction.

saying, "I see nothing I can accomplish here." Hoffman refuses to change academic entrance requirements, as has been done at Yale and Harvard, to let in a quota of minority-race students. By state law the Board of Regents has the authority to cut or eliminate fees for up to 10 percent of the student body, to be judged by family financial need. This provision has never been used.

In the spring of 1970, Hoffman initiated a Save Our Students (SOS) program to assist in this area. It was initially funded by student property deposits and very small individual donations. Its purpose was to provide tutors to assist students graduating from poor high schools. As the funds dwindled the University applied for a Federal grant to extend SOS. However, the University refused to change admission requirements or provide for "remedial instruction." Consequently, the federal grant was denied and SOS is dying.

While the University Personnel Office officially maintains itself as an "equal opportunity employer," hiring is still done on the basis of approval by the area supervisor. The result has been that Blacks and Chicanos are channeled into the $1.60 hourly grounds and maintenance jobs. The result of this policy is demonstrated in the case of a fully qualified Black man who applied for a position on Traffic and Security (T&S). After being interviewed by Mr. Haner in T&S, he was told that they were looking for "an older man." Two weeks later, the Personnel Office, unaware of Haner's racist rejection, called the man at home and asked how he liked his new job. Pressure was put on Haner and Chief Sterling Baker and the man was hired. Today T&S interviews are still conducted and Mr. Haner is still employed as supervisor in the T&S Department.

Though the University of Houston sits in the heart of the Third Ward, it refuses to recognize the needs of the surrounding community. Outsiders are not permitted use of campus facilities. One may recall that at Columbia University in 1968 the people of Harlem were "given" a back door entrance to the College gymnasium. In 1971 all UH athletic facilities

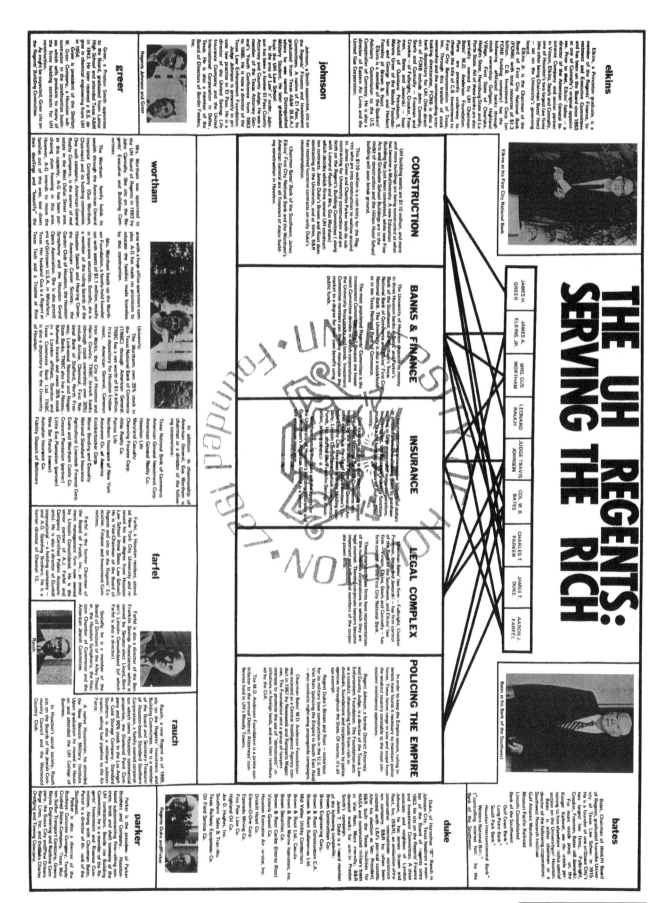

are closed to nonstudents. Even children, lacking any parks, are not allowed to play outside the athletic fields. Presently the University owns a small partially-wooded grass area on the corner of Cullen and Elgin Streets, west of the main campus. Though many neighborhood children play there, the University is currently negotiating for the eventual sale of the land to private enterprise.

Another form of racism lies in the University plans for expansion into the Third Ward. The Campus plan for the 70s prepared by Coulsen Tough (V.P. Facilities and Operation) calls for the acquisition of the land on the corner of Elgin and Scott Streets. This land is presently occupied by over 80 families, most of whom are Black and have low incomes. Upon acquisition of the area, all housing will be destroyed so the athletic fields may be expanded. Campus planner Bill Wright hopes "that H.U.D. will find a new place for these people to live."

Sexism

No administrator in the University is a female. Women faculty members' salaries, on the average, are lower than their male counterparts. The position of Vice-President for Student Life and Dean of Men are on equal footing, but the position of Dean of Women is under the V.P. for Student Life. Women in Traffic and Safety are given desk jobs or positions as Patrol-women. As such, their job status is lower and their pay ($5,040) is much less than the starting salary for a Patrolman 1 ($6,750). Furthermore, women are only allowed to work in daylight hours and are not permitted to carry arms as does every man.

In a personal interview. Senior V.P. McElhinney explained that the sexist administration and regulations of the UH dorms will continue until "the norms and mores of our society change." -30-

Colonel Bates, Chairman of the Board of Regents

Randy Chapman • January 30, 1971

Colonel W.B. Bates is chairman of the Board of Regents of the University of Houston. President Hoffman has commented that "No one has ever exercised a greater sustaining influence over UH." Because of his extreme influence over the University ("No board is stronger than its chairman" — Bates), a complete study of the views of the regent should include not just the financial man but all his aspects in order to understand the composition and policies of the University.

Business Tycoon

Bates, a graduate from UT Law School in 1915, is a founder of one of Houston's two largest law offices (Fulbright, Crooker, Freeman, Bates & Jaworski) which occupies four floors of the Bank of the Southwest Building, consisting of 140 lawyers, all engaged in corporate law practice. Bates and his partners have been very influential in Texas politics. Although he served in the Army in World War I, Bates' rank of Colonel is an honorary title from service on the election staff of Texas Governor Dan Moody. Bates' name appeared in a 1962 endorsement for Democrat Jack Smith for probate judge. Prior to that Bates' name appeared with Frank Horlock, Jr. (Pearl Beer), Jaworski, Bellows (construction) and Tellepsen (construction) in an endorsement for Bob Casey for Congress. Prior to his election, Bates' firm contracted to handle legal affairs for L.B.J. After his election, according to Bates, Jaworski was considered for Attorney General and served on the President's Commissions for the study of campus unrest and prevention of national violence.

Bates is the Advisory Chairman to the Bank of the Southwest (assets of $666 million). Affiliated banks, by stock ownership, include Gulf Coast National, Western National, and Houston Intercontinental National Banks. Though not having the lowest bid, they are the depository for the Houston Independent School District. They are also a depository for UH construction funds. Roy H. Cullen, C.T. Parker, and Bates' law partners Jaworski and Buck also sit on the board of the Bank of the Southwest.

> 'No one has ever exercised a greater sustaining influence over UH.'

Bates is a director of Missouri Pacific Railroad and he sits on the board of directors with Aaron Farfel on Lloyd Bentsen's Lincoln Consolidated. Bates is also a director of the Anderson Clayton Subsidiary, Gulf Atlantic Warehouse.

Besides his corporate links. Bates is a member of several conservative societies and social clubs in Houston. These include the Sons of the American Revolution, the Sons of the Republic of Texas, the Philosophical Society of Texas, the Huguenot Society, the River Oaks Country Club, and the Petroleum Club.

Bates is a trustee, along with Hoffman, of the tax-free San Antonio-based Southwest Research Institute. SWRI picks up theoretical university-related research and applies it to "practical" uses. A majority of SWRI research, both in dollar and volume amounts, is being conducted for the government. Besides being involved in fuel, weapons, and biochemical research for the U.S. Army, SWRI claims credit for a "seismic system for detecting shallow, man-made tunnels" which is now used against the Vietnamese. They have also developed an ultrasonic system of personal intrusion detection. Besides their employment in S.E. Asia, these devices are now used around strategic utility systems (anti-bombing) and along the Mexican-U.S. border to detect "wetbacks" and marijuana smuggling. SWRI also maintains an "Applied Economics Laboratory" with a Houston branch and the institute reports that it does work for a U.S. Government agency which does not wish to be identified (CIA?).

Bates is a director of the Texas Research League and is Vice President and director of the Texas Medical Center. He is also a director of the Clayton Foundation for Research (assets $21 million), which specializes in biochemical research.

Bates' main source of financial control lies in his position as vice president and trustee to the M.D. Anderson Foundation with assets of $31.4 million as of December 31, 1969. Bates, who is the personal attorney for Anderson Clayton "from the beginning,"

has been on the foundation since its creation. In fact.
Freeman, Bates, and Jaworski hold three of the four
trusteeships for the foundation, the fourth being the
chairman of the Bank of the Southwest (and U.T.
Regent), A.G. McNeese. The trustees have financial
control of millions of dollars in stocks without being taxed because of the foundation structure. The
foundation owns stocks valued at over two million
dollars each in First City National Bank, Bank of
the Southwest, and Anderson Clayton. Other large
Houston interests held include Tenneco, American
General, South Park National Bank,
Texas Foundaries, and Western National Bank. Lesser stock is held in 14 other
local banks.

When the M.D. Anderson Foundation became publicly known in 1967
as a conduit for CIA funds, *Newsweek*
suggested that the lack of White House
comment was the result of Jaworski's
close association with LBJ. (Also involved in CIA funds was William P.
Hobby, Jr. of the Hobby Foundation,
who was a UH regent at that time.)

"We worked in promoting in underdeveloped
countries a rule of law, instead of a rule of men... and
we continued to make contributions in that area...
We didn't help them — we just passed it through...
We would still be happy to help them of course... I
certainly can't see anything wrong with it. Do you?"
— Bates

The Regent

Bates and Cullen were originally members of the
Houston School Board and sat on the advisory committee to the Houston Junior College. Acting on their
advice, the School Board designated for Houston
Junior College the board of 15 regents with Cullen
as Chairman and Bates as vice chairman. Until 1963
Bates reports that the regents were "more or less selected by Mr. Cullen and me." Since Cullen's death in
1956, Bates has been the chairman of the board. Most
of the UH regents selected by Connally in 1963 were
on the Bates-named board. Also Hoffman's nomination for president in 1961 was a selection by the 15
members of the Bates-Cullen board.

It is easy to see Chairman Bates' influence on the
procedures and governance of the University.

Rather than paraphrase these views, they are stated
by him as follows:

On Hoffman:

I think he has done a tremendous job.
We stress the fact that the legislature
charges the Board with the duty of
maintaining the school and keeping
peace and order on campus and the
Board has delegated that authority to
him and we look upon him to do it. We
realize ... that the responsibility is his;
not the faculty, not the student, but it's
his to keep peace and order on campus.

> ### 'I'm afraid they don't do as much screening as they should for communists.'

It has always been my policy
that the Board of Regents of a
college act as the board of directors of a large corporation.

On Faculty:

The Administration should be
very careful in recommending
to the board faculty members
and other personnel because we
don't have time to investigate
them.

I'm afraid they don't do as much
screening as they should for communists. That's what I told Dr. Hoffman.

The deans make the investigations. The
deans ought to be more careful in their
investigations before making recom-
mendations to Dr. Hoffman for approval.

On student role:

I think the university is doing a good
job of filling posts in downtown Houston. Students are wise. Some think they
should run the university. I don't think
they should go to the university if they
think they are all that smart.

The Senate should not try to run the
university. They should be concerned
with students, not administrative affairs. What do they know about running the school? You can't have but
one head and one governing body; not
in business or in school. We look to
Hoffman, not students or faculty to

run the school... Hoffman represents the Board well.

I think our public is disgusted with the students... the Board has a difficult time getting money. Students should act responsibly.

I think the people of Houston have been very generous (financially) but students haven't responded as they should.

On free speech:

I can't tolerate rioting. There is no place for rioting... If something happens, well they (downtown police) ought to be called in immediately. I don't think he (Fultz) was as aggressive as he should have been when Governor Smith was here... "1, 2, 3, 4; we don't want your fuckin' war"... students who say this should not be tolerated. There is no place at the university for obscenities... I feel the university should review films (shown on campus).

On War and University Compliance:

Nixon didn't get in the war. He's trying to get out in a way which... People should appreciate his way. I'm for his program. I think (in the beginning) we should have bombed the hell out of them (the communists).

If a school is owned by the public, it must defend the state. Hell, I'm for it (military research).

I see no reason why we should not accept the money. R.O.T.C. is the University's obligation to serve the State...

On serving surrounding communities:

(Asked why UH didn't integrate until 1963) "We probably didn't have any applications before that." (Asked about lowering admission requirements to let in more minority race students) "I don't think you can build a great university by lowering standards. If they're ambitious, there are plenty of

junior colleges. Why should they have any more right to use university facilities?"

Asked why, after students invited Mark Rudd to speak, UH got an order preventing him from speaking:

He should not have been permitted on campus. Men who come to UH should speak as educated people. Why should Rudd be invited to tear down the university built by the public? The state should not provide the platform. SDS has no place on campus.

Jane Fonda has no business speaking ... It is the responsibility of the Administration to prevent... Only activists are at these events who aren't interested in the country, just raising hell.

-30-

Ad: May 25, 1971.

Brown & Root: How to Build an Empire

Victoria Smith and Jeff Shapiro • April 27, 1971

In 1919, Herman Brown and Dan Root began building roads in Texas; today, 50 years later, Brown & Root does the planning, landscaping, architecture, engineering and construction of roads, steel mills, chemical plants, and a multitude of other industrial facilities throughout our expanding world.

From the icy waters of the North Sea to Lake Maracaibo in sunny Venezuela, from the plains of Texas to the sand dunes of the Middle East, we serve progress the world over.

That's Brown & Root talking. The promo piece appeared in the 1969 Fiftieth Anniversary issue of *Brownbuilder*, a slick company magazine for the construction and engineering company. The magazine also boasted that this massive construction and engineering company is "building the world over."

Who can doubt it? Brown & Root has experienced remarkable growth over the last five decades, with interests and influence reaching far beyond the scope of the construction industry, to petrochemical, petroleum, and banking concerns, to name a few.

The powerful Brown brothers, Herman (now deceased) and George (still with us) have vaulted amazing obstacles over the last 50 years in pursuit of fortune and influence. They have emerged victorious from battles with the Internal Revenue Service, the U.S. General Accounting Office, members of the U.S. Congress, and the Texas labor movement. And they have made many friends along the way, like Lyndon B. Johnson, former Texas Gov. John Connally (now Secretary of the Treasury), the late Texas Rep. Albert Thomas, plus some of the biggest legal and business figures in the country.

Today Brown & Root is the second largest contractor in the world, according to the *Engineering News-Record*, with $1,344,600,000 worth of building contracts in 1970. It ranks among the top 10 in foreign contracts, at $187.5 million, with jobs in 31 foreign countries.

The company claimed revenues of $514.7 million in 1968. One of its larger subsidiaries, Texas Eastern Trans-

mission of Houston, was worth $1.54 billion in the same year.

Brown & Root has functioned since 1962 as an independent subsidiary of the Halliburton Co., a Dallas-based oil field service company. In 1962, the Browns placed their company interest in the tax-exempt Brown Foundation. Herman Brown was ailing, and the brothers transferred their money to avoid heavy death taxes, according to George Brown. Later that year, Herman Brown died, and Halliburton bought the company from the Brown Foundation, reportedly for some $36.7 million. Halliburton, with revenues topping the billion-dollar mark in 1969, is one of the largest firms of its kind in the country.

> **Today Brown & Root is the second largest contractor in the world.**

The move helped consolidate Brown & Root's many important ties to the oil industry.

So, you see, we're talking about a lot of money and a lot of power — power in Texas, in Washington and all over the world. And Brown & Root is based right here in Houston, with offices on an 88-acre tract at 4100 Clinton Drive, near the Ship Channel.

This company built or helped build Rice Stadium, the Gulf Freeway, the NASA Manned Spacecraft Center, naval bases from Corpus Christi to Spain, highways, bridges and roads throughout the world, a number of offshore drilling and production platforms, NATO air bases in France, a 504-foot dam in Thailand and dozens of facilities in Vietnam, including Danang and Cam Ranh Bay. And that's only the beginning.

Right now, it looks as though Brown & Root is involved in the construction of isolation prison cells for the Saigon government, off the coast of South Vietnam.

A news item in the *New York Times* concerning this project prompted us to probe deeper into the activities, past and present, of Brown & Root. And once we got started, we couldn't stop. We're still going. The examples of peculiar power pacts and dubious dealings in this vast operation seem endless. What you're reading is an account of what we've pulled together so far. (We'll be back with more next issue.)

New Prison Compounds

The construction of the three new blocks of isolation cells on Con Son began last February, according to a re

Demonstrators with replica of 'tiger cage' built in Vietnam by Brown & Root.

lease from the Dispatch News Service International. The contractor is a massive construction consortium known as RMK-BRJ (that's Raymond, Morrison, Knudsen, Brown, Root and Jones).

RMK-BRJ is under a $400,000 contract, with funds to be provided by the American government.

Con Son Island made the news last summer when two U.S. Congressmen and others, on a fact-finding tour to Vietnam, discovered a secluded group of prisons called the "tiger cages." The Americans, who stumbled across the tiger cages almost by accident, found the prison conditions wretched and the treatment of prisoners barbaric.

The cages were built in 1939 by prison labor under the direction of the French. The prison, the existence of which the Saigon government has kept secret for years, is used to confine South Vietnamese political dissidents.

For a more graphic description of conditions in the tiger cages, read the testimony of a former inmate elsewhere in this issue.

Whether the new prisons will be any better than the old is not yet known. According to the Dispatch News Service, a definite aura of secrecy surrounds the project.

"Anyone who takes a camera to Con Son will be terminated immediately," the RMK-BRJ project manager is reported to have said. And anyone can see that the project is getting little publicity.

The plan, it seems, is to build three cell blocks, each partitioned into 96 isolation cells with an outer wall of concrete block, a barbed wire perimeter fence with security gates, a kitchen, and a dispensary.

The project reportedly will employ prison labor, with skilled workers receiving 200 piasters (72 cents) per week and unskilled, 150 piasters (55 cents) a week. "There is some concern that the prisoners will not be in good enough physical condition to do a 'full day's work,'" according to the release. "Discussion is underway about the possibility of providing special extra rations for those who work on the project."

The descriptive information was provided to Don Luce, of the Dispatch News Service, in the form of five memos by persons who wish to remain unidentified. Luce, a 10-year resident in Vietnam, broke the tiger cages story to the media in this country after he accompanied the U.S. Congressmen to the island. Since then, his press credentials have been revoked by the Saigon government for visiting "a restricted area without authorization."

RMK-BRJ, headquartered in San Bruno, Cal., began construction work in Vietnam in 1962. Actually, Brown & Root didn't join the consortium until 1965. Morrison-Knudsen of Boise, Idaho, is the consortium's sponsoring firm for this and other construction in Vietnam. Morrison-Knudsen gets 40 percent off the projects and the other firms get 20 percent.

We had hoped to get more information on the prison project when we went to talk with Ben H. Powell, Jr., general counsel and a senior group vice president for Brown & Root. (See related story in this issue.) But Powell said he knew nothing about the project, as Morrison-Knudsen is managing the construction. He indicated that he had not even heard of it. We do have a copy of the Department of the Navy contract authorizing RMK-BRJ to proceed with construction, however.

The Brothers Brown

Inspired by the discovery that a Houston company was part of a group building prisons in Vietnam, we decided to examine the historical development of Brown & Root.

Some of our readers may know the story, but we would guess that the majority do not. It's a classic tale of power, politics, and money, and one well worth telling.

It's interesting to note that one of the best ways to study the Brown brothers is to find a book on Lyndon B. Johnson. Where there's Lyndon, there's George and Herman, and their careers are inextricably intertwined.

It all started when Herman Brown, son of a central Texas storekeeper, started to work on the roads. In 1914, the man for whom he was working went broke and couldn't pay his wages. So Herman ended up with 18 mules plus some equipment, and went into the road business for himself. In 1919, he and his brother-in-law, Dan Root, formed a partnership and began to build roads.

A few years later, Herman's younger brother George, who had been studying geology at the Colorado School of Mines, joined the company. Root died in 1929, but the Brown brothers decided to leave the company's name as it was.

Things were pretty shaky at first for the young company, but, by the time the 1930s depression hit, the Brown brothers were already making invaluable political contacts, among them attorney Alvin J. Wirtz.

Alfred Steinberg, in his book on Lyndon Johnson, *Sam Johnson's Boy*, quotes an unidentified associate of Wirtz on the subject. "During the depression things went so sour for them (the Browns) that creditors took away their equipment, and they were at the point of bankruptcy. At this low ebb Wirtz helped them land a paving contract in Guadalupe County where he had lived, but this didn't help them because they lacked the trucks and equipment to fulfill the contract. So Wirtz stepped in and got the Travis County Commissioners at Austin to lend them, illegally, Travis County equipment to complete a state road contract in another county." He adds that the equipment was returned and all was well.

> **In 1936, Brown & Root got its first big federal contract.**

In 1936, Brown & Root got its first big federal contract —construction of the Marshall Ford (Mansfield) Dam on the Lower Colorado River near Austin. Brown & Root bid low; unrealistically low, as it turned out, because costs soared to four times the original bid during the construction, a phenomenon that was to become habitual in future jobs. Wirtz, who by this time was Brown & Root's attorney and general counsel for the Lower Colorado River Authority, had a hand in helping the Browns to win the contract.

Wirtz was also developing a close friendship with a young schoolteacher, Lyndon Johnson. With Wirtz' aid, Johnson began his political career in 1931 as congressional secretary to the wealthy Texas Rep. Richard Kleberg (of the now-legendary King Ranch fortune). Johnson moved on to become director of President Franklin Roosevelt's National Youth Administration (NYA). It was through Wirtz that Johnson first met Herman Brown.

In 1937, Johnson was elected to fill the unexpired term of Texas Rep. James P. Buchanan, who died in office. Attorney Ed Clark, of the Austin law firm Looney and Clark, handled Johnson's campaign. Looney and Clark served for many years as the Brown brothers' lobby in the Texas legislature.

We have to understand that, while Johnson and Wirtz were dedicated New Dealers and the Brown brothers quite conservative from the beginning, political ideologies never seemed to get in the way of politics, so to speak. The Brown brothers sailed through the 1930s, winning a number of New Deal construction contracts, with Johnson and Wirtz backing them up.

When World War II broke out, Brown & Root was designated as one of the primary contractors for a huge naval air station at Corpus Christi. It cost the government nearly $100 million by the time it was completed, a figure more than three times the original estimates. Johnson was a member of the House Naval Affairs Committee at the time.

Suddenly, in 1941, the Browns were offered a number of major shipbuilding contracts from the Navy. So they built a $6 million shipyard on the Houston Ship Channel, established the Brown Shipbuilding Co. and proceeded to turn out the big boats, even though "nobody in the company had ever seen a ship built," according to the company's own autobiography in *Brownbuilder* magazine. And as they began to turn out hundreds of destroyer-escorts and landing craft for the Navy, the Brown brothers moved their main office from Austin to Houston.

By the end of World War II, the Browns had done more than $350 million worth of shipbuilding work for the Navy and ranked sixty-eighth by volume among prime war suppliers, according to David Welsh in "Building Lyndon Johnson" (*Ramparts* magazine, 1968).

By this time, Brown & Root was a pretty big operation—big enough to help friend Lyndon Johnson in his 1941 campaign for the U.S. Senate, following the mid-term death of the incumbent. Johnson lost the bid to Gov. W. Lee (Pappy) O'Daniel.

Brown & Root was big enough to help friend Lyndon Johnson in his 1941 campaign for the U.S. Senate.

Brown & Root found itself in trouble with the Internal Revenue Service the following year when IRS agents began investigating the company's excessive contributions to Johnson's campaign disguised as tax deductions, in the form of bonuses to executives of Brown & Root subsidiaries. The IRS claimed that the "bonuses" were then turned over to Johnson.

The influential Wirtz intervened with the IRS commissioner, who called off the investigation for several months, but ordered it resumed in 1943. Despite various forms of harassment, the IRS agents persisted in their investigation and within months were ready to take action: a proposed tax charge assessment of $1,062,184, a fraud penalty of $531,002 and a decision to ask the Justice Department to initiate prosecution procedures against Brown & Root for political donations to Johnson's campaign.

Some weeks later Wirtz and Johnson visited President Roosevelt at the White House. The President requested and received a full report on the investigation from Dallas and, within three days, the proposed tax charge and fraud penalty were abandoned and the total assessment lowered to $372,000. The criminal prosecution proposal was dropped. And so was the whole incident, until columnist Drew Pearson turned up the story, along with the IRS records, in 1956.

But the Brown & Root tax records had disappeared, never to return. Wirtz' anonymous associate in Steinberg's book comments: "Some years later when there was talk of reviving the issue, all papers involved were removed from a fire-proof building in Austin, dumped into a Quonset hut, and went up in ashes when the Quonset hut was leveled by bursting flames."

We mentioned this incident in our interview with Brown & Root General Counsel Ben Powell. Hasn't this sort of thing cast Brown & Root in a bad light?, we asked. And how much has politicking contributed to Brown & Root's success?

"Brown & Root, despite any of the history and in the face of repeated reruns is still one of the largest contractors in the United States," Powell said, rather defensively. He noted that Johnson had been out of office for three years and Brown & Root continues to expand. "This should show that there is some intrinsic good in the ability (of Brown & Root) to serve the country," he said.

After the War

Johnson finally made it to the Senate in 1948, after he beat Gov. Coke Stevenson, in what appears to have been a fraudulent runoff in the primary. Johnson won by a margin of 87 votes, after 202 additional votes for him arrived late from Precinct 13 of Jim Wells County. Johnson was placed on the ballot.

Stevenson immediately appealed the decision to the federal court, charging Johnson with fraud. His attorneys turned up evidence showing that the extra votes had come from a local graveyard and from Mexico, just across the border from Jim Wells County. U.S. Dist. Judge T. Whitfield Davidson issued an injunction, denying Johnson a place on the ballot.

A frantic attempt to overturn Davidson's injunction ensued, backed by Democrats on all levels. John Connally, a Brown & Root attorney and a partner of Wirtz, choreographed the action. They took the case straight to the U.S. Supreme Court, where Abe Fortas, later a Supreme Court justice, led the defense. Alvin Wirtz, along with Ed Clark, held down the fort back in Texas.

Justice Hugo Black issued an order to stay the Davidson injunction. Johnson was back on the ballot, and he handily took the November election.

As Johnson was gaining a healthy foothold in Washington, Brown & Root was edging into that vital postwar industry, oil. The

old agricultural Texas with its politics of cotton was no match for the new politics of petroleum.

The Browns took a shrewd and necessary step in the right direction when they purchased the government-built Big Inch and Little Big Inch Pipelines in 1947 for Brown & Root's newly formed Texas Eastern Transmission. Texas Eastern became the first major cross country natural gas transmission system, channeling Texas oil and gas to the rich East Coast market.

Rowland Evans and Robert Novak, in their book, *Lyndon Johnson: The Exercise of Power*, write: "New powers in the oil and gas industry, and already linked to Johnson, they (the Browns) quickly plunged ever deeper into Democratic politics and became Lyndon Johnson's personal vehicle for a lateral movement into the center of the new oil power."

Brown & Root had learned a good deal from its World War II projects and moved rapidly into the postwar reconstruction era. The company's first "reconstruction" job was the building of naval and air force bases on the island of Guam. (Welsh notes that Guam is "now a major logistical base for the Vietnam war.") Millions of dollars worth of additional military contracts soon followed.

In the early 1950s, Brown & Root was joining other contractors to build multimillion-dollar NATO air bases in Europe. They teamed up with Raymond International and Walsh Construction Co. to tackle a $357 million cost-plus contract from the Navy for a series of large military installations in Spain.

> ## Brown & Root was edging into that vital postwar industry, oil.

Art: Kerry Fitzgerald, August 28, 1969.

When the project was completed in 1962, the consortium of Brown-Raymond-Walsh was among the top 40 prime military contractors.

Texas Labor Takes On Big Boss

While the Browns exercised considerable influence in Washington, they never ignored their home state powerhouse, the Texas Legislature. Brown & Root's unprecedented control over the legislature in the 1950s was an invaluable weapon in the company's relentless battle against organized labor.

When we asked Chris Dixie, Houston labor attorney who fought Brown & Root in the courts for years, about the Brown lobbies, he exclaimed, "The lobbies! Man, they had the law firm of Clark and Looney which was the nearest thing to proprietary owners of the Texas Legislature you ever saw! Everyone will tell you that Brown & Root was undoubtedly the most powerful single factor in Austin when it came to lobbying activities in the government." (Ed Clark managed Johnson's first Congressional campaign and was later appointed his ambassador to Australia.)

In the early 1950s, when Texas trade unions tried to organize Brown & Root's workers, Herman Brown got a law through the legislature banning the "closed shop" in Texas. (Closed shop means that all employees of a company must hold union membership, as a condition of work.)

And when the unions tried to picket a number of Brown's jobs, he went to the District Court in Austin and won an injunction against the 92 unions involved. The court also enjoined the unions from organizing boycotts against Brown & Root customers and from using "unfair lists," presumably to cite the company as an anti-union employer.

Football fans might be interested to know that one of those picketing sites mentioned in the court decision was Rice Stadium, built by Brown & Root in 1950.

Another noteworthy point: one of the pro-labor attorneys facing Brown's clique of Austin law firms was Bob Eckhardt, now a U.S. Congressman from Houston.

Herman Brown's power in the Texas legislature and his success in blocking labor activities was a cause of great concern to some. Former Texas newspaper editor Hart Stillwell, writing in *The Nation* in 1951, declared that politically Brown "is already the most powerful man in Texas and close to bossing the entire state."

Brown & Root has never relinquished its stand against organized labor.

Right now, Southwestern Pipe Co., a Brown & Root subsidiary, is appealing in the Fifth Circuit Court a National Labor Relations Board decision accusing the company of unfair labor practice.

The employees held an NLRB election in 1966 to unionize as a local of the United Steelworkers of America, AFL-CIO. The union and the company have met several times in negotiation sessions. But Southwestern Pipe has remained adamant in its refusal to recognize union representation for its employees, to the extent that the management maintains the company will shut down before it will recognize the union.

The employees staged a walkout in July of 1966 and were promptly terminated. They abandoned their pickets in September, at which time they offered to return to work. The management replied that all the jobs were taken (by scabs) and the former employees would have to wait their turn. A few were reinstated.

Why the Browns have so persistently resisted attempts by the unions to organize Brown & Root workers is not quite clear. The company claims that it does as much or more for its employees as a union could do. But if the employees decide they want a little change here and there, and they decide to walk out, they may well be walking out for good.

Brown & Root evidently wishes to maintain direct control over its work force and doesn't want any powerful labor organization wedging in between.

...

Epilogue

We don't consider this piece an example of heavy muckraking, but rather a compilation and interpretation of material that has been printed elsewhere before.

We think Americans should study corporations like Brown & Root because they generate the breathtaking power that is largely responsible for the sorry state America and the world is currently in. And this is not the last you will read about Brown & Root in the pages of *Space City!* -30-

> They never ignored their home state powerhouse, the Texas Legislature.

space city !

·formerly space city news·

vol 1 no 13	jan 17 – 30, 1970	houston, texas	20¢
			25¢ out of town

Cover: Art by Kerry Fitzgerald. January 17, 1970.

Space City!
Special Reporting

Cover: Art by Kerry Fitzgerald, May 23, 1970.

ENVIRONMENT

Art: Kerry Fitzgerald, June 20,1970.

The Rape of Galveston Beach

Judy and Dennis Fitzgerald • January 17, 1970

GALVESTON — Galveston feels like a very old town — some parts decaying gracefully, others just decaying. As you drive through shaded streets of crumbling, once-elegant homes, pick your way along the wharves and fishing docks, pass almost without notice the deserted, grass-covered World War II gun emplacements, the smell of history mingles with salt water air.

This is the island once inhabited by the fierce Karankawa Indians. In the early nineteenth century the pirate Jean Lafitte had his headquarters here. And still rumors persist of buried booty and Spanish treasures.

Most of the gold nowadays though is brought over from the mainland, jangling in the pockets of tourists. On a sunny summer weekend 50,000 or more pale bodies may be seen lying shoulder-to-rump along the water's edge. They share at no expense, thanks to the Texas Open Beaches Act, the pleasures and discomforts of sun and surf and sand. They also consume prodigious quantities of Pearl beer, Prince's hamburgers, Coppertone, and Enco regular. Some make a weekend of it in one of the many motels or hotels which line Seawall Boulevard, perhaps taking their evening meal at Paul's Golden Greek Restaurant.

The atmosphere is low key. This is no Miami Beach. The tourists are catered to of course; there are plenty of curio shops, where the kids can buy sea shells and surfer t-shirts; there's a small amusement park and beachside

stands for renting inner tubes and surf boards. But mostly it all looks like it just sort of happened. There's no grand design or master planner behind Galveston's response to the tourists. At least not yet.

The city of Galveston centers itself at the eastern end of the island. The port, the downtown business area, and the urban residences all rest within about a third of the island's area. Suburbia has made tentative feelers westward, but until recently there wasn't much construction at the west end of the island. And still there are large grassy fields, populated only by grazing cattle and horses. Slowly, however, that image is changing.

Lately, the crowds have become too big for the limited facilities. Traffic stacks up. Often you have to drive miles to find an open stretch for your beach blanket. During the summer, litter accumulates faster than the cleaning crews can remove it. The Houston megapolis has been expanding incredibly, and Galveston, as the nearest salt water recreation area, hasn't kept pace.

Stepping into the beach, an organization named Timewealth Corp. (formerly Jamaica Resort Corp.) has been buying up land on West Galveston Island, subdividing it into lots, and erecting an assortment of "resort subdivisions."

Driving down West Beach you find in quick succession a half-dozen little suburbs on stilts: Spanish Grant, Pirates Beach, Jamaica Beach, Sea Isle, Terra-Mar Beach. They spring from the fields and push their way up to the beach, taking all that the law will allow and sometimes a bit more.

The Texas open beaches law permits private ownership of beachland but requires that beach areas be open to the public, that there be open access along the beach, and that structures not be built closer to the water than the vegetation line (that rough line above which the tide never rises, and therefore along which plant life etches a tenuous border).

Galveston's stilt-towns are only occasionally in open technical violation of the Open Beaches Act, but they represent a growing and continuous effort to subvert the spirit of that law.

At one time or another during the past several years the various developments (all are owned by Timewealth, except Pirates Beach) have erected barricades along the beach to block through traffic, staked off roads beside the subdivisions to permit traffic passage but discourage parking, or thrown up signs declaring a certain section to be a "private" beach. They have also constructed buildings set well in front of the vegetation line.

At many places the developers have built bulkheads parallel to the water and as much as 100 feet below the vegetation line. These bulkheads are miniature concrete or wooden sand dams, which have the effect of moving the vegetation line closer to the water, thus enlarging the area of legally private property.

Timewealth has also found a loophole in the law, which grants cities the right to control traffic along beaches — though not to prohibit traffic. Professing a concern for public safety, the corporation has erected barricades which channel traffic through the areas fronting their developments. The barricades also discourage stopping in those areas. It has been proposed by Timewealth on several occasions that vehicular access to these areas be blocked entirely and that private parking lots be built back off the beach (and a small parking fee charged, of course).

The more flagrant of these acts, such as blocking the beach entirely or placing a building squarely in the middle of the beach, have been fought and for the most part de-

feated by a loose-knit group called People for Open Beaches. They have sent letters and photos to newspaper, city, county and state officials; circulated petitions; and made enough noise to slow down Timewealth's takeover. But it's a losing battle.

There's nothing very sinister about Timewealth's operations. It's simply a matter of money.

Money is made by buying something for a little and selling it for a lot. If you're only a mediocre businessman, you can make enough money to get by. But if you have some imagination, a persuasive sales pitch, and a little working capital, you may realize the alchemists' dream of turning sand into sand dollars.

For instance. People need open space for recreation. But the sun shines, the sand blows, and the ocean rolls in — all with very little help from real estate developers. So the task is to surround a natural, but unprofitable, commodity with all sorts of artificial, but profitable, accessories.

You build hotels, restaurants, amusement parks, apartment complexes, shopping centers, yacht basins, etc. etc. You make certain areas inaccessible to the public, thereby creating the illusion of exclusive rights, which are marketable at higher prices. You buy a lot of advertisements in newspapers and magazines and on TV, which imply that this new construction is something special, exciting, "in."

If you do all this artfully enough, pretty soon people begin to feel like it's not enough just to pack a lunch, drive down to an isolated part of the beach, and spend the day basking in the sun. And if you do all this hugely enough, people may not be able to find an unsullied stretch of beach, even if they want to.

THE RAPE OF GALVESTON BEACH

Art: Kerry Fitzgerald, January 17, 1970.

It's a wonderfully profitable concept. You spread insecurity by creating artificial "needs"; then you exploit that insecurity. And people think you're doing them a favor.

At least, some of the people think you're doing them a favor. There are others who aren't so sure. Free beaches are open to everyone. But commercialization of recreation areas and the expensive, fancy trimmings which that implies create at the least an intimidating atmosphere and often, positive denial of access to those who can't afford the price.

There are alternatives. A few years ago a state park was established on West Galveston Island. Unfortunately, this modest accomplishment will be swamped by the eventual domain of Timewealth.

West Galveston Island could be transformed into a beautiful and uncomplicated retreat for thousands of harried city dwellers.

Of course, it won't be. There will be more summer homes, hotels, yacht basins and hot dog stands. Only a few weeks ago Timewealth acquired a 10 percent interest in the Houston Sports Association, the company that brought you Astroworld. Speculation is that in not too many years they may also bring us Island-World.

Timewealth is America. A Jack- in-the-Box on every corner, a parking meter at every curb, a Coca-Cola in every icebox, and an insatiable craving in every citizen.

Timewealth is America, the company soon to bring you World-World. -30-

Art: Bill Narum, April 20, 1971.

Your Garbage and Mine

E. F. Shawver, Jr. • May 25, 1971

Not the least of the problems now threatening our metropolitan existence is that of disposing of the some 4,000 tons of garbage produced each day in Houston.

The problem has many aspects: technological, social, economic, political, and psychological, and is inseparable from the larger environmental and city management problems which face any modern city of appreciable size.

One may get rid of garbage by dumping, burning, burying, or reusing it. These days there is general agreement that the sanest solution is to reuse as much as possible and to compact and isolate the residue. The technological problems involved in this or that phase of solid waste recovery have for the most part been solved but at least in Houston the larger problem of setting up an integrated system of garbage recycling industries has hardly been dented.

At this stage the material is no longer garbage but raw compost. It is dark brown, somewhat like peat moss in texture and only faintly and not unpleasantly odorous. From the agitators the compost is passed to the three regrinding mills. It is then screened, dried, and either bagged or conveyed outside to a storage pile. The total capacity of the digestors is 1,600 tons.

As I mentioned above, the mechanically-picked paper collected by the cyclone is unsuitable for ordinary paper recycling process because of the large quantity of plastic film and plastic-coated paper it contains. (U.S. Gypsum is presently the largest paper recycler in the country but they are unable to use any but clean, uncoated paper. Uncoated paper has been recycled in New York City for years but these plants are also unable to process plastic-coated drinking cups, milk cartons, paper plates, and so on.)

A few weeks ago, I visited the Metropolitan Waste Conversion Co. composting plant located on Lawndale, within nose-shot of the Houston Ship Channel. The sulfurous odor pervading that area does not emanate from Metropolitan which has been shut down since last April with little chance of ever reopening. While it was in operation, Metropolitan handled some 360 tons of city garbage per day. A smaller, 50 ton-per-day plant is in operation at Largo, Florida, while a 150 ton-per-day facility is under construction in Gainesville, Florida. The company's failure in Houston is attributed to difficulties in marketing their primary product (compost), the lack of supporting industries capable of using other garbage by-products, and the failure to work out a viable agreement with the city.

I was given a guided tour of the plant by Frank Dolan, a Metro executive and longtime home-composter, who explained the basic process and pointed out a few of the company's problems.

Incoming trucks laden with garbage pass through a weighing station to the rear of the plant where they deposit their loads inside a shed. Under the agreement Metropolitan had with the city, garbage could not remain in this shed for longer than 24 hours. The dumping operation is organized to allow the orderly transfer of the fresh garbage to a conveyor which carries the material inside the plant.

There it is moved along a vibrating conveyor to the picking tables where items unsuitable for grinding (tires, large metal or plastic items and so on) are removed and separated. Corrugated paper, an important part of industrial but not of residential garbage, is also removed at this stage and baled up to be sold to paper recycling plants. The picked-over garbage is then put through the primary grinder. After this grinding, a magnetic conveyor belt pulls out ferrous metals which are passed out of the plant into waiting railroad cars to be taken to Proler Steel Co. for recycling.

If the material is sufficiently pure at this stage it may be put immediately into the secondary grinder. Otherwise, it may first be run through a system called the "classifier" in which lighter components such as paper, rags, and thin plastic are pneumatically removed. The debris thus separated is blown through a forced-air system called the "cyclone" after which it is concentrated in bales. This mechanically separated "gunk" paper is not suitable for ordinary paper recycling because of the high percentage of thin plastic which inevitably remains. A process described below using heated solvents makes

Art: Kerry Fitzgerald, May 25, 1971.

such material potentially valuable — but the market is not presently open to Metropolitan.

Whichever route is taken, partially purified garbage from the secondary grinder is conveyed to the digestors in an adjoining building. These are two pairs of 350-foot-long concrete rectangular troughs open at the near end. Along the conveyor which runs between each pair runs a device (called a "tripper") which diverts the ready-to-be-composted material on the conveyor into the digestors on either side. Thus, the material is laid down in layers to begin the composting process.

The conversion of purified garbage into compost is by natural, bacteriological action. The process is controlled by an air-injection system which provides the proper oxygen level to keep the bacteria happy and fogging nozzles to hold moisture constant. The tanks are ordinarily emptied every six days by means of large scooping machines on rails called "agitators."

This technological difficulty has been overcome by a new, patented process called the Poly-Solv method used by the Moore Paper Co. According to Ron Pierce, Moore Paper's office manager here, this is a closed, highly efficient process whereby the plastic component is separated from the paper fiber by means of organic solvents and steam. The fiber, of course, is then available for making new paper. The solvent is recovered by distillation and the plastic residue is used to supplement the fuel oil which supplies the energy for the still and steam generator.

Unfortunately, Moore Paper Co. does not now have a mill in Houston. The actual recycling by the Poly-Solv process is done by the Riverside Paper Corporation in Appleton, Wisconsin, which is too far away to do Metropolitan much good.

Another major by-product of the Metropolitan operation is junk rubber of which some two million tons is thrown away each year in the United States. This material cannot be ground up with the type of grinder used by Metropolitan and — along with the five million tons each of glass bottles and plastics which Americans discard yearly — it is not compostable.

Research currently underway at Texas A&M has indicated strongly that all of this presently unusable material can economically be converted into a road-building material actually superior to the asphaltic concrete mixture now in wide use. Dr. Douglas Bynum, an Aggie research engineer, has experimented with pulverized rubber, glass, and plastic to produce crack-resistant foundations and toppings for roads in College Station, apparently with very good results. Unstable soil conditions in conjunction with expansion and contraction produced by normal temperature variation cause roads constructed of more conventional materials to break up over a longer or shorter length of time.

Bynum's rubber and asphalt mixture can be used as a foundation to isolate the road from expansion-contraction cycle in the underlying soil, thereby increasing the lifetime of the riding surface by as much as 400 percent.

The glass component (from which the rough edges have been removed by tumbling with ball bearings) is less subject to thermal effects than the gravel now used in road building. He has also discovered that pulverized plastic improves the bonding of the asphalt to other components of the aggregate. These new materials can be applied in less time than conventional ones, do not require new equipment and, because thinner layers are required, cost no more.

What I have presented in this article is much too skimpy to be called a description of an ideal recycling system for metropolitan solid wastes, but perhaps it may serve to suggest the sort of integrated industrial system which will one day have to come into being if our cities are not to become buried beneath their own garbage. The $2 million junk heap on Lawndale shows how difficult it is for a single company, no matter how good its partial solution to the overall problem may be, to break even, let alone to make a profit.

As I said at the outset, the technological problems have been already worked out to the point where an economically viable system of mutually supportive recycling industries is theoretically possible. Other aspects of the garbage problem — and the political aspect in particular — will be the subject of articles in the near future. -30-

Pitfalls of a Landfill: Oh, Garbage!

Thorne Dreyer • May 4, 1971

"Houston has a solid waste crisis." That's what Mike Noblet told City Council April 28.

Which is nothing new or surprising. Everyone knows that our fair city's been having its troubles trying to figure out what to do with all the garbage. But Noblet, who is president of Earthworks, Inc., the environmental action group at the University of Houston, has a plan. Recycling, he says, is the answer to the trash question.

Houston presently gets rid of its garbage by the "landfill" method. That means digging a big hole, then slowly filling it up with garbage and, when it's full to the brim, covering it with dirt and making it into a park — or something.

There are three landfill sites which receive city-collected garbage: at Pinemont and Ella; at the North Loop and Kirkpatrick; and at Holmes Rd. south of Almeda.

Reed dump is proof of the pudding: landfills are indeed a fire menace.

But a garbage crisis has developed because the three sites are filling up fast, new landfill sites have not been located and contracts have not been awarded.

But if Noblet, and other ecologically-minded citizens, had their way, there would be no more landfills. As Noblet points out, the only real benefit of a landfill is the park that will eventually be created atop the trash. But there are problems even with this. Like, "few citizens will desire to play atop a mountain of garbage." Also, cost of maintenance will be high, and the sites are likely to be distant from population centers, thus lowering their value as parks.

And there are other significant problems with this form of garbage disposal. Noblet points out some of them: future development possibilities for the land are diminished; they cause sanitary problems and are potential sources of water and air pollution; they endanger the surrounding water table; and they are a fire hazard.

The pollution potential of landfills has been pointed out by county engineer Richard P. Doss. The County Commissioners Court recently approved a new one-year lease of a 25-acre county landfill located off U.S. Hwy. 90 near the San Jacinto River. Doss, speaking before the commissioners, said that the sandy soil around the dump has created a significant water contamination problem in the area. To prevent future garbage from polluting, the county will have to build a dike and cover the present dump with at least six inches of clay, before dumping future trash. The dump will cost the county $140,000 this year.

As to Noblet's fire hazard claim, one need only check out the old, abandoned Reed Road dump. On second thought, don't check it out. Fire Chief C.R. Cook has asked the public to avoid the site because of the danger. The fire has been smoldering for weeks, but has not been put out because of squabbles between City Council and property owners Tom and Virgil Reed. (Councilman Homer Ford said April 20, that the situation is "explosive and dangerous" and that the City Legal Department was keeping the Fire Department from putting out the fire because this might be prejudicial to the city in a possible lawsuit with the Reeds.)

Ad: November 11,1971.

The city finally decided April 27 to extinguish the fire. Chief Cook said the fire has probably burned out huge underground chasms, and that putting it out would be "a long drawn-out process."

Anyway, Reed dump is proof of the pudding: landfills are indeed a fire menace.

Noblet's final point about landfills is the simple and obvious one that folks just don't want a garbage dump, landfill — or not in their neighborhood.

Noblet then discounted the second alternative means of garbage disposal: incineration. It creates odor and sight problems. (Drop by the Holmes Rd. incinerator sometime.) Emissions are likely to violate the Texas Clean Air Act. The coolant must be treated to avoid violation of Texas Water Quality Board standards. And it's expensive: $13 a ton, all things considered.

So, what is the answer to Houston's garbage dilemma? Noblet suggests recycling, or resource recovery.

"The benefits of recycling are almost endless. A majority of resources in solid waste can be recycled through a resource recovery plant, including paper, cardboard, aluminum, steel, glass, and rags, all of which can be sold to defray some of the operating costs of such a plant.

"The organics in solid waste are used to create compost... an excellent soil conditioner which can be sold at a profit."

The plant would use a finite amount of land, would have minimal odor, and no air and water pollution. And the net cost is only $6 to $7 per ton.

Noblet points out that Houston had a resource recovery plant on Lawndale St. from 1965 until last year. Metals generated from the Holmes Rd. incinerator were sold for reuse; but, since the unit resumed operation this year, metals have merely been landfilled.

And, as to money, there are matching funds available through the Resource Recovery Act of 1970. "This act," according to Noblet, "changes federal government policy concerning solid waste management. The former policy was burn it or bury it, while the new one emphasizes maximum recovery of resources from solid waste. The Resources Recovery Act is funded with $462 million. Houston will be able to receive matching funds. . ."

It all seems to make sense, yes? But, alas, it doesn't appear that good sense is the fuel on which our city government runs. -30-

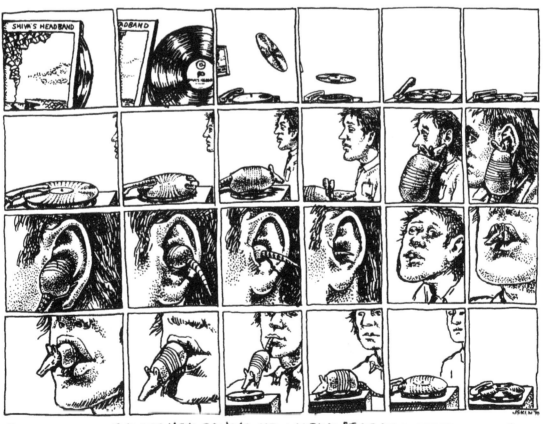

PICK UP A COPY OF SHIVA'S HEADBAND'S NEW ALBUM, "TAKE ME TO THE MOUNTAINS" AND GET AN ARMADILLO IN YOUR EAR!

Ad. Art by Jim Franklin, August 22, 1970

ECONOMICS

Analysis: Brr! Nixon Puts Freeze on Economy

Gary Thiher • August 24, 1971

Once upon a time, in an age more full of simple faith than our own, it was widely believed that the capitalist economy was a wondrous and largely perfect machine. One that insured the production of the cheapest and finest goods available — and always in just the right quantity. According to this theory, there were innumerable producers of goods who all competed for the favor of the consumer. This sovereign consumer, a paragon of good sense, sorted among the goods offered him and purchased only those of highest quality and lowest price. So any unscrupulous manufacturer who tried to get away with making shoddy, high-priced products would soon find he had no customers; and so the best was always available for the least possible cost. The capitalist machine could not produce too many goods for, if supply began to rise above demand, the price would fall and thus consumption would increase. So the amount of goods made and the amount wanted always equaled one another.

This blissful conception pleased Americans immensely — especially politicians. Succeeding administrations clung to this view tenaciously through an amazing number of healthy depressions until finally Herbert Hoover was given a definitive lesson in its untruth. Demand and supply, alas, could get so out of step that as demand fell, supply would be cut back. And when producers cut the number of their employees due to lessened production, the demand would fall still further. Now the theory maintained that the law of supply and demand would hold for labor too, since it was treated as just another commodity. Supposedly, when unemployment was high, and thus the demand for labor low, the price of labor would fall until it became profitable for businessmen to purchase all the available labor, so the system should stabilize only at full employment. But the Great Depression provided something in excess of 10 million exceptions to this rule.

Enter John Maynard Keynes. Mr. Keynes was a Cambridge economist whom the believers in the old theory thought tremendously wicked and subversive. Mr. Keynes taught that this flaw of falling demand and consequent depression could be corrected by a dash of public power to the private enterprise system. Through fiscal policy and budget expenditures, the government could keep purchasing power (and thus demand) at a high enough level to keep the factories going and employment high. And when necessary, the government could reverse the process and hold down inflation. Thus, in recessionary times, the government was to lower interest rates and spend a great deal itself from borrowed money, so that the total amount of purchasing power remained high. Inflation called for higher interest rates, higher taxes and lower spending.

> **These twin economic evils are supposed to alternate, but lucky Nixon has them both.**

Now this theory did indeed work better than the old one. Government spending zoomed up (mostly for war, unfortunately) and the country didn't have any more great depressions, though it did not eliminate a lot of minor ones.

Still, as Richard Nixon has learned, the economic machine was not perfect even yet. Previously, people thought that the economy could maintain full employment with the help of government deficit spending, and that the only price it would have to pay would be steady inflation. Well, the Nixon administration has seen plenty of inflation at a rate of some 6.6 percent a year. But, strangely enough, this has been accompanied by a constantly high unemployment rate as well. These twin economic evils are supposed to alternate, but lucky Nixon has them both. Unemployment runs currently at 6 percent nationally with some local rates rising to a depression-like 10 percent or more. The worst of all possible worlds.

In addition to the continuing high levels of government spending, the inflation is caused by what is called the wage-price spiral, a sub-species of the vicious circle. Large corporations, and the large unions which have grown up to fight them, are essentially outside of any effective market. Though some smaller sectors of the economy are guided by market influences, the backbone of the system (auto, steel, etc.)

is composed of firms too big and few in number to be significantly affected by laws of supply and demand.

In fact, just the reverse is true; these giant corporations exert influence over the rest of the economy. Thus, even though much of the economy is in a slump with unemployment and underproduction, the big corporations can keep prices up. Unions respond to inflated costs of living by demanding higher wages. Then the corporations raise prices further, causing another increase in living costs and bouncing the ball back to the unions. And so comes about the present most peculiar situation: recession and inflation.

President Nixon's plan for dealing with this situation for the first two years of his administration consisted of doing nothing. Nixon is conservative, and conservative politicians have always held as a fundamental principle that the free enterprise economy was perfect and could only suffer from governmental meddling. But it has become clear that Nixon could not get re-elected with the economy faltering. And so expediency has scored yet another victory over principle with the president's announcement of his new "game plan."

The only way to put an end to the persistent inflation, short of a full scale depression, is to control wages and prices directly by law. Thus, on August 15, Nixon imposed a 90-day freeze on wages, prices and rents. Previously, the Kennedy and Johnson administrations had flirted with an informal kind of wage and price control in the form of presidential guidelines. The chief executive requested industry and labor to voluntarily follow these standards and would sometimes use the power of his office to bluff down those who infringed upon them (as with Kennedy and the steel industry). This has come to be called "jawboning," and Nixon has given it a try during his first years in office. But jawboning has proven not only informal, but also ineffective. Inflation continued.

What the administration will propose for the end of the three-month freeze is presently unknown. Both Nixon and Treasury Secretary John Connally have indicated they do not want to continue wage and price controls. But the strategy can only be effective if permanent. If the controls are dropped, nothing will prevent the inflationary trends from reasserting themselves. Nixon, of course, is ideologically opposed to permanent controls which are a feature

Nixon's plan for dealing with this situation consisted of doing nothing.

of the sort of central planning practiced in socialist economies. (In spite of this, many good liberals support permanent controls.)

Nixon's other domestic proposals have to do with combatting the recession aspect of the present dilemma. These consist mostly of a variety of tax breaks, primarily to business. He wants a 10 percent investment tax credit for business (to allow them quicker depreciation benefits on equipment purchases), removal of the 70 percent excise tax on automobiles and an increase in the allowable personal income tax exemptions put into effect one year ahead of schedule. The tax credit is designed to encourage business to invest in new equipment the use of which will create new jobs and help pare down unemployment. The removal of the excise tax will make cars cheaper, and the added personal exemptions will put more disposable income in the pockets of consumers. Both these measures aim toward increasing consumption and spurring the creation of new jobs to meet added demand. These steps will have to be approved by Congress, but congressional comment indicates general support for Nixon's moves.

In apparent contradiction to these anti-recession measures, Nixon also announced that he will cut federal spending in this fiscal year by $4.7 billion and reduce federal employment by 5 percent. These moves are billed as anti-inflationary, but they seem unnecessary with the wage-price freeze. And they will certainly cause some unemployment both directly through the firing of federal workers and indirectly through the lessening of demand caused by the spending cut.

Business leaders have virtually all reacted favorably to the new economic policy. And Wall Street showed its approval when the stock market jumped 20 points the day after the president's announcement. The measures have aroused outright defiance from the nation's normally quiescent labor leaders, however. This is partly because the tax measures clearly favor industry over the poor working stiff, and because the controls do not extend to interest rates and profits.

The administration strained its labor relations even more when it announced a request that all unions end any strikes in progress and not start any new ones during the 90-day freeze. The accompanying implication that the administration thought it could force the unions to comply if they didn't do so voluntarily did little but enrage union leaders. Only one major union, the Teamsters, has pledged to comply with the government's request. Others, including the United Auto Workers, the Longshoremen, and the AFL-CIO have all stated that they will continue strikes in progress and start new ones when appropriate. (Some local AFL-CIO unions, such as the rubber workers here in Houston, have complied with the no-strike request in spite of the stance of the national leadership.)

At no time in recent history have relations between government and labor been so strained.

In terms of historic importance, the president's measures dealing with the international economy probably rate even higher than his domestic measures. In his August 15 message Nixon announced that the United States would no longer keep its pledge to redeem foreign-held dollars in gold and also that all imports into this country would hereafter have an added 10 percent surcharge tax. The removal of the dollar from the gold standard has put the currency situation of the entire non-communist world in flux. Since the Bretton Woods agreement in 1944, the United States has maintained the equivalency of $1 to 1/35 ounce of gold. This has made the dollar the peg upon which the currencies of the capitalist world hung. International transactions were measured in terms of dollars because the U.S. pledge to redeem dollars in gold made dollars stable relative to all other currencies.

Now the value of other currencies will float relative to the dollar depending on market determinations.

> **At no time in recent history have relations between government and labor been so strained.**

This will in effect result in other currencies rising in value relative to the dollar (which is overvalued). This amounts to devaluation of the dollar, which is precisely Nixon's intention. Devaluation of the dollar will make American exports cheaper in foreign markets and, conversely, foreign imports more expensive in America. It will increase U.S. sales to the rest of the world and limit foreign sales in this country.

Of course, this will happen only if other countries allow their currencies to float freely on the market, and thus rise in value compared to the dollar. Some European countries are already doing this — chiefly Germany, whose mark has been floating on the market for several months anyway. Others, notably France, have balked at being so accommodating to the United States. Nixon's policy, however, was aimed more at Japan than any other country. And Japan has so far refused to allow the yen to change in value. Since most businesses think that the pressure of the U.S. move will force Japan to allow the yen to rise in relative value, they have been cashing in large numbers of dollars (which would decrease in value during devaluation) for yen (which would rise). But the Bank of Japan has maintained the old exchange rate rather than allowing the yen to rise in value in the face of increased demand.

Japan does not want revaluation for reasons already mentioned: if Japan's currency rises in value, its exports become more expensive here, and ours cheaper there. Japan is one of the major exporting countries in the world, and it presently sells a full one-third of its exports right here in the U.S.A. — as every owner of a Toyota, Honda, Yashica, or Sony can easily appreciate. Though the United States sells a lot in Japan, we have suffered a trade deficit; Japan sold more to us than we did to them. The United States hopes a cheaper dollar will reverse this deficit. (This competition with Japan pre-dates World War I.) Japan is resisting, though most think it will have to revalue the yen. Until that time, Nixon has still narrowed the American mar-

Ad: November 18, 1971.

VOLUME II / NUMBER 27 / JUNE 1, 1971 / HOUSTON, TEXAS / 526-6257

LBJ (see p. 3) & KKK (see p. 6)

Art: Bill Narum, June 1, 1971.

ket to foreign goods with the across-the-board 10 percent surcharge on imports.

Now the U.S. concern with valuation stems from a general problem of trade balances. Not only was American industry having problems with Japan, it was beginning to suffer a trade deficit with the whole rest of the world; generally, this country was buying more from other countries than it sold to them. This unique situation had not occurred for many decades. And it pointed to the faltering of what historian William A. Williams called "open door imperialism."

Since the end of the 19th century, American leaders have realized that the nation's industry had to have markets for surplus goods and capital because the domestic market could not absorb it all, and the nation had no way to make it do so due to the lack of a planning facility. In competing with already established imperial powers, America espoused the principle of the "open door" (for all countries' goods and capital). American leaders theorized that growing American economic power would then allow this country to stake out large areas for its own informal empire. And so it has. The United States continues to fight increasingly difficult small wars to maintain this empire. This in itself represents a failure of strategy since the open-door plan was designed to avoid the need to fight for empire. Even worse, there appears little point in fighting the wars if the imperial nation is suffering the same poor trading balance which the empire itself was supposed to remedy. (Of course, one of the reasons for the trade imbalance is the outflow of resources necessary to pursue the war.) In other words, America has found itself killing its sons in order to defend a money-losing business.

So Nixon's abrogation of the gold standard for the dollar represents his attempt to put the empire back in the red, to reduce the growing trade imbalance. The plan will probably have a short term beneficial effect. Coupled with a systematized wage and price control, it could give the government better control over the economy and help avoid future difficulties. Corporate leaders have welcomed Nixon's move, and there is little reason to believe that wage-price controls won't come, if not now, at least in a few years. And as long as the federal government continues to fulfill its functions as the coordinating committee for corporate interests, business can only gain from the service. It already demands it more and more — as in the case of Lockheed Corporation. Recent history demonstrates that, capitalist or communist, modern economies demand a good deal of planning and management. And corporate interests would be the last to want to lose their profits and powers through bad management.

From the broader viewpoint, however, the early appearance of trade difficulties and intractable wars seems to confirm the trend toward a faster pace of historical events. And this steadily quickening current may sweep the U.S.A. on and off the stage of imperial history more swiftly than any of its predecessors. -30-

Ad: Art by Kerry Fitzgerald, June 1, 1971.

HEALTHCARE

Good Health: Not a Luxury

Karen Kaser • August 4, 1971

In 1969, President Nixon publicly acknowledged the healthcare disaster present in America and overnight, healthcare became an "in" issue for politicians and the polite public. As the cost of health services has outstripped even the middle-income wallet, the powers-that-be have started to worry about who will foot the soaring bill.

As a response, several plans for national health insurance have been initiated. Each claims to solve the problem, which the planners see as financial, but none seriously confronts other parts of the crisis. An understanding of these issues and the proposed solutions is important, since we are all affected by them.

What is the crisis? One of its facets is our system of priorities. Years ago, we discovered antibiotics and vaccines capable of completely wiping out diphtheria, typhoid fever, paralytic polio, whooping cough, undulant fever, rheumatic fever, and tuberculosis. Our doctors know how to prevent tetanus and diseases caused by malnutrition and bad sanitation. Yet billions of dollars are poured into research of rare diseases and developing organ transplants, projects which benefit only a handful of people, while thousands of people die yearly from the above-mentioned diseases.

This imbalance is reflected in health statistics. In 1950 the U.S. mortality rate ranked fifth among the nations of the world; in 1961 it dropped to eleventh; in 1967 it was seventeenth; and at present it is twenty-second. The infant mortality rate for whites is 19.7 percent; for non-whites 35.9 percent and the average infant mortality rate ranks behind more than a dozen other industrialized countries. Also, more mothers die in childbirth in America than in 100 other countries.

Amazingly enough, the most highly technologized country in the world has fewer beds for its population (9.1 beds per 1,000 people, a figure unchanged since 1934) than many "undeveloped" countries. Furthermore, the ratio of doctors to population was 1-568, 50 years ago, 1-709 in 1966, and was only this high because of large-scale importation of foreign doctors.

The hospitals themselves are in worse shape than the cure they provide.

The average American's accessibility to needed medical care is less than in most European countries because of high costs, shortages, maldistribution of personnel and facilities and inadequacies of insurance coverage. Recent studies by the National Committee on Chronic Illness disclosed that 50 percent of significant illness in the total population during a given year is not medically treated.

Even though not enough attention is devoted to diagnosing illnesses, some medical attention has been proven unnecessary. According to a study conducted by Columbia University School of Public Health and Administration, of 60 hysterectomies (a very serious operation in which a woman's reproductive organs are tied off) performed in New York City, 20 were judged absolutely unnecessary and the "advisability of the operation in another 10 percent was seriously questioned."

Not just in New York City do doctors fatten financially off this situation. It is estimated that 9,000 people a year die from unnecessary operations and surgery performed by unqualified doctors in U.S. hospitals.

The hospitals themselves are in worse shape than the cure they provide. In 1964, a United Hospital study of 58 voluntary hospitals in New York City found that only 17 percent met the full requirements of the U.S. Public Health Service.

The most annoying fly in the ointment we're getting is that the price of a healthy body is increasing beyond nearly everyone's ability to pay. In the past five years, physician's fees have increased 32 percent — twice the increase in the average cost of living. Also, between 1964 and 1969, the cost of a day in the hospital climbed 84 percent. All told, the average American family now spends 5.4 percent of its total budget on healthcare — 30 percent more than it did in 1950.

While family budgets seek relief, the health industry has few complaints. Profit returns after taxes last year amounted to $2.65 billion, with over a half going to physicians and surgeons and nearly one-fourth going to the drug industry. Those who doubt that the business is healthy should check the stock market. As one stockbroker advised his customers in May 1969: "Steady growth of the health industry … is as certain as anything can be."

In response to the public outcry, however, the health providers must now find new methods of financing. Medicare and Medicaid boosted the health industry's profits but the glaring disparity in medical care between rich and poor still exists. Now that the majority of Americans are being out-priced, several national health insurance plans have been proposed to better meet the medical needs of the people.

Three major types of plans have been put forth for universal or national health insurance.

The AMA Plan is a system of income tax credits which encourages people to voluntarily purchase private health insurance. An individual who purchased health insurance would have the right to deduct a certain fraction of the insurance premiums from the income taxes he pays the federal government. This would be set up progressively so that the poor would have insurance completely federally financed while the rich would not be funded at all.

Because it entails no cost controls and interferes least with the present health delivery system (both patients and providers would continue to deal directly with insurance companies), this plan is expected to be favored by commercial insurance companies.

The Rockefeller Plan espouses mandatory purchase of private health insurance, differing from the AMA Plan in its universality. Insurance premiums for working people would be paid by employer-employee contributions, while the unemployed and poor would have premiums paid by the government.

This plan, as the AMA Plan, does not involve reorganization of the health delivery system and thus only provides a new system of financing. Just as with Medicare and Medicaid, it is likely that neither of these plans is capable of covering all those insured because there are no provisions for cost control.

The Reuther plan calls for the federal government to act as insurer for everyone. It would be paid for by employer, employee and government contribution: tentatively two-thirds of the cost would come from employer-employee and one-third from general tax revenues. This plan differs from the other two plans in that it calls for a new administrative apparatus to administer the program and acknowledges the need for reorganization of the health delivery system, such as incentives to encourage group practice, regional planning and cost controls. Thus, this plan has been dubbed the most progressive of the three types.

None of these plans attack the problem at its roots. In addition to not solving the financial problems they are designed for, they do not seriously approach the other real problems mentioned earlier.

A workable national health insurance plan must provide for the following:

1. Totally free medical care — if taxing is the method of financing, it must be done progressively so that the rich pay a higher income percentage than the poor.

2. Deny healthcare as a profitmaking enterprise — no one should build wealth from the people's ill health. This would keep costs at a level the government can afford.

3. Community clinics and decentralized control — the most efficient system is flexible enough to fulfill the needs expressed by each community.

4. Break down the health worker hierarchy — qualifications for medical traineeship should not be on the basis of sex, race, or previous education. Direct pathways must be open so that hospital workers can become doctors, nurses, and other health personnel.

5. Preventive medicine — a good system provides for prevention and elimination of those conditions which promote ill health. This includes consideration of housing, sanitation, food, safety, and other living conditions.

It is doubtful that these provisions will ever be legislated, for they strike sharply at America's racism, sexism, and, in fact, the system of capitalism. If we want good health as a right rather than a luxury, we must do whatever necessary to achieve these demands. HEALTH WORKERS UNITE! -30-

Ad: November 21, 1971.

SPORTS

Ali

Jeff Shero • August 4, 1971

If Muhammad Ali were a trout fisherman, a surfer, a pole vaulter, or even a city councilman, he'd still attract crowds. Boxing has nothing to do with it. Boxing's merely the craft, the escape route, of someone who grew up in the ghetto.

It's the person in this case who possesses the allure. After the defeat in the Frasier fight, newsmen followed him everywhere. Ali was the hero. Frasier traveled Europe with a singing act and the public responded as if he had leprosy.

The Ali-Ellis matchup in Houston was really a nothing fight. An ex-champion versus his old sparring partner. Not even a grudge between them. Yet everyday hundreds paid to watch Ali train. The show was as much the attraction as the boxing. Ali at half speed, spouting poetry and inventing impromptu guerrilla theater, is a better show than Bob Hope at his best, and is at least as good as Spiro Agnew.

After each sparring session Ali would converse with reporters in his dressing room, almost as some apprentice guru complete with a hint of a fattening mid-section. The questions would come from every field, and he would slide wittily from the merits of Marciano's jab, to the contradictions in acquiring material objects and living a spiritual life. Sometimes his discourse would be spellbinding; for instance, one man out of 200 finds his purpose, and how most waste their lives as spectators, daring, experiencing, living nothing.

One of the promoters told me Ali, product of the fine "separate but equal" black schools of Louisville, Kentucky, could read at best poorly. But every day the best sports writers of America, men jaded by the annual rise and fall of champions and given to a certain cynicism, would listen attentively, almost expectantly, to Ali's ideas and put-ons.

And Ali, sweating and completely naked, save for a casually draped towel, would produce a new angle or story for the newspapers every afternoon. But the bounce was gone. Maybe it was having his title taken away in his prime by a gaggle of elderly white men on the Boxing Commission, or maybe it was too many years of dull training sessions in steamy gyms all over America.

But there was a faint hint of tiredness around Ali's eyes, and often the stories would be serious and instructive rather than the "He'll take his dive in five, and that's no jive, because I'm the quickest man alive," enthusiasm of earlier years.

In the dressing room, it was clear Ali was not hungry for the glory of another title or out to prove himself. He was now very much a veteran, at times trying to regain the flow of adrenaline, and at times talking fondly of a home life after retirement.

> **Ali was not hungry for the glory of another title.**

I'd never hung around boxers or their training sessions before. My good sense had told me it was a dull and brutal activity. Syndicates of men investing in the poor — mostly blacks and Chicanos — on the basis of their ability to knock another man senseless. At the same time, I was filled with the mythology of the ring: Norman Mailer articles describing the stark loneliness of the combat, where a man exhausted from being beaten, swollen and wracked with pain, faces himself nakedly and from inner recesses of the spirit summons the will to endure, and conquers his opponent.

Quickly it was clear the myth was wrong. There were characters, crusty and wizened, who hung around the training camp. And it was probably true that an occasional man found himself in winning or getting beaten in the rings. But the rodeo circuit or the meeting place of deep-sea divers would probably be more interesting. For the most part the world of boxing seemed repetitive and dull.

It was easy to see why a man of Ali's intelligence would be tired. And after some 15 years of it, bored and ready to move on to another level of life.

The Pageant

The intimacy of training led, of course, to the studied pageantry of fight night. In many ways, the training had been the more revealing aspect. The fight itself is a theatric event. The jet set deplanes, the Astrodome scoreboard sparkles like some acid head's ultimate trip toy, reporters drink and trade predictions, television crewmen take practice shots on the prelim fighters, spectators dressed to kill, strut through the aisle being seen.

The smart fight press predicted Ali between six and eight rounds. Worldly Dick Young from the *New York Daily News* picked Ali in 12, saying something like, "He'd be a fool to finish it too soon. Then you couldn't sell the film rights for anything and they should be worth $300,000."

Prior to Ali and Ellis, the closed-circuit crowd was beamed a match between Mexican heavyweight champion Manuel Ramos, and Terry Daniels from Dallas. It turned into a passion play with Ramos flattened in the third round, but somehow getting up to be battered for seven more. He was bleeding from the mouth, nose, and a cut over his eye; blood would shower across the ring with every solid punch to his head.

With reflexes slowed after too many years in the ring, Ramos wanted to go down, yet he refused to fall. So through puffed eyes he carried his pain and sadness like a flagellant doing the stations of the cross. Waiting. Waiting for an honest knockout punch. Never receiving deliverance and continuing to suffer.

By the end you couldn't help but be suspicious that the referee hadn't stopped it because the promoters wanted a bloody brawl to satisfy the closed-circuit television folks. If Ramos went down fast, and then Ali were to end his fight in the first few rounds, the out-of-town crowd would feel they hadn't got their money's worth in blood and action.

Of the Ali-Ellis fight itself, there's not much to say that hasn't been written. Ellis is a good fighter and a decent man who very much wanted to win. He's good, but Ali still possesses greatness, so in the end he lost. Knocked out on his feet, and helped to his corner in the twelfth, tears came to his face when he realized he'd failed.

Ali, for his part, was cautious, and probably surprised even himself when he discovered his legs would last through 12 rounds of dancing.

At the end Ali had his friend Jimmy Ellis knocked out on his feet from a fine flurry of punches. Only Ellis's determination kept him standing. Ali stepped back and set himself to cream the defenseless Jimmy. But he looked into Ellis' eyes and his expression changed. Maybe Ali was struck by the existential absurdity that he was making a half million dollars for an hour's work of beating up his friend in front of 30,000 cheering spectators. Or maybe he'd gone beyond that aggressive hunger that allows you to risk maiming another for fame.

Whatever the reason, Ali rose above the tradition of the boxing ring. He dropped his hands, and

Jimmy Ellis. Photo by Cam Duncan. August 3, 1971.

Muhammad Ali. Photo by Cam Duncan. August 3,1971.

Jumpin' Gerrymanders! Legislative Districting

Molly Ivins • January 13, 1972

Special to Space City!

AUSTIN - By jiggering around with the boundary lines of almost any given legislative district, one can ensure that some folks' votes count for more than other folks' votes. One not only can, but one has, and that is why there are lawsuits over redistricting.

Minorities are most apt to be screwed and easiest to screw by the jiggering process and that is why three minorities — blacks, browns and Republicans — have sued the state of Texas over its redistricting plans for the state Senate and the state House of Representatives.

The combined cases were heard in Austin before a three-judge federal panel; the panel is expected to rule on them possibly as early as January 20. No matter what the judges decide, the losers are expected to appeal the decision directly to the Supreme Court before February 7, which is the filing deadline for state candidates.

Perhaps the key point to be settled is the constitutionality of multimember districts as used in Texas. Every urban area of this state except Houston is a multimember district.

Say, for example, that the numbers work out so that every 10,000 people in the state get to elect one state representative. And say there are 100,000 people in your city, which should mean that the city will be divided into 10 districts, each of which will elect one representative. But it doesn't work that way.

Instead, your city is considered one big district rather than 10 small ones and your one big district gets to elect 10 representatives who run at large.

Now what that almost always means is that minorities don't get represented. Say there were 20,000 blacks in your city, 10,000 Chicanos, and 10,000 Republicans. If the city were divided into 10 small districts, presumably it would end up with two black representatives, one Chicano, and one Republican. (It is simply assumed, generally correctly, that members of minorities live close together and vote as a

> **Minorities are most apt to be screwed by the jiggering process.**

bloc.) But if the minority candidates are running at large in a district of 100,000 voters, their 10,000 or 20,000 supporters simply can't outvote the Democratic Anglo majority.

The Supreme Court ruled last spring in an Indiana case that multimember districts are not unconstitutional per se. In order for the one-man, one-vote ruling to apply and overturn multimember districts, it is necessary to prove that such districts really do discriminate against minorities — and that is what most of the testimony in the current suit concerned.

The defense was headed by Leon Jaworski, the Houston legal heavy who is also president of the American Bar Association. Jaworski said in court that he had volunteered to defend the suit. His courtroom style is notable largely for its pomposity. In mid-hearing, he was somewhat set back by the ruling of another three-judge panel in Alabama that had just overturned multimember districts there. In addressing himself to this new ruling, Jaworski said, "The very idea of suggesting to this court for a moment that there is some comparison between the State of Texas and the State of Alabama, with the leadership it has had, is hard to understand."

Earl Luna, a troglodytic reactionary who is the chairman of the Dallas Democratic Party, handled the segment of the case dealing with black plaintiffs from Dallas and tried to prove that there just ain't no such thing as discrimination against blacks in Dallas. The results were interesting.

Luna put a black precinct chairman on the stand who said, yessuh, blacks surely did choose their own candidates in Dallas. Luna also called Bill Clark, a former county chairman who is, naturally, white. Clark was so confident about the ability of Dallas blacks to make their own political decisions that he was able to tell the court just how many blacks and browns would be on the next Democratic slate in Dallas.

In one of the more dramatic moments of the case, Luna questioned Zan Holmes, the only black among

Dallas' 15 representatives. Luna reminded Holmes that he had had no opposition in his House race last year and then asked Holmes if he didn't consider that proof that there was no discrimination in Dallas. Holmes responded quietly, "I don't know why nobody ran against me. Maybe it was just Dallas paying its respects to its token black."

Dr. Clifton McCleskey of the University of Texas gave a lucid explanation of how multimember districts work against minorities. He noted that it is not only a matter of dilution of numbers, but also a matter of excluding minorities from participating in slate-making and coalition forming, because the rules that govern those processes were set up before blacks and browns were permitted to participate.

But multimember districts are not the only kind of line-jiggering to be found in Texas' redistricting plans. Rep. Curtis Graves of Houston brought one of the suits heard in Austin. Graves charged that Barbara Jordan's senate district (which Graves wants to run in) was redrawn to dilute black strength.

This is the simplest way to dilute minority votes. If, for example, a district is 80 percent black, all you have to do is draw a line right through the middle of it and put each half into a predominantly white district.

There was still another lawsuit in play at the Austin hearing, but the plaintiffs didn't make much noise. That suit was in fact a phony: it was brought by some Dallasites close to Earl Luna. They sued the state on the redistricting question, asking for single-member districts, but what they had really planned to do was to get the case heard in Dallas by a conservative judge who would give an adverse decision. One rather mischievous attorney for the black plaintiffs issued an interrogatory to those who had brought the spurious suit, asking them whether they actually wanted single or multimember districts. After a day, the group came up with a long statement that hemmed and hawed and then said they'd like the multi, if constitutional, please.

(Ivins is co-editor of The Texas Observer, a weekly news journal published in Austin.) -30-

Art: Fortier, April 27, 1971.

Kindergarten is Kid Stuff

Dennis Fitzgerald • June 5, 1969

Well, I sure feel better now. It isn't often I feel l like whistlin' and stompin' because of what that school board does, but they've done some mighty straight shooting this time. And I want to thank them for a fine and noble action in abolishing kindergarten.

I can remember like yesterday all the things I learned in kindergarten. I learned how to lie down on the floor and keep my eyes closed even if I wasn't tired, because old Mrs. McCurdy said I was tired and she was the teacher so she ought to know.

Art: June 5, 1969.

I learned how to color without getting across the lines, and I learned the true and exact way to draw a cat. Coloring across the lines meant that you were messy and that you hadn't learned the true and exact way to draw a cat. Coloring across the lines meant you were messy and that you hadn't learned the right way to do things. Drawing cats different from how Mrs. McCurdy showed us on the board was wrong because they probably would look too much like a horse with whiskers.

I also learned about indoor voices and outdoor voices. Indoor voices are very quiet so you can hardly hear them, and outdoor voices are everything that's left over. If a lot of people got mixed up and used the outdoor voice inside, that was bad, because Mrs. McCurdy didn't have such a good outdoor voice (it squeaked a lot). Then Mrs. McCurdy would make us all be quiet because she couldn't hear herself think and nobody was listening to her and everybody was speaking without being called on.

I learned how you weren't supposed to get mad, or cry, or get too excited, or go to the bathroom without asking first. Hitting people was another thing. You couldn't hit another boy because that was bad, and you couldn't hit girls because they were girls.

All in all, I learned a lot of things that were very useful because everyone else was learning the same thing, and that made it a game to see who could learn the best and make Mrs. McCurdy be nice to you.

Though, of course, having Mrs. McCurdy be nice to you wasn't the only thing. Some of the other boys didn't like her much and they used to squinch up their faces and imitate her voice saying, "Now, who knows what this is?" They were the bad boys, and every week or so Mrs. McCurdy would choose one of them to be a sacrifice and he would have to go to the office — which was the worst thing that could happen to you.

That was my first acquaintance with the Applied Nameless Fears Theory. Going to the office was never so bad as just thinking about it. I'd have done almost anything to avoid being sent to the office. Later on, I came to feel the same way about making bad grades, and especially flunking. In high school they added communism, marijuana, and pre-marital intercourse to my list of Nameless Fears. I was beginning to have an awful lot of things to worry about.

And that's some of the reasons why I think the school board is doing a fine thing by cutting out kindergarten. I think Mrs. McCurdy might not have been so nervous, and I might not have had so much to try to unlearn later, if we'd both just skipped kindergarten altogether.

Of course, the school board might not see things exactly that way, apparently being more concerned with saving money, but then I'm not one to quibble over why they do what they do so long as they do what they do. It seems to me that a concerned citizenry might even convince the board — before August 20 when they have to put in next year's budget — that there could be a considerable savings in also eliminating first grade, report cards, all current textbooks, and the compiling of secret lists of "troublemakers."

We might in fact start a whole grassroots movement, which we could call "Citizens for No School," and which could have some fancy motto like, "Where miseducation prevails, any subtraction is a welcome addition." There could be marches and rallies and barbecues, and we could all sing, "I've got plenty of nothing, and nothing's plenty for me. " That would be something.

In time, maybe all the kids could unlearn enough kindergarten so they could be mad or happy if they felt like it; and they could learn that using your out-

door voice indoors isn't nearly so bad as being afraid of saying what you want to say.

Today kindergarten, tomorrow the military-industrial complex. -30-

`DOPE`

Mary Jane: She's in Trouble With the Law

Karen Northcott • August 24, 1971

In a time of wide-spread reform, Texas' dope laws still belong in the Dark Ages; the new state LSD law is a fiasco; Lee Otis is in there fighting; and, is dope really legal in San Francisco? Read on!

Marijuana: "Stepping stone to heroin … got to get the pushers 60-day minimum … 50-year maximum … less than two ounces is still the sale of a major quantity, gentlemen … mandatory life sentences for pushers … they all began with marijuana … a duty to our sister states to stop the flow of drugs … addiction to marijuana… preying on the innocent … opening the doors …" — Legislative references to marijuana during an attempt to pass a marijuana reform bill in the sixty-second Legislature.

Travel and Southern regional magazines delight in referring to Texas as the land of contrast. And indeed it is. But to me the contrast does not lie in the miles of sandy beaches or the miles of mountains nor the acres of desert but in the contrast between the jury that sentenced Lee Otis Johnson to 30 years in prison for giving away a single joint, and the jury that sentenced a confessed murderer to two years on the same day.

Texas is virtually the only state which will continue to send marijuana users to prison.

Simple first possession of any amount of grass is a felony in the Lone Star State. Those convicted of a felony can go to prison; those convicted of a misdemeanor only go to the county jail. A marijuana felony is a special breed of felony. It carries a minimum penalty of two years and a maximum that allows the authorities to do whatever they want, short of execution, with anyone caught with any amount of marijuana, and in most cities the jury will do whatever the prosecutor asks.

In 1970, the federal government and more than 25 of the states classed marijuana possession as a felony. Today, 11 states and the federal government have adopted misdemeanor penalties, instead. Michigan, Pennsylvania, Rhode Island, and Massachusetts are in the process of reforming their laws during their current legislative sessions. Only Alabama and Texas remain. Texas' legislature had the chance to reform, but passed it up. Alabama's legislature is still in session, so there may be hope.

Five neighbor states have adopted misdemeanor penalties of not more than a year in jail. They are Ar-

FRIENDS BUSTED ?

222-1550 MILE HIGH BONDING

kansas, New Mexico, Mississippi, Georgia, Louisiana, and Oklahoma.

The minimum sentence in Texas is twice as long as the maximum sentence in any state that borders Texas.

West Virginia doesn't even send people to jail. And Mississippi, of all places, Mississippi, just passed a maximum of six months for possession of any drug.

The Texas Legislature killed House Bill 549, introduced by Rep. Raul Longoria of Edinburg, which would have reduced the penalty for marijuana. The bill applied only to first-offense possession. It didn't alter the laws concerning sale, nor did it affect any other drugs. It provided penalties of seven days to six months in jail, a fine of $250 to $1,000, or both. To satisfy district attorneys who argued that if possession were made a misdemeanor, they would have no felony weapons to use against the pusher who comes to town with a shitload of grass, the bill made possession of more than 16 ounces "with the intent to sell" a felony.

Amendments were offered. The most outrageous, introduced by Jack Ogg of Houston, struck the entire misdemeanor section. Ogg's amendment provided that a defendant could, after a felony trial, ask the court to reduce his sentence to a maximum two-year misdemeanor. The court could not grant the request unless the defendant was able to prove, among other things: 1) that he was under 21, 2) that he possessed less than two lids, 3) that he did so "for the purpose of experimentation," and 4) that he had never used marijuana at any time before his arrest. Even if these things were proved, the court could still disregard them if it so desired.

An Austin attorney, Griffin Smith, writing for *The Texas Observer*, described the three-ring circus of the Legislature during the debate for H.B. 549 with the hysterical attitudes of the legislators:

> The hysteria blooming into comedy after a while, until one recalled that hundreds of young Texans who might have had a fair shot at a productive life were sitting in prison for an act that carried nothing more than a one-year fall term in any neighboring state, nor indeed, in any state within 500 miles. And that hundreds more were on their way, despite the prison director's protests that they were not like the hardened crimi-

nals, that they didn't belong in his prisons, that sending them there just made matters worse.

Told that the Texas marijuana law should be changed because it is notoriously unjust, their response was simply, "No, it shouldn't because marijuana is against the law."

'They keep talking about experimentation, when it's really a lifestyle.'

To most House members, the drug problem conjures up images straight out of 1949 movies. Their world is populated with sinister men in black raincoats who slink around "hooking" good kids on reefers. ("The lowest form of human life," intoned Rep. Joe Salem gravely, "are those who would sell marijuana. They are the Cosa Nostra. They are the Mafia.") Children buy a clumsily rolled cigarette on the playground during recess to "experiment." No one uses marijuana but "experimenters" and hippies, most of whom are political radicals anyway.

Wholly ignored is the fact — for it is a fact — that marijuana is about as common as bourbon in any college dormitory. Wholly ignored is the fact that marijuana usage has become, wisely or unwisely, a socially-acceptable activity to many business and professional people under the age of 30. Everything must be made to fit the image. As Representative Farenthold said exasperatedly, "They keep talking about experimentation, when it's really a lifestyle."

Middle class white kids rarely go to jail for first time possession in Houston. One percent go to jail and only five percent go to trial. The usual sentence is four to five years probation. The expense is great. There is a $5,000 to $10,000 bond to stay out of jail (with $500-$1,000 going to the bondsman). The going rate for a lawyer is $2,500.

The authorities have the power and the jurisdiction to do whatever they like to anyone caught with marijuana. The laws are not enforced fully or fairly. Political activists, freaks whose lifestyles violate the sensibilities of the traditionally-minded conservative Texans, kids too reckless, unlucky, or stupid to avoid getting caught, and poor blacks and browns bear the brunt of the arrests.

District Attorneys throughout Texas use the marijuana laws for imprisoning people they consider to be dangerous whether whatever makes them "dangerous" is against the law or not.

South Texas and Dallas are known for harsh penalties where the color of skin, political differences, and lifestyles have resulted in severe sentences for first offenders. A few years ago a poor Chicano man in the Valley was given 99 years for possession of a pound.

Law and order forces have been frequently prosecuting activists under the marijuana statutes. Some of the past arrests include the following:

- The most notable and outrageous is that of black activist Lee Otis Johnson of Houston. Johnson, a SNCC organizer, was arrested for possession and giving away a single joint. He was acquitted of possession and given 30 years for the passing of the joint. District Attorney Carol Vance prosecuted the case himself, after having left virtually all other cases to his 50 or so assistants. He asked for 20 years and the jury gave him 30.

- Pfc. Bruce Peterson, then editor of the *Fatigue Press*, underground paper at Fort Hood in Killeen, was found guilty of two counts of possession of marijuana by a general court-martial November 5, 1969. He was sentenced to eight years hard labor and given a dishonorable discharge.

Peterson previously served nine months in Leavenworth prison on a marijuana conviction. He had been involved in anti-military actions at Fort Hood and frequented the Oleo Strut, a Killeen GI coffeehouse.

Peterson was arrested along with four other persons by the Killeen police on August 23, 1969, for possession. A small sack of alleged grass was found in a borrowed car that he was driving.

Later the charges were dropped for all but Peterson.

On September 7, Killeen police arrested Peterson again on suspicion of possession. They didn't find anything on him, but they took a sample of lint from his pocket, sent it away to be analyzed, and report-

A poor Chicano man was given 99 years for possession of a pound.

ed that it contained traces of marijuana. The combined total of grass from both arrests was not enough to roll a joint with, so the police didn't have a case against him. (Under the de minimus precedent, a person must have enough dope on him to get high in order to be convicted in a civilian court.) The Killeen police turned their evidence over to the army brass, and Peterson was court-martialed.

During the court-martial the prosecution didn't produce any grass as evidence. A witness from Waco testified that he had analyzed the evidence and that, yes indeed, it was the killer weed.

But, he added, the amount had been so small that it was destroyed during analysis.

- Joshua Gould, Oleo Strut proprietor, was arrested for possession. The police had only a few seeds and grains which they alleged to have found in his car. The case was dismissed.

- In late June, 1970, four blacks from the University of California at Santa Barbara were charged with possession while traveling through Dallas and were presented to the town as captured black militants. The jury took less than 15 minutes to convict them. Two received probated sentences and two were sent to prison for two years. Not long after they were sentenced, the judge, Judge Gossett, was quoted by fthe *Dallas Morning News* as saying, "We had pretty good reason to believe that they were members of the Black Panther organization, dedicated to the overthrow of the government by revolution, but we couldn't prove that."

The judge's son was arrested that same year for possession. According to Dave Beckwith, a former Houston newsman, his trial was mysteriously hustled out of Dallas to Monteg, where Louis Holland, a close personal friend of Gossett's, is the presiding judge. The boy got two years probation.

The judge's son's sentence of two years probation is the customary penalty for nonpolitical whites who fail to have the charges dropped or the case indefinitely continued. In Texas, except in cases where the defendant is thought to be an important pusher, someone who is sent to jail for possession or sale of a small amount of grass is more than likely black or Chicano, and someone who is sent to jail for a long time is likely to be the kind of man the district attorneys consider dangerous. -30-

Art: Kerry Fitzgerald, June 1, 1971.

Advice to Dopers

Brian Grant • November 22, 1969

ADVICE
TO DOPERS

Q: What drug can you buy at a drugstore to stop a trip when it turns bummer?

A: None of the widely effective contrahallucinogens — including Thorazine, Stelazine, Melaril, Navane, Nardil, Tofranil, Librium, Elavil, Vivactil, Aventyl, and many others — is available without a prescription. A few over-the-counter drugs have been effective for a few people, but I suspect that the psychological effects of taking something like Compoz outweigh the chemical ones.

Many of the tranquilizers and anti-depressants listed above are available from underground sources (or by prescription) and the time to obtain such drugs is before you need them. A few fast-working trip terminators should be part of the pharmacopoeia of any responsible acid head, particularly if you have contact with beginners or if you plan to drop around unfamiliar people or surroundings.

The best protection against a bad trip is proper preparation, not more drugs. A beginner who knows his guide and his surroundings and who has been reassured that what he is experiencing is (1) temporary, he will come all the way back and (2) "normal"—he's not the first person who ever felt so strange — will rarely have an unpleasant trip.

Experienced heads usually follow a few rules to assure a desirable environment. First, when in doubt… don't. There is always another day. Second, minimize the responsibilities: If you have dinner to cook or errands to run, get them over with before you start. Third, avoid unanticipated hassles. If obnoxious friends drop over just as you are coming on, politely send them away. You can call them tomor-row, but right now you want to preserve the situation you have chosen.

This does not mean that one should hide in his pad to avoid distractions; some of the finest settings are turbulent and chaotic; Sunset Strip on Saturday night, Mardi Gras Tuesday, the magic weekend at Woodstock… the idea is to select the environment and swing with it. Just have a friend along to screen out the hassles and do the driving when you venture out into the world.

Q: I've heard that hyperventilating boosts a high. How does this work?

A: Deep, rapid breathing can more than triple the free oxygen in the blood stream. This causes a brief period of hypermetabolism all over the body, and is experienced as a flash reminiscent of cocaine activation. It has nothing to do with "boosting" a high, however, but it is felt more intensely when stoned, just like most sensations are.

Q: My girlfriend has been having flashbacks for several weeks since taking LSD one time in September. How long will these things last and what can we do about it?

A: You have not given me enough information. There are three general classes of flashbacks: sometimes synaptic matrices have been reimprinted during the period of serotonin level reduction. If so, the normal process of recovery will require cognitive reeducation and could take weeks.

Other times the brain has learned a trick for adrenochrome production paired with specific triggering stimuli. Adrenochrome is related to the tryptamines, but usually requires exhaustive discipline for its generation (such as fasting on a mountain top while chanting sacred poetry and contemplating your navel). If this is the case, she needs only to develop conscious control of the triggering mechanism to turn it off and on at will. I have been seeking this kind of mastery for some time, and envy her.

Another possibility is that she consumed sufficient calories during and before her trip that traces of LSD escaped deterioration in the form

Art: Gilbert Shelton, October 26, 1969.

of subcutaneous fat, which is being randomly released along with blood sugar. A crash diet with exercise for a day or two will burn it off.

All of these categories are still pretty theoretical, and there are other theories. If things don't stabilize soon, get a message to me to contact you personally.

Q: I've heard of some kind of acid called Blue Smear. Could you please tell me what this is made of and what effects it has on you? P.S. Please let everyone know all this crap will really mess you up
— I'm experienced.

A: I have never encountered Blue Smear. (You might be thinking of Blue Cheer, which was LSD-STP in large bluish caps, but this has not been around in some time.) It helps if you describe the pill.

P.S. Children, it is true. This crap can really mess you up. LSD is my religion, and I believe that it offers the greatest vehicle for human growth and development yet discovered; but it is nonetheless the most powerful drug known to science, and it can be dangerous.

To derive the most from LSD, it should be approached with understanding and respect. Gobbling hallucinogens for the kick of feeling weird and grooving on the pretty colors is great fun. Cool. Outasight. But the rush and the fireworks are only a trivial part of what it's all about. Youth, in its fearless impatience, plunges in, consuming massive doses, wiring in to seven-day trips by hawking every two hours, mixing incompatible drugs and furiously grasping at the next colossal kick; and in the process, completely missing the boat.

It's not the magic pill, it's in your mind. Slow down, let your mind take shape, then explore it. Please, please people: don't use LSD as a status symbol ("You took 2,000 mikes? Well, I've taken 3,000!") or as a ticket to acceptance or an escape from boredom or an implement of psychological suicide. No one should be harmed by LSD … but a list of casualties is beginning to mount. **-30-**

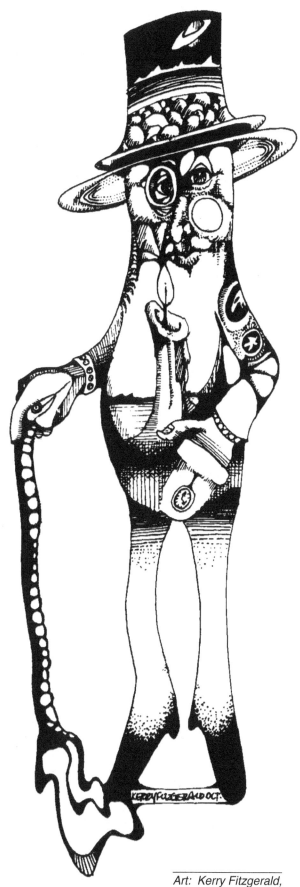

Art: Kerry Fitzgerald,
January 31, 1970.

RED COYOTES

Red Coyote Tribe Going Whole Hog!

Thorne Dreyer • November 14, 1970

The Red Coyote Tribe of Houston is getting its shit together. We've had three large planning sessions and, most recently, a picnic-volley-ball game-pow-wow.

We have adopted (with a few slight modifications) the program of the White Panther Party. (It appears elsewhere in this issue.) The most significant change was the addition of explicit support for the Gay Liberation struggle which was not specifically mentioned in the White Panther program. We also changed several mentions of "man" or "mankind" to "humanity" or "people."

Organizationally, the most important aspect of the tribe is the small work groups, some of which have already been established. The purpose of these is to get people involved in ongoing work and play together. Big mass actions and bullshit meetings are not enough. We have to work together on a day-to-day basis, building revolutionary survival institutions for our people and confronting the decadent institutions of the death culture.

Some of the groups that are happening or will soon be happening:

• Hard Drugs. This group will attempt to fight the flow of killer drugs like smack into our community. This will be done through an educational campaign, through work with Inlet Drug Crisis Center and possibly setting up or helping with a halfway house for heroin addicts.

• Agit-Prop. To spread the word about the Tribe and to aid communication among Coyotes. Also to do basic educational work around political issues. People are trying to get a mimeograph machine. Most exciting idea is a Street Sheet — a spontaneous mimeo newspaper that would come out whenever there is anything to report, with news of busts, political and cultural gatherings, and so on.

• Guerrilla Theater. The guerrilla theater affinity group will be heard from! 'Nuff said.

• People's Medicine. Will educate the community about medical problems (VD, street first aid, etc.) and will aid in setting up medical clinics and other institutions that serve the people. Now working with Peoples Party II and other groups in establishing the Carl B. Hampton free clinic in the Third Ward.

• Child Care. Establishing a day care center in the Montrose area, and possibly a breakfast for children program. Projects like these to be peopled equally by men and women. Also support for Peoples Party II breakfast program, when that gets going. Suitable location needed for Montrose project.

• Action Committee. To plan major together activities that pull in lots of folks around some political event. See discussion of Hog Calling Contest later in this article.

Art: Kerry Fitzgerald, November 14, ,1970.

And there's more. Like a study group is being set up, to meet regularly and discuss political questions. And the ongoing work of such groups as Switchboard and *Space City!* that see themselves as a part of the tribe.

There are several immediate things in the works that involve everyone in the Tribe. Like finding an office. Switchboard needs a new place and people thought it would be good to get an office together. We want very much to be in the Montrose area, and would prefer a big two-story house. If anybody has any ideas, contact Switchboard immediately.

There are also two major pow-wows coming up around Thanksgiving time.

On November 23, the Red Coyote Tribe is sponsoring the Second Annual International Hog Calling Contest and Jamboree at the University of Houston.

That same day (what a coincidence) Atty. Gen. John Mitchell is scheduled to speak on campus (though it's quite likely they'll send a less prestigious representa-tive from the Justice Department, if they think things might get too lively — remember Preston Smith).

There are no more details about the Hog Calling Contest presently available.

Then, on Thanksgiving day, November 26, there will be an all-day FREE rock festival at Of Our Own in the Village. This spectacular event has been dubbed the Red Coyote Honky-Tonk Hoe-Down and Howl-In. The slogan will be "Coyotes eat turkey too!" The bands will be announced later. Should be a far out event and all good coyotes should certainly be there.

So, there you have it. The Red Coyote progress report. If you're interested in getting involved in the Tribe, and especially in any of the ongoing projects, DO IT! For information on the Tribe, call Switchboard (522-9769). They can give you details about actions and will take your name and number if you're interested in specific projects.

Be a Coyote. It's fun, and good for you! -30-

Red Coyotes Greet Spiro: $100-A-Plate Riot!

Victoria Smith and Thorne Dreyer • January 30, 1971

Houston hippies got unruly and Houston pigs ran amuck Thursday night, January 21, at the Asshole-World Hotel right here in Space City. Seems Spiro came to town, to give the Vince Lombardi award to the college football lineman of the year. The event was a wear-your-best-duds $100-a-plate dinner. (And the mashed potatoes were probably cold, too.)

A large number of irate citizens — mostly of the young and scraggly variety — also made the scene. We thought there were close to 1,000; the commercial media said 400. Thirty-seven (including a *Chronicle* reporter — heaven forbid!) ended up in the clink, mostly for "creating a disturbance." We'll present gory details of that action later in this here article.

It was certainly appropriate that some of those present that night should have had justice meted out to them. Only one mistake: the real criminals were inside the hotel, not in the streets. The fat cats dining on $100 catered teevee dinners and Agnew's succulent metaphors, getting rich off sneaky stock deals; they're the ones creating a disturbance.

The event was theater. Red Coyotes wore gory grease paint death masks or righteous war paint.

A genuine pig's head was carried around on a stake. It was to be presented to Agnew ("Ham of the Year") in a special awards ceremony, but Spiro did not show to accept the honor.

Several demonstrators carried large NLF flags, and signs in the crowd ranged from "Spiro Eats Cow Patties" to "Red Coyotes Say: Support the PRG" (Provisional Revolutionary Government of South Vietnam). The crowd sang, chanted, and played kazoos.

The whole scene was a mixed metaphor. People were joyous, yet angry. We expressed our outrage at Agnew the war criminal, while, at the same time, laughing at Spiro the buffoon, Spiro the Foot-in-Mouth.

A Red Coyote press release had said:

We must always confront and express our righteous anger against the puppet

The real criminals were inside the hotel, not in the streets.

masters of the Death Kulture. But we must also rejoice in the birth of our new community, that we not become like them with their stone-frozen frowns.

We mourn for the Vietnamese, slaughtered at countless My Lais, whose land has been decimated by napalm and Amerikan defoliants. But we celebrate the spirit of the Vietnamese people, who throughout hundreds of years of fighting against outside aggressors with superior technological capability, have continued to exhibit a fantastic determination and will to win back their country and preserve their culture.

Perhaps the most significant aspect of this demonstration, as compared to previous Houston pow-wows, was the militancy of the participants.

It wasn't just a few ringleaders who were chanting and pig-baiting and carrying on. The crowd was, on the whole, young, spirited, and together.

People shouted "One, two, three, four, we don't want your fucking war" with gusto. Two popular chants, "Free Lee Otis," and, "These pigs killed Carl," were mentioned in the *Chronicle*, followed by a paragraph explaining who Lee Otis and Carl Hampton are. This was great: militant hippies voicing strong support for black revolutionaries!

As the evening wore on energy began to dwindle and it became clear that the demonstration needed some directed action, some clear target. It was nearing 8 p.m., Spiro's scheduled speaking time, and there was talk of moving off the sidewalk towards the hotel doors.

People stood facing each other across Kirby — shouting, chanting, laughing. We began parading back and forth across the street, defying traffic as well as the police.

"Food should be free, you shouldn't have to pay $100 a plate for it," a sister shouted to the crowd. People responded with cheers and cries of "Right on!" But attention never became focused on the big-

AGNEWS IS BAD NEWS

INSIDE THE U OF H ...p. 13-20

Cover: Space City!'s Dennis Fitzgerald at Agnew demonstration, January 30,1971.

wigs inside; the confrontation was clearly brewing on Kirby Drive.

A few cars passed by during this time, and most of the drivers seemed dumbfounded by the spectacle before them. But the crowd went wild with elated cheers as a black bus driver guided his empty vehicle along the street, with a clenched fist and a smile of solidarity on his face.

Suddenly a fierce chant of "One, two, three, four, we don't want your fucking war!" swept through the crowd and the folks moved joyfully into the street. It was our war cry and we were literally dancing to it. The steady rhythm of the chant was as captivating as the sounds of a rock band.

But this festive, defiant scene was short-lived. The pigs got spooked. After all, it was about time for Spiro to pontificate and, who knows, we just might've all danced our way into the Grand Ballroom and stolen the show!

A paddy wagon sped past a line of waiting patrol cars into the crowd; the police started grabbing people, as whirlypigs soared menacingly overhead. [Houston Police Chief] Herman Short, who apparently decided to forego the pleasure of hearing Spiro's wise words, joined our little gathering. Short later told newsmen that some hippie threw a bottle against the side of the paddy wagon and thus initiated the fray. But everyone we've rapped with insists that the first busts preceded the flinging of the mysterious bottle.

Few of our warriors went to jail quietly and peacefully. "I couldn't believe the militance of the scene," a sister who was busted in the early stages of the fracas later told us. "Everywhere I looked, people were fighting."

The main battleground was smack dab in the middle of the street, rather inconveniently near the open door of the first paddy wagon. Dodging passionate cries of "Fuckin' pigs!" police severed large portions of the crowd from the action, making it increasingly risky for people to move in and offer support for their sisters and brothers.

Some folks in the early battle escaped into the crowd, but were pursued and captured. A small number got in their licks and safely disappeared.

We saw police grab one young girl (later identified as 16-year-old Debby Sirman) and, in trying to

tame her, rip off her shirt. Naked to the waist, she was dragged into a patrol car behind the paddy wagon. According to Mark Bell, a 14-year-old brother whom police mistook for a girl and put in the car with our shirtless sister, the pigs didn't give her even so much as a coat.

Mark gave her his jacket. He said the pigs hit her over the head with a flashlight while she was in the car. Debby later talked to *Space City!* about the brutal treatment she and two of her friends received (see interview elsewhere on these pages).

Several witnesses described incidents of unnecessary police brutality, both during and after the initial busts. Police swung flashlights and wielded cans of mace to subdue demonstrators.

Police started grabbing people, as whirlypigs soared menacingly overhead.

Dennis Fitzgerald, a *Space City!* staffer, said he was knocked to the ground outside the paddy wagon and treated to the unique experience of a pig's booted hoof grinding itself into his face and forehead before he was hoisted by his kinky blond locks into the van. His bandaged and bruised mug remains ready evidence of his story.

Some police, observers say, had their handguns drawn. A patrol car came screeching up on the esplanade, in the process ejecting the pig in the passenger seat, who skidded several feet along the ground to the accompaniment of loud cheers from the crowd. This officer quickly grabbed for his pistol while the other jumped out, brandishing an M-16 rifle.

Houston Chronicle reporter Mel Freeland was quoted in the *Chronicle* as saying that he saw police strike demonstrators with their flashlights, "but could not see whether the police had been provoked or abused." He also said that several protesters in the paddy wagon were bleeding from head cuts.

Freeland was among those who were simply picked out of the crowd for arrest because the pigs thought they were ringleaders, or didn't like their looks, or whatever.

Another was Rod Marks, 19-year-old Rice student, who told *Space City!* that he was pissed off at being busted "because I didn't have anything to do with the violence."

He said he was on the sidewalk on the hotel side of the street during the melee. His one offense apparently was to scream at the police who were vamping on a sister.

Separated from his Rice friends. Rod decided to leave. He was running across the parking lot toward his car when two pigs jumped out and grabbed him. He was flung to the ground and dragged off.

When they got him to the police van, he said, the pigs slammed him against the closed doors several times, knocking him out cold. He came to in the moving paddy wagon.

Although he had enough money with him to get out of jail, Rod was not released until 7:30 the next morning.

Rod also said he talked with the driver of a car who was busted along with three passengers as they were attempting to leave the area. Police pulled them over near Kirby and the South Loop. They yanked the driver out of the car and started beating on him, leaving him with a busted lip.

The four were charged with loitering (in a moving car!) and abusive language.

Bryant Tiertont, 17, a student at Jones High, told us he was sitting on the curb, on the far side of Kirby, when an officer began baiting him. Tiertont decided to split and began walking down the sidewalk. The pig came after him, grabbed him, and dragged him off to the paddy wagon.

Tiertont and several other people witnessed one amazing incident of blatant piggery. The police had demonstrators on the far side of the street pinned up against a fence; they were forbidden to cross the street. One brother, who was pretty freaked with the whole scene, politely requested permission from an officer to walk across the street to his car. The pig finally relented and said okay, go on

Art: Sheridan, October 31, 1970.

across. As soon as the guy stepped into the street, Tiertont said, the pig and several buddies jumped him, beat on him, and threw him into the paddy wagon.

We might add here that several people we talked to went through some real changes as a result of the events of January 21. One brother, who intentionally steered clear of the fighting in the middle of the street because of his pacifist instincts, was very freaked by the pig's actions and impressed with the way many people responded. "I'm not so sure," he told *Space City!*, "that I won't be in there fighting next time!"

Mel Freeland, the aforementioned *Chronicle* reporter, was minding his own business and doing his journalistic thing covering the street battle when a police sergeant pointed to him and declared, "I want that one!" Freeland was hauled off to the van, protesting that he was a reporter for the *Chronicle*. (He had the proper credentials, including a special lapel badge.) His arresting officer replied, "I don't give a damn who you are."

We spoke with Freeland (whose hair is long for a member of the "legit" press) at the police station just after his release. We concluded that the police may have gotten him mixed up with *Space City!*'s shutterbug Doyle Niemann (there's a vague resemblance — and all longhairs look alike). Doyle had had a run-in with police in the early stages of the demonstration.

He was taking pictures, along with other newsmen, outside the Grand Ballroom about 6:30 p.m., before the pigs moved the crowd back to the Kirby Dr. sidewalk A plainclothes officer asked Niemann who he was taking pictures for. "*Space City!*," said Doyle. "*Space City!* is no newspaper," said the pig, ordering him to cease and desist.

Later, Doyle was in the street taking pictures of the crowd when the same pig confronted him and pushed him onto the sidewalk. Doyle regained his footing and snapped the cop's picture. The officer lunged at Doyle, grabbing at his camera and breaking the flash attachment. Doyle suffered a deep cut on his finger and he later heard that the pig cut his hand, too. "I certainly hope so," said Doyle.

A photographer for the University of Houston *Daily Cougar* left the demonstration with a swollen mouth and an eye irritation from mace, although Chief Short told the *Cougar* that officers were not carrying gas. Pacifica radio newsman Gary Thiher was flung up against a car in the melee. Also, several *Space City!* staffers were roughed up and hauled off to jail.

All in all, the police did a fairly efficient job of clearing the area, although it did take a goodly amount of time. And it may be that if Spiro saw anything at all, he just got a good sense of how effective the Houston men-in-blue are at preserving law 'n order to protect him from the people.

There is no doubt however — despite reports in the commercial media — that many of the banquet-goers were well aware of the demonstration. Pacifica's Mitch Green interviewed some of them as they were entering the ballroom. One crotchety old fellow said, "That's not a demonstration, that's treason ... you got about 16 commies over there and they're all pros, too."

And on and on. It was a great group — real Agnew fodder.

Incidentally, the police gave no formal warning before the bust began. Customary procedure in such matters allows for an announcement over a bullhorn, ordering demonstrators to disperse within a certain period of time or such-and-such will happen (busts, gassings, shootings, or whatever). Teargassing is usually the next step. But, in this instance, it appears that the Red Coyotes had the only bullhorn in town.

Because of such negligence and because of the unnecessarily heavy-handed techniques deployed by the police in breaking up the demonstration, the American Civil Liberties Union (ACLU) is considering filing suit against the Houston Police Depart-

ment. Should the suit, indeed, happen, David Berg will be the attorney.

James Calloway, chairman of the ACLU, told *Space City!* that he thinks police should have given demonstrators that small stretch of Kirby Drive, by setting up roadblocks. He said he thought such action should have been part of security for Agnew's visit.

> ## One crotchety old fellow said, 'That's not a demonstration, that's treason.'

People who were brutalized or who witnessed pig atrocities should get their stories and names to ACLU via Switchboard at 526-3666.

Anyway, by the time all the real action was over, those of us remaining were pretty intimidated, but hopping mad. The pigs had chased some of us into the Holiday Inn parking lot and had the rest lined up against the fence across Kirby. Some folks were bemoaning the fact that the whole crowd hadn't mobbed the pigs and others felt we shouldn't have allowed them to fight us on their own grounds, that we should have been better guerrillas.

But the police action had sufficiently dampened our spirit and courage, so, reluctantly and hurling curses at the low-winging whirlypigs, we departed.

Thirty-seven people were busted — 17 were charged with disorderly conduct, 11 with loitering, and four with using abusive language and loitering. Bond for most was $25.

Also busted was the pig's head. (Remember the pig's head?) The pig-on-a-poke was brought into Riesner Street (to the delight of those in the lobby, we are told), and was stored in a refrigerator. Later, both Cam Duncan and Jim Shannon, upon release, demanded the pig's head as their personal property. And it was (justice will out) returned to them. (Tongue sandwich anyone?)

In retrospect, one aspect of the demonstration was unfortunate; too much of the furor was directed at the police and not enough at Agnew and his cronies inside. Surely the Houston oinkers are worthy of derision, but they certainly aren't the ones pulling the strings.

It would probably have been better, in terms of attacking the real enemy, if folks had been busted trying to get closer to the hotel with its assembled piggery, rather than in attempting to take Kirby. Much of the problem was the physical layout: we were far away from the hotel, half of us on the sidewalk, the rest across the street on the esplanade. And the Houston pigs were in the center ring.

Another reason, we'd guess, that so much was directed at the police, is that a majority of the freaks came well-equipped with a hatred for Houston's finest. Their personal experiences had already made the police a logical target for their frustrations.

Much of the thrust of the demonstration itself was aimed at the war in Indochina. One of the main organizers of the event was the Vietnam Action Project (VAP) of the Red Coyote Tribe. VAP is joining with other groups throughout the country in a concerted effort to revitalize the anti-war movement, now when the danger of escalation seems so real.

A leaflet headed "Vietnam Will Win!" was distributed by the Coalition to Confront Agnew. It was signed by the Harriet Tubman Brigade, the John Brown Revolutionary League, Houston Gay Liberation Front, Houston Health Coalition, and VAP. Excerpts follow:

> Agnew is a hypocrite and a liar. He speaks at $100 a plate dinners to combat cancer, but represents a government that spends billions on a war that enriches the rich and kills the poor — billions that could be spent on serving the people, including cancer research. ...

> Nixon/Agnew know well that there is massive opposition to the Thieu-Ky regime in South Vietnam. U.S. withdrawal and real Vietnamization would mean immediate collapse of that regime ... Against this background, the peace program of the Provisional Revolutionary Government presented by Madam Binh in Paris in September, 1970, becomes the only viable basis for peace in Vietnam. The PRG Eight Point Proposal responds to the real needs of the Vietnamese people and also answers every question raised by the U.S. negotiating team in Paris, while providing the United States with a mechanism for safe withdrawal of all our troops. ...

> The U.S. is not getting out of Vietnam. There is speculation that Nixon and Laird will soon resort to the use of "tactical" nuclear weapons in Vietnam. The military will disengage from

Vietnam only when it is forced to do so through action at home by the American people as well as on the battlefield by the Vietnamese. Agnew certainly does not speak for the people of the United States ...

> We must work to transform the movement against the Vietnam war into the broadest possible movement of black, brown, red, yellow and white Americans. Only then will the war in Indochina end. And only then will the reconstruction of America begin.

If you are interested in getting into the struggle against Amerika's involvement in Indochina, take note: the Vietnam Action Project is scheduling a meeting for Sunday, January 31, 2 p.m., probably at the *Space City!* office. Call 526-6257 for details. We'll talk about more ways we can bring the issue of the war into the living room of every Houstonian, through educational activities and militant actions.

Remember Agnew!

Seize the Time! -30-

Art: January 16, 1971.

PRISONS

Prison Advocacy

Karen Northcott

Frances T. Freeman Jalet Cruz was an outlier. A 57-year-old white woman who advocated on behalf of prisoners within the walls of the Texas Department of Corrections (TDC). She came from the North. The good ole boys of the TDC did not know what to make of her. She visited her clients more often than others did. Her visits lasted longer than they deemed appropriate. She became a central figure in the prison reform movement in Texas, filing lawsuits challenging solitary confinement, the denial of religious freedom to inmates, censorship of their mail, the arbitrary withdrawal of an inmate's good time, and the building tender system. One official declared that prior to Ms. Cruz all of the lawyers had been "nice" and "cooperative."

Her exposure of the TDC and its brutal policies towards inmates added to the court record that ulti-mately led to prison reform ordered by the Federal Court in the '80s. Three inmates at the urging of the TDC filed a complaint against her that was heard in a Federal Court in a case that lasted six weeks. These inmates alleged that she conspired with some of her clients threatening the security of the prison system by teaching revolutionary ideas, by endangering prison morale and by fomenting revolution thus denying them some of their privileges. They sought to ban Ms. Cruz from the TDC and to halt her work on behalf of inmates. These inmates later recanted and dropped their lawsuit. Ms. Cruz and 12 inmates filed a counterclaim and won.

Austin
May 2021

Up Against 'The Walls'

Karen Northcott • May 18, 1972

We, the people of the convicted class, locked in a cycle of poverty, failure, discrimination and servitude; DO HEREBY DECLARE, before the WORLD, our situation to be unjust and inhuman. Basic human rights are systematically withheld from our class. We have been historically stereotyped as less than human, while in reality we possess the same needs, frailties, ambitions and dignity indigenous to all humans. Our class has been unconstitutionally denied equal treatment under the law. We are the first to be accused and the last to be recognized.

We hereby assert before the tribunal of Mankind that our class ought not to be subject to one whit more restraint, nor one ounce more deprivation than is essential to implementing the constructive purposes of the criminal law. Prisons should no longer be dim, gray garrisons designed to isolate human waste. Rather, they must mirror the outside world if we are to harbor any hope that its residents will ever rejoin it. In that spirit, we demand the restoration of our constitutional and human rights…
— *United Prisoners Union Bill of Rights*

Frances T. Freeman Jalet Cruz, a Houston attorney who represents the convicted class in its struggle to win constitutional and human rights through the courts, is now facing a legal battle of her own.

Three inmates of the Texas Department of Corrections (TDC), Robert Slayman, Donald Lock and Freddie Dreyer — have filed a complaint against her under the Civil Rights Act, alleging that she conspired with some of her clients to threaten the security of the prison system by teaching revolutionary ideas, to endanger prison morale and foment revolution, thus denying them some of their privileges.

Mrs. Cruz is one of only two Texas attorneys who have filed suit against the TDC concerning solitary

Houston, Texas : April 27-May 3, 1972 : 25 cents

On Trial:
Frances Jalet Cruz

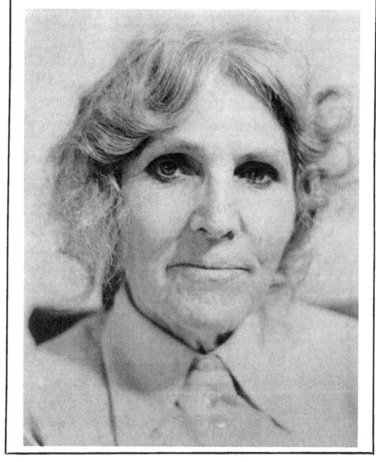

Cover: April 27,1972.

confinement, the denial of religious freedom for inmates and censorship of mail.

The trial, now in its sixth week in U.S. District Judge Carl O. Bue's court, involves issues which will set precedents for cases to come.

The exposure of the Texas Department of Corrections and its policies towards the inmates has been added to the court record and, as a result, all subsequent prison litigation in Texas will be shortened because of the availability of this information on prison rules and regulations.

The authority of the prison system to discredit an attorney for disagreeing with her/his professional conduct is being tried.

The near tyrannical power of the federal trial judge is being exposed and recorded. In this trial, Bue has set aside all ordinary rules of evidence concerning hearsay, leading questions and self-impeachment by a witness. They just don't apply.

Bue also handpicked the lawyers for the three inmates. Tom Phillips, head trial lawyer for Baker-Botts, was Crawford Martin's campaign manager; Martin is a defendant in the countersuit brought by Mrs. Cruz asking for $150,000 damages.

Bue also appointed Donald Eckhardt, a trial lawyer for the firm of Royston, Rayzor and Cook, as lawyer for the plaintiffs. Eckhardt is a partner in Bue's old law firm. Max Jennings, the other appointed lawyer, has his law office on the same floor of the same building where Bue officed in private practice. Thus Bue is well acquainted personally with the lawyers — lawyers whose positions lend respectability to the plaintiffs.

The judge has also guaranteed that the expenses of the trial for the inmates will be paid for by the federal government by allowing them to proceed in forma pauperis. He refused to allow Mrs. Cruz to proceed in forma pauperis, although at the time the suit was filed she was living in poverty as a VISTA volunteer, as required by federal law. As a result, the expense of the lengthy trial is borne by the participating defense lawyers — Bill Kilgarlin, Stuart Nelkin, Henry Rosenbloom, Bill Kimble, David Berg, and Fred Grossberg — and the American Civil Liberties Union, which will be bankrupted unless large sums of money are raised.

The three inmates — Slayman, Lock and Dreyer — are asking the court to bar Mrs. Cruz from the TDC and to halt her work with prisoners.

The near tyrannical power of the federal trial judge is being exposed.

One of the plaintiffs, 27-year-old Robert Slayman, was paroled during the course of the trial and vanished soon after. It is unlikely that the TDC will make the same mistake with Dreyer and Lock and parole them while the trial is still in progress.

The testimony of the inmates alleges that Mrs. Cruz, through her intermediary in the prison, Fred Arispe Cruz, solicited clients and then urged them to take part in a conspiracy to turn the prison system around. (Much has been made both in the trial itself and reportage of the proceedings that Mrs. Jalet, 61, married Fred Cruz, 32, after securing his release from prison on a writ of habeas corpus.)

Lawyers for the plaintiffs have paraded witness after inmate witness, some of them former clients of Mrs. Cruz, who testified that she was causing riot and revolution within the prison system. All of the witnesses spoke in generalities and could pinpoint nothing.

In Slayman's deposition, summarized by attorney Tom Phillips, he alleges that one of Mrs. Cruz's clients told him an Attica was needed at TDC and that an incident like the throat-cutting of three San Quentin guards was also needed.

Another inmate, Julius Perry, 40, testified that he fired Mrs. Cruz after she told him prison riots are sometimes necessary "to open the eyes of the public."

Perry testified he told Mrs. Cruz — at the Wynne Unit in Huntsville in 1971 — that he hoped prison riots such as last year's rebellion at Attica would never occur in the Texas system.

He said Mrs. Cruz replied, "Sometimes we must suffer to open the eyes of the public."

Jim Foster, 29, said he was told in 1968 in the Eastham Unit that Fred Cruz inspired inmates to make trouble and was backed up by a "woman lawyer up north."

The final witness for the plaintiffs was Warden C.L. McAdams, who has been with the TDC since 1948 at various units. McAdams testified about the improvements in prison conditions, dating from the arrival of O.B. Ellis in 1948 and continuing under the present direction of Dr. George Beto. McAdams also testified about his first and subsequent meetings with Fred Cruz.

McAdams said that the prison was changed from an inmate run system — rife with dope, sex, perversion, and knives — to a modern institution where inmates may enter a two-year college program, learn trades, and rehabilitate themselves.

To illustrate the changes in the prison system McAdams showed pictures of the early prison depicting the poor living conditions, the poor working conditions, and the inadequate laundry and shower facilities. To emphasize the great changes which have since taken place, McAdams then showed pictures of the prison facilities taken in 1968 which show the modern area of the cell block, the prison chapel, the hospital, the schoolroom, the laundry, and the sewing room.

(All these improvements are really nothing more than better buildings built by money appropriated by the state legislature.)

His first encounter with Fred Cruz came as the warden was called to quell a "riot" in the unit inmates call "The Shamrock," he said. McAdams described Cruz as "not caring anything about anybody but himself and he strictly did not like work — work was a nasty word in his mouth."

McAdams testified that Mrs. Cruz made an inordinate number of visits to the prison to see her clients. After each visit, he testified, the inmates were restless, edgy and tense. She would even demand to see a prisoner who was being held in solitary confinement, he said. "After one or two visits from Mrs. Cruz," he said, "there was more work stoppage, more fights, more tension, more men in solitary."

The warden acknowledged that Mrs. Cruz's clients, members of the "8-hoe squad," are in a segregated wing, isolated from the other inmates and denied privileges such as use of the recreation room, the TV room, the usual writ room (where inmate legal work is written) in order to protect them.

His first encounter with Fred Cruz came as the warden was called to quell a 'riot.'

The defense lawyers cross-examined Warden McAdams at length concerning his attitudes towards prison discipline, homosexuality, Mrs. Cruz, and the "Ellis Report."

McAdams testified that you couldn't have a prison run by the inmates, that the warden must have complete control and that control is guaranteed by strict discipline. He repeatedly compared the inmates to children who must be punished. He acknowledged, however, that it would not be unusual for him to sit on the three-man disciplinary committee which tries the inmate for an infraction of one of the many obscure prison rules and regulations. Thus, he serves, the defense lawyers pointed out, as both the judge and the appellate body. He denied that his conception of prison reform includes the denial of a man's self-respect and dignity and the instilling in the men an attitude of fatalism and defeatism.

The warden also denied that there is a policy of mistreatment of any inmates found engaged in homosexual acts.

McAdams also testified that he felt no personal enmity towards Mrs. Jalet, even though she was the first lawyer to file suit against the TDC attacking the building tender system, the denial of religious freedom, the use of solitary confinement and the arbitrary withdrawal of an inmate's good time. "Prior to Mrs. Cruz, all the lawyers have been cooperative and nice," he said.

The warden testified that there was no truth whatsoever in the "Ellis Report" — a report of prison brutality at the Ellis Unit. The report was written by Mrs. Cruz while she was working for the Dallas Legal Aid Services, based on information supplied by inmates.

Art: Febuary 14, 1970.

The defense has brought forth witness after witness to cite instances of prison brutality involving Warden McAdams, building tenders, and other prison officials; the pettiness of the TDC rules and regulations; the arbitrary way in which inmates are summarily punished; and the harassment and intimidation to which Mrs. Cruz's clients are subjected.

Witnesses for the defense have cited many instances of prison brutality. Homosexuals, they say, are made to stand naked in the hallway in front of the chow hall, holding each other's penises in their hands. Homosexuals have had Whitfield salve, a salve with an acidic base, poured over their genitals. Men are strung out naked, handcuffed to the bars of the cells, feet off the ground, arms spreadeagled in crucifixion style. Building tenders and trustees carry iron pipes, blackjacks and knives and do the Warden's dirty work. There were also stories of men run down in the field by horses and of nighttime beatings.

Clyde Sewel, 38, testified about an escape attempt and its aftermath. "Three men commandeered a squad truck and tried to escape. The warden supposedly shot them. When we went to eat, three men were lying in front of the dining room, blood was running down the hallway. One man was unconscious. We had to walk through blood to get to the dining room."

Lorenzo Davis, a Black Muslim, testified he had heard that Dr. George Beto, director of the TDC, has ordered that all Muslims be killed. Davis also testified that building tenders carry knives, pipes, and blackjacks which are kept in the desk drawer of one of the prison officers. Davis said that he had spent 21 days in solitary confinement during which time he was only offered pork, which his religion forbids him to eat. Therefore, he subsisted on water alone, suffering a severe weight loss.

Davis spoke of his apprehension about testifying in Mrs. Cruz's behalf. "I expect my death after my testimony," he said quietly. He was not the only inmate to voice this fear. Ernest Ivy testified that he doesn't know what will happen to him for testifying against the TDC. "I know there will be repercussions. I may be beaten; I may be killed."

The inmates testified to having seen other inmates beaten by the building tenders. They said the tenders are the flunkies of the prison officials. Many could not give the names of inmates they had seen beaten by the trustees because it is against prison rules to talk with inmates on another wing and thus they had no way of knowing the names of many of those they saw beaten. Witnesses repeatedly testified that they saw the plaintiffs, Lock and Dreyer, get a prison official to open up an inmate's cell and then beat him.

One former inmate, Sylvester Perez, described the pettiness of the prison rules and regulations as "playing with your mind and your life." Once, while in solitary, he said, he chewed a hole in his arm, hoping to hit an artery and have to go to the hospital at Huntsville.

He hoped to reach Dr. Beto there, he said, and tell him he couldn't do his time at Eastham, where the guards and building tenders were so brutal. "All the bitterness and hatred build up where you get to the point where you don't give a damn," Perez said. "They push you to the edge."

The inmates testified to the prejudicial manner in which their disciplinary hearings were often held. It is not extraordinary for an inmate's punishment, to be handed down arbitrarily. An inmate often signs a piece of paper after he is released from solitary confinement saying he is guilty; not before, but after.

All of the defense witnesses testified that they had been threatened merely for being a client of Mrs. Cruz's. James Estes Baker testified that he had been told that, "as long as Mrs. Jalet was my attorney, I could expect to get into trouble." He said Freddie Dreyer told him, "as long as Mrs. Jalet was my lawyer I could expect to be beat up." Baker also testified that he had seen a directive of Dr. Beto's which ordered all of Mrs. Jalet's clients to be moved to Wynne Unit and be segregated. They are all on the Wynne Unit and are segregated.

Baker was not the only witness to testify to such harassment and intimidation. Ernest Ivy, Lorenzo Davis, Donald Kirby — they all testified that they had seen that they would never get any good time unless they dropped Mrs. Cruz as their lawyer.

The trial, now in its sixth week, is expected to last for two or three weeks longer. More testimony attacking the Texas Department of Corrections as creating an inhuman, sadistic, and brutal prison life is expected. As is more testimony depicting Mrs. Cruz's clients as liars, authority-haters, malcontents and troublemakers. As is more testimony characterizing Frances as an opportunistic lawyer taking directions from "up north," one who conspires with her clients to foment revolution within the Texas Prison system. -30-

> **Witnesses for the defense have cited many instances of prison brutality.**

Frances Jalet Cruz Trial Comes to an End Will They Have to Go on Alone?

Karen Northcott • June 1, 1972

Half a man's life is made up of the time he devotes to labor. Whether in prison or on parole, we are compelled to work for a living. Work is the major provision of a people. If we do not work, we steal. If we steal, the chances are we will be returned to prison. If we cannot find work in a system that does not provide work for everybody, we are sometimes returned to prison on a parole violation. We, as members of the convicted working class, are twisted and mangled in the vice of a cruel system that cares little for human life. We are the last to be hired, the first to be fired. We are compelled to dance at every turn: we dance for a parole, and we dance for a job while on parole. In the widening class struggle in America, we prisoners are the lowest of low. We are the wage slaves outside and inside. ...

We are still daily being psychologically tortured by the nebulous but spirit crushing reality of the indeterminate sentence law, we are still political pawns in the game of power, profit and political debts incurred by the governor and the director of corrections ... We are still being paroled back to the identical poverty and degradation which has been a cycle in our lives of poverty, prison, parole and more poverty, and we are still returning to prison at the same recidivism rate as before ...

WE ARE STILL STRUGGLING ALONE.

United Prisoners Bill of Rights

Six weeks of testimony ended Friday, May 26, in the trial of a Houston attorney who has spent the last seven years seeking to assure inmates of the Texas Department of Corrections (TDC) that they do not have to struggle alone.

Three inmates of the TDC — Robert Slayman, Donald Lock, and Freddie Dreyer — originally filed a complaint against Frances Freeman Jalet Cruz under the Civil Rights Act, alleging that she conspired with some of her clients to threaten the security of the prison system by teaching revolutionary ideas, to endanger prison morale and foment revolution, thus denying them some of their rights. The inmates are seeking to bar Mrs. Cruz from the TDC and to halt her work with prisoners.

The trial has been a complicated and controversial one, the credibility of the witnesses hard to discern. U.S. District Judge Carl O. Bue took the case under advisement, saying, "Frankly I've never seen a case like this before. One of the problems a judge runs into is familiarizing himself with the myriad areas of the law with which he has had no contact. For the past six weeks, as a member of the judiciary, I have felt that I have lived in another planet."

During the first three weeks of the trial, two of the plaintiffs, Donald Lock and Freddie Dreyer, testified that Mrs. Cruz, through her intermediary Fred Arispe Cruz, solicited clients and then urged them to join a conspiracy to take over the prison. The two also testified that Fred Cruz had threatened to kill them if they did not drop their suit seeking to bar Mrs. Cruz from the prison system.

Prosecution lawyers, Thomas Phillips, Donald Eckhardt, and Max Jennings (See *Space City!* Vol. III, No. 47) paraded witness after witness who backed up Lock and Dreyer's allegations, that Mrs. Cruz was causing riot and revolution within the prison system.

One of the plaintiffs, 27-year-old Robert Slayman, was paroled the second day of the trial and vanished soon after, abandoning his suit.

Lock, in a tearful and emotional about face Monday, May 22, reversed his previous testimony and asked that his suit be dismissed without prejudice. In a trembling voice, Lock said, "It's a lie. Mrs. Jalet has done nothing. She's tried to help me. She's tried to help the entire prison population."

Lock further testified that he had been pressured by TDC officials, W. Dee Kutach, assistant director of the TDC; Warden C.L. McAdams; and Lloyd

Hunt to file the suit. "They (prison officials) didn't come out and tell me to file it," he said. "But you just get used to the way these people talk and you know what they mean. I knew that filing the suit was my only way out."

Kutach said Lock's allegations are ridiculous and "under no circumstances has he been pressured."

Lock called Dr. George Beto, director of the TDC, a "phony" and described prison life as "pure hell." Inmate guards (building tenders) beat other prisoners at will, especially those unable to buy protection, he said. Lock said he saw inmate guards take a friend of his, Robert Oliphant, and beat him. "He yelled and begged and they beat him and put him in a straitjacket and tied him to a cell."

> ### 'They beat him and put him in a straitjacket.'

He testified that prison officials, specifically Warden McAdams, knew of the brutality. He called McAdams a "sadistic, sick man."

Lock said most of the inmates at the Wynne Unit feel the presiding judge in the case "is fixed" and that one of the plaintiff's attorneys "was paid $50,000 under the table."

He further testified that Dreyer told him he was "going to terrorize defense attorneys, Bill Kilgarlin, David Berg, Stuart Nelkin, Henry Rosenbloom, Fred Grossberg and Bill Kimball, when he gets out of prison in five and a half months."

Lock said he feared for his life because of his testimony and was placed in protective custody in the Galveston County Jail by Judge Bue. "If given the chance they would kill me," he said in a voice strained with emotion. "I think they would do it kind-of-legal … like, put me in a field, pull me out, shoot me, and say I'd been trying to escape."

The inmate said the third plaintiff, Robert Slayman, "set up Mrs. Jalet to buy time." He said that Slayman had "beat the State" referring to Slayman's receiving his parole and then splitting from the suit.

Lock acknowledged he had "been living the good life" of a building tender since filing the suit. He said that after he agreed to participate in the anti-Cruz suit, he had the power to have guards fired and to get other building tenders thrown into or taken out of solitary.

Frances Jalet Cruz, who had been sitting at the defense table shuffling through files, writing notes to her attorneys, sat quietly, hands clasped, eyes cast downward during Lock's emotional testimony. She

then took the stand and described in a subdued voice how she first came to Texas in 1967 as a Reginald Heber-Smith Fellow to practice poverty law with the Austin Legal Defenders Society. It was while she was in Austin that she received a letter from Fred Cruz asking her assistance in appealing a 1961 robbery conviction.

Mrs. Cruz was eventually fired from the Austin legal services project after the project's director, Hamilton Lowe, was informed by Beto that she had been giving assistance to inmates in the TDC. Lowe regarded this as improper since the office was not allowed to handle criminal matters, only civil. Mrs. Cruz pointed out that her assistance had been in purely civil matters. (She had written a letter to the Board of Corrections upon hearing that Fred Cruz was in solitary confinement, stating that solitary confinement was cruel and unusual punishment and violated the Eighth Amendment of the Constitution.)

Mrs. Cruz went on to testify of her subsequent jobs at the Dallas County Legal Aid Society, and the Texas Southern University Legal Aid program. It was

Ad: June 5, 1969.

while she was working in Dallas that she gained two more inmate clients, Bobby Brown who Judge Sarah Hughes asked her to represent and Ernest Ivy who had written asking for her assistance. Mrs. Cruz lost her job in Dallas, once again under fire from Beto.

In October 1968, Warden McAdams informed Mrs. Cruz that she could no longer visit her clients at the Ellis Unit. This ban was in effect until March 1969. On October 15, 1971, Beto issued an order to all wardens in the TDC to prohibit Mrs. Cruz from visiting any of her clients. This ban followed Beto's testimony in a suit filed by Mrs. Cruz in federal court, challenging the practice of arbitrary removal of an inmate's good time without due process and the censorship of mail.

Mrs. Cruz denied any prior arrangement with Fred Cruz to bring adverse publicity to the Texas prison system. She also denied the allegations that Fred had solicited clients for her: "I have many more requests for assistance than I can possibly respond to."

Mrs. Cruz also denied ever tacitly encouraging or suggesting, even by her silence, that any clients of hers should create an atmosphere of violence in the prison.

She acknowledged that she had experienced a considerable drop in income upon acceptance of the Reginald Heber-Smith Fellow and her subsequent enlistment as a VISTA volunteer. She has not been able to accept any new clients since October 1971; thus causing serious financial difficulty, she said.

But, she continued, she knew of no other source for the inmates to turn to for assistance in civil matters. Mrs. Cruz described her role as an important one in assisting inmates to assert their constitutional rights, to let them know that they had such constitutional rights. "The importance of an inmate being able to say I have a lawyer is great," she said. "To men who are cut off from the outside world, having someone to write to who is interested in helping them is important."

Tom Phillips, during his cross-examination, hammered away at Mrs. Cruz's conception of what a prison should be, her "abnormal" relationship with her clients, and her attitude towards George Beto.

Phillips described Frances' conception of a prison as a "home for broken souls." "Let's put these men somewhere," Phillips proposed, "these men who killed, raped, robbed, and call it a home for broken souls."

When Mrs. Cruz stated she felt inmates should be paid for their work, Phillips exclaimed, "I want to bring you down to common plain-talking language. Do you mean wages should be set through collective bargaining?"

Phillips questioned whether the relationship between Mrs. Cruz and her "so-called clients" was a normal lawyer-client relationship. "Isn't it true that you got advice from jailhouse lawyers rather than giving advice to them?" Phillips queried belligerently. "Are you telling this court that all you have done is exercise a normal attorney-client relationship?" (Many of Mrs. Cruz's clients have become excellent prison lawyers and have cases pending litigation in the federal courts.)

She has not been able to accept any new clients since October 1971.

Upon being questioned about Beto's proficiency as director of the TDC Frances said, "As an administrator, he is enlightened, highly regarded and well known; as an individual with knowledge of prison rights, he is reactionary."

Fred Arispe Cruz testified in a loud, clear voice (despite his recent hospitalization for pneumonitis) of continual harassment by TDC officials throughout his prison life because of his numerous suits against the TDC.

Cruz testified that Warden R.M. Cousins choked him and threatened to "knock my brains out" if he continued to remain a client of Mrs. Cruz. He said the choking incident occurred last year as he was being placed in solitary confinement for complaining he had been cursed by a guard. He said he was confined without clothes despite the fact he had the flu.

He said that Warden Cousins, trembling and shaking with anger, told him, "I'm tired of letters from that nigger-loving lawyer of yours. No lawyers are going to take over my prison. If you don't stop. I'll send you home to your mother in a pine box."

Cruz testified he was placed in solitary confinement on another occasion after he was beaten by two building tenders and hospitalized for 12 days.

He once refused an assistant warden's offer of freedom from prison if he would drop his lawsuits against the TDC, most of which are class action suits, he said. Cruz said he believes George Beto "has a personal dislike for me because I made him look bad in all my writs."

He testified he believes Freddie Dreyer's motivation for filing the suit was an attempt to stifle Frances' efforts to dismantle the power structure of the building tender system. "He would lose his influence over the prison population," he said.

Cruz denied ever having advocated change by force or violence. "I respect the legal process, this is the best way to affect change," he said. He also denied having acted as a runner for Mrs. Cruz in a conspiracy to take over the prison.

Phillips, during cross-examination, questioned sharply a doctor's statement saying Cruz had pneumonitis or "respiratory distress." Phillips contended Cruz passed out after a long day of drinking bourbon with old prison friends.

Warden C.L. McAdams and Beto were the prosecution's rebuttal witnesses. "Warden Mac," as Phillips continually referred to him, alleged after a visit from Mrs. Cruz, the inmates were restless, edgy and tense. "After one or two visits from Mrs. Cruz," he testified again, "there was more work stoppage, more fights, more tension and more men in solitary. He brought a chart which depicted the number of men in solitary confinement month-by-month at the Wynne Unit. In October 1971 there were 29 inmates in the hole; in November, 69.

The letter barring Mrs. Cruz from visiting her clients was issued in mid-October, the implication being that this caused the upsurge in the number of inmates in solitary. Defense attorney David Berg proceeded to go through the daily strength unit in which the names of the

inmates in solitary is recorded. For the month of November, 41 of the inmates in solitary were non-Cruz clients; 12 were clients of Mrs. Cruz.

During cross-examination the warden denied allegations from a series of witnesses that he had ever kicked an inmate, ordered an inmate to be kicked, ordered an inmate to be ice-bagged, kept any inmate in solitary over

Art: Bill Narum, August 17, 1971.

15 days, punished inmates caught in a homosexual act by making them stand in the hallway in front of the dining hall, holding each other's penises in their hands, or shot three inmates who attempted to escape and then placed them in front of the dining room where other inmates would have to walk through a pool of blood.

McAdams called Fred Cruz "the whole, sole cause of the trouble at the Wynne Unit. He is the instigator of the trouble, the inmates have been drilled and drilled by Fred Cruz," he said.

Beto testified for more than three hours describing Cruz as a "nonconformist who looked at other people as being stupid." Beto said he met Fred Cruz 10 years ago when he became director of the TDC. He said Cruz had an "insolent attitude" and "refused to conform to rules."

"I tried to counsel him to avail himself of the opportunities of education. I tried to help him," Beto said. He added that Cruz ignored his advice.

Beto rejected allegations offered by numerous witnesses that building tenders exercised guard functions and carried blackjacks and other weapons. "Guards themselves are not armed," he said. He vehemently denied that brutality was permitted and said that while building tenders sometimes break up fights, they use only their hands.

Beto said he first became disturbed about Mrs. Cruz when she wrote him a letter January 1, 1968. The letter, read during cross-examination, acknowledged cordial treatment by prison officials when Mrs. Cruz visited the women's unit at Huntsville.

The letter read in part, "whatever I saw was pleasing (though I imagine some areas of the prison not open to the public are not so pleasing.)"

Beto claimed no part of the Goree Unit or any other prison is not open to inspection by touring groups or individuals. (These tours were labeled "a farce" by many of the previous inmate witnesses.)

He stated Mrs. Cruz's visits to the prison were "very numerous" compared to other lawyer-client relationships, "that she spent unusual periods of time alone in a room with Cruz and that the wardens complained that she was a disturbing influence on the prisoners."

Beto, scheduled to retire as director in August, spent most of his time on the stand defending his administration. He said he has upgraded the stan-

dards for prison employees and instituted training and education programs for the inmates. "My philosophy of prison administration in Texas is three-pronged: work, discipline and education."

Defense attorney Bill Kilgarlin during cross-examination attacked Beto's attitude and manner of dealing with Mrs. Cruz, saying Beto resented her criticism of his administration and her filing suits attacking the department's policies. When pressed, Beto could not cite any proof that Mrs. Cruz had instigated or caused any incident of violence.

Kilgarlin also implied that Beto's main function is as a lobbyist and politician with the legislature and that he carries favor with state bar officials.

The defense attorney quoted from a television program suggesting Beto has a reactionary attitude toward "liberal do-gooders." Beto has said, he testified, that "some do-gooders have criticized us for using inmates for stoop labor. I said that less than 3,000 are doing this and a good many taxpayers in this state are engaged in stoop labor."

Judge Bue, before he took the case under advisement, indicated he intended to write a fairly broad opinion with an encompassing analysis of the prison system.

Defense attorneys said, after the trial, they felt good. "We found so many loopholes, so many fallacies in the prosecution's case, that we feel optimistic," Kilgarlin said. "What we hope for is an indictment of the prison system. That is what the evidence warrants." -30-

> **Beto has a reactionary attitude toward 'liberal do-gooders.'**

Ad: Art by Bill Narum, May 4, 1971.

Freedom's Just Another Word For Nothing Left To Lose

Karen Northcott • June 29, 1972

Prisoners at the Harris County Rehabilitation Center cell block 1A1 recently refused to return to their cells, tied open the individual cell doors, barricaded the entrance to the cell block, and presented a list of 17 demands, only to be met with two rounds of tear and nausea gas.

The prisoners' demands centered on food, medical care, the right to receive the Black Panther and Muslim newspapers, the right to have legal books available, censorship of mail, visitation rights, and the absence of exercise facilities. The center director, Capt. W.C. (Buster) Doolin, characterized the demands as "nonsense."

The list of grievances is nonsense to Capt. Doolin, but it may not be to a federal court judge. U.S. District Court Judge Sarah Hughes ordered sweeping changes in the operation of the Dallas County Jail on June 5. Her decision may force other Texas jails, as well, to comply to the 1957 state law outlining jail standards.

Hughes called the Dallas County Jail, "a factory for crime... turning people loose on the streets of Dallas who are more criminal than when they were put in jail." She ordered:

- Enough cells to accommodate inmates equal to the largest number of jail prisoners during one day in 1972;

- Solitary confinement cells to be not less than 40 square feet and to include a bunk, commode and lavatory;

- Padded cells for mentally ill persons;

- An outdoor exercise area and recreation program, perhaps using the jail's roof for the required outdoor space;

- Enough jail guards to handle security without resorting to the use of inmate assistance.

She also ordered the Sheriff's Department not to open or censor inmate mail addressed to courts, attorneys, parole officers, government agencies, or the press; not to destroy reading material owned by the inmates; to hold advance hearings on proposed pun-

Hughes called the Dallas County Jail, 'a factory for crime.'

ishment of more than three days in solitary confinement and to bar persons from visiting prisoners without the inmate's consent.

Three days after Hughes handed down her decisions, Dallas County Jail officials were back in the courts, this time on a contempt-of-court charge for not acting immediately on some of the jail reforms. The judge decided not to cite Sheriff Clarence Jones for contempt, but she put him on notice that she would enforce her ruling. She accused County Judge Lew Sterret and the County Commissioners of being more concerned about the expense of jail reform than about the substance of her order.

The grievances of the inmates on cell block 1A1 will more than likely form the basis of a lawsuit charging that the Harris County Jail and the Harris County Rehabilitation Center directly violated the guidelines set out in the 1957 state statute and Judge Hughes' recent order.

The Rehabilitation Center housed, and I use the term loosely, 1,350 inmates on June 23; it was designed to hold 1,031.

Solitary confinement cells do not measure 40 square feet. Five "ringleaders" of the disturbance in cell block 1A1 were placed naked into a single isolation cell, about 4x8 feet, following the two nights of disruption.

There are no padded cells for the mentally ill prisoners.

There is no outside exercise area and no recreation program. Albert McKinney, "ringleader," complained of the lack of exercise, saying, "If you're here for two years, you're just here for two years and you never see the sun."

Lt. Joe Ford, deputy director of the center, blamed budgetary restrictions for the lack of an exercise program. He said that there is no possibility of providing an outdoor exercise area unless more manpower is provided. Doolin estimated the cost of such a program would run as high as $100,000. He said he had asked the county commissioners for the $100,000, and his request was turned down.

Inmates do function as guards at both the Harris County Jail and the Rehabilitation Center. The prisoners said a "goon squad" of other inmates has the tacit permission of guards and jail officials to beat and intimidate prisoners. "If another inmate gets into a fight, they can't do nothing, but if a guard beats up on somebody he might get charges filed against them," according to McKinney.

Mail, both incoming and outgoing, is censored. Doolin defended the censorship because of past attempts to smuggle in narcotics and pornography. He said mail to judges and lawyers is "only scanned."

He told *Chronicle* reporter Al Reinert that they had "to cut out greeting cards altogether. They were taking those felt-covered cards and soaking them in watered down heroin and mailing them. The prisoners would get them, re-soak them and get enough for a couple of hits," Doolin continued.

Under the present rules, an inmate upon entering the center lists five people with whom he wishes to correspond. He can neither send letters to nor receive letters from anyone else, and is allowed to send only three letters a week. He is allowed to change the list of five once a year.

There are no such things as advance hearings on proposed punishment of more than three days in solitary at either the Harris County Jail or the Rehabilitation Center. Seventeen "instigators" of the two nights of disturbance were placed in solitary; some were moved to the Harris County Jail where security is stricter. "I expect to put them in isolation for a couple of weeks, or maybe four weeks," said Doolin without mention of any disciplinary hearing.

Doolin said the reason for the restriction of the number of letters is the lack of personnel to censor more than that a week. Ford said he didn't know why prisoners are limited to the five persons correspondence list. "That rule was here before I got here and I don't really know why it's like that," Ford said.

The inmates also complained of the lack of adequate medical care. One inmate — a Vietnam vet with war injuries who has been waiting seven months for a trial — complained that he was unable to get medical attention and had stopped receiving disability checks from the Veterans Administration because he could not get to the VA hospital for a physical.

Johnny Coward said he could get nothing but one dry bandage per day to put on a bleeding gunshot wound in his heel.

The inmates are skeptical; Frazier is just another 'promising John' to them.

Inmates also complained of poor dental care. "They don't ever treat anything," one said. "All they do is pull, pull, pull."

The inmates characterized the food served in the Rehabilitation Center as "cold, not nutritional and inadequate." Only the inmates who work on the prison farm — about 300 of the more than 1,300 inmates — eat in the prison cafeteria; the rest are served in their cells from meal carts. By the time the food gets to them, it's cold.

Officials at the Rehabilitation Center say this is one grievance they are attempting to remedy. Instead of waiting until all carts are loaded before delivering the food, they are now trying to stagger the deliveries so that it gets to prisoners as hot as possible.

Chief Deputy Loyd Frazier met with some of the prisoners to discuss their grievances. He called some of the grievances "legitimate" and said that steps would be taken to remedy them. The inmates are skeptical; Frazier is just another "promising John" to them. Frazier's words are "just promises, we haven't seen any changes yet," one inmate said.

The Harris County Rehabilitation Center is not a prison, but a detention center. Most of the inmates have no final convictions. Approximately 70 percent are awaiting trial; 20 percent are awaiting final results of appeal. So why treat them as convicted criminals, they ask, if they're not?

"They would never have been indicted if someone didn't think they were guilty," said Doolin. -30-

Ad: Febuary 14, 1971.

LABOR

Sticking With the Union

Sherwood Bishop

When I first began volunteering at *Space City!*, I was living in Pasadena and working at the massive Shell Oil refinery nearby in Deer Park. I had been elected as a union steward in the Oil, Chemical, and Atomic Workers Union (OCAW), and had taken "Young Unionist" training classes offered by the AFL-CIO. During one class, one of my heroes, Texas State Senator Barbara Jordan, came to speak to us. A few days later, I was bussed to Austin with a group of young union members and escorted around the state capital. While sitting in the gallery overlooking the Senate chambers, Senator Jordan looked up at the gallery, recognized me, and beckoned for me to join her on the Senate floor. That was the high point of my young life and she won my heart forever. Before I first visited *Space City!*, I had gone through the OCAW strike of 1968 and had become a gung-ho unionist.

Most of the workers at the huge combined refinery and chemical plant were white men who had replaced women who had worked there during World War II. At the war's end, the women were fired. There were also many Black men working there, most of whom had been hired during the war. In 1967, as some men began retiring, Shell hired young replacements, including me, for the first time in decades. I worked one day as a laborer, then was surprised to receive a promotion to "operator" on my second day. My wage was almost doubled. This happened to all the new hires.

Over time, I noticed that the (older) Black Shell employees were still classified as laborers. The older Black workers had mostly (maybe all) dropped out of high school to get jobs at the refinery. After the war, the Black men at the refinery weren't fired and replaced by white men, but the company and the union had agreed on a scheme to keep them from being promoted. The union-approved contract stated that workers could not become operators if they didn't have a high school diploma. Over the decades, that status quo had been accepted.

> **Senator Jordan beckoned for me to join her on the Senate floor.**

After learning this, I began trying to organize a union educational program where workers could earn a GED. I assumed that the union would support any program that would enable members to increase their incomes. I was shocked when the union refused to help, or even to allow the GED program. I hadn't realized that the status quo kept Black workers from competing with white ones for higher paying jobs. Not only did the older white workers object to the program, but many of the Black ones did too, fearing that their jobs might be imperiled if the white men's seniority was threatened. I began feeling like an outcast.

I had become good friends with a Texas Southern University pharmacy major named Mickey Leland. He'd been a Black separatist but had decided that he could accomplish more if he worked with whites, and within the political system. We were part of a small group in Houston who were trying to improve poor neighborhoods.

Mickey had grown up in Houston's Fifth Ward, as Barbara Jordan had before him. He was much more knowledgeable about the pervasiveness of racism and less naïve about unions than I was. I learned a tremendous amount from him.

One day I showed him a copy of the first issue of *Space City!* that another friend had given me. We visited the *Space City!* office together a few days later. I had just finished working and was wearing my coveralls and steel-toed shoes. I don't remember what Mickey was wearing, but he usually dressed stylishly and was probably wearing a suit. I'm sure we seemed a strange duo to the *Space City!* staff, but they were friendly and respectful. We were both highly impressed by *Space City!*

As I became more frustrated with unions and with working within the system, I became radicalized. Within a few months, I had joined the *Space City! Collective*. Mickey was moving in a different direction, though we remained friends. In 1972, he was elected to the Texas House of Representatives. In 1978, after Barbara Jordan developed multiple scle rosis, Mickey was elected to fill her seat in the U.S. House of Representatives where he served until his death in 1989.

Space City!'s coverage of unions and labor issues reflected the same conflicts that Mickey and I faced. *Space City!*'s coverage was strongly supportive of workers struggles and strikes.

Houston was an industrial center with its proximity to refineries and a massive ship channel. Organized labor was a force to be reckoned with. The newspaper had first-hand reporting on a strike at General Electric, a strike at Southwestern Bell Telephone Company by a CWA local, a United Steelworkers strike at the Koenig Iron Works, and on a strike of the American Bakery and Confectionary Workers Union. The paper also covered demands made to the city council by 200 Houston firefighters.

Danny Schacht reached back to buried Texas history to report on the militant East Texas lumberjacks who organized with the Industrial Workers of the World (IWW). An article about striking restaurant workers at the Houston Club went beyond the demands for higher pay. The club for the city's elite did not allow Black members, but the majority Black workforce served food for members in the club's Plantation Room.

The paper had excellent coverage of an Economy Furniture strike where most of the upholsterers were Latinx. The Economy strike in Austin lasted many months and forged lasting progressive alliances. The better-known United Farm Workers' strikes in California and Texas were also transformational, building Latinx solidarity and alliances. *Space City!* reported frequently on the Farm Workers' organizing activity as well as the national boycotts of California grapes and Texas Rio Grande Valley lettuce, and covered César Chávez's 1971 visit to Houston.

There was also frank coverage of racism, sexism, and other conflicts within unions. An article in the first issue of *Space City News*, "Radical Rumblings: Workers on the Move" by Victoria Smith discussed racism in unions in California, West Virginia, Michigan, and New Jersey. In "Steel Strike: Scab 'Freaks,'" Jeff Shapiro and Mike Heinrichs wrote of young "longhairs" who crossed picket lines during a strike of Latinx Steel Workers in Houston.

San Marcos, Texas
June 2021

Texas Labor History:
Lumberjacks in the Piney Woods

Danny Schacht and Raymond Ellington • June 19, 1969

In the Piney Woods of East Texas and Louisiana, around the years 1907 to 1913, the tycoons of the lumber industry were seeing "terrorists," "agitators," and socialists behind most every tree.

Those labor agitators, as they were called, were the men who cut the timber, worked the sawmills and daily faced the prospect of losing life or limb in the humid pine forests. They worked hard for what little they got, and when pushed would yield only so far before deciding it was time to do something about their situation.

Joyce Kornbluh writes in *Rebel Voices*:

> Unlike the lumberjack of the Northwest, the southern lumber worker was usually a "horn-guard" or "sodbuster"

— a local farmer who worked seasonally in a sawmill or lumber camp to eke out a living. About half the labor force were Negroes who, like the white farmers, lived in company-owned housing in lumber camps or mill villages. In many places where the semi-monthly payday was ignored, workers in need of money borrowed it from their employers at usurious rates of interest. When they were paid, it was frequently in scrip, redeemable only at high-priced company stores.

For years those Piney Woods were torn indiscriminately to shreds by axes and saws. Lumbermen were worked 10, 11, or more hours a day, were paid such

Art: June 19, 1969.

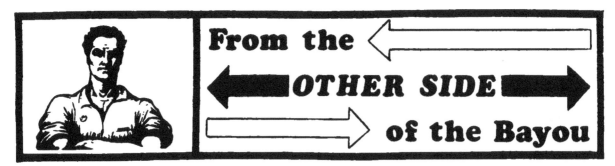

low wages it was hardly possible for a man to support himself, much less a family.

There was an empire being built on sawdust and sweat, and the businessmen of the Southern Lumber Operators' Association (organized in 1907 to combat unionism) were stacking up the profits. The Kirby Lumber Company, the American Lumber Company, and others showed little concern for the lands they were leaving in ruin or the men who slaved in their pine tree sweat shops.

The lumber corporations had great wealth, and with this wealth came political power — power that stretched from the hastily constructed mill towns to the bustling state capitals.

Among the workers, who lacked a voice in that power, support began to grow for the People's Party and the Progressive Movement. But strong opposition from big business quickly dashed any hopes for legislative reform, and men turned in increasing numbers towards unionism and the Socialist Party.

With help from agrarian allies, Louisiana lumber workers formed the independent Brotherhood of Timberworkers in 1910. Al Emerson and Jay Smith formed the first local of the union in Carson, Louisiana.

The immediate response of the Southern Lumber Operators' Association was to declare open war on the Brotherhood. It initiated a seven-month lockout, blacklisting 7,000 of the most active union members.

For its part, the Brotherhood demanded $2-a-day wages, a 10-hour work day, bimonthly payment in lawful U.S. currency, freedom to trade in independent stores, reduced rents and commissary prices, and the right to meet together on union business.

In May 1912, the union's first convention was held in Alexandria, attended by delegates from all of the organized locals. A keynote speaker at the convention was "Big Bill" Haywood, organizer for the In-

dustrial Workers of the World (IWW), or Wobblies as they were better known.

Haywood was surprised to see no Negroes at the gathering, and when he was told that it was illegal to hold interracial meetings in Louisiana he replied:

> You work in the same mills together. Sometimes a black man and a white man chop down the same tree together. You are meeting in convention now to discuss the conditions under which you labor. This can't be done intelligently by passing resolutions here and then sending them to another room for the black men to act upon. Why not be sensible about this and call the Negroes into the Convention? If it is against the law, this is one time when the law should be broken.

The blacks were invited into the convention which voted three to one to affiliate with the IWW National Industrial Union of Forest and Lumber Workers. Black as well as white delegates were elected to attend the 1912 Wobbly convention.

Meanwhile, the Lumber Operators' Association was taking stronger actions. A Benefit Trust Fund was organized to give compensation to struck owners. The owners were instructed to close down all mills "infected" with unionism. Burns and Pinkerton agents were hired to spy on the union.

The lumber companies attempted to vindicate themselves as defenders of God and country by instigating the formation of Good Citizens Leagues. These were composed mainly of hired punks and some local merchants — similar in content, outlook, and methods to the Ku Klux Klan, an organization which had been used not only to terrorize and murder black people but also to suppress the workers' efforts to organize unions.

There was an empire being built on sawdust and sweat.

Like the Klan, the Good Citizens Leagues operated in a cowardly fashion, striking at night to shoot up houses containing men, women, and children. The League attacked union men only when it was safe that their number would insure an easy victory.

When a pro-union speaker tried to rent lecture halls or auditoriums, he found that none were available. If he persisted, the local sheriff would inform him that he was not welcome in a "Christian community," and that the sheriff could not long guarantee his continued safety in that "Christian community."

At the Galloway Lumber Company in Grabow, Louisiana, company guards shot and killed three strikers who were taking part in a union meeting on a public road near the town. The Brotherhood returned the guards' fire.

After the shootout, a coroner's jury charged officers of the company with murder, but the Grand Jury indicted 62 members of the union for conspiracy to murder and issued no indictments against company officials or guards.

The union members were imprisoned for three months in a jail known as the "Black Hole of Calcasieu" in Lake Charles. When the case reached the courtroom, a jury took only one hour to find all of the union members "not guilty."

Testimony revealed that company officers had distributed guns to the guards and encouraged them to get drunk before the union meeting. Also disclosed was the fact that the Brotherhood was honeycombed with company detectives, including one who had stolen the union's records and membership lists.

By 1913, the repressive actions of the Lumber Operators' Association and their Good Citizens Leagues had continued and killed the struggle of the hardworking, underpaid lumberjacks. This could not have happened without the help of the courts, the local "law enforcers," and the so-called good citizens. -30-

Photo: Sue Mithun, January 31, 1970.

On the Picket Lines at GE

Sherwood Bishop • January 31, 1970

The beginning days of the 1970s find over 150,000 women and men, members of 13 different labor unions, on strike against a common enemy which they have fought constantly over the years — the General Electric Company. The times have changed a lot in the past few decades, but many things remain nearly the same.

Back in 1946, there was a nationwide strike of GE employees, much like the struggle today. People were fighting then for the same simple things they need and demand today — reasonable working conditions and decent pay for their work. The small group of powerful company owners were trying to starve their employees into crawling back to work. The company claimed, among other things, that they were "fighting inflation." Two years later, in 1948, "Generous Electric" was convicted of conspiring with Nazi Germany's Krupp corporation to fix prices.

Twenty years later, they're still "fighting inflation." Twenty years later, they're still fixing prices.

In 1947, GE Vice President Lemuel Boulware began the official company policy of offering a wage increase of a few pennies and refusing to negotiate. In 1968, there were over 400 small strikes against GE because of its refusal to arbitrate differences with its employees.

In 1960, GE was convicted of unfair labor practices for refusing to bargain collectively with workers. In 1970, GE has just filed an appeal to overturn that court decision.

Four members of the present GE Board of Directors were at the top of the military establishment during the Eisenhower administration when the Vietnam war was being planned. General Electric is still making millions by selling weapons to the military.

Today, General Electric is the fourth largest industrial corporation in America and the second largest defense contractor. According to Loyde Hailley, IBEW Local 716:

The scabs? Most of them are young boys going from one job to another or student dropouts going to work and back to school later maybe. They don't seem to even know what a strike is. They ask us, "Are you on strike? Is everybody on strike?"

At Hailey's plant, only six of the 240 workers, both union and non-union, have gone back to work.

One guy in there is up for retirement soon, and they (GE) scared him that he wouldn't get his retirement. There's no way they can do that, but they brainwashed him.

The issues in the present three-month-old strike are simple. The workers are demanding better wages and working conditions. They want a cost-of-living clause in their contract so that inflation won't reduce the buying power of their wages. Because of inflation, wages in 1969 bought less food and clothing than in 1966!

A demand which is of particular interest to the workers in Houston calls for the elimination of geographical wage differentials. This means that workers in Houston will get the same pay for a certain job level as a worker up north.

A few of us talked recently with some of the strikers at picket lines near Houston area plants.

Give them some support by visiting picket shacks at 4435 West 12th, 3530 West 12th, or 23 Japhet off Clinton Drive.

And support the nationwide GE boycott by refusing to buy GE and Hotpoint Products. -30-

Twenty years later, they're still fixing prices.

Adi June 20, 1971.

Photo, Sue Mithun. January 31, 1970.

Scab 'Freaks'

Jeff Shapiro and Mike Heinrichs • September 5, 1970

In any strike, the strikebreaker is the handiest villain (after the management, of course): he is cutting the workers' throat for his own temporary gain. So, when I heard, early in August, that a strike by a principally Chicano steelworkers' local was being broken by long-haired freaks who were crossing the picket lines to work. . . well, that was not the sort of situation you liked to hear about. *Space City!* oughta hear about this, I thought. I decided to do a story.

Naturally it took several weeks for me to stir myself to any sort of investigation; by this time other people had heard about the story as well. So, what follows is a composite of what we all learned.

The strike began in the first week of July. Some 155 workers of Steel Workers Local 6831 have withdrawn their labor from the Koenig Iron Works' two local plants. For the past three years a contract had been in effect which included a no-strike-no-lockout agreement. The contract expired in June, and the strike was called during the negotiations for a new contract.

The issues of the strike are these: first, the company wants the prerogative to fire any worker who they think is responsible for a slowdown or curtailment of production. This firing is to be done without recourse to any sort of grievance proceeding. Thus, the management and not the union would be the sole judge of who is to be employed.

Second, the company proposes that in event of a dispute which brings on arbitration proceedings, the losing party would be required to pay the full costs of arbitration. Under the old contract these costs were shared equally by both parties. Furthermore, the management wants a court recorder to be present at these proceedings. Court recorders come as high as $150 a day (or $1.50 a page) and this would make the cost of arbitration prohibitively high for a small union.

The union did not agree to these terms and has now been on strike for nine weeks.

A few weeks ago, a Pacifica reporter went to the plant to interview the freaks who were scabbing. He found that most of them were college students who had little idea what the strike was about and, usually, didn't care. Their indifference is ironic in view of the fact that prior to the strike the company had tried to fire one of the workers because of his exceedingly long hair. The union had come to the freak's defense and forced the factory to retain him.

I had heard that there was a lot of ill will among the strikers toward the freaks, but by the time we visited the two factories, the workers' feelings seemed to have softened. Most of the longhairs had left and gone back to college. "We could have ended the strike long ago if they hadn't come in," one striker told me, but his bitterness appeared to be at odds with itself, and not as deep as it might have been. He and his fellows seemed to differ about (what they presumed was) the students' ambitions to go to college and better themselves.

An unfair and intimidatory contract; the workers on strike; a bunch of freaks/straights with stylishly long hair, ignorant of all the issues, breaking the strike, not caring; and the workers, bitter at the scabs, but deferential to those who were lucky enough to go to college.

There is little the public can do to support the strikers — the Iron Works sells its products (boxes and equipment parts) to the City of Houston, the Texas State Highway Department, Houston Lighting and Power, Houston Natural Gas, and all of these government bodies and monopoly utility interests are not susceptible to the usual public boycott.

Neither the *Chronicle* nor the *Post* has reported on the strike, though the *Post* boasts "the country's best labor reporter" on its staff. Koenig, approached by the Pacifica interviewer, said that the strike was "none of the public's damn business." The *Post* and the *Chronicle* have, however, accepted want ads from Koenig advertising for scabs. The union has also been hampered by a court injunction issued by Judge Touchy (the same who issued the injunction against MAYO during the church occupation). This time the injunction forbids picketing by any more than two strikers, who must maintain a distance of 50 feet between themselves. Neither can the strikers talk to or detain a strikebreaker. -30-

Art: October 17, 1970.

Workers Strike at Ritzy Houston Club

Randy Chapman • December 23, 1970

Members of AFL-CIO 251 (Hotel and Restaurant Workers) are on strike against the unfair labor practices of the Houston Club.

The Houston Club, located on the top floor of the Texas Bank of Commerce, is a gathering point for Houston's ruling elite with "Junior Memberships" starting at $1,500 monthly dues. No blacks are included in the membership, but nearly all of the 132 striking workers are black.

The strike was called after the club management failed to negotiate over a four-month period of 16 sessions. The union, which was formed on July 8, is not recognized as the "official" bargaining agent by club management. However, the union is recognized by government mediators who intervened without success. Then on December 4, a strike vote was called and passed unanimously by the 124 members voting.

On December 14, workers received letters demanding that they go back to work or be replaced. On December 15, workers were told by registered letter that they had been replaced.

Meanwhile, the club continues to operate. Luncheons are now buffet, and customers have to wait longer. Management has called in ex-employees and has used office personnel and supervisors and their families to tend the floor. Peakload was contacted, but they honored the picket line. Clayton Woodbury, an employee of four years and the strike spokesman, reports that scab labor is being tunneled in from other buildings and scabs are now given garage parking privileges and are allowed to use the front elevators.

Employees start at $1.60 per hour and wages scale to $2.50. Wages is not one of the issues, however, but rather how employees are paid. Members are told not to tip, as a 15 percent gratuity is added to their bill, but this 15 percent goes to the club and not to the waiter. Employees feel this deceives people to believe the 15 percent goes to those who serve them.

Scab labor is being tunneled in from other buildings.

Clayton reports, though, that the strike "is an issue of power, not wages." Workers want the power to establish rules for working conditions, including rules to prevent arbitrary firings. They also want power to eliminate racist hiring and promotion policies. For example, the same club that hires 100 black people to work in the "Plantation Room" has no black people in the front office. Also, "service personnel," mostly blacks, are supposed to use different dressing rooms from managers and supervisors.

The strike continues. There is no strike fund and most families are poor. Some may be evicted. However, the strikers' plea has not been for donations, but for sympathetic people to come down, possibly bring sandwiches, and give picketers moral support by showing we're behind them. -30-

Art: Judy Binder, January 30, 1971.

Lettuce Growers Talk

Bill Chandler • May 11, 1971

Thirteen representatives of those lettuce growers who signed sweetheart contracts with a Teamster local in Salinas, Cal. last summer have been meeting with the United Farm Workers Organizing Committee, AFL-CIO, since Tuesday, April 27.

This is the first significant development stemming from the 30-day moratorium on the boycott of lettuce produced under those sweetheart contracts, and a hopeful sign for the Farm Workers.

The moratorium was called after the Teamsters signed a pact with UFWOC on March 26, giving full jurisdiction for organizing farm workers to UFWOC, and admitting the obvious, that UFWOC represents lettuce workers.

The action by the Teamsters followed six months of embarrassment and pressure. First the lettuce workers walked out of the fields protesting Teamster contracts, drawing nationwide support. Then people all over the nation began boycotting "Teamster" lettuce.

During the moratorium, the Teamsters asked the growers to release them from the sweetheart contracts and to recognize UFWOC. As a result of the moratorium the growers have agreed to meet with the Farm Workers, a giant step in the right direction.

Whether the meetings will produce signed contracts is still another question. But UFWOC has shown its good faith by extending the moratorium beyond the scheduled April 26 deadline to give them a chance to resolve the issue through negotiated and signed union contracts with the Farm Workers.

However, while the moratorium has been in effect, lettuce boycott activists have been after the remaining lettuce growers (numbering more than 200) who are not involved with the Teamsters, but who have refused to recognize the Farm Workers.

Of those, 11 were listed as top priority for boycott attention. Each grower ships produce under many labels so a list of growers and labels would be too lengthy to print here.

The growers' names do appear on each box (usually in small print). The following list should make it easy to identify "ultra-scab" lettuce: Palo Verde Farms, Hi-Life Farms, Abatti-Kirkorian, Del-Mar Packing, Hogue Produce, J.R. Norton, Senini-Arizona, Tri-Produce, J.A. Wood, Pleasant Valley Farms, and Santa Clara Produce.

The Farm Workers need your help in a massive store-checking campaign to keep this lettuce out of Houston. Visit the grocers, restaurant managers, and personnel in other institutions in your neighborhood. Then call the lettuce boycott office at 522-8142 or 524-9404 with this information: 1) brand on hand when visited, 2) which produce house supplied them, and 3) will they agree to cooperate with the boycott and order the Farm Workers Eagle label on their next lettuce shipment?

And when the moratorium ends, no store should handle non-UFWOC label lettuce. The Farm Workers and boycott activists will be asking the stores to sell only Farm Workers lettuce and when the moratorium ends, the chains that demonstrate the most ardent unwillingness will be picketed.

Farm Worker Fiesta

Farm Workers and local supporters of the United Farm Workers Organizing Committee lettuce boycott held a *fiesta campesina* Saturday, May 1, in Moody Park.

The celebration was preceded by car caravans starting from several areas of the city and converging at the fiesta. They stopped along the way at several chain stores to check if UFWOC lettuce was available and if not, demanding that the store handle it.

The crowd at the fiesta, which numbered about 800 people throughout the day, heard a speech by Texas Farm Worker leader Antonio Orendain. There were skits performed by the new *teatro boycoteo* and music by local Chicano bands, including the Saints and Singers.
-30-

Art: July 4, 1970.

Venceremos Brigade and Cuba

Cam Duncan

The first article published by *Space City!* on international issues was about the Vietnam War. The second — "Yanquis to Cut Cane in Cuba" — was by the regional organizer of the Venceremos Brigade, Brian Murphy, and announced the Brigade's first contingent to Cuba in November 1969.

Space City!'s broad coverage of U.S. foreign policy and Third World liberation movements for decolonization and self-determination included pieces on wars in Vietnam and Southeast Asia and others on the U.S. anti-war movement, described elsewhere on these pages. Most of the stories on global liberation concerned revolutionary struggles in Latin America, including the Puerto Rican independence movement, in-depth articles on Allende's Chile, Bolivia, Brazil, Mexico, and Venezuela.

But the foreign country that received the most attention in the pages of *Space City!* was Cuba, an indication of the growth in the early 1970s of an important U.S. movement in solidarity with the goals of the Cuban revolution. Of the 13 stories about Cuba published during the paper's three-year run, six were penned by *Space City!* staff and contributors.

The Venceremos Brigade was an international solidarity organization that sent multiethnic delegations of volunteers to Cuba to materially support the Cuban revolution by working in sugar harvests and in construction projects. Though Venceremos ("We will win") initially emerged from the mostly white New Left, the early organizing of the Brigades made an effort to appeal to people of color within what some have called the "U.S. Third World Left."

With the goal of building people-to-people links between Americans and Cubans in order to undermine Cold War tensions between the two nations, the Brigade stood for an anti-imperialist foreign policy of U.S. progressives. It soon became the largest Cuba solidarity group worldwide.

The Brigade's vision of a world shaped by international solidarity and people-to-people aid was a sharp rebuke to U.S. diplomatic policies that aimed to isolate and punish Cuba. In the collectively-written piece by five Houston participants on the fourth Brigade — two of them *Space City!* staffers – *brigadistas* denounced the U.S. trade embargo against Cuba that, while seeking to strangle the island's socialist economy, had harmed mainly the Cuban people.

Brigadistas also challenged the ban on travel to Cuba by U.S. citizens, a policy begun in 1961 after Washington broke off relations with Havana. As a *Space City!* staffer, I joined the Fourth Brigade contingent, eager to see for myself whether our movement's egalitarian values — that led us into the streets — were shared by Cubans building a socialist society, and what we might learn about the impacts of their revolution. This political journey led me and 230 *brigadistas* to violate the warning on our U.S. passports that stated they were "not valid for travel" to the "restricted countries of Cuba, Mainland China, North Korea, and North Vietnam." The prospect of doing manual labor with

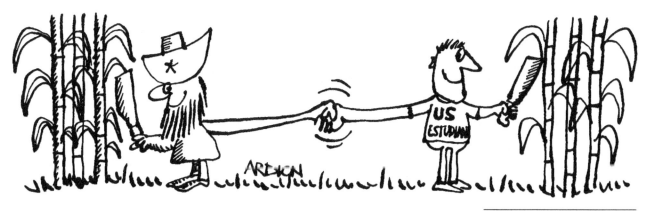

Art: Ardion, January 31, 1970.

ordinary Cuban workers meant we were more likely to see the real Cuba than if we sat in formal meetings and speeches. We co-authored the two "Venceremos" articles reprinted in this section.

Another goal of the Brigade — and of *Space City!*'s coverage of the project — was for American radicals to "have the opportunity to work with revolutionaries from such places as Guinea Bissau, Indochina, and Uruguay," as stated in the organization's recruitment flyers. The camps for foreign volunteers in Cuba served as meeting places beyond the reach of U.S. government power, allowing activists to make their movements known to Cubans and other international volunteers.

Many of us, especially those who were white, had become radicalized during our participation in the anti-Vietnam War movement. But all of the Americans had experienced the horrific media images of the war's destruction. We were inspired by our face-to-face meetings with the Vietnamese National Liberation Front fighters who worked next to us cutting sugar cane and fertilizing citrus trees in Cuba. The Vietnamese asked the brigadistas to keep on building the U.S. anti-war movement. "Your country is trying to kill our people, destroy our nation," an NLF captain told members of the Brigade in Cuba. "We will fight to victory and we are thankful for your support."

Sherwood Bishop, a member of the *Space City!* Collective and a participant with one other Houstonian on the Third Brigade, wrote in the December 12, 1970 *Space City!* about the personal impact he felt when a Vietnamese delegation visited their *campamento*:

> A group of nearly 100 Indochinese men and women stayed with us for a week. They ranged in ages from teenagers to people over 60, but they all showed a beautiful amount of respect, trust and love for one another and for us. We all felt guilty waiting for them to reach our camp. We knew what our country was doing to them and their country, and that we hadn't been able to stop the war. But they never showed anything less than affection and respect for us and never even hinted that we weren't doing our best to stop the genocide against their people.

Houston volunteers visited Cuba on three different brigades during 1970-72, returning home to present slide shows at solidarity events at the University of Houston and community forums and to write about their experience during the two-month stay on the island. We screened Saul Landau's film *Fidel* to raise money for the next brigade.

One of the Houston Brigade organizers, *Space City!* Collective member Susan Mithun Duncan, edited the eight-page *Space City!* Cuba supplement in July 1972, and wrote about the revolution's history and the urgent need to support self-determination for Cuba. Contributor Tina Phillips penned a compelling story in that issue about visiting innovative new day care centers, a major project of the revolution.

Space City! coverage of the Brigades included frank discussion of internal political differences in the volunteer camp, especially regarding gender roles and racial tension. More than any other

Houston volunteers visited Cuba on three different brigades during 1970-72.

Arti Nuoa, January 31, 1970.

cause, racial frictions complicated the Brigade's early efforts to become a coherent representation of what we optimistically termed the American "movement."

The Venceremos Brigade continued to send a delegation to Cuba — coordinated with Pastors for Peace Friendship Caravans to Cuba — every summer through 2019. As with earlier groups, these brigades worked in agriculture or housing construction. Sugar cane harvesting was discontinued because it became mechanized in the 1970s. The Brigade was an important forerunner of larger mobilizations of U.S. activists against Washington's foreign policy, especially the growing solidarity movements in the 1970s and 80s.

I considered Cuba not so much a model to be imitated, but rather a revolutionary setting where I could test my capacity to function collectively and my commitment to work for radical change in the U.S. For six weeks in Havana province, our brigade which encompassed the entire breadth of the movement had to live in close quarters and work together in a structured and collective way. What happened to us in Cuba and the way we responded to the challenges of that daily struggle in the volunteer camp was a major turning point in my life and gave me an insight into the strengths and weaknesses of our movement.

I returned to work in U.S. solidarity movements with revolutionary forces in Chile, Puerto Rico, and El Salvador, and spent three decades as an educator in the U.S. and international labor movement. The Brigade's aim to shape the internationalism of the U.S. Left through contact with the Cuban revolution has impacted social justice movements in multiple ways. That vision of intense transnational exchange continued to inspire me, not only in radical organizing but in political, service and education work of many kinds, ever since.

We need as much now as we did then—new systems and vision. Our country needs to overcome its arrogance and isolation. *¡Venceremos!*

Santa Fe, New Mexico
July 2021

Sherwood Bishop along with two volunteers plants citrus tree on Isle of Youth, Cuba. Photo by Sue Duncan.

¡Venceremos! Houston Brigadistas Talk About Cuba

Houston Brigadistas • August 4, 1971

We intend to light the shadows that surround this vicious operation — to drive from these shadows the missiles — in human form — which have been fashioned on that Communist island and fired at America. We want our people to be aware of the direct chain which reaches from Cuba into our cities, our campuses, our conventions, our lives — and which threatens the life of this Republic.

—Sen. William O. Eastland

When the distinguished Senator from Mississippi opened fire on the Venceremos Brigade in March 1970, he reminded the U.S. Senate that what had been a "comparative trickle" of persons visiting Cuba in the 1960s now "threatens to become a flood." As Fidel Castro has commented concerning the fear of the imperialists who see revolutionaries plotting everywhere, "It's true! It's true!"

The interest of North American radicals in the "First Free Territory of the Americas" has indeed taken a profoundly new direction. Only a few years ago direct contact with the Cuban Revolution was limited to the few left-wing journalists and political exiles who toured the country at the invitation of the revolutionary government. Now over 1,500 young North Americans have traveled to the "Communist island" — not as official guests, but as volunteer workers in the Cuban cane and citrus fields.

The difference is more than numerical. It represents a qualitative change in the "foreign relations" of our movement with the liberation struggles of the Third World (the underdeveloped countries of Latin America, Africa, and Asia). What is new is the mass collective involvement of white radicals, blacks, Puerto Ricans, and Chicanos, of men and women from urban and university communities as well as from small towns.

Even more important is the fact that this involvement has led to our direct participation in the work of socialist revolution. All of us found ourselves in a situation which called for a higher level of political consciousness, collective organization, and discipline than we have ever had to develop at home.

This is the first of two articles by Houston people who recently returned from the Fourth Venceremos Brigade to Cuba. The second article will appear in next week's Space City!

Five Houston people returned home in late May from a trip to another world. We were four white men and one Chicano, part of the fourth Venceremos Brigade ("Venceremos" means "we will win" and is the title of a book by Che Guevara). The brigade of 230 North Americans was about evenly divided between women and men and ethnically representative of the movement in the United States — Blacks, Chicanos, Puerto Ricans, Asian-Americans, Native American Indians, and whites.

Ages ranged from 16 to 40, with most of us in the early 20s. A few were fluent in Spanish, some not at all, and most of us fell somewhere between. Some of us were students, some movement journalists, most part of that small army of unclassifiable, unsettled transient youth thrown out by a decaying society which can no longer claim our allegiance nor absorb us. We went to see, to experience, to search.

The Venceremos Brigade was conceived jointly several years ago by Cubans and U.S. revolutionaries. It gives North Americans a way to demonstrate concretely our solidarity with the Cuban Revolution, and the international socialist revolution of which it is a part; and to experience that Revolution first-hand.

For the Cubans, the Brigades provide several benefits:

1. Additional labor in a small, underpopulated nation with an acute labor shortage — a result of the Revolution's success in providing full employment for the first time in Cuba's history.

2. North American allies who will return to the heart of imperialism and tell their people about Cuba, exposing the lies and distortions of the U.S. government and Eric Sevareid. Hopefully, this will help to ease Washington's anti-Cuban policies, which have tried to crush the Cuban revolution through armed invasion, internal subversion, economic blockade, and diplomatic isolation.

3. The brigade provides for Cuban communists — true internationalists — a chance to keep informed about the developments in the United States, to learn from and to teach their American comrades.

Since the imperialistic blockade has abolished direct travel from the United States to Cuba, we were forced to go first to Mexico City and then fly via Cubana Airlines to Havana (we returned by way of Canada, a six-day trip on a Cuban ship). We worked seven weeks in the cane fields of the Reuben Martinez Villena sugar mill near a small town in Havana province and then were given a two-week tour which took us from one end of Cuba to the other.

For the work, we were divided into brigades of about 25 North Americans and eight Cubans each. The Cubans who worked and traveled with us were generally young university students or recent graduates, both women and men. "Wherever the Revolution needs me," most would answer when we asked them where they would like to work. There were two students from the Language Institute in Havana in our

brigade, future English teachers who saw the Brigade as a chance to practice their English; two agriculture students; one philosophy instructor; an organizer for the Communist Party; and our jefe (chief) was a 30-year-old party member who had been Cuba's ambassador to Algeria and now worked in foreign relations in Havana.

We worked the normal 44-hour Cuban week, getting up about 5:30 AM Monday through Saturday, leaving for the fields at 6:30, working from 7 to 11, resting in the hot midday, and returning to work (except on Saturday afternoons) from 3 to 7 PM. The work consisted of cutting sugarcane with the "Australian method," in which the cane field is burned the night before it is to be cut (only the leaves and chaff burn, making the stalks much easier to cut and stack). This was the first year that this method was used extensively in Cuba, since burned cane must be milled within 36 hours of cutting to avoid loss of sugar content and the harvest has only now become mechanized enough to accomplish this.

We were housed in canvas tents with bunk beds, sleeping 10 to a tent by brigade — the Cubans slept together in their own tents. Cold showers became real treats after the temperature rose to the nineties each day.

We ate together — light breakfasts, heavy lunches and dinners — in a large dining hall; there were also mid-morning and mid-afternoon breaks for merienda (snacks). The diet was heavy with starches and sweets, lots of rice, beans, soups, guava; some fish, beef, or spam; few green vegetables; no milk; and occasional treats of Cuban beer or ice cream. (Cuban ice cream is outasight!)

The camp had a first-aid station, infirmary, dentist, barber, post office, library, laundry, supplies station (which issued us all the work clothes we needed), recreation hall, basketball

Cuban workers construct homes for fellow workers.
Photo by Sue Duncan. July 20, 1972

and volleyball courts, press tent, outdoor stage for cultural events, a combo, and a wide-screen theater for outdoor movies — all free. Music, either recorded or played live by the camp combo or visiting groups, blared constantly from the PA., ranging from the hair-splitting Cuban reveille, *De Pie!* (On your Feet!) at 5 a.m. to the Stones to Aretha to traditional Cuban folk-songs to soupy romantic mush. Cubans have a very musical culture to say the least.

Activities at the camp during non-working hours included a too-full schedule of films (Cuban documenta-ries and some full-length features were beautiful; they also dig Charlie Chap-lin and showed a few American flicks); forums by the directors, visiting Party officials or experts on this or that as-pect of the Cuban economy; presenta-tions by visiting revolutionaries from Vietnam, and Portuguese-dominated Africa, on the state of their struggles against impe-rialism; panels on the black, Chicano, Puerto Rican, Asian-American, Native American, GI, women's, and Gay Liberation movements, etc. — most requested by the Cuban comrades, who have an insatiable appetite for information about nearly everything (but not about homosexuality and Gay Liberation, about which they are as uptight as North Americans); parties, dances, musical groups or other cultural events, including an Afro-Cubano troupe which did a dance based on old witch-doctor rites, often with beer or *guachipoopa*, a rum drink; trips to the beach or into nearby towns; and weekly production meetings at which we dis-cussed our work, problems, criticized ourselves and set quotas. All events except the production meetings were voluntary.

* * * * *

Our tour took us through five of Cuba's six prov-inces and most of the largest cities — Havana, Matan-zas, Santa Clara, Camaguey, Holguin, and Santiago de Cuba. We traveled in a caravan of 12 buses, led by a sound truck which announced our arrival as we passed through many *pueblos*. We stayed in school dormi-tories or warehouses equipped with bunk beds. The Cuban countryside we passed through was mostly flat or low rolling hills, dotted everywhere with palms, covered with cane fields, *bennequin* or grazing cattle (the Revolution is now in the final stage of breeding a third-generation hybrid from the Cuban zebu and im-ported Holsteins which will give both milk and meat).

The mountainous regions, the Sierra Maestras in Oriente Province and the Sierra del Escambray in Las Villas, are beautiful and rugged — perfect for the guer-rilla activity launched there by Fidel and Che in their armed struggle against former dictator Fulgencio Ba-tista. More spectacular than the countryside was the Cuban sky — brilliant clouds, rainbows, sunrises and sunsets, and striking combinations of pinks, oranges, yellows, and red.

The special thing about Cuba is not the geography or even the skies, but the people and their Revolution and the new society they are trying to cre-ate from the ground up. Everywhere we saw signs of a people on the move, new schools, technical institutes, trac-tor stations, mechanized dairy farms, artificial insemination centers, dams, factories, new housing projects, and even new towns for workers. Cuba still has tremendous problems, but we were constantly reminded that they are the problems of development — not the problems of stagnation faced by many of the Third World countries still under the thumb of American imperialism.

Our tour took us through five of Cuba's six provinces and most of the largest cities.

We visited schools, including a secondary school in Camaguey; the Universities of Santa Clara and Santia-go; and teachers' training schools at Topes de Collan-tes and Havana. We went to two factories — a brand-new fertilizer plant near Cienfuegos and a sugar mill. We visited two work camps of the Centennial Youth Column (CYC), a corps of young Cubans who have volunteered to work three years at the hardest jobs in Cuba, such as cane-cutting and citrus; and went to Playa Girón (the Bay of Pigs), site of the CIA-spon-sored invasion of Cuba in 1961.

We visited the Moncada in Santiago, an army bar-racks under Batista which was unsuccessfully attacked on July 26, 1953, by revolutionaries led by Fidel — now converted into a museum of the Revolution in one wing and a school in the other; the farmhouse out-side Santiago where the attack on the Moncada was planned, now a historical exhibit taken care of by an old man whose son was killed in the attack; and the small cabin in Mayari Arriba, now also a historical ex-hibit, which served as Raul Castro's headquarters in the Second Front of guerrilla activity against Batista.

We swam on the white Caribbean beach and camp-ground of Jibacoa, formerly a resort of the rich but now used for international youth conferences; several times revisited places which before the Revolution had been monopolized by rich Americans and the Cuban bourgeoisie but are now open to the Cuban public.

Everywhere we went, we were free to talk to people. The usual format of our visits to schools, factories, work camps, and forums was an introductory presentation followed by a question-answer period, after which we could roam at will, individually or in groups, and talk to students, teachers, workers. In Havana, Santiago, and Camaguey we had several hours or a full day on our own. Different people went to daycare centers, hospitals, art galleries, restaurants, ice cream bars, government ministries, the Chinese, Korean, North Vietnamese, and PRC embassies, universities, Party headquarters, ICAIC (the Cuban film Institute), radio stations, bookstores, centers of the Committees for Defense of the Revolution, food rationing centers, *Poder Local* (local government) offices, etc.

The people we met were equally diverse. We were often approached by students who handed us their blue books of English exercises to read and correct. Some *brigadistas* were approached by *gusanos* (counterrevolutionaries waiting to leave Cuba, literally "worms"), who badmouthed the Revolution. Everywhere — except among the more sophisticated city folk of Havana — we attracted spontaneous street crowds of curious, mostly young Cubans, who had dozens of questions about us, the Brigade, our movement in the United States, rock music, sex. They were eager to know our opinion of Cuba.

We were often reassured that they make a sharp distinction between the imperialist U.S. government, their enemy, and the American people, who are not. We spoke with many *Cubanos* who had lived in the States — usually in Miami, New York, or Chicago — but returned to their homes after the Revolution to join the struggle.

* * * * *

In one sense, Sen. Eastland is right: There is a "direct chain" which reaches from Cuba — and Vietnam — "into our cities, our campuses ... our lives." And for the "Republic," which Eastland represents it poses a most distinct threat. The chain links rebellious students and white youth with the inhabitants of Ameri ka's barrios and ghettos who are collectively rising up in defense of the original high ideals of this Republic.

It is no accident that the Black Panther Party concludes its Ten-Point Program with the opening paragraphs of the Declaration of Independence, or that Ho Chi Minh modeled the Constitution of the Democratic Republic of Vietnam on this same Declaration. The ideals which inspired these manifestoes are just demands of any people invoking the rights of life and liberty.

When Fidel says, as he did to the second contingent of the Brigade, "We are a species representative of the problems of millions of inhabitants of the world," he is affirming the bond which links the Cuban people to the struggle of the oppressed everywhere to demonstrate that the rule of imperialism is finite — and the power of national liberation infinite.

We absorbed much of this Cuban spirit of internationalism.

We absorbed much of this Cuban spirit of internationalism, and we also learned about the self-discipline and solidarity necessary to make a new society here in America. If in the belly of the monster we find ourselves still weakened by the values of an exploitative system, it only means that we face a more complex struggle to unify ourselves around our common goals.

One *brigadista* concluded: "Revolutions are not made by liberated people. They are made by people who understand the possibility of liberation, but who know they must clear the ground of oppressive institutions if they are to realize that possibility."

And if for the moment the power of Eastland, Nixon, Agnew and Co. and their "silent majority" seems overbearing, we should recall Fidel's reminder: "As we were telling some members of the Brigade this afternoon, at the university where we studied there were about 30 anti-imperialists among the 5,000 students. We must be optimistic."

¡Venceremos! -30-

Salvador Allende

A Crack In The Imperial Armor

Art: April 13, 1971.

¡Venceremos! Houston Brigadistas Talk About Cuba: Part 2

Houston Brigadistas • August 10, 1971

We have vivid memories of our work in the cane fields of Cuba. Riding through the countryside in open-air trucks at 6:30 in the morning. Watching the sunrise on the way to the fields. Starting work each day when the fields were still wet with dew. Joy at the signal for our midmorning *merienda* (snack) when we could stretch out on stacks of cane in the baking sun.

Climbing on the truck at the end of the day, feeling like we'd done something good and useful. Teaching our Cuban comrades country songs on the trucks and learning Cuban songs from them. Feeling a growing sense of solidarity between us as North Americans and the Cubans we worked with every day.

Cutting burned cane wasn't as hard as cutting green cane, which was done by the first two Brigades last year. Still, the long hours, the back bending, the blistered hands — this was harder, more routine, and more sustained work than many of us had ever done before.

We felt in our bones and muscles and heads that the regular, physical, outdoor work was good for us. But we were not used to it, physically or *mentally*. Our experience in the United States has left us with a distaste for regular work because here it is associated with careerism, conformity, materialism, competitiveness, and top-down hierarchical structures. We are not turned on by most of the types of work offered to us in the United States — helping corporations make money, selling people things they don't need, or helping a giant military machine repress people from the Mekong Delta to Kent State University.

But in Cuba we were working for the people. The sugar cane we cut will be milled into refined sugar to feed the Cuban people as well as to exchange in foreign trade for other things which will raise the general standard of living — not profits which will line the pockets of rich businessmen and politicians. This awareness of the different meaning of work under socialism involves quite a consciousness leap, and few of us made it completely. The headaches, upset stomachs, sprains, allergies, rashes, and numerous other symptoms we developed in the fields were telling testimony to our physical and psychological unreadiness for hard work.

So, our work taught us some things about ourselves, but also about Cuba, about socialism, about underdevelopment, and about the everyday life of many workers and *campesinos*. Socialism in an underdeveloped country means *work*! Hard, physical muscle-work and the equally necessary mind-work of planning, coordinating, organizing. Socialism does not automatically solve the problems of economic underdevelopment. *It merely creates a context in which solutions become possible.*

Our seven weeks of field work gave us some *feeling* (not just an *idea*) of the daily experience of many Cubans — as well as millions of other people in the underdeveloped world and some, such as migrant workers, right here in the United States. (It is possible to exaggerate this empathy-four weeks of hard work obviously is not the same as a lifetime.)

The emphasis on work, on maximizing production, pervades every phase of the Revolution, and should always be kept in mind in any analysis of the Revolution's record. Some examples:

1. A constant theme in all levels of Cuban education is that the student must be brought into contact with production and technical things. The Cuban ideal of "integral education" combines work, technical study, and ideological development.

2. The emphasis on production has significantly changed the position of Cuban women. Although the Revolution has not attacked the old Latin double standard head-on, it has attempted to make women fully productive members of society by opening to them many new educational, work, and political opportunities. Universal free day care centers, maternity leave, equal pay for equal work, and other policies provide positive encouragement for women to take advantage of these new opportunities.

> **Cutting burned cane wasn't as hard as cutting green cane.**

Many women work in the fields, but also 50 percent of Cuban doctors are now women.

3. Finally, the emphasis on production — combined with a severe labor shortage and the Revolution's humanitarian desire to free people from shitty work — means full speed ahead on automation. The recently invented Henderson Harvester, a product of Cuban technology and ingenuity, is expected to mechanize two-thirds of the cane *zafra* within the decade, liberating thousands of Cubans from millions of hours of backbreaking work, and freeing them for work in other sectors of the economy.

The fact that the Revolution has released and channeled a tremendous amount of energy among the Cuban people doesn't mean that they didn't work hard before the Revolution, in capitalist Cuba. They did — when they could — when their labor was needed by the rich North American and Cuban landowners and capitalists who controlled the Cuban economy and saw it as a means of enriching themselves.

During the *zafra* (harvest) the campesinos worked for 12, 14, and 16 hours a day for subsistence wages, creating sugar profits which wound up in New York banks, paid for the high living of the Havana bourgeoisie, or greased the palms of politicians in the incredibly corrupt Batista dictatorship. After the *zafra* ended, the campesinos were likely to be without any work at all for half the year, creating mass unemployment and depressed living conditions in the countryside.

Now, the wealth Cuba's workers create comes back to them in the form of free medical care, free education, better housing at lower rents or none at all (rents have already been abolished in much of the country's housing, may not exceed 10 percent of the occupant's earnings in the rest, and are scheduled to be abolished nationwide in the near future), free telephone service, cheap mass transportation, and guaranteed food rations. Or it is plowed back into the economy in the form of dams, factories, machines, or other long-term investments which will yield even greater benefits to their children and grandchildren.

Most of us, after coming back from Cuba, will probably return to the way we used to live. It's not an easy thing to change your way of life completely, to transform your feelings about physical work.

But after a few months, people are going to start thinking about the meaning of the work they're doing in terms of what they learned from the Cubans — that is, about thinking in a collective way, about understanding struggle and internationalism. They'll be asking themselves if they're really making a contribution toward destroying Amerikan imperialism and building a revolution in this country.

They'll know that internationalism isn't just a slogan. It doesn't mean just putting "Support the PRG" at the bottom of a leaflet. Internationalism can only mean that we're all in the same struggle. It's doing it. It's understanding that the Cubans and the Vietnamese feel unity because they're both struggling against U.S. imperialism. Support and unity cannot be abstract. It means doing it when you get back.

- Houston Venceremos Brigade Contingent

Several Houston people have just returned from Cuba, where we worked with other North Americans in the fourth Venceremos Brigade. We worked seven weeks in the cane fields of Havana province, and then were given a two-week tour of Cuba which took us from Havana in the west to Santiago de Cuba in the East. We are available to talk to classes, clubs, conventions, or informal groups about our experiences and observations in the First Free Territory of the Americas. Write Venceremos, 1217 Wichita, Houston 77004, or call 526-6257. -30-

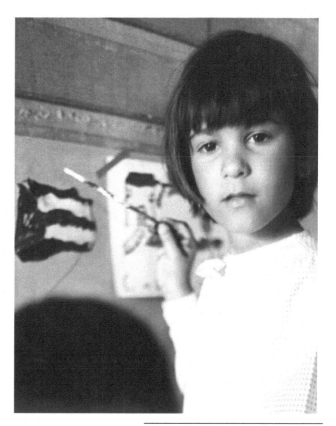

Photo: Sue Duncan, July 20, 1972.

Childcare in Cuba

Tina Phillips • July 20, 1972

In the United States, no real system of childcare is available for the people. Most day care centers are privately owned and serve only families of high income levels. The few centers open for working women are invariably understaffed, the children are undernourished and often beaten. There is little concern for the child's development as a human being.

During my visit to Cuba this spring I visited a day care center in a newly-built town in the country called Vado del Yeso. I spent the entire afternoon at the center playing with the children, looking through their books and materials, and talking to the coordinators and staff of the center.

Several of the women who worked there were mothers that lived in the town and the majority of them belonged to the Federation of Cuban Women. They explained to me that at the triumph of the Revolution a national plan was completed for the construction of day care centers as a major project of the Revolution. These were to provide not only a healthy and stimulating environment for the children, but also to free the women from the home so they could work, study, and participate in all aspects of the Cuban society.

Day care centers were built in factories and work centers in both large and small towns. They have played and are playing a major role in the liberation of the Cuban woman.

Children in Cuba maintain a very important position — "the new men and women of the revolutionary society, the strength and future of the Revolution." The centers are organized to allow a child to develop as freely and as fully as possible. Creative toys, books, and art materials provide a stimulating atmosphere inside, while a large playground area outside furnishes an outlet for a child's need for physical exertion.

Teachers and staff are carefully selected and trained to work in the centers, and are quite proud of the responsibility placed upon them.

The centers are kept impeccably clean and sanitary; the children are taught to take the responsibility of keeping their center clean. Vaccinations and preventative medicine are provided for each child, as well as diapers, clothes, food, and toys. These services are provided free to all Cubans.

However, there is a more important and essential aspect to the Cuban childcare centers than the many material benefits and services which are provided. The children learn and experience from the very beginning the reality of the world in which they live. They learn to face and deal with problems in their daily lives, to learn from their mistakes and their successes. Their books are not about Jane, Dick, and Mary competing with each other, but tell of the life of the children of Vietnam, the numerous cultures and tribes in Africa, and the daily struggles of their own people. -30-

Students perform scenes from Cuban history. Photo by Cam Duncan. July 20, 1972.

Birth of the Revolution

Susan Duncan • July 20, 1972

On July 26, 1953, 120 men and two women attacked the Moncada Barracks, a large military camp in Santiago de Cuba. The action was a military failure. Seven were killed in the attack and Batista's army rounded up, tortured and killed 70 others, some of whom were men, women, and children who had nothing to do with the attack. Shocked by the bloodbath, Cuban liberals persuaded the army to grant trials to the rebels. Fidel Castro, the young leader of the group, was one of those who survived to be put on trial.

During his trial Fidel explained the attack on the Moncada, stating that no other way was open to change the Cuban government. He not only denounced the violence and corruption of the Batista dictatorship and the conditions existing under it — the poverty, unemployment (a million from May to December when the sugar harvest was over), lack of education and medical care for the poor, the starving peasants with no land and the uncultivated land of the large corporations and the rich — but he also established the essential steps of a program to deal with these conditions. He talked about agrarian reform, diversification of agriculture, scientific farming, reforms in education, medicine and housing policy, industrialization, nationalization of the foreign companies, economic and political independence, and a government with justice and equality for all Cubans.

Fidel was sentenced to 15 years in jail and the others to lesser terms. Public pressure forced Batista to grant amnesty to the prisoners in 1955. They were released to an enthusiastic welcome by the Cuban people and then went to Mexico to prepare again to topple Batista.

The Moncada attack may have been a military defeat, but it was a political victory.

Batista had come to power in 1933, through seizing control of the army. He ruled Cuba directly or through one of his men until 1944, when his candidate was defeated in the elections. He retired to Florida (with the millions he had made since 1933) and returned to Cuba to take over the government in a military coup in 1952 when it was obvious he didn't have a chance of winning the elections. Fidel, then a 25-year-old lawyer, responded to the coup by filing an airtight case against Batista accusing him of treason and sedition. Despite the evidence, the court was unable to reach a guilty verdict. With a dictatorship replacing elections and the traditional parties' and the courts' subservience to the privileged preventing them from doing anything about Batista or any of Cuba's problems, the only solution lay in organizing the people to fight.

Ad: Art by Dennis Kling, June 22, 1972.

The Moncada attack may have been a military defeat, but it was a political victory because it showed the Cuban people that there was something they could do to change their situation. It showed them they did not have to be passive to dictatorship and exploitation and that there were people willing to take the risks to create a better society. It was the beginning of the building of a revolution.

Thus today, the 26th of July is the biggest holiday celebration in Cuba. We are celebrating it here too in solidarity with the Cuban Revolution. Why? Because the Moncada action and the Cuban Revolution were not just an attack against the Batista dictatorship and the conditions maintained by the rich of Cuba, but also and more significantly, an attack against U.S. imperialism, a system which exploited Cuba and prevented her from developing — just as it does in so many other countries around the world.

Cuba fought for years for independence from Spain only to shift to the control of the U.S. Large North American corporations moved in and turned Cuba into an appendage of the U.S. economy — a gigantic sugar plantation providing the U.S. with sugar (and the North American plantation and refinery owners with high profits from the cheap labor) and an outlet for American manufactured goods, which went to the local elite who could afford them. U.S. interests owned or controlled the most important business operations in Cuba and dominated her internal market and foreign

trade — 75 percent of Cuba's exports and 80 percent of her imports were monopolized by the U.S. The U.S. corporations were just following good business principles (profits) for them, but they were draining off any possibility for economic development of Cuba.

Along with the economic domination came political domination — Batista represented the U.S. interests in Cuba. There was no way to reform the situation in Cuba (even if the government and the wealthy it represented had been willing) without running into conflict with U.S. interests. This is the situation underdeveloped countries all over the world face today.

Whether we agree with the content of the Cuban Revolution or not, we should support its right to exist. We should support the Cuban people's right to self-determination — their right to run their own country without the approval of U.S. corporations and the U.S. government. And we should take a stand against the U.S. continuing to interfere in the affairs of other countries.

July 25-27 there will be a conference on Cuba at the University of Houston. There will be a display of posters and photography from Cuba, film and slide showings, and speakers. The films from Cuba will be shown Tuesday at 8 p.m. and Wednesday at noon. The slide show and talk, given by Houstonians who have been to Cuba with the Venceremos Brigade, will be Wednesday at 8 p.m. -30-

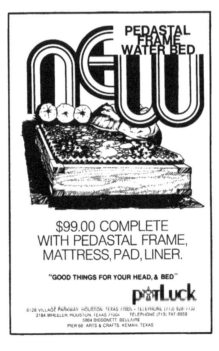

Ads: (left) Art by Bill Narum, February 17, 1972; (center) February 24, 1972; (right) July 6, 1972.

Space City!
Electoral Politics

SPACE CITY!

25¢

Houston, Texas : July 27-August 2, 1972

35¢ out of town

Miami Beach: 1972

Cover: July 27, 1972.

Sissy Farenthold:
Houstonians Rally for That Woman

Giles Corey • May 4, 1972

Hermann Park seems the right place to have a rally for Frances Farenthold, matching the green motif of her campaign and the greening of the governorship she hopes to accomplish. And also, I tell myself Tuesday evening, May 2, as I park along the crowded drive in this small island of green in Concrete City, symbolic of the limited base of support she has — the long-haired young, their liberal parents, a sprinkling of blacks and browns, and assorted mavericks.

An omen shakes my she-can't-win cynicism: The turquoise Ford in front of me has a Farenthold sticker centered in its rear window and on its bumper, a sticker with the old red-white-and-blue legend, "America: Love It or Leave It." Weirdness. Is something happening here?

> **Her campaign has style, and the style is symbolic of substance.**

First glance at the crowd confirms preconceptions. It looks like an audience at Hofheinz Pavilion waiting for the Big Group, milling back and forth, parading the trappings of the counterculture, seeing and being seen. Not a political rally, except for the scattering of campaigners for lesser offices wandering aimlessly, almost as if stoned, through the uncharacteristic political crowd.

Dare you stick out a hand to this tie-dyed mass and ask for their vote? It seems uncool, the campaigners sense, and few try.

There are a few more blacks in the crowd than one might expect, a few more shorthairs and grayhairs and straights of various descriptions. And some who obviously labor for a living in heavy industry. But

Photo: Thorne Dreyer, June 1, 1972.

as night envelops the crowd, the contradictions fade from view. The spirited jazz of the Kashmere High School stage band seizes the air, and maybe you can count all those who don't quite get off to the music and free barbeque.

A decent young conservative reporter who is spending the week with Sissy for one of the major dailies reinforces my cynicism.

The other day, he says, Farenthold spent four crucial morning hours having her hair done (isn't that just like a woman?) and spent an evening in Corpus Christi with her husband recuperating from getting up at 4 a.m. The campaign is, well, amateur, he sighs. A lady who chauffeured Farenthold around for a day some weeks back told me how tired she was then. A little of that came across on the recent statewide public broadcast network live hookup in which the six gubernatorial candidates were quizzed and Sissy kept forgetting the question by the time it came to her and kept blowing chances to slam Barnes.

But her campaign has style, and the style is symbolic of substance, like the green motif. No billboards:

dumb, maybe, but principled. High school kids in green T-shirts, white pants, and Farenthold derbies move through the crowd collecting litter in big canvas sacks.

Isabel Lipschutz declines to sing the Star Spangled Banner as requested ("It's not that I'm not patriotic, it can't be sung," she explains) and substitutes Woody Guthrie's populist-patriotic ballad, "This Land Is Your Land." It fits.

Sissy will be the kind of governor Texas not only needs but has never had.

A middle-aged, middle-American steelworker sitting in an aluminum lawn chair next to me on the hill facing Miller Theater agrees the National Anthem is hard to sing and stops talking during the ballad, the first music of the evening he has so honored. Maybe just because of what it's standing in for, although the rendition is beautiful and moving.

He's for Farenthold, he says, "because of corruption in Austin. We need a change there bad."

A 24-year man at Armco Steel, he's recuperating from heart surgery, he says, and has been doing a little traveling around the state to relax. "North Texas, East Texas, everywhere I go people I talk to are for this lady. I believe she'll win."

The convalescing steelworker would vote for Briscoe if Sissy weren't in the race, but Briscoe's a millionaire and the steelworker has suspicions about where some of that money may have come from. He thinks it's going to be a runoff between Farenthold and Briscoe, "and if she gets in the runoff she'll win."

What about Ben Barnes? "People feel like he knows something he's not telling. A man in his position so close to things for so long. . ."

"We can make a woman governor of this state," the steelworker says. "Wallace's wife did it in Alabama — she made a good one."

No, he tells me, quizzical at my question, he doesn't own a turquoise Ford.

The music's over and the tributes are rolling in. Leonel Castillo, Houston's new Chicano controller, intones about "the fantastic need for reform" and leads the audience in the Viva clap (a steady beat building to thunderous applause which he says he learned from César Chávez). Zollie Scales of the black Harris County Council of Organizations, which gave a dual endorsement to Sissy and Barnes says it's time for a

Ad: May 4, 1972.

Photos: Thorne Dreyer. June 1, 1972.

change. Mrs. C. V. Adair, an ancient, crusading, and deeply respected black precinct chairwoman, says the absentee voting is strong for Farenthold. "Sissy will be the kind of governor Texas not only needs but has never had," she says.

The crowd has been building and is losing patience. Farenthold's people estimate 10,000; one television news report says 10,000; another, 30,000. Who can tell? The 10,000 guess seems reasonable and is double expectations.

"We want Sissy. We want Sissy. We want Sissy," the crowd demands with rhythmic claps. Her introducer promises they will get her soon, and then tells them there are four lobbyists for every legislator and who Sissy's famous ancestors were and how she is in the tradition of Texas's populist-reformer governors like Sam Houston, Jim Hogg, and James V. Allred.

Finally, Sissy, under a huge, emerald green FARENTHOLD sign framed by two emerald green trees that look like inverted shamrocks.

Forget the stories about how tired she is. Forget the cynicism. She is electrically alive and sparkling and full of frijoles. "Six months ago this wouldn't have been believed," she says, gazing out on the crowd.

Farenthold says she knew that when she was elected state representative that Chicanos weren't represented in state government because 49 percent of her Corpus Christi district was Mexican-American, and she says she knew blacks weren't represented.

"But what I learned in my two terms in Austin was that most Texans weren't represented."

She entered the governor's race "because I did not intend to sit on the sidelines wringing my hands and let the office go by default to the present Lieutenant Governor, the 'boy wonder' groomed, pampered and protected for 12 years by those who need special favors from the state."

The state's voters, Sissy says, have through her campaign been made aware of Barnes' "failure to protect the public interest."

She calls tax reform the number one issue: "You have the three of them over there and Farenthold here. I am for a tax on big business profits. Let it be fair but let them pay their share of the burden."

Thunderous applause.

She reminds her listeners of "the Barnes bread tax that would have taxed groceries. Smith and Barnes

were both part of that tax package and I doubt if Briscoe even knew about it."

Consumers pay too much for electricity, gas, and telephone service, Sissy says, "because utilities go virtually unregulated in this state."

More thunderous applause.

> **'We seek one class of citizenship for all and one system of justice for all.'**

She makes her traditional call for full financial disclosure and says the heart of it is disclosure of the income tax return. She has done so. The others have ducked, she says, and Barnes hasn't even filed income tax this year.

"1972 is a time for insurgency," she proclaims. "We seek one class of citizenship for all and one system of justice for all."

The choice, she concludes, with characteristic modesty and precision, "is between a wheeler-dealer from Brownwood, a bowl of pablum from Uvalde, and me with all my imperfections."

The audience goes wild. The Hofheinz Pavilion crowd demands an encore. "We want Sissy, we want Sissy ..."

She obliges, returning to the mike with a single sentence: "We have within our grasp the ability to accomplish the political coup of this decade."

I leave entranced and elated, feeling that if she can touch a chord in my too-jaded soul, and in the populist steelworker's and his spiritual kin, and in the kids and the grandmothers and the other mavericks and working stiffs who want a governor who is both honest and smart — well, then, maybe we will accomplish that coup. And then who can say what miracle might happen? -30-

[In 1968, Frances "Sissy" Farenthold was the only woman serving in the Texas House of Representatives. In 1972, she was nominated for Vice President at the Democratic National Convention in Miami Beach and came in second to presidential candidate George McGovern's choice, Sen. Thomas F. Eagleton of Missouri. Farenthold ran spirited campaigns for the Democratic nomination for Governor of Texas in 1972 and 1974, both times finishing second to the eventual winner, Dolph Briscoe, and helping to coalesce the growing progressive forces in the state. In 1973, Sissy was elected the first chair of the National Women's Political Caucus.]

Photo: Cam Duncan, May 4, 1972.

New, Improved Wallace Holds Court in Houston

Cam Duncan • May 4, 1972

Bless George… and remember that the one who serves Thee, reigns… One God, One Governor, World without end, Amen. — Rev. Robert Ingram, Invocation, Wallace Campaign Rally

Ridicule, Righteous indignation, and empty Rhetoric were the three "R's" preached at George Wallace's campaign rally at Houston's Music Hall on May 2. Emphasis was on the latter. Speaking before national television cameras, a refined Wallace gave his standard pseudo-populist "anti-platform" on busing, tax relief, labor, law 'n order, and welfare.

Wallace also unveiled a brand new issue he had dug up to propose to the Democratic Platform Committee: to strengthen our legal system. Supreme Court judges would be reapproved or

rejected every six to eight years, and federal district judges would be elected by voters in their district. Such a plan would be enacted through constitutional amendment. A good solid issue, ignored by his opponents, that will appeal to liberals and conservatives alike.

With his new strategy to pressure the Democratic Party to the right rather than build a strong third-party threat, the swaggering Wallace of the past has calmed his bombast and spread his appeal. We heard no mention of race, other than a brief condemnation of busing, no communists were cursed (although "ultra-left-wing liberals" were), there was no right-wing fanaticism and none of the revival atmosphere of past campaigns. George has got a new young wife, Southern belle Camellia, and a new slick self-confidence that makes it easier to believe what he says. If you don't listen too hard.

Wallace was in Texas to remind his supporters to vote Democrat in the May 6 primary and, more important, to vote for Wallace delegates at the precinct conventions. Wallace hopes to take a chunk of Texas' delegates at the state convention June 13.

The crowd which streamed into the Music Hall 3,000-strong included a few people decked out in expensive clothing, but most wore cheap suits or open-necked shirts. Their clothes, their faces and hands, and their voices showed them to be a crowd of working people and small businessmen. (There were no radicals picketing outside, as at Wallace rallies in other cities.)

Vendors in the lobby sold Wallace records, bumper stickers, buttons, hard hats, straw (plastic) hats, *The George Wallace Story* ($7.95) and flags: American, Confederate, and Texas. "Show your colors on national TV, show your colors!" barked the vendors. Another huckster opened a traveling salesman's suitcase and displayed colorful right-wing paperbacks.

The crowd was mainly over 35, many white-haired, but there was also a sizeable number of teenagers. Few of these seemed to be committed Wallace supporters; they had come to "check it out."

The swaggering Wallace of the past has calmed his bombast.

14 VARIETIES OF CHARCOAL BURGERS
ROLANDO'S
Burger Factory

Another ROLANDO'S opening soon at Kirby and Kipling.
PHONE ORDERS TAKEN!!

OPEN MON.-SAT.   11a.m. to 10p.m.
1739 RICHMOND   tel. 528-8865   KLING

We saw only one black face in the crowd, and he was a newsman. Lots of thick accents — and Billy Grammer of the Grand Old Opry played "The Eyes of Texas" and "Under the Double Eagle." Almost an old-time political hoe-down, but the crowd was a little reserved and Wallace's style too smooth.

The most fervent in the crowd were those drawn by the busing issue. They carried such signs as "No Busin' for Usun." But most spectators were of a slightly different stripe from the anti-busing activists. They feel that Wallace is the first politician in a generation to speak for them. Several older people compared him to Roosevelt. "They called Roosevelt a radical too," one white-haired woman said. A man mused on the ITT scandal — "ITT has no more votes than anyone else," he said, apparently seeing Wallace as a crusader — against the power of the monopolies.

Wallace played up to these sentiments in his 45-minute speech. Over and over, he hit at his familiar message: "The working people, the business people, the farming people of this country are sick and tired of a faceless bureaucracy running things." Wallace struck again and again at the unrepresentative nature of American politics, as no other candidate has been willing to do. "In Washington there are offices after offices where there's an Assistant to an Assistant to an Assistant to an Assistant — and he's getting $40,000 a year — and he doesn't have anything in his briefcase but a peanut-butter sandwich."

Wallace repeatedly voiced the sentiment of millions of voters that the candidates (except for himself) are fakers. "They turn their heads so far speaking on both sides of an issue that they get slipped disks." He correctly pointed out that the "anti-war" candidates all voted for the 1964 Gulf of Tonkin resolution, but then, after involving American boys in the Indochina War, they wouldn't let them win and now they want to withdraw. He made much of the fact that these politicians now say the Vietnam War was a big mistake; an error, Wallace pointed out, so costly in American

Photo: Cam Duncan, May 4, 1972.

lives and dollars that the guilty politicians should not be easily forgiven.

The six major candidates, he said, have been in the Senate a total of 109 years, "and they're all talking tax reform. But in those 109 years, what have they done about tax reform?" He appealed to the crowd's sense of powerlessness. "Send them a message," he cried. "You are silent no longer."

George Wallace has been able to move many politicians in his direction — it was just after Wallace's victory in Florida that Nixon made his anti-busing speech. But the character of Wallace's proposals represents no real solution to the problems of the white, older crowd at the Music Hall, much less to the problems of black and brown workers who were quite notably absent.

His program, by now familiar, is to cut back government spending. Although he mentioned the problem of unemployment, he has no solution for it, except fake economics to the effect that lower tax-

His rhetoric presents the 'businessman' as another victim of 'big government.'

es would stimulate buying and thus create employment. His program is against — against giveaways to "countries that spit in our face" and to "welfare loafers," particularly those 250,000 heroin addicts in New York who are on welfare.

Wallace carefully avoided cutting himself off from the political center, which he hopes will continue moving in his direction. On foreign policy, he sounded like a cold war liberal, opposing cuts in arms spending but favoring "negotiations" and supporting the Marshall Plan which had "stabilized the free world." A far cry from 1968, when Wallace and running mate Curtis LeMay called for bombing Vietnam "back to the Stone Age."

But the most notable aspect of Wallace's oratory was what was absent from it. Over and over he repeated that he speaks for "the working man, the businessman, the farmer." But he had very little to say on labor issues.

Wallace emphasized that he has been a strong friend of organized labor. But he did not mention his own

Photo: Cam Duncan, May 4, 1972.

labor record as Alabama governor, like his steadfast opposition to all efforts aimed at repeal of Alabama's "right to work" law.

His rhetoric presents the "businessman" as another victim of "big government"; thus he avoids saying anything very concrete about the huge corporations. And although he referred to the fact that the other candidates, as senators, have brought us to the brink of economic chaos, Wallace said nothing about Nixon's wage controls, made no statement on controlling prices, said nothing about the efforts in Congress to curb the right to strike, made no reference to the need to organize non-unionized workers. Opposing busing, he offered no program for improving schools or other social services.

Although Wallace is able to put voice to the frustration of his audience, frustration at their powerlessness and their declining living standards, his program would actually cut back the few benefits which poor people now have, while offering nothing to replace them.

On the busing issue, Wallace said little. He took a swipe at Nixon, calling him just as dictatorial as Mao Tse-tung for not seeking the people's opinion on busing. This, however, was tucked away in the middle of his speech. The most enthusiastic audience response came when Wallace eulogized J. Edgar Hoover ("one of the finest law enforcement officials that our country ever saw") and praised Houston's police force and its Chief Short.

As a result, the rally had an anti-climactic quality. The outpouring of emotion against busing, which a large part of the crowd must have expected, never came. Wallace, knowing he has the anti-busing vote in his pocket, was carefully projecting an image that could appeal to the many people in the crowd who share his opposition to busing but are also concerned about other issues.

The result was that the rally did not really display the expected flavor of a right-wing hate session. It was, in many ways, a typical American campaign rally — the people yearning to believe in this one candidate who promises he is different from all the rest, who promises that he will give them a voice.

This atmosphere was part real, part deceptive. The rally did represent an upsurge of people who feel established politics has ignored the common man — and it has. This white electorate is one which, this year, could respond equally to a progressive or a reactionary call, provided both dress in populist slogans.

An example was the reaction of one youth who said he thought a Wallace-McGovern ticket would win; he didn't care which of the two topped the bill. Asked if there weren't a contradiction here, he replied that the Georges stand for the same things. In rhetoric this is often true.

Wallace's remarkable success so far is an indicator of the potential power of independent politics. Yet Wallace is the biggest fake of all the candidates. Despite his rhetoric, he himself is dependent on support from big business interests; he is able to give a voice to voters' frustrations, but is unable to offer a constructive program.

The kind of independent politics which could offer a real alternative — based on the common interest of working people, black, brown and white, against the employers and their parties — is not in sight this year. -30-

[Gov. George Wallace of Alabama ran in the 1972 Democratic presidential primaries but his campaign was put to an end when on May 15, 1972, he was shot in Maryland by Arthur Bremer, paralyzing Wallace for the rest of his life and putting a virtual end to his national prominence. Wallace was the fourth-longest-serving governor in U.S. history, ending his fourth term in 1987.]

Jerry Rubin on George McGovern

Thorne Dreyer • May 4, 1972

This year's presidential campaign has been full of surprises and unexpected turns. Such things as heralded Democratic front runner Ed Muskie fizzling like a birthday balloon sprung a fast leak. The consistently strong showings George Wallace has made throughout the primaries. And the emergence of George McGovern, battling the Hump for Democratic king of the hill — his amazingly widespread and energetic organization, and his unexpected clout at the ballot box in communities ranging from affluent urban suburbs to blue collar strongholds.

Much of McGovern's core of strength has come from the peace movement and from young kids, many of whom wouldn't have been caught dead in the arena of electoral politics a few months back. There's a children's crusade that rivals that of McCarthy four years ago; perhaps one with less simplistic idealism and a little more sophisticated savvy. Maybe it's because McGovern has been able to do something that the Left in this country has dreamed about in its rhetoric but failed to achieve in its actions. McGovern (as is Wallace) is appealing to a long untapped native American populism, is merging the war with other issues basic to our survival as a people, and appears to be forging an unholy alliance encompassing hard hats and hippies.

Perhaps his key failure has been his inability to strike a deep chord in black America; so far, the Hump appears to be pulling in the bulk of the black vote. The McGovern folks feel this is due to a lack of exposure in the black community, and they think this tide too will turn.

Their hopes have been boosted by recent endorsements from such as black legislator Julian Bond, Operation Breadbasket's Jesse Jackson, and Ralph Abernathy of SCLC.

Anyway, all this is intended as a lead-in to the latest, and perhaps one of the most interesting, surprises of the '72 campaign. Yippie leaders Jerry Rubin and Abbie Hoffman have publicly endorsed McGovern and are encouraging young people to work for his election.

They have expressed reservations about George, to be sure, and it would be wrong — they'd be the first to say it — to consider them the spokesmen for the freak/left movement in this country. But it's certainly a turn of events worthy of note: especially when you realize that four years ago, during the Democratic Convention, Hoffman and Rubin were in the Chicago streets — and were later convicted for conspiracy as a result of their actions. Their verdict at that time — and there were many of us with them — judged the electoral process to be totally corrupt; to work within it was seen as futile and, indeed, a cop out.

We called Jerry in New York last week and talked to him live over the air during the Briarpatch show on Pacifica radio. We asked him just why he and Abbie had thrown their support to Honest George. Following is part of his response.

> 'Humphrey and Muskie are just the Democrats' versions of Nixon.'

We feel the Nixon administration is just disastrous for everybody and is leading us to genocide — ecological and human genocide — and that we really have to defeat Nixon... Humphrey and Muskie are just the Democrats' versions of Nixon, and we certainly don't want another Humphrey-Nixon race. The only candidate we're supporting is McGovern.

Jerry Rubin, photo by Thorne Dreyer.

McGovern has said that he would get every American soldier and every piece of American equipment out of Vietnam within 90 days after being elected. McGovern is represented by grassroots people across the country and McGovern is running an honest campaign. So, McGovern is coming across as a left-wing candidate.

By supporting McGovern, we're contributing to the defeat of the traditional Democratic Party and Republican Party. And we're giving the electoral system sort of one more test... We're organizing people around McGovern based on his stands on the issues. We have no illusions about McGovern. Any politician put in certain situations is gonna sell out — gonna become corrupt — and that may happen to McGovern too.

And if McGovern should by luck get elected, we'll be on the other side of the street. . . We're gonna be watching very carefully what he does, because he would be the representative of corporate capitalism and he would be commander-in-chief of the armed forces.

But if we all unite, we could give a stinging defeat to Nixon and Humphrey and Muskie and put our candidate in office. And McGovern will then know that he was put into office by us; he'll be responsible to us and maybe, maybe there's some hope of changing this country — at least of ending the War in Vietnam, which has gone on too long for human beings to bear.

We don't throw our support totally behind McGovern — but in a battle between McGovern and Nixon, there's just no choice. And the Left has to survive in this country. I think more people will listen to us — the Yippies — if we're involved in a campaign to elect a left-wing candidate — than if we're just on the sidelines saying the whole thing's a phony, the whole thing's a sham... We've gotten some flak (from some people on the left), but that's okay. It'll just get people talking.

And if McGovern is not nominated in Miami — if they have the audacity, the nerve to nominate Humphrey or Muskie or someone like that — then it'll be a deep revolutionizing, radicalizing experience for young people and will just further deepen the contradictions in the country. -30-

Art: Bill Narum, July 13, 1971

Miami Beach: The New Politics Are Pretty Weird

Thorne Dreyer • July 27, 1972

In 1968, thousands of demonstrators were bloodied in the Chicago streets while inside the convention hall Mayor Richard Daley mouthed anti-Semitic slurs at Sen. Abe Ribicoff, and a party controlled by bosses and hacks handed the presidential nomination to Hubert Humphrey.

In 1972, many of those same demonstrators were delegates. Mayor Daley was sent packing and Sen. George (They Said It Couldn't Be Done) McGovern won a first ballot nomination. After his acceptance speech, not long before sunrise Friday, July 14, the delegates to the Democratic Convention joined together and sang "We Shall Overcome."

Is the Democratic Party becoming truly a party of the people?

Is the Democratic Party becoming truly a party of the people? Or have we witnessed the crowning achievement of cooptation in our century? Or maybe a little of each?

Here I am, sitting in my humble living room on Willard Street in the heart of the Montrose, banging away on the old typewriter late Sunday night prior to Space City! publication. I've been back from Miami Beach a week and this, my inevitable "Miami piece," has been teasing my consciousness most every minute of every hour since my return. Every time I hop into my Volvo for a spin to Richwood, there it is: sitting next to me in the front seat, waiting, smiling.

I've been sleeping a lot, trying to hide from it, but it finds its way into my subconscious and flitters through my dreams like a mischievous butterfly. "Dreyer," it says. Firmly. With conviction. "You ain't getting away. And you know it. That deadline's approaching. It's getting closer every minute. Face it, baby."

"Uh, yeah," I admit sheepishly. "You're right. No question about it. Just let me make a sandwich, and read the paper ..."

You see, dear readers, here's the problem. There were 8,000 representatives of the news media swarming around Miami Beach. They appeared out of nowhere, like ants when you leave a piece of baloney on the kitchen table. Wherever you turned, there was some dude with a tag, dangling from a piece of elastic around his neck, and it said, "Media." And it meant. "Media."

Now, these folks had a job to do: they were there to cover the Democratic National Convention. To report the facts, as they happened. Problem was, there were fewer facts than there were media. So, they hovered around hotel lobbies, waiting for a slice of baloney to be thrown their way. When meat was scarce, they became vegetarians, savoring the condiments: looking for anything they could get their teeth into. They sought all the angles, dissected every aspect of the scene in all its complexities, even fell to interviewing each other.

All of which is to say: most everything has been said. I have proof. Scattered about the table on which I type, mingling with the near empty coffee cup and the rather incongruous yellow vase with its five zinnias spying on me, are CLIPPINGS. I clipped them. From the *Miami Herald* and the *Miami News. The Washington Post. The New York Times. The New Orleans Times-Picayune. The Boston Globe.* The *Houston Chronicle* and *Post. Newsday. The New Republic* and *Newsweek*.

Included therein are thousands of inches of copy. I stayed up all night — I guess it was Wednesday — clipping them. Not reading, just clipping. I thought they might be useful, as reference material. And it's true, I guess. Here I am, referring to them already.

Anyway, what all that has to do with this *Space City!* report on the convention is just this: I plan to babble. You already know who won. You know that the sessions went into the wee hours. You know that the Democratic Party has been taken over by a bunch of weirdos and the old guard is freaked. You know what Walter Cronkite looks like.

So, I'm not going to give you a chronology or an in depth on-the-scene report, or even, for that matter, a well thought out and internally consistent overview replete with historical parallels and inspired predictions. Not ol' Thorne. I'm just going to touch on some of the things that interest me and, I hope, might be of concern to the kind of folks who read this paper.

Some things I should tell you about myself, so you don't get misled into thinking (fat chance) that this is objective journalism. First, I come out of a milieu known as the New Left. For several years now I've considered myself a radical, attended and organized demonstrations, shouted obscenities at bureaucrats, that kind of thing. In '68, I attended the Democratic Convention in Chicago — in the streets. I wasn't a McCarthy kid; I thought Gene mushy and electoral politics in most any form a cop out. I was running in the streets in 1968, and writing stories for Liberation News Service about the piggish goings-on.

Well, I'm 27 now (or will be within days after this issue hits the streets). I've mellowed some, I guess. And the times have most certainly changed. I registered to vote this year, for only the second time in my life. I attended my precinct convention. (A year ago, I didn't even know there was any such thing.) Before I knew it, I found myself in San Antonio at the Texas State Democratic Convention, as a delegate from my District (15), committed to Sen. George McGovern. And I went to Miami Beach, to join the media hordes, because it seemed to me that something pretty important was happening … something crucial to many of the precepts we in the "movement" have clung to … and I wanted to try to figure it out.

Probably the most important question the convention raised for me and, I believe, for a large percentage of the McGovern-committed delegates and onlookers, was the issue of Pragmatic Politics. Sacrificing ideals because you're playing to win. The key difference between George McGovern and the party's previous white knight, Eugene McCarthy, is that McGovern has put together a political organization fit to kill. Watching it at work in Miami Beach simply dazzled the eyes. *Newsweek* quoted a McGovern higher-up: "We had absolute control of that convention floor. We played it like a violin."

And when that meant breaking a promise to the women's caucus to support the South Carolina credentials challenge, Pragmatic Politics won out. And when it meant voting down an abortion plank that clearly had the support of a majority of the delegates, had they voted their consciences, Pragmatic Politics was king. And when it meant putting off restructur-

'We had absolute control of that convention floor. We played it like a violin.'

ing the party to appease the old guard, Pragmatic Politics was the victor.

McGovern was already recalling some of his bets, moving perceivably to the right. Like announcing, to the astonishment of many, that he would leave some troops in Thailand (which, after all, is not a part of Indochina, we learn) until all the POWs are returned. Like pushing through a militaristic position on Israel, to appease the "Jewish vote."

Nicholas von Hoffman writes left-wing commentary for *The Washington Post*. He was disgusted. "Seen looking miserable: California delegate sitting with his head in his hands on convention floor saying, 'I think I'll go back on the streets.'"

Hoffman ends his July 14 column discussing anti-war leader Dave Dellinger. "McGovern would never have been nominated without the people Dellinger led on the streets, but he walks around here unrecognized … I tell him that if McGovern sends the boys to Thailand, he will see to it that their dog

TYRANNOSAURUS NIX - STEGAGNEWS US

tags are stamped out in the shape of the peace symbol and that they will be permitted to salute their officers by flashing the 'V' sign."

The McGovern organization's decision not to support a Platform Committee minority report on abortion created perhaps the greatest bitterness, leading to verbal battles among delegates. Actress Shirley MacLaine, a delegate from California who worked hard for McGovern in the primaries, thought a pro-abortion plank would hurt McGovern's chances.

She was verbally assaulted by women's activist Gloria Steinem and New York Congresswoman Bella Abzug. Said Bella: "A sister never goes against a sister. This cannot be tolerated! She does herself an injustice." MacLaine later said, "I'm not going against Bella. Sisters have a right to have pragmatic politics as well as personal principles."

Sissy Farenthold spoke in favor of the abortion plank and, after the word went out to vote "No," was the only member of the Texas McGovern delegation to break discipline and vote "Yes." Also breaking discipline on this issue was McGovern economic adviser John Kenneth Galbraith who, in addition, supported Sissy in her run for the vice presidency.

Chris Treviño, who was an alternate from District 15 in Houston, was extremely upset about the abortion vote. She told *Space City!* that Houston delegate David T. Lopez felt that he could not, in conscience, vote against the plank. He was then, according to Trevino, asked to sit out the vote, and agreed. Chris said that she was deliberately passed over as a replacement for Lopez because the Texas McGovern leaders knew that she too would not vote as instructed.

The McGovern forces felt that McGovern already had a significant "crazy radical" image to overcome with middle-American voters, and that placing inflammatory issues such as abortion on the platform would make the task just that much more difficult. Their opposition argued that McGovern had gained solid support from women who considered him liberal on abortion and that an increasing number of Americans believe abortion should be a decision between a woman and her doctor (57 percent, according to a recent poll).

And, as Galbraith put it, "There are two important functions here — one, to get the right issues into dis-

> **McGovern already had a significant 'crazy radical' image to overcome.**

cussion, and another to get your man elected. This is one issue that simply has to get into discussion."

The issue of abortion, and controversial questions, did get into discussion at this Democratic Convention, and that's a far cry from the past. And, even though the minority report on abortion was defeated, the platform contains a comprehensive plank on women's rights. A New York delegate, a male doctor, told *The Washington Post*, "I can't believe it. These issues never came up before at a convention and they are vital. No matter if they lost, it reasserts women's rights as important issues not to be ignored."

A minority report asserting the rights of homosexuals was defeated by a voice vote and some proponents reacted with bitterness. After the vote, one gay man shouted, "You turn your back on us, McGovern, and we're not going to vote for you." Former New York

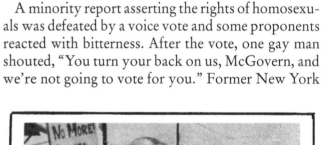

Ad: May 4, 1972.

Congressman Al Lowenstein watched several gays walk out after the vote and said, "I feel so sorry for them. I think they were extremely brave." He caught up with them before they left and said, "I just want to tell you a lot of people voted with you. What you did was a useful and important step. It takes time."

The Washington Post quoted a Wallace delegate from Alabama: "Hey, sugar, that McGovern won't carry a damn state in America. These damn people supporting him are dragging him right in the ground." And a delegate from Washington state: "This is embarrassing and degrading. It's disgusting they allowed such a thing in the first place."

The significant point here has to be that the question of homosexuality was given an open forum by a major political party; this has never happened before. Two delegates spoke from the rostrum, declaring their homosexuality. Madeline Davis of Buffalo, N.Y., said, "We are coming out of our closets and coming out on the convention floor to tell you and all people in America to put an end to our discrimination."

A small group of gay activists sat in the next day at the Doral Hotel, McGovern headquarters. They said they were extremely disappointed that the minority report was rejected but, a spokesman told us, they would certainly support McGovern over Nixon.

Another report popular with many delegates but defeated by McGovern forces was a radical revision of income tax laws proposed by Senator Fred Harris from Oklahoma. Another plank that was defeated was the National Welfare Rights Organization's (NWRO) demand for a guaranteed income of $6,500 for a family of four. A contingent of poor people had made its presence known throughout the convention and some 150 were in attendance in the galleries when the vote was taken. The proposal which went to a roll call vote, gained the support of approximately one-third of the 3,000-plus delegates. I was with the NWRO folk, who held up signs and cheered throughout the vote, and found them to be, on the whole, pleasantly surprised that they got such significant support at this Democratic Convention. I think the poor peoples' forces went away, though certainly not satisfied, at least confident that they had made their point and had been listened to.

The convention did support, by a vote, a proposal calling for "allocation of federal surplus lands to American Indians on a first priority basis."

After the abortion stand, the thing that probably caused the most disillusionment with McGovern was his July 11 statement on POW support. It reaffirmed his commitment to be out of Vietnam 90 days after assuming the presidency, but added, "While I am fully confident that there would be no such need, I would also retain the military capability on the region — in Thailand and on the seas — to signal and fulfill our firm determination on this issue. This is the only cause for which I would retain any U.S. forces in or adjacent to Southeast Asia."

Many McGovern supporters — delegates and non-delegates — considered this to be a betrayal of his previous position. Perhaps 200 demonstrators, led by the Progressive Labor Party-dominated SDS, marched on the Doral Hotel and were denied entrance by a cordon of police. This was one of two times during the entire Convention that a violent confrontation seemed possible. Word was sent from McGovern headquarters that the police should allow the protesters to come into the hotel. Then, according to *Newsday*, "McGovern people ordered the hotel not to permit police to enter and evict the youths; the McGovern men threatened at one point to sue if the hotel allowed police to come in and if an ugly confrontation resulted."

> **It reaffirmed his commitment to be out of Vietnam 90 days after assuming the presidency.**

DINOSAUR FABLES PART 3: THE BEGINNING

PATIENCE-SOON AS HE STEPS IN THE TAR PITS WE'LL RUSH OUT AND WHOMPSHIT OUT OF HIM.....

Art: Bill Narum, August 10, 1971

The SDSers, joined by a contingent of Zippies, a militant split-off from the Yippies, proceeded to jam the hotel lobby, blocking stairways and elevators, and demanding an appearance from McGovern. This particular demonstration, from our perspective, succeeded primarily in alienating delegates, media people, and anyone else who got caught in the mess.

McGovern advisor Fred Dutton and Kathleen Kennedy, daughter of the late Robert Kennedy, spoke to the crowd. At about 8:20 p.m., as convention proceedings were getting underway down the beach, McGovern came downstairs and spoke to the crowd. This move was reported to be made in the face of strong protest from secret service men. McGovern told the demonstrators, "I know you have been here for a long time because there are things you feel very deeply about. I'm here to hear what you want to say. Every person has a right to be heard."

Thorne Dreyer, photo by Robert Hauge. July 27, 1972.

McGovern himself could not be heard very well, however — or seen, for that matter. Half of McGovern's time in the lobby was spent in an attempt to create some order, as everyone was standing and shouting at once and media especially were blocking the view. McGovern responded to questions about the war, an SDS racism petition, marijuana laws, abortion, and the indictment of Vietnam Veterans by a grand jury in Tallahassee. McGovern's statements were consistent with his previously stated positions on the issues, and certainly did not please all the demonstrators. But his apparent earnestness and his willingness to face them won him, I believe, a solid plus.

He ended his visit with the sitters-in by saying, "I can't possibly agree with all of the demands that I know are in the minds of many of you here. You do hold different positions on some of these issues than I do... so let's have an understanding that while we do disagree on some of these questions, there isn't

any disagreement at all about the desperate need to improve communication in this country."

The only other time a significant confrontation was threatened was on the opening night of the convention, July 10. At 6 p.m. about 2,000 people marched from Flamingo Park several blocks to the convention site to attend a rally sponsored by the NWRO. They filled up the street in front of the Convention Hall and heard speeches by Rev. Ralph Abernathy of SCLC, Dr. George Wiley, executive director of NWRO, Gloria Steinhem, Dr. Benjamin Spock, and Inamu Baraka (formerly Leroi Jones).

The Abernathy-led poor people's forces were demanding 750 seats inside, and everyone began chanting "Open the Door!" The rally broke up, however, and most of the demonstrators headed back to the park (or into the hall, if they were delegates or media).

A small group, mostly young white longhairs, broke off and headed back for a hoped-for confrontation. A group of about 100 pushed against a chain link fence and a 50-foot length of fence suddenly collapsed from the weight of the demonstrators.

There was a lightweight tussle, several cops were slightly injured, and a number of young people were maced. It was over quickly, followed by an extended period of milling around by the several hundred who remained. During this time there was heated debate about the tactics involved, with NWRO leaders and many others arguing for a return to the park. Poet Allen Ginsberg came through intoning "Aaah" (not "Ohm") and led a group off; the Krishna Consciousness freaks led others away chanting "Hare Krishna." A fairly persistent group of young whites who were itching to do some trashing were eventually won over by the argument that the poor peoples' groups had organized the rally, had the most to win/lose from the events and that their leadership should be followed.

There were demonstrations outside the hall on other nights — all peaceful. And there was a continual living demonstration at Flamingo Park, where hundreds camped at night and thousands gathered during the day. There were highly visible contingents of poor people, Gay Liberationists, Yippies, zippies, Viet Vets Against the War, Jesus freaks, and SDSers, and they variously pontificated, threw feasts, smoked grass, and went swimming (at times *au naturale*).

Flamingo Park, when it isn't being invaded by such hairy hordes, is a gathering place for the Miami Beach old set. And Miami Beach is literally packed to the gills with senior citizens, many of them retirees from New York and environs. The Youth International Party, in its preconvention publicity, made much of a budding alliance between young freaks and old folk, even staging a symbolic wedding of the old and young. We were somewhat skeptical before arriving, thinking this smacked of PR gimmick. But we were amazed to find that a lot of rapport had indeed been established in this area.

Apparently there had been a great deal of fear on the part of most old people, anticipating an invasion of flea-ridden, obscenity-spouting Neanderthals. And there certainly were some who believed them to be exactly that, once there in the flesh. But much of the fear was broken down, and the Yippies made a conscious effort to relate to the old people in a sensitive and respectful manner. When I was walking the Miami Beach streets, 10 old people beamed at me for every one who sneered.

There was also some fear of confrontation with the Cuban exile community, but little tension materialized there, either.

One of the most striking aspects of this convention was the way in which the "nondelegates" — as they were tagged — were incorporated into the whole scene, rather than being placed in conflict with it. Police Chief Rocky Pomerantz, Mayor Chuck Hall, youth representatives, and the Democratic Party officials worked together to maintain a generally cool scene — though the City Council originally opposed this approach. Chief Pomerantz kept the police in low profile; there was no overreaction at times of potential confrontation, nobody was busted for grass, the cops in general seemed less uptight than any I can remember. It was a far cry from Chicago 1968, to be sure. As for the Party, it exhibited an amazing

ability to incorporate anyone with an axe to grind into the convention process. There were continual demonstrations and caucuses of all sorts in the hotels and meeting halls, all week long. And almost every interest group had at least one spokesman proselytize from the Party podium sometime during the four days of the convention.

One night, delegates raised a massive banner on the convention floor: "Stop Bombing the Dikes." Another night, a large banner proclaimed, "Support the Lettuce Boycott." In fact, if the convention did nothing else, it gave the National Farm Workers Organizing Committee a boost into the national consciousness. Delegation after delegation introduced themselves from the floor with something like, "California, the delegation that is boycotting lettuce, casts its votes . . ." Teddy Kennedy, when he spoke Friday morning prior to McGovern, addressed the delegates as "fellow lettuce boycotters."

One of the more interesting and less noted actions taken by the Convention was a "Special Order of Business" passed Thursday night, which called on the Nixon administration to quash subpoenas issued against members of the Vietnam Veterans Against the War. The resolution was presented by VVAW members and delegate Edwin Selby of Dumont, N.J. It read:

> The issuing of subpoenas to at least 21 leaders of (VVAW), directing them to appear before a federal grand jury in Tallahassee and apparently timed to coincide with this Democratic Convention, represents an attempt by the Nixon Administration to deny to the Veterans their most fundamental constitutional rights to express their dissent and opposition to the War in Southeast Asia.

> The Democratic Party strongly condemns this blatantly political abuse of the grand jury to intimidate and discredit a group whose opposition to the war has been particularly moving and effective.

> We formally call upon the Justice Department to withdraw immediately the

Ten old people beamed at me for every one who sneered.

subpoenas served upon the Veterans so that they may stage their protests at the national political conventions free of harassment.

The resolution passed on a voice vote.

For those of us who were in Chicago in '68, perhaps the biggest moment of the convention was the unseating of Mayor Richard Daley's delegation. Granted, it may have hurt McGovern's chances to win over the Boss as a teammate, but this was one instance where sweet revenge just simply had to be savored. According to Mike Royko, columnist for the *Chicago Daily News*, Daley was warned months ago that this could happen. Daley's response was something like: "Who in the hell is going to throw us out?"

TRB in *The New Republic* describes the delegates as they were "throwing Mayor Daley out on his ear." He goes on, "I confess to a certain satisfaction in this. Four years ago, at the Chicago amphitheater, I went back and redeemed a stick and printed sign from the trashman which proclaimed, 'We love Mayor Daley.' He had hundreds of them printed. His supporters waved them. He made an angry gesture on TV at Abe Ribicoff over the Vietnam peace resolution. He wouldn't let the hippies sleep in the parks and helped to precipitate the riots."

Royko was less enthusiastic. He called Jesse Jackson's speech supporting the challenge a "demaogogic masterpiece ... He poured it on, about how Daley's delegation didn't have enough women, enough Latins, enough blacks, enough young people. Since the building was packed with women, with Latins, with blacks, and with young people, they naturally shared Jackson's indignation. That the delegation led by Jackson and Alderman William S. Singer is short on white ethnics, older people, and working-class people was ignored."

Royko sardonically cut at Jackson, saying that he didn't even vote in the primary. But whatever faults the challenge delegation might have had, there was pleasure in seeing the pompous Boss, who evidently thought he was above the rules, knocked down a notch or two. Daley was so arrogant he refused a compromise that would have seated both dele-

Abbie Hoffman, photo by Robert Hauge. July 27, 1972.

gations, each with half votes. Either he thought he had the votes to win outright, or else he just simply couldn't stomach the idea of sitting down with his political enemies.

There is no question that Daley's active support is important to McGovern, but probably less so than before. Because this is certain to diminish Daley's absolute domination of the Chicago (and Illinois) political scene. Similar is the case of AFL-CIO boss George Meany, who, unlike Daley, refuses even a token endorsement to McGovern. In its Election Special, Sunday, July 23, CBS interviewed a number of lower level union officials and all said they would work for McGovern. The implication — explicit in some cases — was that Meany was losing face and, quite probably, real power, as a result of his refusal to endorse McGovern.

Daley and Meany weren't the only missing faces at this convention. Much less has been made of the fact that a vast majority of the delegates were attending their first convention. Absent, or hovering in the galleries, were many of the old guard of the party. Notably missing, it has been pointed out, was Lyndon Baines Johnson, who sat this one out at the ranch. Lyndon's presidential portrait at the convention was stuck off in a corner, obscure and out of sight of the television cameras. Nobody missed LBJ much this trip. Incidentally, if there is any question concerning Lyndon's love for George McGovern, Irving Wallace, writing for the *Chicago Sun Times*, quotes close Johnson friends saying, "Lyndon absolutely loathes McGovern."

In attendance, but generally ignored, was Sen. Eugene McCarthy. And that was kind of sad. I never was too hot for the Clean Gene trip, but you've gotta give credit where credit is due. McCarthy was the hero of four years past and his contribution to what happened in '72 should not be minimized.

Very much on the scene this time around were Hubert Horatio Humphrey and Edmund Muskie, two Democratic politicians whose stars have quite likely risen as high as they'll ever go and will dip now to just above sea level. Humphrey has "Loser" stamped on his forehead in dayglo paints; Muskie has established a kind of legacy for his chronic indecision. The Muskie joke around Miami hotels was that you don't get into the same elevator with Ed, because he'll spend 10 minutes trying to decide whether to go up or down. By the time Muskie decided to climb

aboard Hubert's "Anybody but McGovern" movement, most of his delegates had jumped ship and were supporting the McGovern forces on the California vote. When he finally bowed out, Humphrey coined a new term:

"I'm not going to be a hangdogger," he promised. No crosses count? Anybody but McGovern, huh? How about a ticket of John Connally and Benedict Arnold?

Absent, or hovering in the galleries, were many of the old guard of the party.

Of course, you should probably ignore all that. After all, we're supposed to be bathing in the cleansing spirit of party unity. You've got to forgive me: I'm new to this whole thing and I still can't tell the difference between spirits and ghosts.

Which reminds me of the Texas delegation. Maybe Muskie has trouble making decisions, but Dolph Briscoe performed the lulu of the century. He cast his vote for George Wallace and George McGovern in the same sentence. That's going out of your way for the sake of unity! What is unclear is how Briscoe managed to get himself in such a pickle. It would have been an easy out to cast his vote (and those of his entourage) for Scoop Jackson; that's what Jackson's campaign was all about, anyway. Briscoe succeeded in alienating everyone, and getting himself in something of a sticky situation concerning the governor's race. As the delegates returned to the Lone Star State, it was clear where the alliances fell. Briscoe had kissed and made up with the Wallaceites.

Let's see, who's the Raza Unida candidate? Ramsey Muniz.

The Texas vote, before the switch, was Wallace, 52; McGovern, 41; Jackson, 32; Chisholm, 4; Muskie, one. In the vice presidential race, those getting a significant number of votes from Texas were Sen. Eagleton, 50; Clay Smothers, 45; and Sissy Farenthold, 22. Smothers was a black Wallace alternate from Dallas who made his own nominating speech. A number of Texas McGovern people did not vote for Sissy because they felt the presidential candidate should have the right to pick his running mate. There was a significant minority at the convention who did not share those sentiments, however, and several persons campaigned vigorously for the post, including former Governor Endicott Peabody of Massachusetts and Senator Mike Gravel of Alaska. Some delegates were disgruntled with the way McGovern picked Eagleton and thrust him on them at the last minute. And the Na tional Women's Political Caucus was still hot under the collar about the South Carolina and abortion votes.

The candidacy that caught fire was that of Frances (Sissy) Farenthold, whose recent race for Governor of Texas, in the words of Gloria Steinem's nominating speech, "put together a coalition of working people, Chicanos, blacks, middle-class people and young people and changed Texas." Sissy's nomination was seconded by Houston School Board member David T. Lopez, black Mississippi civil rights leader Fannie Lou Hamer, and former N.Y. Cong. Lowenstein. She also gained support from Rep. Bella Abzug, John Kenneth Galbraith, and historian Arthur Schlesinger. She got 407.04 votes, second to Eagletons 1,741.81, and came out of the convention with national political clout.

Incidentally, other figures of note receiving at least one vote for VP included Jerry Rubin, Eleanor McGovern, Dr. Spock, Ralph Nader, one each for Fathers Philip and Daniel Berrigan, Martha Mitchell, Archie Bunker, and CBS correspondent Roger Mudd.

The vice-presidential balloting was one of the few times in which some levity was injected into the proceedings. The media has made much of the fact that the sessions were lengthy and dull; of course, zany floor demonstrations, maybe a few fistfights would make for good copy but not necessarily a harmonious, Democratic convention.

There was another period in the proceedings, though, when things would sometimes get interesting. That was during the roll call votes. After being recognized, the state chairman would often introduce his state with some spiffy descriptive phrase like "New Mexico, the Land of Enchantment," or "Florida, the home of Daytona Speedway." Groovy things like that.

But often the chairman would take advantage of the floor time for some political message. By far the most common messages were the previously mentioned affirmations of non-lettuce eating. Oregon even pointed out that it was the state delegation that refused to allow lettuce to be served on its airplane. And then there was, "Massachusetts, the state that calls for an immediate end to the bombing of the dikes in North Vietnam."

Some states sought brownie points: "Montana, the state that cooperates with the Chair by staying in its seats, votes ..."

At one point, into the wee hours, North Carolina voted several (I don't remember the exact number) orders of ham and eggs. And, at 4:14 a.m., the first night — er — morning, we heard, "The Kentucky vote is 36 yes, 10 no, one asleep ..."

If things continue in the directions they've been heading, we figure that by, say, the 1976 Democratic convention, it's going to be pretty strange. Like, we can picture the chairman of the California delegation taking a deep toke off her joint, then intoning into the microphone, "Sensual Chairthing. California, the state that supports the Weatherman Underground and believes that revolutionary armed struggle is imminent, casts the following vote ..." Or, Alabama: "Honorable Chairthang. The Confederate State of Alabama, the state that supports the patriotic vigilante terrorism of the Ku Klux Klan, votes ..." Boggles the imagination.

Anyway, that's the convention scene. It's all over with and the party has its nominee, George McGovern, and everybody's saying, "No way!" Well, not everybody. Some are optimistic. Sylvan Meyer, editor of the *Miami News* says: "It will be easy for friends and opponents alike to underestimate the soft-spoken and relaxed Sen. McGovern ... George McGovern is a formidable, well-organized candidate with a potent platform, backed by a political party whose back-home leaders think they genuinely played a role in his nomination and have a duty to perform for him and themselves. He's no pushover and no Goldwater. Richard Nixon must know that."

In an editorial, *The New York Times* said,

> With the nomination of George S. McGovern, as with the composition and character of the National Convention that chose him, the Democratic party has taken a refreshing turn in American political life . . .
>
> If Senator McGovern is right in stating, as he did in his acceptance speech, that the United States is entering a period of remarkable ferment comparable to that of the eras of Jefferson, Jackson and Roosevelt, this is the new Democratic wave that at the grassroots is sure to have something to say about it. Theirs is the voice primarily of youth, the intellectuals, the disadvantaged, the minorities, but above all of those who in Mr. McGovern's words "are not content with things as they are" — more interested in constructive change than in passive compromise, in pushing forward to new positions than in giving vent to old frustrations...
>
> The ticket chosen last week is — irrespective of polls or soothsayers — a sturdy one ...

Of course, for every *New York Times* editorial like the one above, there are uncountable prophesies of doom. But the McGovern people just smile and keep on truckin' — like they did back when people (like me) said, "No way! He'll never get the nomination."

They say he's got committed grassroots workers throughout the country. They say the party regulars and the labor machinery are already coming around. And they say they're going to register so many new voters that it can be won without the old guard, if necessary; creating a new electorate, they're calling it.

Tom Wicker wrote, in the July 16 *New York Times*:

> The so-called Democratic "split" that sent some labor leaders and party regulars home disgruntled from Miami Beach can hardly be a worse handicap

for Mr. McGovern than the Chicago convention was for Mr. Humphrey in 1968. The 1972 nominee is not carrying an unpopular President on his back, nor defending an indefensible war; he is riding a tide of change that, if not yet irresistible, is clearly rising; he has put together an attractive ticket that promises to pull the Democratic party more or less together by November.

But what about the people who were disillusioned at the convention, who were dismayed by McGovern's moves toward the center, disenchanted with the Pragmatic Politics of the McGovern organization. Aren't they the ones who've carried him this far? Will they drop out, or be less enthusiastic in their support?

Perhaps a hint of an answer came three days after the convention, Monday, July 17, in Miami. The Peoples Party, a New Left-oriented group which has been touting Dr. Benjamin Spock as its presidential candidate, held its southern regional convention and endorsed Sen. George McGovern over Dr. Spock by a 3-1 margin.

> **But what about the people who were disillusioned at the convention?**

On the CBS Election Special Sunday, there was an interview with a young man who was identified as the only paid McGovern worker in Atlanta at this time. His name is Howard Romaine, and the last I knew, he was working for *The Great Speckled Bird*, Atlanta's underground paper.

I ran into Gregorio Salazar at Big City News the other night. Greg is the former fiery spokesman for the leftist Mexican American Youth Organization (MAYO) and ran for the school board last year. We discussed the convention; Greg said that he and Yolanda and Walter Birdwell, also former MAYO leaders, were generally impressed with McGovern and might drop by campaign headquarters and "lick some envelopes" some time.

The other night I was talking with one of the leaders of the Texas McGovern delegation. She was bemoaning having to vote against her conscience at the convention, but is resolved to the Pragmatic Politics situation, and is optimistic about the chances here. "Of course, once we get McGovern elected," she said "we might have to get ourselves involved in a Dump McGovern movement." Who knows?"

As for myself, I don't quite understand all the freaking out. I basically don't have any faith in American politicians. They have to make compromises; they have to sell pieces of their soul in order to be electable. That's the name of the game; it's basically corrupt and corrupting. George McGovern is a slick politician, but I think he's more honest than most. He's got to be clever, getting himself elected and maintaining as a liberal in a conservative state.

I think people should work within the electoral political arena at this time. Therein lies much power to bring about change, and there certainly are changes that need to be made, and quick, if we are to survive on this planet. We just shouldn't lose our perspective, for power also lies outside the political arena, on the streets and in the community. It is the movement for social change in this country that put McGovern in the seat and that has changed the face of the Democratic Party.

The right of women to control their own bodies will not be won in the Democratic party, though it might someday be implemented through that vehicle. Likewise, the antiquated sex and drug laws that oppress us. When the movement is strong enough, when enough people have been reached, those issues will be in the Democratic Party platform, and they will be winning issues.

In the meantime, I'm supporting George McGovern, not because he or his platform are the embodiment of my beliefs, but because I think Richard Nixon is a very dangerous man and needs to be rooted out, and quick. And because I think a McGovern administration would be qualitatively different; he'd get us out of Vietnam and would, I believe, be reluctant to engage in other such adventures; he would give working people a better deal; he'd ease repression and give us more room to operate, to breathe; he'd be less in the employ of big business (though certainly not free of its corrupting influence).

And he's no Messiah (I never could go for the `); he's low key and when he's confused about an issue, he doesn't come on like he's got it all together.

Which gets us back to that opening question: is this progress or cooptation. And the answer is, both. If you get bought into it, you're lost. If you stay outside and ignore it, you're ineffectual.

Support George McGovern, and any other progressive candidates you can find. But keep a cool head. At least, that's my intention.

End of pontification section.

End of article. -30-

Ad: November 11, 1971.

The Wichita Street gang. Staff photo by Bill Metzler, June 6, 1970.

Space City!
Reflections

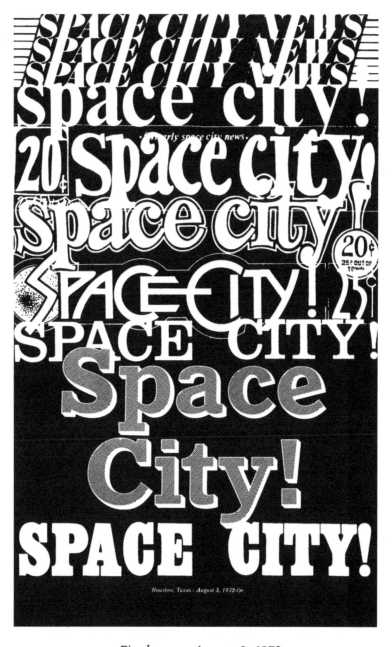

Final cover: August 3, 1972.

The House Next Door

Jeff Nightbyrd • August 3, 1972

MIAMI BEACH — It wasn't much of a house. Just one of those fading, paint-peeling, Montrose wooden affairs which rested next door to ours. There was a space underneath the front for the dogs to settle in the hot afternoon, a couple of quart Jax bottles as companions. The shrubs around it hadn't been trimmed in several years, and they grew all helter-skelter, providing good hiding places for insects and birds. Inside there was a faint smell of cat piss. No matter how hard the floor was scrubbed with miracle cleansers, the faint cat piss odor endured — a relic, I suppose, of some artist's or hippie's pet two or three dwellers removed.

For a while, Hayseed slept on a waterbed surrounded by psychedelic head comix in the front room. You could always find him there any time up till noon. Redhaired Marie, who had to be out every morning by eight for work, slept in back. Sometimes in the quiet of the late night, when I lay restless blue, or with loneliness too heavy in my head, I would creep across the yard and knock on her screen. Marie would wake up groggily and I'd crawl through the window. We'd sleep together close and the existential anxiety would slip away till another day.

It wasn't much of a house. But one day Texas Art Supply which owned the land, bulldozed it down, leaving a huge flat scar. We had heard it was coming and called several times, but we always got a businessman, instead of an artist, who told us neighborhoods had to give way to parking lots and progress. For three days Thorne had nightmares that they were going to cut down the huge shade tree in the front yard, but the bulldozer only wounded it a couple of times. Afterwards, the gray-haired lady across the street who was even older than the tree, would stand on her lawn, staring at the gouged earth and shaking her head warily.

Not much of a story. It's happening all over the Montrose. Businessmen tearing down houses, pouring cement, greedy for money and calling it progress.

They tell me in the year 2000 Houston is going to be larger than New York City. I hope not. All this thoughtless progress leads to disaster. In the Northeast, the electricity fails, the subways break down underground, the streets are filthy with unpicked-up garbage, the noise and air pollution stages causing constant edginess, and many days you can't breathe the air. New Yorkers

joke that they don't trust breathing air they can't see. It's gallows humor.

Unplanned growth is a cancer. It may create profits, but it destroys the goodness in a place to live. The mentality of the powerful in Houston is more skyscrapers instead of trees, freeways and cars instead of buses and bicycles, more commodities, more consumerism. The connections Texans once had with the land are forgotten in a mad mindless rush for more and more. It's the mentality of being Number One. It's a view which sees life's worth in quantity rather than quality.

The alternative community is at a stage of resistance, because in Houston, unlike New York, the old business mentality is operating in a boomtown. When you get some distance away, it's clear that apathy prevails because individuals have a sense of powerlessness. Hip culture smells of defeat, and remains in the beatnik withdrawal of the '50s rather than the activist engagement of the '60s. *Space City!* and other things failed because too many people laid back beatnik-style while wishing them luck.

> **The connections Texans once had with the land are forgotten.**

Luck doesn't change things. Building a strong community and culture does. Farenthold's victory in Houston proved that there is a basis for a coalition of forces for change. But electoral politics doesn't build for the future; it's too tied to an individual and the time limits of the campaign. People who are worried by *Space City!*'s demise should work for everything from bikeways and food co-ops to anti-war actions and music at Liberty Hall. It's all related.

Until people realize that there's a better future in getting together, rather than in downers and escapism, then more cars will clog the streets, the hot air will get harder to breathe, people will feel more isolated, and businesses like Texas Art Supply will tear down the Montrose to build plastic apartment houses and parking lots.

I admit it wasn't much of a house next door, and it did smell of cat piss, but it represented life.

[Jeff Nightbyrd is organizing for the Youth International Party in Miami Beach. In a previous incarnation, he was known as Jeff Shero, did the late nite show on Pacifica and contributed to Space City! *Jeff, Dennis and Judy Fitzgerald, and Thorne Dreyer, were all founders of* The Rag *in Austin and Jeff went on to start* Rat *in New York.]*

Aaahhh!!!

Thorne Dreyer • August 3, 1972

Well, I must say this is pretty weird. After three years of publishing this rag, riding out its birth traumas, sitting up nights with its tangents, muddling through the heavy changes, we've decided to blow it all off. I mean, this is it. We're unabashedly, unashamedly, *folding*.

Last week, when we said this would be our final number, we weren't bluffing, we weren't putting you on. We weren't secretly praying for some last-minute low-flying angel to drop a bundle of manna (or even Peking gold) in our laps. We had no illusion of pulling it out in the bottom of the ninth.

In fact, the decision was sort of uplifting, like finally scratching that elusive itch. The catharsis of decisive action: Aaaahh! We had been feeling it in our guts and it added up in our heads: a nice clean act of *hari-kiri* seemed in order.

And we know two things for sure already. The coroner hasn't even gotten here and the preliminary autopsy's already in. One: we made one hell of a mark on this city. Two: we failed to consolidate our fleeting victories into anything that could last.

There are articles on these pages, written by staffers and former staffers and by those who have watched us with at least slightly detached eyes. They grasp at straws, pulling tentative explanations out of the ether; perhaps you, "dear reader" — whoever you might be — have something to add. Maybe you, in fact, have the piece of the puzzle that's missing; the perspective that makes it all come clear. Probably not, though...

Anyway, we want to make some acknowledgments now. And you, our readers and supporters, certainly come first. Those of you who have followed us from the beginning, or through any period of our schizophrenic existence. (Existential dilemma: does a newspaper exist if no one reads it? If we don't communicate, or at the very least, infuriate, we make no reflection in the mirror.)

We want to pay special tribute to the people who encouraged us, gave us financial aid and spiritual guidance during the early days and at times of cri-sis. Especially Francis Yeager, to whom we owe lots of money and lots more gratitude. And to Benj and Effie Feld, who gathered together friends willing to part with their money, and who helped us pull together our Collective head, when we faced a crisis in February 1971.

Thanks to the nearly 250 people who worked for no pay on this newspaper.

And to so many others. To Phil Ochs (who came here and did a benefit for us) and Don Sanders and all the other musicians and artists who came through in the pinch. To Richard Ames and Maggie Dreyer (It's alright, Ma. I'm only dying.) and Jeanne Gitlin, our far-out typesetter and friend. To Ernest Norris and the folks at the *Forward Times*. To Texan Gilbert Shelton, whose Furry Freak Brothers have found a place in the hearts of all. And to our chief artists through the months — Kerry Fitzgerald and Bill Narum — who worked for love and who could make people laugh or gasp, even when our words lacked clout.

To Bobby Eakin, who has been with us since almost the beginning, but whose bout with hepatitis has separated him from our final days. And to the folks we've dealt with in the community, people like Mike Condray, Lynda Herrera, and Ryan Trimble of Liberty Hall (and the Family Hand); Lloyd Sandel and Jerry Sebesta of Surfhouse; Rick Williams of the General Store; Forrest and Raymond, the Hobbit Hole brothers; Phil Oesterman of Fondren Street Theater; Mike Harvey and Bill Metzler of Sunshine Collage and Of Our Own; Saundra and Chester Wrye of Tao Whole Foods.

To almost everyone at Pacifica, and lots of friends at KAUM and KLOL. To the many dedicated people who have shaped such community organizations as Gay Liberation, MAYO, Switchboard, the Food Co-op, with whom we have worked so closely. And so many other friends whom we overlook or have no room here to mention.

And to everybody in the composite staff box on page 30 — the nearly 250 people who worked for no pay, on this newspaper. Though many are gone, and some would certainly disown us now, and we would disown some, their dreams, their craziness, their commitment, and their ego trips, have been the shaping force on this newspaper.

To our subscribers, we apologize that we are unable to honor the remainder of your subs. We do promise you one thing, though: we won't give out our sub lists to anyone, and, if any of us get another publication going, it'll be coming your way. We would also like to note that a very large percentage of our new subscribers of late have been residents of America's prisons — perhaps we've been getting 10 prisoner subs a week. If anything has been an up in these rather bleak days, it's been the knowledge that prisoners all over this country have been reading our words, and passing the paper on to their brothers and sisters. We are truly sorry they will receive *Space City!* no more.

So, as Pancho Villa says, in the page 31 drawing Kerry sent from San Francisco as his farewell message: "Til we meet again..."

Soon, we hope. -30-

Art. Gilbert Shelton, October 28, 1969.

Space City! Rap No. 2:
How We Started • What We Did • Why We're Folding

Victoria Smith • August 3, 1972

The last few weeks have been some of the busiest I can recall at *Space City!* Seems it's a lot of work, shutting down a newspaper. Whatever impulses we've felt towards sentimentality or regret have been extremely short-lived: we're too busy to look back, and besides the *Space City!* Collective had made up its sometimes-collective mind weeks ago, and we've stuck by that decision.

In case you haven't guessed by now, *Space City!*, at the ripe old age of three and a half years, is folding. This is the last issue. I mean the last, no second thoughts, no surprise resurrections. We're not turning over the name to anyone, we're not "selling out," and wouldn't, even if we had a prospective buyer.

Since we announced our decision last week, people have been calling, curious and sympathetic. They often say things like, "Well, it's too bad you couldn't have kept on going," but I'm always tempted to say, "Why, not at all." In fact, folding seems like the single best idea we've had all summer. We've gone about as far as we logically can with this project. We've wanted to do more with it, to do everything a little better, but, for many reasons, that wasn't possible, and stopping seems an immensely wise move at this point.

For one thing, each of the *Space City!* regular staff members is now free to pursue new projects, some of which may be journalistic. And, there are other reasons why our decision, we think, is the correct one, a voluntary decision reached independent of pressure from any external forces.

But, if you're interested to know why we're folding now, you have to understand why we started in the first place, and what happened after we did. So, a little background.

Space City! (then *Space City News*, altered about

> ### It's a lot of work shutting down a newspaper.

a year later because a UFO newsletter already had registered our original choice of names) published its first issue June 5, 1969. That issue, and the ones that followed every other week after that, were made possible by about $1,000 in reluctant contributions, the bounty of a few generous souls like Francis Yeager, our first landlord, a lot of revolutionary zeal and a collective of six people (Cam Duncan, Susan Mithun Duncan, Judy Fitzgerald, Dennis Fitzgerald, Thorne Dreyer and me, Victoria Smith).

Although it really wasn't so long ago, things were very different in the summer of 1969. Or so it seems to me: I suppose there are those who imagine that things are quite the same, but my life, and the lives of many around me, have gone through substantial changes in those three years.

In 1969, there was such a thing as a "movement"; there was a burgeoning counterculture that seemed at times almost on the verge of "taking over," there was such a word as "revolution," and the Black Panther Party was going to lead it. It is hard to say now whether the movement and all that was really as influential and consuming as it seemed at the time, because for people like us it was simply Life. Our radicalism grew not out of some peculiar notion of stylish rebellion, but out of a sense of frustration and anger at the real economic and social injustices in the world.

Ad: October 17, 1970.

(I have been thinking quite a bit lately about the old New Left, neo-Marxist movement, and I believe that it is impossible for me to communicate to "outsiders" what it really was all about, at least not in these few pages. It was a thoroughly exclusive, intimate experience, something beyond political rhetoric and demonstrations, or even lifestyle.)

At any rate, because we were radicals, perceiving the world in a certain way, and because we believed both in community and communication, and because there wasn't one already, we started an "underground" newspaper in Houston, Texas. Virgin territory for almost any alternative institution. They told us it couldn't be done. We, of course, did it. Never once did we think it couldn't be done, and, as Dennis Fitzgerald suggests elsewhere in this issue, it's a damn good thing we didn't stop to think about it, because if we had accessed the situation in Houston at that time realistically, we'd all probably have split for the four corners of the world.

Houston was a very quiet, but very uptight, place that year. I guess it always had been. The city seemed to be victim of wildly uneven growth patterns: economically, things were good, developing rapidly; but socially, culturally, the city was stagnant and backward. I don't mean simply that there wasn't a "movement" in Houston at that time, although that was noticeably lacking: it was just everything, the whole atmosphere, the arts, the Old South mentality, the way everything was so spread out and disconnected — both literally and figuratively.

Things were just starting to loosen up when *Space City!* first began publishing. Perhaps the first sign of life, such as it was, was the Klan — which seemed to generate spontaneously, armed with the sole purpose of making life and work difficult and dangerous for us — as soon as we were into our fourth issue. Firebombs, concussion bombs, stink bombs (and later on, bullets, pipe bombs, and dynamite, but by that time the Klan didn't bother us much because we were shooting back) plagued us and our friends for months. The legally-endowed authorities, of course, could not and would not protect us.

Much was made of the Klan attacks on *Space City!* and fellow travelers, but actually that aspect of our early existence wasn't nearly as important as the positive things we felt we were helping to accomplish. Since we considered ourselves activists as well as

journalists, we were not content merely to put out a newspaper on a biweekly basis. We had to organize, too.

Out of *Space City!*'s office and/or staff over the years have come such demi-institutions as the high school movement, high school "underground" newspapers, the Food Co-op, Of Our Own, Switchboard, the Red Coyote Tribe, women's liberation consciousness and organizations. (You may never have heard of some of these; they were rather short-lived, but important nonetheless.) We offered draft counseling services (and occasionally inexpert counseling about everything from drugs to abortions, because kids would call us all the time, asking impossible questions); we organized rallies, marches, and demonstrations. (One of our finest, and bloodiest — the two being somewhat synonymous for us at the time — was the colorful Agnew demonstration, so called because the object of the protest was Spiro T. himself, speaking at the Astroworld Hotel in January of 1971. It was replete with guerrilla theater and a confrontation with the cops.)

Space City! also gave a voice to certain radical and revolutionary organizations, perhaps, except for Pacifica, their only media voice: the Mexican-American Youth Organization (MAYO), People's Party II, the Welfare Rights Organization, Gay Liberation. *Space City!* the Underground Newspaper peaked in the summer of 1970, in many ways. Circulation was the highest it has ever been.

Our coverage of the Carl Hampton murder in July of 1970, made us even more controversial than before. (The actual event made us more serious.) The Klan had stopped fiddling around with kid stuff like concussion bombs and was shooting at us by night. We shot back, and for a while it looked as though "armed struggle" might break out any minute. (We had a lot at stake that summer. The Switchboard kids were working out of our offices on Wichita and the place was constantly overflowing with freaks of all descriptions. They'd hang out on the porch at night, and we just knew one of them was going to get shot. What a life!)

The whole movement, from the angry youngsters beating down the doors at rip-off rock concerts to the serious Marxists working to rebuild People's Party after Carl's death, was going hot and heavy. There was action, motion, energy. People bought guns the way

> ## The Klan had stopped fiddling around with kid stuff like concussion bombs.

Art: Gilbert Shelton, January 30,1971.

they buy dope now. (Well some of us bought a lot of dope too, back then.) *Space City!* ran a lot of articles about guns, and revolution, and the Third World.

Whenever we saw a flame, the first thing we'd think about was how best to fan it. But *Space City!* was never able to set the world (or the city) on fire. Maybe there was an old wet blanket lying around somewhere that we didn't know about, but we realized that the times were changing, after the much-hyped Red Coyote Tribe (and its offspring, the Vietnam Action Proj-

ect) failed to catch hold. The Red Coyote Tribe was a sort of umbrella organization, something of a cross between Yippie and the White Panther Party, although very loosely organized, and we had long meetings and volleyball games and picnics and rock concerts and we howled the Red Coyote howl a lot, but the whole thing fizzled. And then all those people got their heads bashed in by city police at the Astroworld Hotel (which was very exciting, but hardly productive), and we decided that since the times were changing, it was time we changed, too. Frankly, we were just getting bored with the old "off the pig" song-and-dance.

And, we were not alone in this sudden change in attitudes. The underground press all across the country, once so central to the youth movement, was losing credibility (and money, what little there was), fast. Some newspapers folded, some changed like *Space City!*, others just kept on keeping on.

So, we took a long break. That was February and March of 1971. We did some fundraising and a little promotion. We reorganized, reconsidered, rethought the whole notion of an "underground" newspaper. We wanted to be more responsive, more honest, more thorough as journalists. We wanted to look hard at injustice in our own city, rather than preaching all the time about the distant Third World. We didn't want to be considered a freaky, shrill underground paper anymore. We made

We wanted to be more responsive, more honest, more thorough.

a lot of changes, and when we made our second debut on April 6, 1971, *Space City!* (by now weekly) was quite a different publication. A cleaner format, cleaner language, a cleaner image in general.

Everything was going great until we all of a sudden went broke. Our original bookkeeper/controller/business manager, Judy Fitzgerald, had left with her husband for San Francisco. Judy had always watched the money like a hawk, but after she left no one really paid all that much attention (we were all such artists, you know). We were putting out these beautiful, colorful, 32-page newspapers, and then, bang, within a week we had almost folded. We couldn't pay our bills, so telephone and electricity services were cut off. The Wichita St. office, which had once been sort of a community center and a real place of business, was almost deserted. How can you put out a newspaper without a telephone?

Ad: June 5, 1969.

We had a little collective staff shakedown, and then began to try to pick up the pieces. It's December of 1971. We are broke, deeply in debt. We have no financial management. In a fit of desperation, we ask Bill McElrath to take over the business end of the newspaper. For no pay. He agrees to help.

Bill's management keeps us afloat but does little to cut into that nagging debt. We cut back on production. No more color, no more 32-page issues, no more $25 a week salaries unless absolutely necessary.

Now, about this time, *Space City!* must have looked rather strange to many of you. You couldn't reach us anywhere, unless you were one of the privileged few who had some staff member's unlisted number. You never saw us, because we spent so little time at the office. Yet every week this newspaper would be on the streets, in newsstands, in your mailbox. Mysteriously. How did we do it? I'm not sure, but it wasn't easy.

The contents of the paper must have appeared rather odd, too. I'm certain we looked, even then, back in January and February of 1972, like a newspaper on the verge of folding, the way we'd change format and editorial leanings every week. We were, in fact, a little confused. Many of us were more than a little overworked. Tensions grew, tempers flared. (Money may corrupt, but lack of it seems to make people behave in angry, detestable ways. Lack of money corrupts, too.)

Political and aesthetic cleavages began to develop, seemingly out of nothing. Mighty egos battered against each other. A major split developed, which culminated in the *Space City!* Collective's firing of McElrath. McElrath and some friends started this other paper called, for some reason not readily discernible, *Mockingbird*, and *Space City!* kept on trucking. (Well, actually we had forgotten how to truck, we'd been limping for so long, and the split made the limp all that much worse.)

We understand now that *Mockingbird* has suffered a split of its own in recent weeks. McElrath, we hear, maintains control of *Mockingbird* and some of his former staff members are planning to start yet another newspaper. Interesting.

Well, we still had our big debt. But there were far more people flocking around *Space City!* at that time, wanting to help, than I can ever remember. But, despite all the good people and well-wishers, despite the few encouraging signs, it became quite apparent after a while that it just wasn't going to fly. Our organization was not tight enough, our energy and morale were hopelessly low. Money was scarce, as usual.

But more than that, as we said in our statement last week, we had just reached the limit. We had tried to make the changes we thought "necessary in order to reach a broader audience," but we only made the changes editorially. The basic change still hadn't happened, and by the time we realized that, it was too late. The structure of our operation, that poor, frail, low-budget, underground newspaper structure, was still there, trying valiantly to sustain all the wild dreams and nonsequiturial tangents that have characterized *Space City!*'s last weeks. It was like we had this house of cards, and every time we'd get all the cards in place, one would fall and then the whole paper edifice would almost collapse. A few cards would remain standing, and we'd start stacking them up again. It was thoroughly frustrating.

So, who knows what the future may hold?

But, as we keep telling ourselves, we have learned a lot in these three years — I think that we know at least what not to do — and well, you know, publishing is something that kind of gets under your skin or in your blood — it's like a benign if chronic disease.

So, who knows what the future may hold? Oh, you may hear some rumors here and there, like *Space City!* people are starting a new newspaper next month, or *Space City!* people are selling the name to Howard Hughes, or *Space City!* people are going to start writing for the UFO newsletter. But, in fact, our future plans are vague and unsubstantive.

So, there's the history, incomplete as it may be. (We've told that story so many times, to all sorts of different people, that we all practically have it memorized, and the only fun in re-telling it is thinking up slightly different ways to say things. Judy and I used to call that particular story "*Space City!* Rap No. 2," although I don't recall what No. 1 was.)

To the faithful among you, the readers who will miss us, who have stuck by us through hard times and cheered us on in good, that's the breaks. We're certainly not blaming you for any of our problems, but we do think it fitting that you should be warned: community institutions, like Pacifica radio, like Inlet, need your support, financial and otherwise. *Space City!*'s gone, but there are others like us still around, if you only take a look. Let them know you care.

I realize that it's a cliche in itself to end an article like this with some famous quote, but so what's wrong with a good old cliche once in a while? Anyway, paraphrase Joe Hill: Don't mourn for *Space City!*, organize. Organize what? Your guess is as good as mine, but all I know is that this city could use some good counterinstitutional organizations. Grow your own. -30-

Not Folding, Just Moving On...

Dennis Fitzgerald • August 3, 1972

SAN FRANCISCO — Upon close inspection, "Buy 'em for a dime, sell 'em for a quarter" does not have that certain ring of enduring greatness such as embues "I lift my lamp beside the golden door" or "Sic semper tyrannis." Nevertheless, there it sits, burned into my brain alongside the most heroic, the most pithy, the most cherished phrases of Western civilization. And though the thought sends a nervous shudder down my anti-capitalist spine, I have to admit: That's my kind of poetry.

Lamp lifting being an honorable profession since Diogenes, and tyrants, as always deserving their comeuppance, there was but one clarion call with the strength to move hoards of hungry hippies to the street

> **I am of very mixed emotions about that last big deadline in the sky.**

corners and freeway onramps of Houston. And that, friends, is the test of great literature.

Before going any further here, I really ought to level with you and admit that this is my fourth draft of this thing. I'm having a terrible time. First, I wrote down all these humorous anecdotes, but that seemed too frivolous. Then I gave it the thoughtful political analysis treatment, but that seemed too heavy. Finally, I wandered off into a mood of "Ah, but those were the years," but that seemed too "Ah, but those were the years." Frankly, I'm becoming very confused about just exactly how you stop a newspaper.

You see, *Space City!*, I am of very mixed emotions about that last big deadline in the sky. In one sense I'm glad to see you go like this: a nice, clean, self-inflicted zappo to the jugular. Neat. All colors flying. And damn the mainsail. None of that embarrassing lingering on, having to face the knowing smiles, the half-muffled sniggers at birthday parties and other social occasions.

But then I think, is it really over? Is this it? The end, nothing more, kersplat, fribble, — 30 —? Oh, it can't be. Who's going to feed that army of seven million roaches living in the kitchen? Who's going to curse the air conditioner for being a worthless noisemaker? Who's going to assure that the right size of liner tape is never in the box, and that the graphics file will continue to defy organization? There are some things which can't be simply folded up and forgotten.

It's a dilemma.

One thing I think I won't do is zip up my serious face and tell you how important *Space City!* has been for Houston. Except that it has been far more than the six people sitting in a living room on Decatur Street three and a half years ago could have reasonably expected. Not that they were especially reasonable folks, but then if they had been, none of this would ever have happened. A minute of grateful silence for the continued existence of people who don't know any better.

Do you know what's nice about those people who don't know any better? (You don't? Well then. I'll tell you.) So many of them just seem incapable of figuring out how hopeless everything is. Right at the point where it ought to be obvious that they've completely exhausted

Art: Gilbert Shelton, January 13, 1972.

all the possibilities in what they're doing, they just start doing something else crazy, all the time talking about free this and free that. Actually, it's annoying the way they don't give up, and if I were in some position of importance, I think I'd do something about them. Already they've simply ruined one perfectly good political party.

You see how hard it is to stick to the point in this thing? Reminds me of one day after a particularly horrendous all-night layout session. A dozen of us were lying exhausted among piles of garbage, a scene fully equal to Art Linkletter's best fantasy, when in strode a uniformed and painfully polite deliveryman with a box of Hostess Twinkies. Seems that one of us in a forgotten moment of consumer advocacy had written a letter complaining about inadequate cream fillings. No cause too small for the people's champion. (I can't remember now what it was that reminded me of that.)

But back to the mainstream of this article. You may recall our mentioning that *Space City!* is folding. Actually, it's nothing like that. Just moving on, that's all. If you don't keep moving you're never gonna find it because you've got it in you all the time. That's a little poesy for the more spiritually inclined among you. Jesus, but some of you people write terrible poetry.

We used to get so much awful poetry, all rhyming and everything, with cadence and strophe and all that stuff. Which is nothing against H.W. Longfellow. "Let the dead past bury its dead," like he used to say.

There, I'll bet I've rubbed somebody wrong when all I wanted to do was praise Caesar, as it were. Maybe I should just leave it at saying that there's going to be a big hole where *Space City!* used to be. But there are so many more beginnings here than there were three years ago, that I suspect somehow Houston will muddle through.

If I were going to express regrets, my biggest one would be that the administration of Welch and Short is outlasting *Space City!* But if there's anything certain at this point, it must be that history has already decided the fate of that breed of men.

Of course, it can't do any harm that we continue giving history a little nudge in the right direction. In the vernacular, that we keep on truckin', with all the love and joy and patience that's seen us along this far, and with that certain kind of boogie that's gonna carry us right on through. If you can dig it.

Seems like a good night to get a little high, pull down all old issues, and catch up on the last three years.

[*Dennis Fitzgerald was a founding member of the* Space City! *Collective. A year ago he and Judy split for the more sensual pleasures of the San Francisco Bay. Their departure was only geographical; they have remained with us in spirit, though they do fuss when we forget to write.*] -30-

In Praise of Space City!: The Paper Revolutionaries

Space City! Staff • August 3, 1972

Tuesday afternoon we went to the post office to pick up the mail. It was one errand among many, all tied to the eminent death of this newspaper: picking up articles discussing our demise, coaxing neighborhood merchants to advertise in the final number, things like that.

So, it seemed kind of ironic when, among the stack of press releases, underground newspapers, and unklassified ads, we noted a review copy of a new book, sent our way by Simon and Schuster publishers. The book, called *The Paper Revolutionaries: The Rise of the Underground Press*, contains some very kind words about *Space City!* We remembered when the author, Laurence Leamer, came through town, maybe a year and a half ago, during better times. We liked

him, and he seemed impressed with what we were doing.

So, as we depart from the scene, we reprint a few of his words as a bit of history:

> To find papers that manage to satisfy both political and cultural radicals, one must travel to the backwaters of American radical life — to nowhere Alabama, Mississippi, or even Houston, America's sixth-largest and possibly fastest growing city. In less than a decade, Houston has shot up out of its Texas provincialism to become a sophisticated center of industry, space and medicine. Houston's middle class

has gone through this change with little of that psychic disintegration familiar in other cities, and these good citizens fairly bubble with a Junior Chamber of Commerce pride. There is another Houston though — a world of black, Chicano and poor-white ghettos; of business and political leaders manipulating Houston's future like a Monopoly game; of drugs and ennui in the suburbs; of hippies and assorted longhairs building lives within the confines of the city limits. This is the Houston that *Space City!* has covered since June 1969 ...

Space City! is unabashedly radical. Among its founders are Dennis and Judy Fitzgerald and Thorne Dreyer, native Houstonians who cut their teeth beginning Austin's *Rag*. The *Space City!* layout pays obligatory obeisance to McLuhanism, but the paper remains highly print-oriented. There is a solid intelligence to the reviews and cultural articles, an intelligence that doesn't pose as brilliance, draping itself with literary flourishes or obtuseness. It is a radical journalism grounded in fact. There have been major muckraking and numerous articles challenging the conventional wisdom, either above or underground. ...

Space City! has had a special importance in Houston since the city is a sprawled-out, Texas version of Los An-

The Paper Revolutionaries
THE RISE OF THE UNDERGROUND PRESS

$2.95

By Laurence Leamer

> **'Space City! is unquestionably one of the strongest underground papers in America.'**

geles. The paper holds the radical community together. To do this it avoids the hairsplitting ideological politics of other prominent radical forces ...

Leamer describes the reorganizational break from mid-February to early April 1971, reprinting the Letter from the Collective we ran upon return. He then comments: "There was nothing apocalyptic about the changes but they were enough to revitalize the paper and the staff collective and to make *Space City!* unquestionably one of the strongest underground papers in America."

It's weird to read those words while working on our final issue. Maybe Larry Learner should drop back through and do a follow-up; we could all use a little help putting this whole experience into perspective. -30-

Art: Gilbert Shelton. March 9, 1972.

Art: Rick Sharp, October 3, 1970.

Cast, in Order of Appearance:

Space City! Staff Box • August 3, 1972

Names appearing in *Space City!* staff box (other than Collective) from June 1969 to August 1972.

Jane Manning	Carol Courtney	Ellen Blumenthal	Bobby Eakin
Carolyn Kendrick	David Courtney	Judy Weiser	Dwayne Miller
Bob Northcott	Bill Casper	David Williams	Star Gibson
Bidy Taylor Lomax	Sherwood Bishop	George Banks	Diane LaGuarta
John Lomax	Nancy Sweeney	Bingham Murrah	Mike Heinrichs
Andy Prindall	Tracy Oates	Bill Murrah	Terry Balch
Doug Bernhardt	Bartee Haile	Dewitt Standard	Suzi Somppi
Gavan Duffy	Bryan Baker	Sharon Lynn	Jeff Shero
Danny Schacht	Bill Metzler	Lee Andrews	Kelly Erin Fitzgerald
Raymond Ellington	Barry Lesch	Brian Grant	Michele Toth
Tom James	Steve Wittmarsh	Puppy Cat	Jean Croce
John Ferguson	Lisa Johnson	Skippy	Nancy Simpson
Kerry Fitzgerald	John Dunham	Vince Johnson	Marigold Arnold
Mike Bishop	Hugh Grady	George Bradley	Suzi LeBlanc
Bob Stogsdill	Sue Grady	Delores Ray Frenzel	Roger Elkin
Ham	Shagnasty	Lyn Eubanks	David Ross
Gary Chason	Hunt Hawkins	Vicky Radowsky	Fred Higdon
Randy Chapman	Mike Love	Doug Friendenberg	Bill Knight
Melinda Chapman	Gerri Pressnall	Marjon Rowland	Bill Narum
Stuart Gitlin	Bill Katzenberg	Pete Rowland	Ron Young
Karen Kaser Casper	Bobby Minkoff	Julie Mendes	Marie Blazek
Greg Salazar	Alex Rodriguez	Brand	Juliette Brown
Lyman Padde	Kay Bennett	George Kimmels	Danny Sepulvado
Elsie Padde	Ron Jarvis	John Schaller	Jeff Jones
Guy Mendez	Pooneil	Kathleen Webster	Karen Northcott
Larry Gorman	Whiskers	Larry James	Tom Hylden
Hal Owens	Pearl Chason	Susie James	Steve Welzer
Jeff Shapiro	Jeanne Gitlin	Chris Debremaecker	Vicki Gladson
Don Rhodes	Susan Simms	Charles Parmaley	Carter Beasley
Trudy Minkoff	Galapoochie	Lillian Ceruana	Connie Mendez
Darlene Burlson	Ron Dornbusch	Greg Peters	Ernie Shawver
Carol Rhodes	Bill Corbin	Doyle Niemann	Rick Price
Jody Batemen	David Fuqua	Pat Cuney	Russ Noland
Ron Gregory	Peggy Sullivan	Margaret Hortenstein	Crystal Krietzer
John Edson	Don Trepanier	Scribner	Gwenn Spriggs
Gary Thiher	Dave McQueen	Paul Scribner	John Persons
Judy Hansen	Patricia Smith	Terry Gunesch	Molly Bing
Ron Murfkin	Tough Louie	Doug Gunesch	Noelle Kanady
Larry Waterhouse	Stubble	Walter Birdwell	Mark Wilson
Richard Atwater	Elizabeth Marsh	John York	Jim Dennison
Tony Grant	Craig Campbell	Lee Baum	Dennis Kling
Wolfgang von Padde	Julie Duke	Jim Shannon	Becky Noland
Dan McCauslin	Harrell Graham	R Hartman	Wallace Author
Mike Zee	Alice Embree	Rick Sharp	John Hale
Brian Murphy	Susan Tillman	Wesley Frenzel	Mickey Montana
Melissa Young	Chris Tebow	Melody Frenzel	Eddie Reed

Beth Reed
Jerry Sebesta
Saundra Wrye
Lloyd Sandal
Ralf Williams
Trey Wilson
John Goodwin
Bill McElrath
Burnet McElrath
John Carroll
John Sayer
Clarence Kemp
Jane Striss
Joel Tammariello
Rick Fine
Tino Ochletree
Susan Montgomery
David Crossley
Paul Samberg
Bill Dennig
Richard Hoover
Zengi

Alex Stern
Henry Fernandez
Ann Jorjorian
Joel Barna
Scout Schacht
Robert Finlay
Benny Lauve
Jamie Yeager
Ebenezer Cooke
Mark Johnson
Patricia Gruben
Dave Benson
Jamie Vaughan
Peggy Murphy
Jane Polaski
Roger Black
Giles Corey
Scoop Sweeney
Tary Owens
Steven Moffitt
Barbara Duff
Martin Chapman

Sara Pendleton
Elizabeth Campbell
Tom Flowers
Gary Brant
Diane Morin
Lynn Dennison
Al Morin
Rick Johnson

Original Collective
Judy Fitzgerald
Dennis Fitzgerald
Victoria Smith
Thorne Dreyer
Susan Mithun Duncan
Cam Duncan

Additions
Sherwood Bishop
Bryan Baker
Richard Atwater
Delores Ray Frenzel

Doyle Niemann
Star Gibson
Susie Somppi
Bill Casper
Gavan Duffy
Jim Shannon
Bobby Eakin
Susie LeBlanc
Ernie Shawver
Karen Northcott
Noelle Kanady

Present Collective
Noelle Kanady
Richard Hoover
Karen Northcott
Victoria Smith
Zengi
Thorne Dreyer

Cover: Photo by Jerry Sebesta, June 8, 1971.

Acknowledgements

We want to acknowledge former *Space City!* staffers, generous donors, and fellow travelers, who made this book possible, including proofreaders Hugh Grady, Martin Murray, and Sue Wells. Reflecting on the rich history of *Space City!* was a collaborative effort. The newsprint is now frail, but today's technology made it accessible, so we want to shine a light on our process of preserving *Space City!* and making it accessible to the world.

Open Access

As editors, we needed access to a digitized collection of *Space City!* newspapers. That process required a concerted effort. In early 2020, we assembled a near-complete collection with the help of Sherwood Bishop and Dennis Fitzgerald's family members who sent papers from Canada to Austin. The complete collection will be housed at the University of Texas Briscoe Center for American History.

In March 2020, we shipped the newspapers to Jeff Sharpe, our Internet Archive contact in Indiana, to be scanned. COVID-19 intervened, but the digital scans were added to the Internet Archive (shown in the Bibliography) in June 2020, and updated when Sherwood located three missing issues. *Space City!* has been viewed at the Internet Archive more than 9,000 times at the time of this writing.

Working with Peggy Glahn at Reveal Digital, now Ithaka, we then made sure Houston's *Space City!* joined Austin's *Rag* in JSTOR's Independent Voices collection (shown in the Bibliography). Independent Voices is an open-access digital collection of alternative press with more than 1,000 titles. In this way, we have made *Space City!* part of the historical record, accessible to academics, activists, and others, around the globe.

Former *Rag* staffer Hunter Ellinger created a data entry site for *Space City!* as he had for *The Rag*. We added 6,000 entries and gained a valuable contents directory that included authors, subject matter, advertisements, and more. The New Journalism Project collaborated with another Austin-based nonprofit, Peoples History in Texas, to input contents data and co-produce a short video (shown in the Bibliography) to promote the book project. Spencer Perskin, Bluethroat Music, and producer Bruce Hooper let us use Shiva's Headband's "Song for Peace" in that video.

Space City! had some excellent photographers. Thanks to Thorne Dreyer, Cam Duncan, John Lomax III, and the Houston Metropolitan Research Center, we were able to use digital scans from a number of original photographs. We had access to digitized graphics that made the print pop, and artist Kerry Fitzgerald, now Kerry Awn, graced us with a 2021 drawing for the book.

New technology benefitted us in one more way. The digital scans utilized Optical Character Recognition software (OCR), so we were able to convert the 111 original articles included in this book to documents for layout without retyping. It wasn't a moonshot, but it was a leap forward.

Art: Kerry Fitzgerald, August 3, 1972.

New Journalism Project
P.O. Box 16442 • Austin TX 78761-6442

The New Journalism Project (NJP) is a 501(c)(3) Texas nonprofit with three major projects:

- **Rag Radio**, a syndicated weekly show, is broadcast by KOOP 91.7 FM, a community radio station in Austin. Host Thorne Dreyer's book, *Making Waves: The Rag Radio Interviews*, will be published by the University of Texas Dolph Briscoe Center for American History in 2022.
- *The Rag Blog* (TheRagBlog.com), now in its 15th year, publishes a lively selection of art and articles with national and international distribution.
- **NJP Publishing** has published seven books, beginning with the widely-acclaimed *Celebrating The Rag: Austin's Iconic Underground Newspaper* in 2016. *Exploring Space City!: Houston's Historic Underground Newspaper* is now in your hands.

Celebrating The Rag: Austin's Iconic Underground Newspaper
Edited by Thorne Dreyer, Alice Embree, and Richard Croxdale

"A raucous, absorbing excursion back to the 1960s and 70s."
— Kirkus Reviews

Buy it at Lulu.com, Amazon, Ingram

Exploring Space City!: Houston's Historic Underground Newspaper
Edited by Thorne Dreyer, Alice Embree, Cam Duncan, and Sherwood Bishop

"This lovingly crafted compilation... perfectly captures the spirit of the New Left and the counterculture."
— Historian Robert Cottrell

Buy it at Lulu.com, Amazon, Ingram

Contributors

Kerry Awn (Kerry Fitzgerald) drew his first *Rag* cover in 1967 when he was in high school in Houston. His artwork adorned the first issue of *Space City News* and continued to enliven the paper until the last issue of *Space City!*. He moved to Austin in 1970 and went on to become a part of the Austin music/arts community involving himself in art, theater, standup comedy, and music. A former longtime cast member of Esther's Follies, founding and current member of the Uranium Savages, former Funniest Person in Austin winner, member of the "Armadillo Art Squad," the Austin Visual Arts Hall of Fame, and the Country Music Hall of Fame in Nashville. Kerry is now living in Alpine, Texas, pretty much still doing what he's always done: drawing, painting, and breathing. You can usually find him at the West Pop (a West Texas branch of Tex Pop Museum of Popular Culture) in Alpine on 6th Street, or out at Rancho 709 growing rocks and cactus.

Jude Binder contributed artwork to *Space City!* and *The Rag*. Binder is a multi-talented artist, trained in classical ballet, modern dance, Afro-Caribbean, folk, mime, clogging, and clowning. She majored in painting and printmaking during her three years of study at the Pennsylvania Academy of Fine Arts, and has added costume design, mask making, and wood-carving to her credits. She moved to West Virginia in 1973, and founded Heartwood in the Hills in 1982, a school dedicated to nurturing creativity. Binder has received many honors in West Virginia for her commitment to arts and education and for her film, *Field of Flowers*, about domestic violence.

Walter B. Birdwell (1942-2017) was born in Missouri and graduated from the University of Missouri. He served in the Army 112th with Military Intelligence, was bilingual, and was sent to Austin, Texas, where he was exposed to political groups like SDS and realized his Army assignments required spying on civilians. He became a political activist opposing the war in Vietnam and working with MAYO. From 1967 to his death, he dedicated his time to resisting wars that he considered imperialist.

Sherwood Bishop was the first person to join the original six members on the *Space City!* Collective in late 1969. He went to Cuba in 1970, on the Third Venceremos Brigade. In the early 1970s, he was director of the Houston Peace Center and of the Houston Committee to End the War in Vietnam. He was a founder and director in the early '70s of Community Bread, a food co-op that at one time had over 20 branches in the Houston area, as well as a communal farm, a full-time day care center, and a "free university." For over 25 years, he has lived in San Marcos, Texas, where he chaired the San Marcos Parks and Recreation Board and the San Marcos Planning and Zoning Commission, and served on boards of other organizations. He was a founder of the San Marcos Greenbelt Alliance in 1998, and is currently serving as its president. Sherwood recently retired as senior lecturer in economics at Texas State University. Since 2014, he has also served as the president of the New Journalism Project board of directors.

Marie Blazek graduated from the University of Texas in 1969, and immediately moved to Mexico City where she taught English as a Second Language for a year. She later became the Women's News Director at Houston's Pacifica Radio from 1971-72, producing feature stories and hosting a weekly talk show. She regularly visited *Space City!*, writing occasional book reviews. Subsequently, she meandered through several career paths, mostly as a professional potter for many decades, with a decade as a public school teacher spliced among them. Most recently she has taught GED classes to Spanish-speaking adults and she continues to produce pottery. Among other accomplishments, she has birthed three sons, raising two; she has bought, fixed up, and sold several houses, written a personal memoir, and she sustains a daily Buddhist meditation practice.

Randy Chapman departed Lubbock in 1968, where he was a square peg in a round hole. While attending the University of Houston, he and his wife Melinda soon connected with *Space City News* and began distributing the paper at UH and later in head shops, newsstands, and community outlets. He soon became friends with the *Space City!* Collective and he later researched the investigative article "Who Rules the University of Houston?" From that life experience, he decided to attend the TSU Thurgood Marshall College of Law and become a public interest lawyer and state level lobbyist. Randy now serves on Austin's Electric Utility Commission and he chairs the board of directors of the National Center on Appropriate Technology.

Gary Chason (1942-2021) was a frequent contributor to both *The Rag* and *Space City!*, writing about film and the arts. Gary was a stage and screen producer and director; much of his work was avant garde, existential, and edgy. He produced groundbreaking live theater productions in both Austin and Houston. He was also a character actor and an acting coach and mentor to many. He gained a measure of fame as a casting director and dialogue/dialect coach for major studio directors like Robert Altman, Peter Bogdanovich, Sam Peckinpah, Michael Ritchie, and Louis Malle, doing the location casting for films like *Brewster McCloud*, *The Last Picture Show*, and *Pretty Baby*. As a dialect coach, Gary tutored people like Jeff Bridges, Cybill Shepherd, Cloris Leachman, Brooke Shields, Tatum O'Neal, and Ann-Margret. He was also an activist, opposing the Vietnam War, and co-founder of the Sexual Freedom League at UT in Austin in 1966. His essay written for this book arrived four days before his sudden death.

Thorne Dreyer, who lives in Austin, is editor of *The Rag Blog*, host and producer of Rag Radio, and a director of the New Journalism Project. He was the original "funnel" of *The Rag* in 1966, and was a founding member of the *Space City!* editorial Collective in 1969, remaining with the paper until it closed shop in August 1972. He was also an editor at Liberation News Service in New York, general manager of KPFT-FM, Pacifica radio in Houston — where he hosted the popular Briarpatch program — and a correspondent for the early *Texas Monthly* magazine. Dreyer worked as a public information officer for the City of Houston under Mayor Fred Hofheinz, owned and operated a Houston political public relations business, and managed a jazz club and several musical acts including popular jazz singer Cy Brinson. He was the son of prominent Houston artist Margaret Webb Dreyer and *Houston Chronicle* reporter Martin Dreyer; his family operated Dreyer Galleries, a major gathering place for activists and creative types. Dreyer is an editor of both *Celebrating The Rag* (2016) and *Exploring Space City!* (2021) and his book *Making Waves: The Rag Radio Interviews* will be published by the Briscoe Center for American History, University of Texas Press, in early 2022.

Gavan Duffy volunteered at *The Rag* off-and-on from 1969 to 1973. During the same period, he volunteered sporadically at *Space City!* and served, from time-to-time, on the staff of Pacifica radio (KP-FT-FM) in Houston from 1970-1976. He returned to the University of Houston to pursue the BA he had

abandoned in 1969. He then earned MS and PhD degrees from MIT and taught from 1985 to 1989 in the Government Department at UT-Austin. After that he served on the political science faculty of the Maxwell School of Citizenship and Public Affairs at Syracuse University, where he is now an Associate Professor Emeritus.

Cam Duncan was a VISTA volunteer community organizer in Houston and a founding member of the *Space City!* editorial Collective in 1969, and wrote the paper's Selective Servitude column on draft counseling and resistance. As a graduate student in economics at UT-Austin, Cam wrote occasionally for *The Rag* and coordinated the Latin American Policy Alternatives Group. He taught labor economics in Puerto Rico and at American University in Washington, D.C.; worked as a labor educator for AFSCME; managed a campaign on trade and the environment for Greenpeace International; and represented union members in North and South America for the global union federation Public Services International and the National Labor College. Cam is a lifelong member of the American Federation of Teachers, a trustee of the Northern New Mexico Central Labor Council, and keeps bees at his home in Tesuque, New Mexico. He helped produce *Exploring Space City!*

Susan Mithun Duncan (1946-2017) was a founding member of the *Space City!* editorial Collective in 1969. Sue and her husband Cam Duncan were community organizers working for Volunteers in Service to America (VISTA) in Houston's Sixth Ward. She studied education at UT-Austin and was a lifelong educator and activist for racial and economic justice. Sue taught secondary history and geography in Washington, D.C. and Puerto Rico and managed school-based programs for nonprofit organizations (afterschool, summer, service-learning, and adult education) in D.C. and Santa Fe. She was Training Director for Amigos de las Americas, a hemispheric youth service organization. Sue worked for solidarity organizations with Chile, El Salvador, and Nicaragua, and was co-founder of the D.C.-Bluefields Nicaragua Sister City Program. After relocating to New Mexico, she was elected to the Santa Fe Board of Education, where she championed bilingual education and advocated for the needs of immigrant children.

Alice Embree helped found *The Rag*, worked with the North American Congress on Latin America (NACLA) and *Rat* newspaper in New York, and contributed to *Sisterhood is Powerful*, a 1970 anthol ogy of writings about Women's Liberation. She was a founder of Red River Women's Press in Austin. After receiving her master's degree from UT-Austin, she served as a strategic planner for the Texas child support program. She has written for the *Texas Observer* and *The Rag Blog*, is a union member, and has been a peace and justice activist in Austin for many decades. She is a director of the New Journalism Project and co-edited *Celebrating The Rag: Austin's Iconic Underground Newspaper* as well as this book. Her memoir, *Voice Lessons*, has been published by the University of Texas Briscoe Center.

Dennis Fitzgerald (1945-2018) said, "I was privileged to be in the delivery room at the birth of *The Rag*. 'Breathe, breathe, breathe!'" Three years later, he helped bring *Space City!* into the world. Dennis was a staff member at the SDS regional office in San Francisco; sales manager for a small import company; co-founder of *Space City!*; communard in Arkansas; assistant city editor at the *Houston Chronicle*; editor of a rural community newspaper near Vancouver, British Columbia; carpenter; sawmill worker and union representative; freelance journalist; and a social and environmental policy manager for a multinational forest company, before his retirement in Canada.

Judy Gitlin Fitzgerald was part of the original *Space City!* Collective and was also a founder of *The Rag* in Austin. After leaving Houston in 1971, she lived in San Francisco, a commune in Arkansas, and Houston with her then-husband Dennis and small daughter Kelly. In 1977, they all immigrated to the Sunshine Coast in British Columbia, a 50-mile stretch of very small West Coast communities reachable only by boat or ferry, amidst the tall trees and lush green of the rainforest, the Salish Sea, and the mountains. Forty-four years later she is still there, living in Gibsons, riding ferries when necessary, writing a bit, volunteering in the community, and doing Tai Chi.

Jim Franklin, an acclaimed surrealist graphic artist, designed many of *The Rag*'s most iconic covers. Called the "Michelangelo of armadillo art," the Galveston native almost single-handedly transformed the lowly armadillo into a symbol for the Texas counterculture. Also an accomplished painter who studied at the San Francisco Art Institute, Jim helped found Vulcan Gas Company, Austin's first psychedelic music hall, and was later resident artist and emcee (in wild costumes) at the famed music and arts venue, Armadillo World Headquarters. Franklin's art appeared in *Space City!*, including the Shiva's Headband ad in this book.

Yolanda Garza Birdwell was born in the state of Tamaulipas, Mexico, and came to the USA as a student in the '60s. She attended Business School and worked at Aramco. She married Walter Birdwell in 1967 and they both became political activists, opposing capitalism and imperialism and working with the Mexican American Youth organization (MAYO).

Molly Ivins (1944-2007) was an iconic figure in American journalism. She was a columnist, political commentator, humorist, and *The New York Times* bestselling author. She was known for her outrageous views and sparkling writing style. Molly and Kaye Northcott co-edited the *Texas Observer* from 1970-76. Molly started out as an intern at the *Houston Chronicle* for three summers, then worked at the *Minneapolis Tribune*. After the *Observer*, Ivins worked at *The New York Times*, the *Dallas Times Herald*, and the *Fort Worth Star-Telegram*. Her syndicated column appeared in hundreds of newspapers. Her book, *Molly Ivins Can't Say That, Can She?* was on the *Times* bestseller list for 29 weeks. She was a three-time finalist for the Pulitzer Prize. She died in 2007 after a seven-year battle with breast cancer.

Karolyn Kendrick (1947-2012) graduated from Rice University in 1971. An activist in the student anti-war movement at Rice, she contributed articles on Houston's power structure to *Space City!* After working as a science writer for *Scholastic Magazine* in New York City, she became a professor of Biology, Botany and Marine Sciences at Pima Community College in Tucson, and received an award as outstanding teacher. She worked with Native Seed Search, an organization dedicated to preserving the native seeds of the Southwest. Karolyn later taught at the Biosphere 2 research lab on ecological conservation in Oracle, Arizona.

John Lomax III (Aka John M. Lomax), grandson and nephew, respectively of pioneering folklorists/authors John Avery and Alan Lomax, carries on a family music tradition that began in 1885. After *Space City!*, he relocated to Nashville and continued his music journalism. He later fashioned careers as an artist manager and music distributor, selling recordings to importers in Europe, Japan, and Australia. Streaming ate his export business so he ramped up his "professional Lomax" persona, giving lecture/performances based on his family's work. He is also engaged in several book projects and is methodically dispersing 60 years of accumulated music materials to various institutions. He is happily married to Rice graduate and retired nurse Melanie Wells. His children, John Nova and Amanda Margaret, are both engaged in creative endeavors, John as a staff writer for *Texas Highways* and Amanda as a freelance artistic photographer.

Carlos Lowry grew up in Chile and lived there until 1974, the year after the military coup. He earned a BFA in Studio Art from Southwestern University in Georgetown. After working as a commercial artist in Dallas, he moved to Austin, joining Interart-Public Art as a muralist. He painted several murals in Austin, including the Varsity Theatre Mural, served on the City of Austin Art and Public Places Panel, and has designed covers for small press books, record album jackets, and many political posters and flyers. He worked for 28 years as an exhibit specialist, graphic artist, web developer, and programmer analyst for the Austin Public Library, retiring in 2011 to devote time to painting. He contributed his design talent to this book.

Adolfo Mexiac (1927-2019) was a prolific Mexican graphic artist, well known for his political-themed woodcuts and serigraphy. He worked with the Taller de Gráfica Popular with artist Leopoldo Méndez. His image of a face with chains across the mouth titled *Libertad de Expresión* was widely used during the 1968 student uprising in Mexico.

John Moretta received his Ph.D in history from Rice University in 1985 and has published several books and scholarly articles on both Texas and United States history including his most recent book, *The Hippies: A 1960s History*, published by McFarland & Co. In 2020, he wrote an article for the academic journal, *Southwestern Historical Quarterly*, titled "Political Hippies and Hip Politicos: Counterculture Alliance and Cultural Radicalism in 1960s Austin, Texas" and his book on that subject will be published in early 2022. Dr. Moretta is a full-time history professor with Houston Community College and also teaches upper-level U.S. history courses at the University of Houston.

Bill Narum (1947-2009), an Austin native, was an artist, illustrator, album designer, poster artist, broadcaster, and a pioneer in video production and computer graphics. Wikipedia calls him a "Texas counterculture icon" and notes that he was "one of the few

non-natives to have lived with the Tarahumara tribe of northern Mexico." Narum served as art director at *Space City!*, making his mark on the look of the paper. He was a founder of Houston underground rock station, KLOL-FM, worked with Houston's Pacifica radio station, KPFT-FM, and was founder of Space City Video. A close friend of Billy Gibbons, he was also the house artist for "that little ol' band from Texas," ZZ Top. Later, he had a video game development company in Austin. He was voted Austin Poster Artist of the Year in the *Austin Chronicle*'s People's Choice Awards and received a Certificate of Appreciation from the City of Austin for distinguished service to the public through his artwork.

Doyle Niemann parlayed his experience with *The Rag* in Austin from 1967 to 1970 into a stint with *Space City News* and, later, *The Great Speckled Bird* in Atlanta. He was the founding managing editor of *In These Times*, based in Chicago. Moving to the Washington area, he worked promoting community organizing, rural advocacy, and nonprofit, labor, and corporate communications. Graduating from law school at 50, he has been a criminal prosecutor in Prince George's County, Maryland, for the last 23 years. During that time, he served two terms on the county school board and 12 years in the Maryland House of Delegates. He has lived in Mount Rainier, Maryland, for the last 40 years and is still trying to figure out what he is going to do when he grows up.

Karen Northcott was a reader of *The Rag* while she was a student at the University of Texas. She was campused (confined to her dorm room) for a weekend after acknowledging possession of *Rag*s in her room. Karen wrote for *Space City!* from April 1971, until July 1972, covering a panoply of issues including the Vietnam Veterans Against the War, sex discrimination at UT, the trial of Klansman Jimmy Dale Hutto, and the Texas Department of Corrections' vendetta against prisoner rights attorney Frances T. Freeman Jalet Cruz. She left Texas in 1973 when she was recruited to the Wounded Knee Legal Defense/Offense Committee in South Dakota where she became an investigator on state-related Wounded Knee cases. Karen moved to Minnesota where she worked at shelters for battered women, ran a law program for women, and supervised Guardians ad litem. She was a member of the Teamsters union. Karen's life came full circle when she worked on criminal cases that arose out of the NODAPL (North Dakota Access Pipeline) struggle on the Standing Rock Reservation in North Dakota alongside allies from Wounded Knee and their children and grandchildren. Karen returned to Texas in 2020, after 47 years in the North Country.

Tary Owens (1942-2003), who wrote about music for *Space City!* and for a time served as the paper's music editor, became a celebrated music historian, archivist, and producer and was himself a musician. Owens received a Lomax Foundation grant to research and record roots musicians in Central Texas. His field recordings are archived at the Briscoe Center for American History at the University of Texas at Austin. According to the Texas State Historical Association, "Owens not only documented the music of [historically important] artists, but also helped revive their performing careers." Tary Owens is in the *Austin Chronicle*'s Texas Music Hall of Fame and was one of the first 10 inductees into the Austin Music Memorial. Owens died of cancer on September 21, 2003.

Gregorio Salazar (1950-1990) was a leader of the Mexican American Youth Organization (MAYO) in Houston. He was an eloquent and smart spokesman and had a great interest in the arts. He was an internationalist who traveled to Europe and Cuba before many of his peers did. An oral history, recorded in 1989, is available to the public at the Houston Metropolitan Research Center, Houston Public Library.

Jim Shannon was active in the high school movement when he was at Houston's Waltrip High and was also involved in the high school underground press. He was among a number of students disciplined by their schools for selling underground papers on campus. Jim wrote about these events for *Space City!* and also wrote about music and other subjects and did design work for the paper. Jim became a member of the *Space City!* Collective. In 1984, Shannon was a juror in the Houston trial that awarded an unprecedented $10.5 billion to the Pennzoil Company in its lawsuit against Texaco that led to Texaco filing for bankruptcy. Shannon wrote about the trial in a book published by Prentice Hall titled *Texaco and the $10 Billion Jury*.

Jeffrey Shapiro was a VISTA Volunteer in Houston between 1968 and 1971, and, during that time, researched and co wrote stories for *Space City!* on the Houston power structure. These stories unearthed the makeup and machinations of the city's powerful banks, law firms, oil, natural gas, insurance,

and real estate interests. He grew up in Chicago and graduated from the University of Illinois, Chicago, with a Bachelor's degree in English and a Master's degree in Journalism from Northwestern University. He was a reporter for a chain of community newspapers in Chicago and an investigative reporter for the Sun Newspapers of Omaha. He was later a program evaluator for the U.S. Government Accountability Office (GAO), specializing in investigations of financial markets and institutions. Since 2008, he has been a writing tutor and teacher at LaGuardia Community college in New York. He is currently completing a memoir-history of the War on Poverty's VISTA volunteer program in Houston, Texas.

Rick Sharp grew up in the southwest area of Houston and attended Westbury High School. He created his first commercial poster at age sixteen for a show by Leon Russell at the Catacombs Club. While still in high school, Sharp created posters for surf shops, head shops, and *Space City News*, and won a poster contest in *Seventeen* magazine. A large Houston record store, part of a national chain, commissioned Sharp to draw a full-page advertisement in *Rolling Stone* magazine. Sharp was honing a craft that would eventually become the flag of a new burgeoning ecological movement in Southern California. Sharp's work was widely reproduced on t-shirts, album covers, concert posters, and magazine advertisements, to name a few. Today, if you walk through shops in Hawaii, you may have seen or purchased Sharp's nostalgic posters on a myriad of products, such as calendars, postcards, tote bags, placemats, towels, and mugs.

Gilbert Shelton is a Houston native. With Robert Crumb, Shelton was arguably the most famous underground comix artist of the '60s and '70s. He is best known for The Fabulous Furry Freak Brothers, which started in *The Rag* in 1968, appearing in the paper through most of its history, and also graced the pages of *Space City!*. The Freak Brothers strip, which was reprinted in underground and alternative publications and comic books around the world, still has an international following, has been translated into multiple languages, and has reached tens of millions of readers. Shelton, who now lives near Paris, France, was editor of the irreverent *Texas Ranger* humor magazine and a founder of Rip Off Press. His other comic creations include Wonder Wart Hog, Fat Freddy's Cat, his comic book, *Feds 'N' Heads*, and *Not Quite Dead*, a collaboration with French cartoonist Pic.

Jeff Shero, later known as **Jeffrey Nightbyrd**, was a major figure in the American New Left, serving as national vice president of SDS and later as a spokesman for the Youth International Party (Yippies). Jeff was a founder of *The Rag* in Austin in 1966, started *RAT Subterranean News* in New York, and was a contributor to *Space City!*. He worked with KPFT-FM, Pacifica Radio in Houston, in the early 1970s where he hosted the popular late-night program, Liferaft. From 1974-1978 Jeff and Michael Eakin published the *Austin Sun*, a paper that served as an early transition from underground to alternative press. In more recent years, Jeff has been involved with the Acclaim Talent Agency. Several of his articles are included in this collection.

Victoria Smith, later **Victoria Marie Holden**, Ph.D. (1945-2008), was a member of the founding *Space City!* editorial Collective and was at the paper through its entire run. Prior to her involvement with *Space City!* Victoria was a reporter at the *St. Paul Dispatch*, worked in the SDS national office where she was the printer for *New Left Notes* (the SDS national newspaper), and then was an editor at Liberation News Service (LNS) in New York. Later in life, she received a doctorate in Mass Communications from the University of Minnesota, graduating Summa Cum Laude. In 1991, she was appointed Associate Professor in the School of Communications at the University of North Dakota. In 1992 she married William Holden in Grand Forks, ND.

Don Snell (1922-2014), a Houston artist known for his expressive and often whimsical figurative paintings, was also a sculptor and photographer. Snell was known for his lively gatherings of artists and counterculture figures in Houston in the 1960s and 70s, and *Texas Monthly* once called him the "Pearl Mesta of the Montrose." He grew up in Kansas City and served in World War II. He studied at the University of Texas at Austin and Tulane University, later teaching at Tulane, Arlington State College, and the University of Houston. In 2010, Snell was awarded the Lifetime Achievement Award from the Austin Visual Arts Association. He died in Georgetown, Texas, in 2014, at the age of 91.

cindy soo, a native-born Houstonian, graduated from Westbury High School in 1970. She wrote for the alternative high school paper, *The Little Red Schoolhouse*, worked with Community Bread, and coordinated the University of Thought, a free university in Houston. In 1972, she moved to Tahlequah,

Oklahoma, as a VISTA volunteer, working with Flaming Rainbow, University-Without-Walls, an affiliate of Antioch University. She relocated to Austin in 1977, where she worked with movie theaters, *The Daily Texan*, and then *The Austin Chronicle*. She is a current board member of the New Journalism Project. Since 2015, she has been active with Lucky Chaos, an Asian arts incubator in Austin.

Trudy Stern [formerly **Trudy Minkoff**] transferred to U.T. in 1965 where she and then spouse Bobby Minkoff moved into a flat on 12th Street above like-minded friends in the basement, Alice Embree and Jeff Shero. She worked on the first issues of *The Rag* and contributed artwork to *Space City!*, some of which is included in this collection. Since those days she has lived in New Mexico, Arkansas, Vermont, many other places briefly, and finally Buffalo, New York. She writes and performs spoken word art in Buffalo where she owned and operated a tea house and worked as a nurse practitioner. She is a Shambhala Buddhist and teaches Miksang — contemplative photography.

Scout Stormcloud [formerly **Scout Schacht**] wrote a record review column for *Space City!* from 1970 to 1972 to help with John Lomax's overflow of music LPs. She grew up in the Heights and OST South and graduated from Jesse H. Jones High School in 1964. She played the clarinet and piano. She attended the University of Houston for a couple of years and worked for the Houston Oilers and FAO Schwartz before moving to Austin in 1972 to volunteer with *The Rag* where she wrote a column called Music Hype. Scout began painting in oil and had her first show in 1980 at the Shown-Davenport Gallery in San Antonio. In recent years she has had shows with the EAST & WEST Austin Studio Tours, Austin Visual Artists Association (AVAA), and the Austin Museum of Popular Culture.

Gary Thiher was among the original group of *Rag* staffers and contributors for several years. Following graduation from UT, he spent several years in marginal left-wing journalism, writing for *Space City!*, and hosting a Pacifica radio show in Houston. There followed a two-year tour of duty as a hippy-pioneer-back-to-the-lander in the Ozarks. Then for a number of years he plied the trade of carpenter/contractor in several cities. In middle age, he obtained a Ph.D. from the University of Missouri and since 2001 has taught philosophy at the University of Central Arkansas.

Bibliography

Books

Abernethy, Francis Edward, Editor, *What's Going On? (In Modern Texas Folklore)* (Austin: Encino Press, 1976), "Texas Tea and Rainy Day Woman," by Hermes Nye, p. 112, 118.

Ayo, Vicki Welch, *Boys from Houston* (Houston: Vicki Welch Ayo, 2013), "Interview with Thorne Dreyer," pp. 414-417.

Burke, John Gordon, Editor, *Print, Image and Sound: Essays on Media* (Chicago: American Library Association, 1972), "The New Journalism" by James Ridgeway, p. 8.

Calonne, David Stephen, *Conversations with Allen Ginsberg* (Jackson, MS: University of Mississippi Press, 2019), p. 50.

Calvert, Robert A., Armoldo De Leon, Gregg Cantrell, *The History of Texas* (New York: John Wiley & Sons, 2020), pp. 395, 526.

Cottrell, Robert C., *Sex, Drugs, and Rock 'N' Roll: The Rise of America's 1960s Counterculture* (Lanham, MD: Rowman & Littlefield, 2015), p. 158, 287.

Dreyer, Thorne, Alice Embree, and Richard Croxdale, Editors., *Celebrating The Rag: Austin's Iconic Underground Newspaper* (Austin: New Journalism Project, 2016), pp. 6, 8, 10, 11, 54, 209.

Embree, Alice, *Voice Lessons* (Austin: Tower Books, University of Texas Press, 2021), pp. 106, 122-123, 131-133, 247-248, 254.

Gershon, Pete, Collision: *The Contemporary Art Scene in Houston, 1972-1985* (College Station, TX: Texas A&M Press, 2018), p. 120.

Hinojosa, Felipe, *Apostles of Change: Latino Radical Politics, Church Occupations, and the Fight to Save the Barrio* (Austin: University of Texas Press, 2021), pp. 120, 124, 186, 218.

Leamer, Laurence, *The Paper Revolutionaries: The Rise of the Underground Press* (New York: Simon and Schuster, 1972), pp. 62, 73, 104-109, 135.

Linfield, Michael, *Freedom Under Fire: U.S. Civil Liberties in Times of War* (Boston: South End Press, 1990), pp. 149, 279, 281.

McMilllian, John, *Smoking Typewriters: The Sixties Underground Press and the Rise of Alternative Media in America* (New York: Oxford University Press, 2011), pp. 131-32, 133, 210, Photo gallery, 9.

Moretta, John Anthony, *The Hippies: A 1960s History* (Jefferson, NC: McFarland & Company, 2017), p. 98.

Newfield, Jack, *Bread and Roses Too: Reporting About America* (New York: E. P. Dutton & Co., 1971), p. 278.

Nord, David Paul, Joan Shelley Rubin, David D. Hall, Michael Schudson, *A History of the Book in America: Vol. 5: The Enduring Book: Print Culture in Postwar America* (Chapel Hill, NC: University of North Carolina Press, 2009), pp. 273-4.

O'Brien, Timothy J., David Ensminger, *Mojo Hand: The Life and Music of Lightnin' Hopkins* (Austin: University of Texas Press, 2013), pp. 213, 264.

Oluwole, Joseph O., *Censorship and Student Communication in Online and Offline Settings* (Hershey, PA: IGI Global, 2015), pp. 154-5.

Peck, Abe, *Uncovering the Sixties: The Life and Times of the Underground Press* (New York : Citadel Press, 1991), pp. 183, 231.

Rips, Geoffrey, *The Campaign Against the Underground Press* (San Francisco: City Lights Books, 1981), pp. 114-115.

Rolling Stone, Editors, *The Age of Paranoia: How the Sixties Ended* (New York: Pocket Books, March 1972), "The Underground Press," by John Burks, pp. 22, 35, 57.

Rossinow, Doug, *The Politics of Authenticity: Liberalism, Christianity, and the New Left in America* (New York: Columbia University Press, 1998), p. 176.

Schaefer, Alan, Joe Nick Patoski, Nels Jacobson, *Homegrown: Austin Music Posters 1967 to 1982* (Austin: University of Texas Press, 2015), pp. 22-23.

Slonecker, Blake, *A New Dawn for the New Left* (New York: Palgrave Macmillan, 2012), pp. 170, 265-6.

Stewart, Sean, Editor, *On the Ground: An Illustrated Anecdotal History of the Sixties Underground Press in the U.S.* (PM Press, 2011), pp. 142, 143, 190.

Streitmatter, Rodger, *Voices of Revolution: The Dissident Press in America* (New York: Columbia University Press, 2001), p. 216.

Trodd, Zoe, Ph.D., and Brian L. Johnson, Ph.D., Editors, *Conflict in American History: A Documentary Encyclopedia. Volume VII: The Postwar and Civil Rights Era: 1945-1973* (New York: Facts on File, Infobase Publishing, Inc., 2010), p. 502.

Wachsberger, Ken, Editor, *Voices from the Underground* (East Lansing, MI: Michigan State University Press, 2011), "My Odyssey through the Underground Press" by Michael "Mica" Kindman, p. ix.

Wachsberger, Ken, Editor, *Voices from the Underground: Insider Histories of the Vietnam Era Underground Press, Part 1* (East Lansing, MI: Michigan State University Press, 2011), "*Space City!*: From Opposition to Organizational Collapse" by Victoria Smith Holden, pp. 299-323.

Periodicals

Associated Press, "Journalists Condemn Terrorism," *Houston Chronicle*, November 15, 1970, p. 2.

Aynesworth, Hugh, "Houston's Civil War," *Newsweek*, May 4, 1971, p. 54.

Bertelsen, Elmer, "Principals See Problem as Student Unrest Grows Here," *Houston Chronicle*, October 26, 1969, p. 59.

Dreyer, Thorne, "What Ever Happened to the New Generation?: Sixties Radicals: What are they Doing Today," *Texas Monthly* 4:11; November 1976, pp. 94, 96, 99.

Dreyer, Thorne, "The Mad Mix: Montrose, the Heart of Houston," *Cite: The Architecture + Design Review of Houston*, 2010, pp. 38-39.

Harper, Fred, "Prof Praises Underground Newspaper," *Houston Chronicle*, January 12, 1971, p. 37.

Houston Chronicle, "14 Subpoenaed in Terror Probe; Klan Members and Exes Included (series of articles), May 26, 1971, pp. 1-3, 9

Houston Chronicle, "Bomb Rocks Radical Paper's Office," July 28, 1969, pp. 1, 23.

Houston Chronicle, "Council Probe of Klan Asked Within Houston," April 8, 1971, p. 77.

Houston Chronicle, "Ex-Klansman Gets Probation in Bomb Case," September 12, 1973, p. 21.

Houston Chronicle, "Judge Rules Student, 17, Was Improperly Suspended by School," June 24, 1971, p. 2.

Houston Chronicle, "Rice Rejects Chicago 7 Figure's Talk," April 2, 1970, p. 20.

Houston Chronicle, "*Space City!* Advertisers Lose Windows," April 9, 1971, p. 2.

Houston Chronicle, "*Space City!* Tab Closing Down After 3 Years," July 28, 1972, p. 2

Houston Chronicle, "*Space City!* Will Publish Weekly Starting April 6," March 30, 1971, p. 12.

Houston Chronicle Washington Bureau, "High Court Upholds Houston School Code," November 12, 1973, p. 3.

Kane, Karen, "Echoes of rebellion and random gunfire: Can it be only 10 years since Thorne Dreyer published Space City News?" *Houston Chronicle Texas Magazine* "Part Two: The '60s: The Young Radicals, Then and Now," December 7, 1980, pp. 10-12, 14.

Mankad, Raj, "*Space City!* Underground," *Cite: The Architecture + Design Review of Houston*, Summer 2010, p. 18.
Same article at *Offcite* (online): offcite.rice.edu/2010/07/20120308155133046-1.pdf

Northcott, Kaye, "Vigilantes Still Ride in Houston," *Texas Observer*, August 29, pp. 10-11.

Redding, Stan, "Dissent is Risky Business Here, As These Dissenters Found Out," *Houston Chronicle*, February 8, 1970, pp. 1, 18.

Siemssen, John, "Remembering Houston's First Alternative Newspaper," *Houston's Other*, Summer 1998.

Singer, Steve, "Scuffles End Rice Students' Protests," *Houston Chronicle*, April 13, 1970.

Wilson, John W., "Ochs, Denim Supply Superb Musical Politics," *Houston Chronicle*, March 15, 1971, p. 14.

[The articles above from the *Houston Chronicle* are representative of scores of articles posted by the *Chronicle*, the *Houston Post*, and other mainstream media outlets during the three years of *Space City!*'s existence, especially concerning violent attacks on the paper, harassment of its vendors, and other related news.]

Online

Bludworth, Michael, "Houston's *Space City! News*: Vintage ads from Houston's underground newspaper." Flickr: www.flickr.com/photos/10659106@N00/albums/72157632950446996/

Dreyer, Thorne, host, "60s Houston Counterculture with Sherwood Bishop and Bobby Ray Eakin," Rag Radio, April 13, 2010.
Internet Archive: archive.org/details/RagRadio2010-04-13

Dreyer, Thorne, host, "Underground Press Historian Sean Stewart," Rag Radio, August, 31, 2010.
Internet Archive: archive.org/details/RagRadio2010-08-31

Dreyer, Thorne, host, "*Celebrating The Rag* editors Thorne Dreyer, Alice Embree & Richard Croxdale speak at Book People," Rag Radio, January 6, 2017.
Internet Archive: archive.org/details/RagRadio2017-01-06-ThorneDreyerAliceEmbree RichardCroxdale/1RagRadio2017-01-06-ThorneDreyerAliceEmbreeRichardCroxdale-RadioEdit.mp3

Dreyer, Thorne, host, "John McMillian, author of *Smoking Typewriters*," Rag Radio, March 4, 2011.
Internet Archive: archive.org/details/RagRadio2011-03-04

Dreyer, Thorne and Sherwood Bishop, "Veterans of *Space City News* talk about underground press in Houston at Zine Fest," Houston Indymedia, June 2009 (audio files) radio.indymedia.org/en/node/17303

Embree, Alice, "Houston's historic '*Space City!*' to get new life," *The Rag Blog*, December 5, 2019. www.theragblog.com/alice-embree-houstons-historic-space-city-to-get-new-life/

Embree, Alice, "Houston's historic newspaper... on the really small screen," *The Rag Blog*, November 25, 2020. www.theragblog.com/alice-embree-report-houstons-historic-underground-newspaper/

Embree, Alice, "Preserve Houston's underground newspaper," *The Rag Blog*, March 9, 2020. www.theragblog.com/alice-embree-preserve-houstons-historic-underground-newspaper/

Embree, Alice, "*Space City!* Lives online, survives quarantine," *The Rag Blog*, June 18, 2020. www.theragblog.com/alice-embree-report-space-city-lives-online-survives-quarantine/

Embree, Alice, "*Space City!* project: Calling all hoarders," *The Rag Blog*, February 12, 2019. www.theragblog.com/alice-embree-space-city-project-calling-all-hoarders/

Houston Public Library Oral History Collection, Digital Archives, "Interview with Thorne Dreyer," July, 15, 1976. Audio files and text. (Substantial content about *Space City!*) digital.houstonlibrary.net/oral-history/thorne-dreyer.php

People's History in Texas and New Journalism Project, "*Space City!* Video" (Promoting *Exploring Space City!*). YouTube. www.youtube.com/watch?v=JlMnXoZKAnM&t=16s

People's History in Texas website: Video about and covers from *Space City!* peopleshistoryintexas.org/space-city/

Plutopia News Network (PNN), "Thorne Dreyer interviewed about *Space City!* and *The Rag*," PNN Live, July 7, 2020. YouTube: https://www.youtube.com/watch?v=1GC89QFyOx8

Scarlet Dukes, "*Space City News* Cover Gallery from the Bill Narum Collection," 1960s Texas Music. www.scarletdukes.com/st/tmhou_press3.html

Digitized set of *Space City!* at the Internet Archive (open access) archive.org/details/newjournalismproject

Digitized set of *Space City!* At JSTOR (open access) www.jstor.org/site/reveal-digital/independent-voices/spacecity-29574752/

Space City! article at Wikipedia: en.wikipedia.org/wiki/Space_City_(newspaper)

Index